Que's 1995 Computer Buyer's Guide

Bud Smith

Revised by
Dave Gibbons

Que's 1995 Computer Buyer's Guide

Copyright © 1994 by Que® Corporation.

All rights reserved. Printed in the United States of America. No part of this book may be used or reproduced in any form or by any means, or stored in a database or retrieval system, without prior written permission of the publisher except in the case of brief quotations embodied in critical articles and reviews. Making copies of any part of this book for any purpose other than your own personal use is a violation of United States copyright laws. For information, address Que Corporation, 201 W. 103rd St., Indianapolis, IN 46290.

ISBN: 1-56529-775-x

This book is sold *as is*, without warranty of any kind, either express or implied, respecting the contents of this book, including but not limited to implied warranties for the book's quality, performance, merchantability, or fitness for any particular purpose. Neither Que Corporation nor its dealers or distributors shall be liable to the purchaser or any other person or entity with respect to any liability, loss, or damage caused or alleged to have been caused directly or indirectly by this book.

97 96 95 94   6 5 4 3 2

Interpretation of the printing code: the rightmost double-digit number is the year of the book's printing; the rightmost single-digit number, the number of the book's printing. For example, a printing code of 94-1 shows that the first printing of the book occurred in 1994.

Publisher: David P. Ewing

Associate Publisher: Corinne Walls

Publishing Director: Brad R. Koch

Managing Editor: Anne Owen

Product Marketing Manager: Greg Wiegand

Production Team: Stephen Adams, Angela Bannan, Stephen Carlin, Maxine Dillingham, Chad Dressler, DiMonique Ford, Aren Howell, Michael Hughes, Bob LaRoche, Malinda Lowder, G. Alan Palmore, Wendy Ott, Kaylene Riemen, Caroline Roop, Clair Schweinler, Nanci Sears Perry, Kris Simmons, Craig Small, Mike Thomas, Marcella Thompson, Tina Trettin, Donna Winter

Publishing Manager
Thomas H. Bennett

Acquisitions Editor
Nancy Stevenson

Product Directors
Anna M. Huff
Steven M. Schafer

Production Editor
JoAnna Arnott

Editors
Heather Kaufman
Chris Nelson

Technical Editors
Tony Schafer
Michael Watson

Figure Specialist
Cari Ohm

Book Designer
Amy Peppler-Adams

Cover Designer
Sandra Stevenson

Editorial Assistant
Theresa Mathias

Acquisitions Assistant
Ruth Slates

Composed in Garamond and MCPdigital by Que Corporation

Dedication

To my ever-supportive father, who's still trying to figure out the "computer" on his bass boat.

About the Authors

Bud Smith

Bud Smith is an experienced computer programmer, systems analyst, and technology writer based in the Silicon Valley. He's previously published four computer-related books, has been West Coast Editor for *Personal Workstation*, and has written for a variety of computer and other magazines. His books and articles cover a wide range of topics, from the cutting edge of future technologies to easy-to-follow descriptions of how to use popular hardware and software.

Dave Gibbons

Dave Gibbons is a former technical trainer and writer for DATASTORM TECHNOLOGIES in Columbia, Missouri, and LaserMaster Technologies in Eden Prairie, Minnesota. He began his professional writing career in chilly Cando, North Dakota, at age 16. Now a freelance writer and consultant, Dave spends much of free time rock climbing on the Internet (dgibbons@bigcat.missouri.edu).

Acknowledgments

Thanks to all the PR reps I've talked with over the past few months and the retailers who helped with pricing (particularly the staff at Mill Creek Computing and MMCS in Columbia, MO). Thanks also to friends at DATASTORM for weird-hours technical guidance, and friends on the Internet for other kinds of weird-hours guidance. Extra special thanks to Nancy, Steve, Jenny, and Ruth at Que, who were supportive and patient, and who work too much.

Trademarks

All terms mentioned in this book that are known to be trademarks or service marks have been appropriately capitalized. Que Corporation cannot attest to the accuracy of this information. Use of a term in this book should not be regarded as affecting the validity of any trademark or service mark.

Contents at a Glance

Introduction 1

Part I: Identifying Your Needs
Chapter 1	Why Get a Personal Computer?	11
Chapter 2	How You Will Use a PC	17
Chapter 3	How a Computer System Works	35

Part II: Choosing a System
Chapter 4	Deciding What Kind of Computer You Want	63
Chapter 5	Choosing a Computer System Manufacturer	77
Chapter 6	Listing of Computers	93
Chapter 7	Deciding What Kind of Video System You Need	155
Chapter 8	Listing of Monitors and Adapters	173
Chapter 9	Deciding What Kind of Printer You Need	197
Chapter 10	Listing of Printers	223

Part III: Deciding What Add-Ons You Need
Chapter 11	Ergonomic Devices	255
Chapter 12	Pointing Devices	267
Chapter 13	Modems and Fax Modems	275
Chapter 14	CD-ROM	303
Chapter 15	Storage	315
Chapter 16	Tape Backup Systems	333
Chapter 17	Sound Devices	339
Chapter 18	Scanners	349
Chapter 19	Feeding Your System	361

Part IV: Buying a System
Chapter 20	Putting Together a System to Meet Your Needs	371
Chapter 21	Making the Purchase	387
Appendix A	Planning for the Future	415
Appendix B	Vendor Information	433
Index	....	447

Contents

Introduction 1
   What This Book Does 2
   Who This Book Is for 2
   How This Book Is Organized 3
   New for the 1995 Edition 6
   Other Reference Sources from Que 7

I Identifying Your Needs

1 Why Get a Personal Computer? 11
   The Benefits of Using a PC 11
      Improving Quality 11
      Saving Time and Money 12
      Increasing Accuracy 12
      Gaining Flexible Storage 12
      Handling Repetitive Work 12
      Opening New Avenues of Opportunity 12
      Having Fun 13
   The Problems of Using a PC 13
      Significant Investment 13
      Learning How To Use It 14
      Tip of the Iceberg 15
   And the Winner Is... 15
   Chapter Summary 15

2 How You Will Use a PC 17
   Determining Your Uses for a PC 17
      Working with Words 19
      Working with Numbers 20
      Working with Money 21
      Managing Data 21
      Communicating with Others 22
      Sharing Work 22

  Creating Graphics 23
  Creating Presentations 23
  Creating and Using Multimedia 24
  Playing Games 24
  Enhancing Your Education 25
  Creating Programs 25
 Where You Use a PC 26
  In the Office 26
  On the Road 27
  At Home 28
  At School 28
 How Many Computers? 29
 Identifying Your Requirements 30
 Chapter Summary 33
 IN THE NEXT CHAPTER 33

3 How a Computer System Works 35

 Hardware 35
  Microprocessors 37
  The Motherboard 47
  Disk Drives 52
  System Unit 55
 Software 57
  ROM Firmware 57
  Operating System Software 57
  Operating Environments 57
  Drivers 58
  Utilities 58
  Applications 58
 How Hardware and Software Work Together 58
 Chapter Summary 59
 IN THE NEXT CHAPTER 59

II Choosing a System

4 Deciding What Kind of Computer You Want 63

 How To Choose an Operating Environment 63
  Your Budget 64
  What You and Your Coworkers Use at the Office 65
  Specific Programs You May Need 65
  How and Where You Plan To Use Your Computer 66

Macintosh, DOS, Windows, or ?	66
Run DOS if You Can	66
The Case for Windows	68
The Case for Macintosh and Power Macs	69
Run OS/2 or NT if You Have to	71
Making a Safe Choice	72
Desktop or Portable?	73
Who Can Use a Portable	73
Portables Take Center Stage	73
Super-Portables: Subnotebooks, Palmtops, and PDAs	74
When a Desktop System Is a Better Buy	75
Chapter Summary	75
IN THE NEXT CHAPTER	75

5 Choosing a Computer System Manufacturer 77

Important Factors in Choosing a Manufacturer	77
Name Recognition	78
Price and Performance	78
Compatibility	79
Service and Support Policies	79
Sales Channel	80
Financial Viability	81
Top PC Manufacturers	81
The Top Three Manufacturers	82
The Second Tier	85
The Best of the Rest	90
Chapter Summary	91
IN THE NEXT CHAPTER	91

6 Listing of Computers 93

Fields for Computer Tables	94
386DX-Based Desktop Computers	96
486SX-Based Desktop Computers	100
486DX-Based Desktop Computers	104
486DX2-Based Desktop Computers	110
486DX4-Based Desktop Computers	114
Pentium Desktop Computers	118
Macintosh 680X0-Based Desktop Computers	134
Power Macintosh Computers	138
Macintosh Portable Computers	140
Subnotebooks and PDAs	146

7 Deciding What Kind of Video System You Need 155

The Video Display System 155
    The Video Adapter 156
    The Monitor 160
Display Standards 165
    Obsolete IBM-Compatible Standards 165
    Current IBM-Compatible Display Standards 166
    Macintosh Display Standards 167
    Software Drivers 169
What To Look for in a Monitor 169
The Right Video System for You 170
Chapter Summary 172
IN THE NEXT CHAPTER 172

8 Listing of Monitors and Adapters 173

Fields for Monitor Tables 174
    Small Monitors Sorted by Screen Size, Resolution,
        and Manufacturer 175
    Medium Monitors Sorted by Screen Size, Resolution,
        and Manufacturer 178
    Large Monitors Sorted by Screen Size, Resolution,
        and Manufacturer 182
Fields for Graphics Adapter Tables 188
    PC-Compatible Graphics Adapters 189
    Macintosh-Compatible Graphics Adapters 192

9 Deciding What Kind of Printer You Need 197

Introduction to Personal Printers 197
Dot-Matrix Printers 198
    How It Works 198
    Price and Costs 199
    Speed 200
    Resolution and Print Quality 200
    Fonts 201
    Graphics 201
    Drivers 201
    Size 201
    Paper Handling 202
    Controls 202

Memory	203
Portability	203
Color	203
Manufacturers	203
Inkjet Printers	**204**
How It Works	204
Prices and Costs	205
Speed	205
Resolution and Print Quality	205
Fonts	206
Graphics	206
Drivers	206
Size	207
Paper Handling	207
Controls	207
Memory	207
Portability	207
Color	208
Manufacturers	208
Laser Printers	**208**
How It Works	209
Price and Costs	210
Speed	210
Resolution and Print Quality	210
Fonts and Printer Control Languages	211
Graphics	211
Drivers	212
Size	212
Paper Handling	212
Controls	212
Memory	213
Portability	213
Color	214
Manufacturers	214
Color Printers	**214**
How It Works	215
Price and Costs	216
Speed	216
Resolution and Print Quality	216
Fonts and Printer Control Languages	216
Graphics and Text	216

    Drivers 217
    Size 217
    Paper Handling 217
    Memory 217
    Portability 217
    Manufacturers 217
  The Right Printer for You 218
    How To Pick a Printer 218
    What Kind of Printer? 218
    Your Main Applications 220
  Chapter Summary 222
  IN THE NEXT CHAPTER 222

10 Listing of Printers 223

  Fields for Printer Tables 224
    Thermal Printers Sorted by Weight 225
    Dot-Matrix Printers Sorted by Number of Pins and Price 226
    Inkjet Printers Sorted by System, Company, and Model 230
    Personal Laser Printers Sorted by Speed, Company, and Model 236
    Office Laser Printers Sorted by Speed, Company, and Model 242
    Color Printers Sorted by Company and Model 248
  Chapter Summary 250
  IN THE NEXT CHAPTER 251

III Deciding What Add-Ons You Need

11 Ergonomic Devices 255

  Easy on the Eyes 256
    Eyestrain 256
    Exposure to Radiation 256
  Hurting Hands 258
  Aching Backs 261
  Overall Ergonomics 264
  Chapter Summary 265
  IN THE NEXT CHAPTER 265

12 Pointing Devices 267
Choosing a Pointing Device 267
Reviewing Manufacturers of Pointing Devices 268
Pointing Device Listing 269
Chapter Summary 272
IN THE NEXT CHAPTER 273

13 Modems and Fax Modems 275
What You Need To Know 276
Making the Purchase 278
Modem Listings 278
Chapter Summary 300
IN THE NEXT CHAPTER 301

14 CD-ROM 303
CD-ROM Basics 304
CD-ROM Problems 305
Purchase Considerations 306
CD-ROM Drive Listing 307
Chapter Summary 314
IN THE NEXT CHAPTER 314

15 Storage 315
Selecting an External Storage Device 315
    How It Works 316
    Price and Costs 317
Listings of Storage Devices 317
Chapter Summary 330
IN THE NEXT CHAPTER 331

16 Tape Backup Systems 333
Backup Background 334
Purchase Considerations 334
Fields for Tape Drive Listings 335

17 Sound Devices 339

Selecting a Sound Card 339
    How It Works 340
    Features to Look For 340
    Manufacturers 341
Listing of Sound Cards 341
Chapter Summary 346
IN THE NEXT CHAPTER 347

18 Scanners 349

Selecting a Scanner 349
    How It Works 350
    Price and Costs 351
    Resolution 352
    Drivers 352
    Size 352
    Manufacturers 353
Listings of Scanners 353
Chapter Summary 360
IN THE NEXT CHAPTER 360

19 Feeding Your System 361

Secure Power Supplies for Your PC 361
Laptop Batteries 366
Chapter Summary 368
IN THE NEXT CHAPTER 368

IV Buying a System

20 Putting Together a System To Meet Your Needs 371

Know Your Operating Environment 371
General-Purpose Desktop PCs 372
    A Mid-Range System 372
    A Low-End Desktop System 376
    A High-End Desktop System 377

General-Purpose Portables 378
　　　　　A Mid-Range Portable System 378
　　　　　A Low-End Portable System 380
　　　　　A High-End Portable System 381
　　　Selecting a Model Based on a Major Application 381
　　　　　Word Processing 382
　　　　　Spreadsheets 382
　　　　　Educational Software, Games, and Multimedia 383
　　　Considering a Used Computer 384
　　　Chapter Summary 386
　　　IN THE NEXT CHAPTER 386

21　Making the Purchase 387
　　　Where To Purchase Computers and Peripherals 387
　　　　　A Brief History of PC Buying 387
　　　　　Computer Dealers 388
　　　　　Mail-Order Vendors 390
　　　　　Computer Superstores 393
　　　　　Consumer Electronics Stores and Departments 396
　　　　　Department Stores 398
　　　　　Vendor Summary 400
　　　More Things To Consider in Buying a System 400
　　　　　Warranties 400
　　　　　Setup 403
　　　　　Phone Support 404
　　　　　Training, Training, Training 405
　　　A Buyer's Checklist 407
　　　　　What Kind of Computer? 407
　　　　　IBM-Compatible Systems 408
　　　　　Macintosh Systems 410
　　　Making the Purchase 412
　　　Chapter Summary 413
　　　IN THE APPENDIX 413

A　Planning for the Future 415
　　　Maintaining Your Computer System 415
　　　　　Maintaining the System Unit 415
　　　　　Maintaining Floppy Disk Drives 416
　　　　　Maintaining Hard Disk Drives 416

Maintaining the Keyboard, Mouse, and Video Monitor	418
Maintaining the Printer	418
Maintaining Your Software	419
Long-Term Troubleshooting Strategies	420
Upgrading Your Computer	421
Adding Memory	422
Adding a Math Coprocessor	423
Upgrading the Processor	423
Upgrading the Hard Disk	424
Upgrading the Keyboard and Mouse	425
Upgrading the Video System	426
Long-Term Upgrade Strategies	426
Repairing a Personal Computer System	427
In-Warranty Repairs	427
Out-of-Warranty Repairs	428
Keeping Pace with New Developments	430
Subscribing to Computer Magazines	430
Joining an On-Line Service	431
Appendix Summary	432
B Vendor Information	**433**
Index	**447**

Introduction

Buying a personal computer today can be an exciting yet confusing experience. The choices have never been greater, and the prices of powerful systems have never been lower. Yet the chances of making expensive mistakes are also high. Major computer makers reprice existing lines constantly and introduce new models several times a year. Some of the most interesting new systems are back ordered for weeks or months; a few have been discontinued before the backlog was ever worked off.

Some mid-size and many small computer makers are in financial trouble. Many of the less expensive systems lack upgradability and expandability that you might find important later. Portable computers are growing in power and capability to the point that many of them are being used for work formerly reserved for desktop systems.

Making the right choices for the parts that make up your computer is a major concern as well. The computer's speed, for instance, may seem to be the most important of the choices you make at the time that you're ordering your system. When you get the system set up, however, you may be more concerned about the size of the monitor you chose than about the system's speed. A lot of elements have to work together to produce a feeling of satisfaction with your system. Hardware choices affect your software options, increasing or limiting the number of things you can do with your computer. Making the right software choices takes as much thought as selecting hardware.

You may be a first-time buyer with little or no computer experience who wants to know what you are getting into before putting down real money. You may be an experienced computer user who is looking to buy an additional system for use at home or on the road. You may be considering upgrading or expanding an existing system to better handle current work or to take on new tasks. You may be a satisfied computer owner who is advising a friend or colleague who has decided to become a computer user.

What This Book Does

Que's 1995 Computer Buyer's Guide gives you the information and perspective to understand the choices you need to make, and then guides you through the steps to making a decision and purchase. It is also a reference that you, your colleagues, and friends can refer to again and again to understand the sometimes dizzying array of choices that are available today.

In contrast to other sources of information, this book covers all the important kinds of hardware and software for personal computer users: Macintosh and IBM-compatible systems, desktop systems, and portables. This book helps you select a type of computer and a brand and model, and then configure the system with RAM, hard disk, video subsystem, a printer, and other peripherals to meet your needs and budget. The book also gives tips on buying, maintaining, repairing, and upgrading your system.

Unlike buyer's guides that appear in computer magazines (or, increasingly, other consumer magazines), *Que's 1995 Computer Buyer's Guide* does not consist solely of long lists of product features and ratings with little explanation as to why you might or might not need the kind of product in question. Instead, this book explains, in understandable terms, what different kinds of products can do and which types of products are best for meeting specific needs. It recommends what you should look for in products in each category—recommendations based on years of experience using these products and similar ones. Finally, this buyer's guide offers specification tables of computer systems and peripherals, organized by category, so that you can easily select the best items for your needs.

In each product listing, you'll find some of the most attractive pieces of hardware (based on price and performance) highlighted so that you can tell at a glance which pieces deliver the best value and most features. The "Value Leader" in each table is not necessarily the least expensive—it's the one that delivers the most bang for the buck.

Who This Book Is for

Most computer purchases today are made by corporate buyers who are responsible for dozens or even hundreds of purchases a year. Most books and, especially, magazines about computing are intended to reach this big, rich market of power buyers. But the very people who created the personal computer revolution—individuals who are trying to do work, to learn, to gain new knowledge and skills—are being left behind. Although some volume buyers will no doubt find this book useful, its main intent is to help put the "personal" back into personal computing.

If you are about to buy a system that you, a family member, or friend will be using, or are looking to upgrade or buy software for such a system, *Que's 1995 Computer Buyer's Guide* is for you. Whether your computer will be used at your job, at home, at school, on the road, or some combination; whether you're committed to IBM PC-compatibles, the

Apple Macintosh family, or are willing to consider either; this book will help you make decisions you'll be happy with now and in the future. The goal of this book is not to tell you what to buy, but to tell you what you need to know to make that decision on your own.

Que's 1995 Computer Buyer's Guide is also helpful to anyone new to personal computing and to experienced users who want to learn more about the hardware they are already using. The information in this book helps you put your computer system into perspective and lays the groundwork for all the decisions you will make about computer-related purchases: the computer system, monitor, printer, and other add-on hardware. As the reader of this book, you benefit by having a wealth of comparative details that help you select the right hardware for your needs.

How This Book Is Organized

Que's 1995 Computer Buyer's Guide is structured so that information to help you determine what you want to do is followed by recommendations and information on the products you need to accomplish your goals. The book is divided into four parts. It consists of 21 chapters and 2 appendixes.

Briefly, Part I, "Identifying Your Needs," explains the basics of computer systems and software and how they are used. Part II, "Choosing a System," provides information and tables regarding computer systems and major peripherals. Part III, "Deciding What Add-Ons You Need," covers many of your hardware options beyond the basic computer, monitor, and printer, including CD-ROM drives, ergonomic devices, modems, and much more. Part IV, "Buying a System," helps you make final purchasing decisions and decide where to buy your system and add-on hardware. The appendixes include helpful information for use after you have made your purchases. The following paragraphs describe in greater detail the contents of each part, chapter, and appendix.

This introduction is intended to let you know what to expect in this book and how to use it to get the information you need. It also points you to things that are new in this year's edition of the book, in case you bought previous editions and want to find the latest information or are simply interested in the changes taking place in the computer marketplace.

Part I, "Identifying Your Needs," is designed to familiarize you with the uses of computers and to describe how the different parts that make up a system work and interact to accomplish useful tasks.

Chapter 1, "Why Get a Personal Computer?" describes some of the ways in which you can use a computer. If you are new to using a computer, or are considering using a system you already have in new ways, this chapter helps you decide what you want your computer to do.

Chapter 2, "How You Will Use a PC," takes you through the different things you can do with a computer. It also provides a fresh look at the usefulness of desktop versus portable systems.

Chapter 3, "How a Computer System Works," provides a basic overview of how each part of a computer system works. It is intended to give you enough technical information to understand computer advertisements and magazine articles describing and comparing products, without burdening you with obsolete information or useless details.

Part II, "Choosing a System," gives you specific information about how to choose software, systems, and peripherals. It describes the choices available in operating environments, computer systems, monitors, printers, and other add-ons. This part includes useful tables filled with specifications, including prices, for each part of the computer system.

Chapter 4, "Deciding What Kind of Computer You Want," helps you focus on some of the most important questions that computer buyers face today. Are you constrained by compatibility considerations to choose DOS or Windows, or is Macintosh a better choice for you? Are you one of the many users who can do most or all of their work on a portable system? These key questions are addressed in this chapter.

Chapter 5, "Choosing a Computer System Manufacturer," gives you some real guidance on the important issue of picking the brand name you'll buy. This chapter will make your computer system choices much easier.

Chapter 6, "Listing of Computers," contains specification tables covering many different kinds of IBM-compatible PCs and the Macintosh, including desktop systems and portables. This chapter, with up-to-date listings of models, configurations, and prices, is one of the key assets of this book. It is an excellent starting point for anyone considering the purchase of a system.

Chapter 7, "Deciding What Type of Video System You Need," gives you detailed background information about how monitors and video systems work and what you should look for in making a purchase. It gives specifics about how your software choices might affect what you want in a monitor, all influenced by how much you're able to spend.

Chapter 8, "Listing of Monitors and Adapters," contains specification tables listing monitors and display adapters. Like the computer listings chapter, it has up-to-date information about products, descriptive information, and prices, making it a great place to start the purchase process.

Chapter 9, "Deciding What Kind of Printer You Need," describes what you need to know about the most popular kinds of printers, how they work, and what features you should look for in making a purchase. It describes how your software choices affect what kind of printer you need, within the bounds of what you're able to spend.

Chapter 10, "Listing of Printers," contains specification tables with the latest information about portable, dot-matrix, inkjet, and laser printers. It will be of great assistance to you in buying a piece of equipment that may well outlast your computer system.

Part III, "Deciding What Add-Ons You Need," explains how many common peripherals are used and what factors you should consider before buying.

Chapter 11, "Ergonomic Devices," contains both descriptive information and specification tables about ergonomically related products. These important add-ons assist you in using your computer without pain, discomfort, or injury.

Chapter 12, "Pointing Devices," covers mice, trackballs, and drawing tablets. The chapter lists specific advantages of each type of pointing device and specifications for popular products.

Chapter 13, "Modems and Fax Modems," shows you the latest cruisers for the infamous "Information Superhighway." Desktop and laptop modems are listed, including specifications and prices.

Chapter 14, "CD-ROM," shows you the things to consider before you buy a CD-ROM drive and lists specifications and prices for popular drives.

Chapter 15, "Storage," introduces you to external and removable hard drives, rewritable optical drives, and other devices to help you store large amounts of data. It explains the advantages and disadvantages of the competing technologies and lists specifications and prices for many popular storage solutions.

Chapter 16, "Tape Backup Systems," explains how (and why) to protect the data on your hard drive from disk crashes. Popular tape drives are listed, including specifications and prices.

Chapter 17, "Sound and Voice Devices," details the options available in the growing PC sound market. It lists sound cards (including MIDI), voice-recognition systems, and voice mail systems.

Chapter 18, "Scanners," lists hand-held and flatbed scanners, both grayscale and color. The main technologies are discussed, along with buying considerations.

Chapter 19, "Feeding Your System," covers options for keeping your computer supplied with power. It discusses power conditioners (to protect your PC from power surges), uninterruptible power supplies, and sources for notebook computer batteries.

Part IV, "Buying a System," brings together the information in earlier chapters to help you make the right purchase decisions and carry them out effectively.

Chapter 20, "Putting Together a System to Meet Your Needs," matches up specific kinds of needs and budgets against the available systems and comes up with examples of systems and peripherals that fill the bill. The listings are of combinations of products, to demonstrate what you might expect to pay when everything has been taken into account.

Chapter 21, "Making the Purchase," describes your options for buying a computer and peripherals. It includes information about your choices as to setup, support, and training.

Appendix A, "Planning for the Future," helps you prepare for life with a computer system. This appendix discusses maintenance, repair, and upgrades to your system.

Appendix B, "Vendor Information," provides the names, addresses, and phone numbers of companies listed in the specification tables in the book. You can get in touch with the companies for further information about the products mentioned in this book, and buy direct in some cases.

New for the 1995 Edition

This book is completely redone for 1995. All the tables have been thoroughly updated and new technologies are discussed. This edition takes recommendations further than previous editions, pointing out value leaders in each category rather than simply presenting tables for you to figure out on your own.

The most important change that has taken place in the computer hardware market since last year's edition is the continuing fall in hardware prices. For many years, the amount of computer power you could get for a given amount of money has steadily improved, but now the whole price structure is moving downward, so that even a high-end machine powered by the latest microprocessor can be had for well under $5,000. Mid-range and low-end machines are becoming fantastically inexpensive. This is a wonderful time to be buying a computer system, if you have the right information at hand to make a good buying decision.

The drop in prices also means a drop in profits, and this situation is leading to consolidation in the personal computer industry. Consolidation simply means fewer kinds of products, sold by fewer manufacturers. The risk of being "orphaned"—buying a system, only to have its manufacturer go out of business—is growing. If this happens to you, you might have difficulties in getting service, support, and parts for your machine. To help you guard against this problem, this book focuses attention on large, profitable computer system manufacturers whose sales are growing.

Another important change since last year's edition is the growing power of a mid-range computer system. This increase has been driven by the continuing drop in prices and the high performance requirements of Windows. Whereas a 486 (or 486SX) was the microprocessor in a mainstream desktop system a year ago, a clock-doubled (or clock-tripled) 486 is used now. Pentium systems are becoming more common, with PowerPC-based Macintoshes and PC-compatibles poised to shake up the market radically. Video performance is being accelerated rapidly, and bigger hard disks and monitors are rapidly becoming commonplace. Portables are also quickly becoming more powerful as users demand the same performance as they get from desktop machines. In today's computer market, you can shop for a very powerful system and still get a bargain.

These major changes—dropping prices and growing computer power in the mid-range—have affected this book. The author is very interested in your reaction to these changes and in your opinions of the book as a whole. Please write the author, care of Que Corporation; send mail on CompuServe, address 72410,2077; or send a fax to (317) 581-4663 with your ideas. These ideas will be used to improve future editions of the book.

Other Reference Sources from Que

Although *Que's 1995 Computer Buyer's Guide* tells you what you should know in order to make an intelligent computer purchase, no book can fill all your personal computing needs. Que Corporation publishes a full line of microcomputer books that complement this one.

If you want general information about computing fundamentals, look through *Introduction to Personal Computers*, 4th Edition, and *Que's Computer User's Dictionary*, 3rd Edition. For IBM and compatible computers, *Using MS-DOS 6.2*, Special Edition, and *Using Microsoft Windows 3.1*, Special Edition, provide information about the most popular operating systems and environments. For Macintosh computers, *Que's Big Mac Book*, 4th Edition, is an all-in-one reference source.

If you are interested in finding out more about how to use a particular software application, you can choose from many Que books for IBM-compatible and Macintosh computers. Que books on some of the more popular applications include *Using 1-2-3 for DOS Release 3.1+*, Special Edition; *Using WordPerfect 6.0*, Special Edition; and *Using WordPerfect for Windows*, Special Edition. You also may consult *Using dBASE IV 1.5*, Special Edition (for IBM and compatibles) and *Using Excel 3 for the Macintosh*, *Using Excel 4 for Windows*, and *Using Word 5.1 for the Macintosh*.

If you are interested in further technical details about computer hardware, examine *Upgrading and Repairing PCs*, 2nd Edition. This informative text shows you how to get the most from your current hardware and how to upgrade your system to achieve better performance from your software.

PART I

Identifying Your Needs

Includes

Why Get a Personal Computer?

How You Will Use a PC

How a Computer System Works

CHAPTER ONE

Why Get a Personal Computer?

This chapter explains the benefits a computer can bring you and some of the problems you can run into when buying and using it.

The Benefits of Using a PC

A personal computer system, although somewhat expensive, is often a requirement for specific business and personal needs. In other areas, the computer is not a requirement, but you can greatly benefit from having one. Although your specific requirements determine what you will get out of the experience of owning a personal computer, some benefits are common to most uses of personal computers.

Improving Quality

There are a number of areas in which you must have a PC to do high-quality work. The best example is probably word processing; a personal computer enables you to get much more writing done in a given period of time and to produce noticeably better looking output with fewer mistakes. Other examples abound, from desktop presentations to multimedia. Anyone in a competitive situation—writing letters to clients, preparing reports and presentations, even turning in a college paper—feels the need to produce work of good quality, and PC-generated output has become the standard in these and other areas. Your purchase decisions will be at least partly motivated by the desire to match or exceed the quality of work produced by others at a reasonable expense.

Saving Time and Money

Many tasks that you can do in other ways, you can do more easily and inexpensively on a PC. If, for instance, you want to plan a trip, you can do the "traditional" legwork, calling travel agencies, airlines, and hotels on the phone, possibly researching your destination in the library. Gathering information this way is hard work, and considering a number of options simultaneously is difficult because of the time it takes to investigate each one. To perform the same task with your computer, you can use a program like the Online Airline Guide or an on-line service like CompuServe to make gathering a wide variety of information and even booking a flight easy and fast.

Increasing Accuracy

Accuracy is a great benefit of using a personal computer. A spell-checking program can eliminate most of the misspellings from written work, and a grammar checker can catch other problems. When you get your formulas set up correctly (often no small task), a spreadsheet can reliably recalculate the same equation dozens or thousands of times without ever making an error.

Gaining Flexible Storage

Many people need to manage large amounts of data in pursuit of their professional and personal interests. Keeping the records of a company on-line can greatly enhance the ability to quickly find needed information. Keeping your personal records on a computer can also make it easy to enter and track a lot of data.

You may or may not need this benefit when you make your initial purchasing decision, but it becomes an important benefit after you have had a computer for a while and created dozens, hundreds, even thousands of different word processing documents, spreadsheets, drawings, and so on. Keep this benefit in mind as you consider your uses for a computer.

Handling Repetitive Work

If you have repetitive tasks that can easily be automated, you can benefit greatly from using a PC. A good example of such a task is sending out a form letter to a list of people, whether it's a Christmas letter or a billing statement. Another example is performing a set of calculations, such as mortgage interest on a loan or the growth of an investment over time, over and over on different sets of data.

Opening New Avenues of Opportunity

Becoming a computer professional of some kind is a goal of many PC buyers. Others want to continue the work they currently do and use the computer to set the quality and quantity of their work apart. Many people who buy computers for home want their kids to have computer experience.

Having Fun

Using a computer opens up a lot of ways to have fun, from conversing with others via an on-line service to playing computer games. Whether it's doing things that are widely known to be fun, or the enjoyment you get from learning about the computer itself, having fun is one of the key attractions of owning and using a personal computer.

The Problems of Using a PC

Although the benefits of using a PC for many applications are indisputable, the problems that it can bring have been ignored or downplayed for too long. Recent studies have asserted that the average computer user in an office spends five hours a week doing various things to his or her computer, and other studies show that some unofficial office "computer gurus" devote half or more of their time to helping others with computer problems, usually with little reward or recognition.

The problems of using a PC are particularly pertinent to home computer buyers. For novice users, there is no computer guru available to answer your questions unless you were very fortunate in who you married, or have a bright and patient teenager in the house who can help. Unlike many office workers, you're not getting paid for the time you spend learning about your system and its software, and the benefits that home computer users get from their systems are often less dramatic than those achieved by a business. (This statement is somewhat less true if you're using your home computer for work.) More experienced users have to handle all aspects of upgrading or repairing their home PCs—they can't fall back on an MIS department like office users can. Pay special attention to potential problems if you're considering buying a system for home use.

Significant Investment

A computer costs a good deal of money—somewhere between a middle-of-the-road television set and an inexpensive car—and the purchase price of a computer is just the first in a series of expenditures. If a monitor isn't included in your system, you have to buy one. You need a printer for output. Although prices are dropping, a good printer can still cost as much as the computer system itself. You have to buy software; the software you want to run has a tremendous effect on the computer system you choose and how much you have to spend on it. On-line services cost a small to medium amount per month, and for the home user, the cost of setting up a suitable work area in your home can be substantial.

You need a lot of benefits from the computer to recoup the amount of time and money you will spend on buying your system and getting it to do your bidding. Let's say that you spend $2,500 for your system, software, and a printer. (Even with today's low computer prices, this figure is low.) If you use the system to produce one 10-page paper or report a month, keep track of your checkbook, and communicate on-line with newfound friends, your hard dollar savings may only be about $50 a month compared with the amount you would have paid someone to type up the paper or report for you through a couple of drafts. At this rate, it would take you over four years to pay back the cost of the computer.

Of course, the hard dollar savings is not the only benefit of using the computer. You may do a noticeably better job of tracking your bills on the computer, and it's hard to put a price tag on the friends that you might make on-line. But offsetting the intangible benefits are hard-to-track costs: the many hours you spend setting up your computer, learning about it, and trying to fix problems that arise. The point is that you need a clear idea of what you're getting into before you buy a computer; make sure that the benefits will outweigh all the costs that you will incur, in time as well as in money.

Learning How To Use It

In addition to a financial investment, you also have to invest time in setting up the computer, learning how to use it, and learning how to use your software. The time you spend learning to use your computer system is worth giving some attention to in advance because it can be an insidious drain on other things you're trying to do in your life. It's not uncommon for new users to become "addicted" to their computers, spending countless hours exploring the different options in their software—especially if they have a modem and a subscription to an on-line service. Computing is a fascinating new world for many people, and it's easy to get lost.

Most computer users don't get much (if any) training in using their systems and software. This means they get less out of the system than they should, and they have a hard time when they need to use obscure features or when problems arise. Unless you already have considerable experience (or easy access to someone who does), you need to include in your analysis of whether a computer is a worthwhile investment for you, the cost of several hours of training courses, plus the cost and reading time for several computer-related books and at least one magazine subscription. Before you start, make sure that you have access to some computer expertise on short notice; find out whether the providers of your hardware and software provide affordable telephone support, and consider joining an on-line service and a user's group.

If you want to get a feel for how hard it can be to use a computer, read the User's Column by Jerry Pournelle in *Byte* magazine for a couple of months; it honestly describes the dozens of hours he spends each month grappling with obscure hardware and software problems. Then remember that he's an expert user and a well-known figure who usually gets top-quality technical support as needed, yet he still spends a lot of time fighting problems; you will spend more time waiting on a help line than he does.

Tip of the Iceberg

Like buying a car, buying a computer system can be the first step into a whole new world of technical gobbledygook, unexpected expenses, and potential problems. But people have over 75 years' experience with cars; the problems are well-known and understood, and a lot of benefits accrue to car makers and service providers who can reduce the overall hassles to drivers. Thankfully, the computing industry is following the same trends, taking much of the hassle out of what could be a pretty intimidating process.

Society is still on the early part of the learning curve for personal computers, and until recently the industry expects users to bring an inordinate amount of expertise, patience, and cash to the problems involved in buying and using them. Not all the wrinkles are ironed out yet, so you may still want to consider deferring your purchase if you're not sure that the benefits of buying a computer system significantly outweigh all the costs and potential hassles associated with owning it. If you do go ahead, as more and more people are doing, be aware that your purchase of a computer system is only the first of many steps on the road to becoming productive with it.

And the Winner Is...

For most people, a personal computer is a worthwhile investment. It increases your opportunities to work better or in other places, to learn, and to have fun. If you avoid the pitfalls described in this book, you can get a lot out of a personal computer.

Chapter Summary

In this chapter, you have learned some of the benefits and problems of using personal computers. You have learned that personal computers can improve the quality of your work, save time and money, increase accuracy, add flexible storage for your records, handle repetitive work, open new opportunities for you, and help you have fun. You have also learned that personal computers require a significant investment of time and money. Understanding these plusses and minuses of personal computers is an important first step in making informed purchasing decisions.

The next chapter explains some of the specific uses you may have for a personal computer, from mainstream applications such as spreadsheets and word processing to emerging applications such as multimedia. It also discusses the importance of deciding where you will use the computer and how this decision will affect your buying decisions.

CHAPTER TWO

How You Will Use a PC

When you enter the computer market for the first time, it's only natural to look for advice from "experts" like your computer-using associates, magazines, and, well, this book. People are always happy to give advice, but as you consult more sources, their advice is more likely to contradict someone else's. For example, when you ask a programmer, she might say, "Get a fast machine with lots of RAM and a huge hard disk and forget about wasting money on a fancy monitor and peripherals." A graphic artist might say, "Get a nice monitor and a laser printer—they're worth the investment." Accountants might advise against a fast machine because of the monetary investment, saying you can get just as much done on a slower, cheaper machine. Magazines lay out arguments for (and against) every possible computer, peripheral, and software. Everyone you ask has an opinion, but many of their opinions are based on what they want rather than what you need.

After listening to advice for a while, it's easy to become frustrated enough to think that nobody really knows what they're talking about and maybe this whole computer business is overrated in the first place. But don't give up. There is one advisor who you can truly trust to have your best interests at heart, and that's you. You know your needs and abilities better than anyone else.

In this chapter, you learn the questions you need to ask yourself when you decide to buy a PC. (Throughout this book, the terms *personal computer* and *PC* refer to any type of personal computer: IBM, IBM-compatible, or Macintosh; desktop or portable.) Take a close look at the checklists at the end of the chapter, even if you only skim through the other parts of the chapter. The checklists help you consider important factors that are often overlooked when purchasing PCs and direct you to other sections of the book that can help you learn specifics before you make your decision.

Determining Your Uses for a PC

For your personal computer system to be worth its purchase price and the other costs associated with it, you must know what you want it to do. What tasks do you want to perform with it? What things that currently take up your valuable time will be done faster and better with the computer? What will it add to your life? The following list describes many of the tasks you may want to accomplish with your PC, and the following sections describe each in more detail:

- Working with words
- Working with numbers
- Working with money
- Managing data
- Communicating with others
- Sharing work
- Creating graphics
- Creating presentations
- Creating or using multimedia
- Playing games
- Enhancing education
- Creating programs

These tasks fall into three categories for each person, depending on their needs. Some may be tasks that you must have a personal computer to do well. If, for example, you work with numbers, becoming proficient in using a spreadsheet program is practically a job requirement. Tasks like this should play the largest part in determining what type of a system you get because they dictate what software you need, and the software in turn dictates what type of system you need.

Other tasks are things that you currently do manually and could do better with a PC. For example, you no doubt manage your own money, and possibly someone else's as well. If you currently manage a moderate or large amount of data on paper, storing it on the PC makes retrieving it, creating reports with it, and other tasks much easier, especially if you repeat these tasks frequently and with the same data.

The third category of tasks are things that you don't currently do, but would like to do on a computer. These tasks are usually the weakest justification for buying a system. For instance, you may want to play games on a computer and explore multimedia. You may spend hundreds of hours and thousands of dollars only to find that a game system would have met your entertainment needs for much less money and that creating multimedia presentations takes a great deal of training and expertise that don't automatically come with the purchase of a PC. Think hard before buying a system or expensive add-ons to meet this kind of need. If your main reason for buying a computer is so that you can tackle totally new tasks like multimedia or programming, consider taking a course in those areas at a local college first. The class will give you access to the proper equipment, and you can get a feel for the task before making a major (and less-informed) computer purchase.

All of these tasks require a suitably equipped personal computer and one or more application programs. The term *suitably equipped* means different things for different applications. Throughout the book, you see specifics about the memory, speed, and peripherals your computer needs to accomplish different tasks. In general, to run a multitasking system (in which you can use multiple programs at the same time), you need a more powerful system than for a single-task operating system like MS-DOS. As DOS programs become more powerful, the suitably equipped system of yesterday may not be sufficient. If this sounds confusing, don't worry—by the time you read through this chapter and the next, you will understand more about what it takes to run the popular operating systems and programs.

A large variety of programs are available for each of the tasks in the previous list. The following sections introduce some of the most important kinds of software. The descriptions are relatively free of jargon and product names, so you can think about your needs and budget before plunging into the greater detail offered in later chapters. Use the following sections to help you determine what you will do with a PC after you purchase it.

Working with Words

Creating letters, reports, manuscripts, term papers, and other documents is one of the best reasons to buy a PC. To do these tasks, you need a relatively inexpensive system and a word processing program. Using a word processing program is not unlike using a typewriter, but word processing software offers significant advantages over traditional typing.

With a word processor, you can correct mistakes just after you make them or at any point up until you print out the final copy of your document. You don't need correction fluid or extra typing paper; just find the mistake, delete it, and type in the new text. Making larger changes in your document is easier too. You can move paragraphs around and add new ones, letting the word processor reformat your document automatically.

Most good word processing programs have additional capabilities. Spell checkers are now standard in even the simplest programs, and grammar checkers are not uncommon. These two tools can eliminate a high percentage of the mistakes you might otherwise make. A built-in thesaurus to help you find just the right word and an outliner to help you brainstorm and manage growing documents are other tools that are available within the more powerful packages or as relatively inexpensive add-ins.

You can accomplish many tasks using a word processor without having to learn much about the program or the computer on which it runs. Just get someone to show you the basics of running the word processor, storing documents, backing up your work onto a floppy disk, and deleting unneeded files (be careful with this one). You can produce attractive documents using a few simple formatting commands.

If your needs are greater and you're willing to invest more time and money, you can go a long way with word processing. Mid-range word processors can now do a great many things that used to be the strict domain of desktop publishing programs, such as importing graphics and text from other programs, and flowing text around graphics. Once you figure out how to set up style sheets (which are like guidelines or rules for the word processor so that it knows how your documents usually look), they can make it easy to modify large and complex documents.

If you bump up against limitations in the formatting, importing, or other functions of your word processor, you can move up to a desktop publishing program. Desktop publishing programs allow precise control of the location of text and graphical elements on your pages, allowing you to create highly formatted documents like sales brochures, newsletters, and annual reports. You can work efficiently with multicolumn documents and very long documents. Experienced desktop publishers are able to create documents that formerly would have required hours of expensive time from print shop professionals, and they can do it at a fraction of the print shop cost. All these capabilities are available to you with an appropriate investment of time and money to develop the necessary expertise and put together the right combination of hardware and software.

Working with Numbers

Spreadsheet programs are now standard tools for all sorts of people who work with numbers. Spreadsheet programs are, first and foremost, electronic representations of pages in an accountant's pad, but a spreadsheet can also help with inventory, production planning, and other applications that deal with finance and numbers. But the spreadsheet program is easily extended to dozens of rows and hundreds of columns, is easily erased, and is programmable so that a number entered into a specific area can be used in one or more predefined calculations.

To use a spreadsheet program, you enter formulas and data into a spreadsheet document, which then calculates results according to your specifications. Then, when you enter a new figure or change a formula, the spreadsheet recalculates all the formulas and displays the new results. Suppose, for example, that you want to figure out the monthly payment on a mortgage given different initial down payments, interest rates (variable or fixed), and the length of the loan. You can enter the numbers for each scenario, and then calculate the results. This what-if feature of spreadsheets gives them a tremendous edge over manual calculating tools.

Not only do spreadsheet programs handle the drudgery of dealing with complicated calculations and eliminate the errors that sometimes come up when the work is done by hand, they can produce graphs of the results. Some programs also do a relatively good job of handling non-numeric data, such as names, addresses, and phone numbers, and combining numbers, text, and graphics into easy-to-understand reports.

Today's popular spreadsheet programs have a tremendous amount of built-in capability. With many of these programs, you can create 3-D worksheets and 3-D graphs, automatically plug data from other computers into your reports, and produce formatted reports of the results. You can do an awful lot with a relatively inexpensive computer system and a low-end or mid-range spreadsheet program, and then upgrade the software and the system if and when your needs grow.

Working with Money

The use of accounting programs has long been one of the primary justifications for computerizing a business. By automating necessary chores like payroll, billing, payment processing, and reporting, small and medium-size companies can attain a level of accuracy and an aura of professionalism formerly accomplished only by their larger competitors.

In the last few years, several software companies have introduced programs that bring this kind of capability to individuals for use in managing their personal finances. These personal finance programs are powerful but easy to use. You enter your transactions regularly, either daily or at the end of a month. Then you can print checks, reconcile bank statements, and compare your progress against financial goals, all with a high degree of accuracy. Other, similar programs make it as painless as possible to calculate your taxes; often, you can link the tax and personal finance programs.

Some of these low-end personal finance and tax programs are powerful enough to handle the needs of a small business and have add-ins available that allow them to take on complicated tasks like payroll. As with other low-end programs, a relatively inexpensive system may handle the work, though you may spend a lot on a good printer and consumables, such as preprinted check forms. Mastering the requirements of these programs early in the life of a small business, or even in the context of a complicated set of personal finances, can make it easy to grow into more capable hardware and software as your requirements change.

Managing Data

Using database management systems was one of the original uses for business computers.

Simple databases (which are technically called *flat-file databases*) that are sold inexpensively or as part of integrated software programs can perform many simple data management chores. These programs often make it easy to build new databases and extract information and reports.

To use a flat-file database, you first define the fields you will use, such as Name, Address, and Phone Number, and then enter groups of information (called *records*). The program should allow you to easily add fields, such as Birthdate, to existing databases, define default values for fields, and create simple to moderately complex reports.

The type of system you need for this kind of work can be very low-end, especially if you only need to store and retrieve text and not graphics. Your needs increase as the amount of data you are managing grows, and you will probably need a faster system if you move up to a more specialized database program (typically called a relational database).

Communicating with Others

Communicating with others is becoming one of the most important, and for many users the single most important, uses of a computer. Communications with others can be divided into three forms:

1. Local-area networks (LANs) that link the computers in a given location to one another so that they can share peripheral devices, such as printers, and exchange e-mail.

2. Wide-area networks (WANs) that extend LANs among multiple locations, to distant cities, and even worldwide.

3. Modem communications that enable a PC user to communicate with other computers and with on-line services like CompuServe and Prodigy over a regular phone line.

Networking takes a wide variety of forms and is usually designed and installed by professionals who have learned much about the subject. In recent years, however, simple, low-cost networks have started to appear. A networking scheme called Appletalk has been built into every Apple Macintosh ever made, and several similar products exist for IBM and IBM-compatible computers. With such technology, non-professionals can create and maintain local area networks.

Communication by modem over phone lines is one of the most exciting and popular things about personal computing. Hooking up to an on-line service is probably the easiest thing to do with a modem, and one of the most rewarding; you connect your modem to a phone line, and then dial up the on-line service. You sign up in a simple procedure (have a credit card or checking account number ready), and then start working your way around the system. You can learn a great deal about your computer or any number of other topics by exchanging messages with other users, searching on-line databases, and **downloading** free software.

> *Downloading.* Receiving computer files over a phone line through your modem.

Sharing Work

Users of networked terminals, such as airline reservation agents, are using a technology called *groupware*. Each user's actions update the system and affect what's available to other users. The term *groupware* is used to mean shared work among people using terminals (which can be full-fledged PCs) linked by a LAN or by modem connections.

You're more likely to use groupware in the context of doing office work than for personal needs. A groupware application is one that allows several people to work on the same document safely (without unknowingly erasing each others' work) and interactively. Lotus Notes may be the prototypical groupware application. To use Notes or similar programs, you attach your computer to the network (usually with a sign-on procedure in which you type your name and a password), join ongoing conversations and projects, respond to queries from other users on the network, and generate your own queries to any of the other users. Programmers can create custom applications specific to the kind of work done by a company or workgroup.

Creating Graphics

Before the advent of PCs and, in particular, the Apple Macintosh, only researchers and the most advanced users were using computers to create graphics. Graphics programs are now widely available, and are becoming easier to use all the time. This category of software includes "paint" programs that allow you to work on-screen as if you were sketching and coloring on paper, and "draw" programs that treat each piece of your drawing as an object that you can edit, manipulate, or delete individually.

To use a paint or draw program, you simply start up the program, select a tool (such as a paintbrush or pencil), and use a mouse to move the tool around on-screen and create graphics. Although paint programs tend to be easier and more fun to use, changing things once you put them into your drawing is difficult. Draw programs take a little more effort to use, but they allow you to easily modify your work. Many word processing and desktop publishing programs include simple drawing capabilities.

To use a paint or draw program, you should have a computer with a graphical user interface (a GUI), such as any Macintosh or an IBM or IBM-compatible running Windows or OS/2. Some paint programs run in DOS, but the other operating systems (which are inherently graphics oriented) offer many more options and typically easier setup.

Such a system already has a mouse and the capability to put graphics on-screen. If you just want to have fun with graphics, a low-end system is fine, but to move up into higher end graphics work, you probably will need a fast computer system with a color screen and graphics-capable printer. Professional graphics programs are notorious for needing a computer with a lot of resources (like RAM memory and disk space, which are discussed further in the next chapter).

Creating Presentations

Creating presentations is an outgrowth of creating graphics. Presentation programs allow you to combine background colors, graphics, and text into effective displays for use with speeches and demonstrations.

With most presentation programs, you pick a presentation format and type in text that appears in simple bulleted lists. You can also change backgrounds, add graphics, and make other changes to the basic layout.

A standard business presentation system has a large color screen and (sometimes) color printing or slide-creating capability. As your needs grow, you may begin to create presentations that are displayed on the computer screen. In this case, you may want to move into more advanced presentation programs and other tools that allow you to create animation and add sound and video, as described in the next section.

Creating and Using Multimedia

"Multimedia," like most buzz words, is an ill-defined term. By definition, a word processor or presentation graphics program that enables you to combine text and graphics is a multimedia program. But the term multimedia is most often used to describe what professionals call *time-based media*—sound, animated graphics, and video, all of which change with time and require synchronization with the clock and with one another to be used effectively.

Multimedia tools are used to produce video output, presentations displayed on the computer, and multimedia applications that a user interacts with on the computer. Some simple multimedia tools now exist that include **clip art**, sound and video clips, and predefined templates to give you a running start on creating successful presentations. But the design and creation of video output and interactive presentations, training programs, and so on is not a trivial exercise. Most computer users will be multimedia *consumers*, customers for learning programs and games developed by professionals and delivered on CD-ROM, rather than multimedia *producers*, the people who create the games and other programs.

> *Clip Art.* A collection of pre-made, general graphics that you can use in your own graphics, word processing documents, and desktop publishing projects. A clip art collection usually follows a theme. For example, it might contain pictures of dozens of different animals.

Becoming a multimedia consumer is getting easier, but you still need to purchase a fast system with a CD-ROM drive, a fast video card (discussed in Chapter 7), and sound output. To become a multimedia producer, you need training, expertise, time, money, and a really powerful system to succeed. The sky's the limit on the amount of time and money you can spend to produce professional-quality output that includes interactivity and special effects.

Playing Games

From the original Rogue, a text-only game played on UNIX systems, to today's multimedia jet fighter and starship passenger simulations, computer games have attracted some of the best creative energies in computing. Some of the best games require powerful systems and expensive peripherals, such as CD-ROM drives, but many games work well on mid-range systems.

Luckily, the same powerful systems that are needed to run graphical environments like Microsoft Windows provide an excellent base system for computer games. High-end games may require a fast CD-ROM drive, a sound card, and high-performance video. Some of the newest games even let you play against others across modems or local area networks.

Enhancing Your Education

Educational programs exist for many areas, from reading and writing to typing and learning a foreign language. Just as most educational programs have an element of fun to them, many game programs have an educational bent. Anyone who's played SimCity or beaten the computer at Railroad Tycoon feels that they have learned something from the experience.

Educational programs for children work well depending on the subject area covered, the age and interests of the child, and the amount of care and work that went into creating the game. If your children want to use "adult" programs, such as word processing, either get a typing program to help them learn to type first or turn them loose on the word processor so that they can try to produce something right away with the hunt-and-peck method.

Although some educational programs run on less-capable systems, a color Windows or Macintosh system that can handle computer games is needed to run most of them. At the high end, you may need a CD-ROM drive and fast video.

Creating Programs

In the early days of personal computing, many enthusiasts went on to become well-paid computer programmers, working in languages like BASIC or database languages. Now, programming for microcomputers is a profession that is increasingly populated by college graduates with degrees in computer science and related fields. Yet whether they realize it or not, ordinary users do a great deal of computer programming, from creating complex spreadsheets and word processing macros through writing SQL programs for database access. You don't need a college education to use the newest crop of programming tools (especially ones like Microsoft's Visual Basic and the many varieties of C++) to write stand-alone programs for use in your company or at home.

You can do some programming in many of today's popular business applications via macros (stored sets of instructions to a particular program or set of programs). You can write more powerful programs within database packages, such as dBASE, Paradox, and Oracle.

If you're interested in programming, start by learning to use one or more productivity programs, such as a word processor, database, or spreadsheet. Then start automating some of the things you do in the course of your daily work and start helping others who have similar problems. If you find you have a knack for this kind of work, consider taking some classes that allow you to further develop your skills. For programmers, the cost of even a high-end system is a small expense compared to the difficulty of gaining the skills to translate user needs into working software.

If you decide to pursue programming, you should be aware that most of today's compilers require a large amount of disk space—sometimes dozens of megabytes. CD-ROM disks are rapidly replacing volumes of printed documentation, so the base programming system needs a fast CD-ROM drive. If compiler speed is important to you, consider a very fast machine with a significant amount of RAM (8M or 16M is not uncommon) and disk space.

Where You Use a PC

Where you plan to use your computer also affects your decisions concerning a PC purchase. The following sections examine several environments in which you may plan to use your system and some of the things you should consider in each case. These environments include the following:

- In the office
- On the road
- At home
- At school

In the Office

Most businesses have standardized on a given type of system, and you should (or will be required to) buy a similar system unless you have a compelling reason to do otherwise. For instance, if the other systems in your office are IBM-compatible machines, you should purchase an IBM-compatible. If you try to purchase a Macintosh instead, the amount of time you spend trying to work with the existing systems and the amount of time your company spends trying to support you could outweigh whatever benefits the computer provides. Luckily, you can minimize this risk if you shop smart. Many systems (such as Apple's Power Macintosh) support *cross-platform* operation, which means they can run Macintosh, Windows, and DOS programs.

Use similar logic in justifying the initial configuration you want to purchase and any later upgrades to it. Find the specific benefits to the company that come from the upgrade. In most offices, you don't have to develop a specific dollar-for-dollar justification, just a few common sense reasons that relate to your productivity.

Most computer users have developed the bulk of their expertise on company time, and you should do the same within reason. Both your employer and you will benefit. Seek out any training you can get and set aside time for learning about your system by reading books and magazines.

Be aware that your productivity in your line of work may not increase greatly as a result of getting a computer. Do not take on the task of buying, learning about, or upgrading a system during times when you have pressing deadlines to meet in other areas of your job. On average, you will probably spend several hours a week doing things that involve your computer system rather than doing work that directly relates to your specific duties. You are more likely to benefit from a rise in the quality of your work than in the quantity of it.

The nature of your job may change somewhat to include new tasks based on your computer expertise. These tasks may not turn out to be the most glamorous or exciting tasks to you, unless it's your goal to become a computer expert. If you do become the most capable user within shouting distance, you may end up spending a significant portion of your time supporting others who grow dependent on your expertise. You also need to develop your own sources of help within the company so that you have someone to turn to when problems arise.

Most people who learn to use a computer do so at work, and most find that the variety of their work and their employability both increase as a result. Be ready to make the investment of time and energy to get the most out of the experience.

On the Road

Getting a computer for use on the road is different than getting one to use back in the office (although you may end up using the portable in the office as well). Portable computers (which include laptops, notebooks, subnotebooks, and personal digital assistants) are regarded as more personal than desktop systems, and people seem to have more latitude in the choices they make. Some people use their portable computer for desktop use as well so that they can put all the computing dollars available to them into one machine. This strategy makes sense because portable computers are more expensive and have more demands placed on them than desktop systems, which are getting cheaper more quickly than portables.

Although it can be pleasant to work in isolation from the office, you will probably want to use your portable computer to receive and transmit data files and even programs. The crucial element for a portable system in a corporate setting is communications capabilities; the acid test of these capabilities is being able to connect to your company's network by dialing in. If you can do this, all the shared computer resources of your company are at your disposal; if not, you're likely to miss important e-mail messages and be dependent on others for sending and receiving files you need to get or have created. Seek out experienced portable computer users in your company to learn how they have solved these problems. When you have the capability to dial into the network, you can work anywhere, even at home, if your job is of the right kind and your employer is agreeable.

Another element that's critical to success on the road is technical support. You're likely to need help at inopportune times and under tight deadline pressures. Make sure that you have with you the phone numbers for all your providers of technical support, both from the companies that made your system and software as well as the in-house resources you have developed. Try new or critical tasks, such as uploading or downloading files, at least a day or so before you actually need to perform them. Be ready to spend even more time learning about your computer than the user of a desktop system; road use is more demanding than working on the system in your office.

At Home

Although many people get a lot of rewards from their home computer system, don't rush right out and buy one until you think about it carefully. It's easy to spend hundreds of hours and thousands of dollars on a system that ends up sitting in a closet. If you're not yet an experienced computer user, do your research up front and make sure that you're comfortable with any buying decision; if you are experienced, you're probably ready to take on a system at home, but you obviously will want to keep a close eye on your pocketbook.

If you are paying for the system yourself, consider extreme measures to keep costs down. If you're planning to bring home work from the office, carefully consider what that work is. For instance, if you only do writing at home, a used or low-end system running DOS and an inexpensive word-processing program that can exchange files with your system at work may be all you need. Similarly, you may be able get by with an inexpensive printer at home, doing high-quality printing at work or at a copy shop that has a laser printer.

In addition to cost, another important issue for using the computer at home is technical support. Keep all the documentation associated with your system and its software so you can call support people and describe your setup and the problem you're having in exact terms.

At School

If you're a student, whether you're living at home or on your own, you may need a computer for word processing. You may also want to use a computer for other functions. Luckily, a basic system with a word processor or integrated software package is inexpensive. Many colleges sell the Apple Macintosh and other systems to students at a discount; a few have a strict requirement that you buy a PC that's compatible with systems used on campus. Ask at the campus bookstore to learn more about where and how you can purchase computers at a discount.

Transportability is an important consideration for students. While true portability—the ability to use the computer on an airplane or in a classroom—is not necessarily a requirement, the ability to take a computer with you from place to place easily probably is. An entry-level portable Macintosh or a mid-range notebook PC will serve a student well and should fit into most budgets.

Most students are on a strict budget. When considering a system for school use, however, make sure to include a modem and communications software, including terminal emulation capability, as part of your purchase. In most cases, you will be able to dial into your school's mainframe or library computer, and even if you can't, you will be able to access a wealth of on-line resources to help with research. (Simple versions of such packages are available cheap or free; ask your fellow students what they use.) Most schools make it possible to log on to their large systems over a phone line, which can be an extremely effective way to do homework and communicate with classmates. You should also include a moderately capable printer, unless you know that inexpensive, convenient printing is available on campus. Then you can get by with a low-end printer for rough drafts and for use in extreme time crunches.

Students can sometimes rely on each other for technical support, but most colleges provide help desks you can call if you need computing help. Make an effort to learn all you can about your system during the school year so that you can solve problems on your own during breaks. As with home users, you should either become somewhat of an expert yourself or identify knowledgeable friends who will help you if you have problems.

Students need at least a low-end system for handling the flood of paper they have to produce. Take advantage of low-cost purchase deals, technical support, and cheap or free computer resources on campus to get the most out of your buying dollar.

How Many Computers?

You may have an automatic tendency to think of a desktop system when you hear the word computer. But more and more users are whittling down the expense and difficulties associated with computer use by making portable systems play multiple roles.

Some people end up with three computer systems: desktop systems at home and work and a portable computer for the road. Maintaining all these systems and synchronizing files between them takes a little work and thoughtful preparation, but is usually manageable.

If you have a portable computer, consider seriously whether you need a separate home system. You may want to have a monitor, keyboard, and mouse at home and plug in your portable machine as the engine for an easy-to-use home system.

A more radical step is to use your portable computer in the office. If you consider this step, you will definitely need a desktop monitor, keyboard, and mouse for the heavy use you will make of the system in the office. Several of the portable systems described in this book offer docks that you can use to hook your portable to desktop peripherals when you come into work. You will also need a way to lock your portable to the desk and ways to connect to the company network both from your desk and from outside locations.

The one-person-one-computer approach may become more popular now that products that support it are becoming available. Keep this way of doing things in mind as you consider your options for a computer purchase.

Identifying Your Requirements

Because you're learning about computer purchasing, it's safe to bet that you're about to spend a few thousand dollars in a highly complex area you know relatively little about. Your chances of success increase greatly if you take the time up front to carefully consider your needs. Follow these steps:

1. Make a list of your needs.

    What do you want the computer to do? Define your objective with focused statements. For example, "To keep track of inventory in the book department." "To help my daughter improve her spelling." "To improve the corporate image by producing higher-quality proposals that include illustrations as well as text."

2. Collect data about your current way of doing things.

    For each of the needs you have listed, collect information about how things are currently done. If the task is currently handled manually or by an outside agency, you may be able to save money with quicker turnaround time or a reduction in expenditures. If computerizing the task will improve quality, what benefit will result? If the task is not currently being done at all, try to quantify the benefits that will come from doing it.

3. Do a little brainstorming based on what you know computers can do.

    Use the list earlier in this chapter to get an idea of what applications of a computer are ones that you would be able to use to do your work better.

By completing these three simple steps, you should be able to create a detailed list of what you want the computer to do. This list gives you a head start in thinking about the issues involved in finding a computer best suited to your needs.

To fine-tune the results you get from the list, read the chapters following this one and refer to the specifications tables before you make a purchase decision, taking into account the following:

- Set priorities for your purchase.

    If you haven't already done so, look around in computer stores to get a general idea of what is available. What features seem most important? What do you think you will need immediately? What can you buy later? For example, you may want to purchase a printer right away but wait a while before purchasing a CD-ROM drive (used for accessing large amounts of information).

- Think of other users.

    Who will be using the computer? Does it have enough disk storage, memory, and so on to meet all the requirements you and others will have? Considering these questions will help you make a choice that works for the long term.

- Consider compatibility issues.

    Do you need to share your data with other people? If so, you need to gather information about their computing environment.

- Consider your experience.

    What are your abilities? What is your previous experience and typing ability? Have you used a computer before? If you don't have much experience, you will need more training and technical support .

- Determine your working environment.

    Where you use the computer affects the type of computer you buy.

- Establish a budget.

    How much money can you spend? Remember that much of your budget will be spent on peripherals, software, computer furniture, training, and other additional expenses.

- Plan for the future.

    What needs will you have in a year or two? For example, do you want the system you purchase now to be capable of running multimedia software later? If so, you may need to purchase more advanced hardware or hardware that can be upgraded easily. You may want to consider a longer time frame, but it's very hard to buy a system now with any confidence that it will (or won't) meet your needs three or more years down the road.

The following checklist summarizes these issues. This list can start you on your way to making the right purchasing decisions.

✔ What do you want the computer to do?

  Help run a business

  Help manage a home office

  Enable you to do at home what you do on the PC at work

  Help with schoolwork

  Entertain

✔ How will you use the computer?

  Only for business-related work

  Only for pleasure

  For business and pleasure

✔ Where will you use the computer?

  At the office

  At home

  On the road

  At school

✔ Who else will use the computer?

  Only you

  Employees

  Family members

  Friends

✔ What do you want the computer to do one or two years from now?

✔ How much money can you spend for the complete system and additional expenses?

  Less than $1,000

  Between $1,000 and $3,000

  Between $3,000 and $5,000

  Between $5,000 and $10,000

- ✔ How much time can you spend up-front to research and make the best decisions? Do you have a few hours a week on an ongoing basis to learn about and make changes to your system?
- ✔ What features are most important?

Chapter Summary

In this chapter, you have learned about some of the many ways in which you can use a PC, including working with words, numbers, and money; managing data; communicating with and sharing work with others; creating graphics and presentations; creating and using multimedia; playing games; enhancing educational opportunities for yourself and your children; and creating computer programs. You have also learned that where you plan to use a computer affects the kind of system you buy and how much you expect to pay. Finally, you have learned how to lay the groundwork for making an informed purchasing decision.

IN THE NEXT CHAPTER

The next chapter provides you with an overview of the major parts of a computer system in terms that both cut through and explain the buzz words that pervade the computing world. The chapter defines each part of a computer system, including different kinds of hardware and various levels of software, and explains how the parts work together.

CHAPTER THREE

How a Computer System Works

This chapter explains what you need to know about your computer system in order to make sense of the terms you will hear while making a computer purchase.

The first part of this chapter covers the system's hardware—the computer's microprocessor, motherboard, disk drives, and system units. The second part of the chapter covers software, with brief descriptions of ROM software, operating systems, drivers, utilities, applications, and how they work together. Understanding the hardware and software building blocks that together make up a computer system can help you purchase the best system for your needs and get the most out of it.

Hardware

A typical computer system is made up of the following major parts:

Part	Description
Microprocessor	Performs all the calculations and functions needed to operate the computer; the "brains" of the system.
Motherboard	Holds the microprocessor, related components, RAM (memory), and expansion slots.
Adapters and Controllers	Provide peripheral devices, such as video monitor and hard disks, an interface to the motherboard. Adapters and controllers may be integrated into the motherboard or housed on electronic cards plugged into the motherboard's expansion slots.
Case	Houses the motherboard, power supply, expansion cards (if any), and disk drives.
Disk system	Includes drive controller(s), floppy disk drive(s), and hard disk drive(s). There may be separate controllers for floppy drives and hard drives, and either or both may be integrated onto the motherboard or on a separate add-in card.

continues

Part	Description
Video system	Made up of the video adapter, which may be integrated into the motherboard or may be on a separate add-in card, and the monitor.
Input devices	Always includes a keyboard and usually includes a mouse or other pointing devices.

In figure 3.1, you can see a complete desktop computer system; figure 3.2 shows a complete portable computer system. In each figure, several of the pieces described above are visible, but the motherboard and the controllers and adapters that drive the visible pieces aren't. The microprocessor, RAM, and expansion slots are enclosed within the case. The video and disk controllers are also inside the case, either integrated onto the motherboard or on plug-in expansion cards. The hard disk and floppy disk drive(s) are inside the case, but the floppy drive has an external opening to allow you to insert a floppy disk; the hard disk usually is connected to an indicator light that comes on when the disk is being accessed.

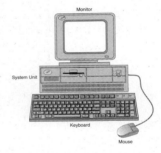

Figure 3.1 *A typical desktop computer system showing the system unit, floppy drive opening, monitor, keyboard, and mouse.*

The monitor either sits on top of the case, beside it, or, for portable systems and a few desktop ones, is integrated into it. The keyboard either sits in front of the system unit or, for portables, is integrated into it; the mouse either plugs into a port on the side of the keyboard (on Macintosh desktop systems) or into a port on the back of the system unit. Portable systems may have an integrated trackball or a clip-on trackball that attaches to the keyboard.

These parts and perhaps some peripherals (see the following chapters on video and printing) are combined to make up different types of systems. The systems that this book discusses are desktop systems, which tend to have more of the controllers on add-in cards and more of the visible parts separate from the system unit, and portables, which have everything integrated.

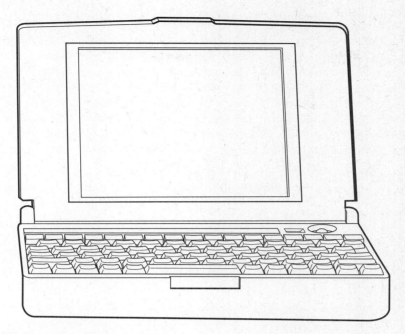

Figure 3.2 *A typical portable computer.*

If most of the preceding has been new to you, stop and take a break before reading on; what follows will take a while to read and understand, and only some of it will make sense the first time through. If you have some experience with using a system and are familiar with most of the things that have been discussed so far, plunge right in. In either case, read through this chapter once before making a buying decision to fully understand the buzzwords that will be thrown at you. Refer to this chapter for more information when you are making a specific system purchasing or upgrading decision.

Microprocessors

The microprocessor chip (also called the Central Processing Unit, or CPU) is probably the most amazing thing in a computer. Its millions of transistors give it a great amount of processing power, and it all fits in an area about an inch on a side. Many personal computers are referred to by the name or speed of their microprocessor. For example, a 486/50 computer is a PC with an 80486 microprocessor running at a speed of 50 Megahertz; a Power Mac 6100/66 has a PowerPC microprocessor running at 66 Megahertz.

Microprocessors belong to several *families*, and different manufacturers may make microprocessors for the same family. Most IBM-compatible computers, for example, use the 80*x*86 family (which includes the 80386 microprocessor, the 80486SX, the 80486, and several others) which was invented by the Intel company, but Intel is not the only company that makes chips for the 80*x*86 family. Other microprocessor families include the Motorola 680*x*0 series (the 68000, 68020, 68030, and 68040, used in many Macintosh computers) and the PowerPC family (PowerPC 601, PowerPC 603, PowerPC 604, with others on the drawing board). Different microprocessor families run different computer code, so the same program usually cannot run on microprocessors from two different microprocessor families. Microprocessor *families* are groups of microprocessors that have some level of compatibility with each other. The family that a microprocessor belongs to determines what software it runs, which is an important characteristic to buyers.

Besides compatibility with other microprocessors in the same family, the major characteristics of a microprocessor are its speed and the number of bits in its internal and external data buses.

Speed

The speed of a microprocessor is measured in Megahertz (MHz), or millions of cycles per second. Typical microprocessor speeds today are 25 MHz, 33 MHz, 40 MHz, 50 MHz, 60 MHz, 66 MHz, 80 MHz, and 100 MHz. Today's microprocessors perform almost all internal operations, such as adding two numbers or moving a quantity from one on-chip storage location to another, in a single cycle. *Superscalar* microprocessors, such as the Intel Pentium or the PowerPC, perform two or more operations per cycle. Getting data to and from RAM takes several cycles, even on superscalar microprocessors.

Most microprocessors communicate with the other components in your computer and perform operations internally (within the chip) at the same fixed rate. This rate is called *clock speed*. *Clock-doubled* and *clock-tripled* microprocessors make the system clock run twice or three times as fast as normal, speeding up processing and memory operations. Operations that demand a lot of processor power, such as recalculating a spreadsheet, benefit from the clock-doubling; operations that demand a lot of data transfer, such as moving a window to a new location on the screen, don't.

The speed of the microprocessor you are using is an important factor in the overall speed of your computer system. The type of microprocessor in a computer system used to greatly affect a system's cost, but only the very fastest microprocessors demand much of a premium these days. Although microprocessor speed makes a big difference, many of the things you do on a computer can be sped up or bogged down by other components. The fastest microprocessors are likely to outpace the rest of your system, so weigh other factors before buying a system with the highest-end, and most expensive, microprocessor.

Number of Bits

A microprocessor has to send data to and receive data from other components in your computer (like memory and expansion cards for the hard drive or monitor), and it has to process data internally (within the microprocessor itself). The microprocessor handles data in the form of *bits*, or *b*inary dig*its*. Each bit can communicate the state of a single piece of information: 0 for off or 1 for on. Bits can be grouped together to communicate more information; 2 bits can combine into any of 4 different values, 3 bits can represent any of 8 different values, and so on (multiply by 2 for each additional bit). By convention, bits are normally grouped into chunks of 8 bits, called a *byte*. A byte can represent any of 256 different values. A 32-bit, or 4-byte, quantity, such as that used by the 80386 and 80486 microprocessors, can represent any of over 4 billion different values.

The number of bits a microprocessor handles externally has a great effect on the system cost; the rest of the system has to handle the same number of bits or perform some workaround to deal with the data in smaller chunks, slowing overall performance. To accommodate this fact, a number of microprocessors handle only half the number of bits externally as they handle internally. Although this setup makes for a cheaper system, the microprocessor is often waiting until two chunks of data come in so that it can assemble one chunk of the size it uses internally.

For instance, the 80386SX has a 16-bit *external interface* but handles data at 32 bits internally. To grab a 32-bit quantity from memory, the 80386SX has to grab one 16-bit quantity, make a separate grab for a second quantity, combine the two quantities into a 32-bit quantity, and only then do its work. By contrast, a true 80386, or 80386DX, has a 32-bit external interface and a 32-bit internal data bus. The 80386SX is described as a 16/32 bit chip because it has a 16-bit interface but processes 32 bits internally. The 80386 is a true 32-bit chip. The number of bits a microprocessor supports has a large effect on system performance. Having a microprocessor with an external interface that's less than its full internal processing capability slows performance by a small percentage, but not enough to make a big difference for most operations.

Compatibility

Microprocessor families have not generally been created from some master plan. Instead, a manufacturer creates the best chip that it can while trying to beat the competition to market. If the chip is a success, the manufacturer then tries to develop a new chip that is *compatible* with—that is, runs all the software created for—the old one, and adds speed and new features as well. Any bugs or poorly conceived methods of operation in the earlier members of the chip family must be supported by newer ones or compatibility, for at least some software, is lost.

By all accounts, the early members of the Intel family of microprocessors (which now includes the 8086, 8088, 80286, 80386, 80486, Pentium, and several others) contained many more bugs, strange operating modes, and design problems than the early members of a competing family, Motorola's 68000 line (the 68000, 68020, 68030, and 68040). But Intel consistently got its buggy, sometimes poorly designed, chips into the hands of computer system manufacturers for testing, and then into production, months and even years ahead of Motorola. As a result, the Intel line now dominates the computing world, and the Motorola 68000 line is being shelved in favor of the new PowerPC.

Compatibility starts with the microprocessor, but certainly doesn't end there. Other parts of a computer system and the different kinds of software that determine the characteristics of a machine all must be at least similar for two computers to be compatible. Many wildly different systems use the same microprocessors but are not otherwise compatible; for instance, now-defunct Commodore's Amiga line used the Motorola 68000 line, but was not compatible with the Macintosh. The IBM PC and PC compatibles are the major family of compatible microcomputers from a large number of different manufacturers, whereas the Mac has had no significant compatible competition up to this point. That's all starting to change, though. Personal computer users have long been asking for computers that run software from many different environments (like Macintosh, Windows, and DOS), and the industry is responding with *cross-platform* solutions. IBM, Apple, and Motorola united to create the PowerPC microprocessor, which can run Macintosh, Windows, OS/2, DOS, UNIX, and several other operating systems.

Intel Microprocessors and the IBM PC

IBM took on two major partners to create the original IBM PC, introduced in 1981: Intel and Microsoft. Intel provided the 8088 microprocessor, the first widely used chip in what later became the 80*x*86 family; Microsoft provided the MS-DOS operating system. The involvement of IBM and the relative ease of developing software for the PC led to the development of a wide variety of powerful, inexpensive programs, such as the original Lotus 1-2-3. These programs were a catalyst for the development of a much larger market for personal computers. Assisted by Intel and Microsoft, who made their products widely available, many companies made machines that ran IBM PC software. The development of the IBM-compatible standard is now in the hands of a whole industry that makes compatible computers and of the customers who depend on them. No IBM-compatible computer can be successful unless it runs the same software as other machines based on this standard.

Intel microprocessors have led the ongoing development of the IBM-compatible standard. Each new, faster Intel microprocessor has led to a slew of new machines and, more slowly, new software that wrings as much performance as possible out of the latest Intel chips. This family of microprocessors now includes, in order of increasing performance, the 8088, 8086, 80186, 80286, 80386SX, 80386, 80486SX, 80486, clock-doubled and clock-tripled 80486s, and the Pentium. Each new microprocessor in the family runs almost all the software developed for previous chips, while adding speed and new features as well.

Software developed for the original 8088 and 8086 runs without modification on all the succeeding members of the family. But software that takes advantage of features of a given microprocessor does not run on previous chips. For instance, almost all new Windows software requires at least an 80386 or 80386SX to run.

The following sections give brief descriptions of the important members of the Intel 80*x*86 family of microprocessors. Read the descriptions of the 8088, 8086, and 80286 for historical background or if you are considering the purchase of the cheapest possible used computer system. Otherwise, start with the descriptions of the 80386SX and 80386 to learn about the Intel microprocessors that can run today's software.

8088 and 8086

The 8088 has an 8-bit external data path and processes data at 16 bits internally. IBM used the 8088 in its first two computers, the IBM PC and the IBM PC XT, and later in some early PS/2s (Models 25 and 30). The 8088 was very popular with system manufacturers because it was easy to build a cheap system to interface with the chip's 8-bit external data path, and the internal 16-bit data path helped the chip perform at reasonable speed. Some systems that used the 8086, with its faster 16-bit external data path, were also introduced. NEC and AMD introduced nearly identical, competing microprocessors. Originally, the 8088 worked at a speed of 4.77 MHz, but later models of Intel and competing chips ran at up to 20 MHz.

Don't buy a system with an 8088, 8086, 80186, 80188, NEC V20, or NEC V30 microprocessor unless you want the cheapest possible system to run one or two undemanding, text-based applications. Even under these conditions, you may regret your purchase later when you want newer software.

80286

The first personal computer to use the Intel 80286 was the IBM AT, which had a clock speed of 6 MHz. Later models of the 80286 ran at faster speeds, especially compatible chips made by AMD. The chip's 16-bit internal and external data buses and fast internal processing made it a winner as a performance upgrade to the 8088 and 8086, but the 80286 was also meant to support advanced software capabilities; software makers, including Microsoft and IBM with the original OS/2 operating system, found these capabilities extremely hard to access. These difficulties were a big part of the reason that OS/2 and early versions of Windows got off to such a slow start in the marketplace.

You should consider buying an 80286-based system only if you want to run one or two undemanding applications. Even then, such a system is unlikely to meet your long-term needs. Look at an 80386 or better unless cost is a critical concern.

80386SX and 80386

Although IBM was the first major personal computer maker to use the 80286 microprocessor, ALR and Compaq were the first to use the 80386. Compaq's 80386-based systems established the company's reputation as a leading supplier of high-performance computers. A true 80386, or 80386DX, has a 32-bit external data path and internal processing unit and runs at speeds as high as 40 MHz. The 80386SX has a smaller 16-bit external data path, which impairs performance to a greater degree on most graphically and numerically intense programs, and the same 32-bit internal processing unit. It tends to be available at lower clock speeds (25 and 33 MHz); 80386DXs are available at these speeds and higher speeds as well.

The 80386 has effective implementations of all the advanced features that were meant to be in the 80286 and more. Besides being much faster than previous microprocessors, the 80386 is also excellent at multitasking (performing several tasks at the same time). This feature is supported by more advanced operating environments like Windows and operating systems like OS/2 and Windows NT. With multitasking, you can have many programs loaded at once and, to the extent that overall performance permits it, have two or more of them actually performing I/O or calculations at the same time.

At this time, mainstream PCs that capably run today's software and that have some hope of running the advanced software of tomorrow, such as Microsoft Windows NT, are based on an 80486SX or better. If your needs and your budget are modest, or you are buying a portable system that will be used only occasionally, or mainly for communications, consider the purchase of an 80386DX system.

For portable systems, look for a version of the 80386 that supports low power consumption (like the 386SL). AMD's versions of the 80386 have been leaders in this area. For desktop systems, look for a system that can later be upgraded to an 80486 if needed. If an 80386DX system meets your current needs, it may be a good investment.

Math Coprocessors for 80386 and Lesser Systems

Intel microprocessors up through the 80386 are relatively slow at performing mathematical functions, such as those required for graphics, recalculating a spreadsheet, and so on. Systems based on these chips can get a performance boost by adding a math coprocessor to the system.

The 8087 is the math coprocessor for the 8086 and 8088, the 80287 works with the 80286, the 80387SX speeds up the 80386SX, and the 80387 accelerates the 80386DX. The speed of the math coprocessor should match the speed of the microprocessor; for example, get a 25 MHz 80387 to go with a 25 MHz 80386. Only software that specifically accesses the coprocessor gets a boost from it. Almost all spreadsheet programs, for instance, take advantage of a coprocessor if one is present. Some graphical programs, such as the sophisticated computer-aided design program AutoCAD, require a math coprocessor.

Math coprocessors are a lucrative and relatively easy-to-produce product, so competition is fierce. Most of the name brands, such as IIT, Cyrix, AMD, and, of course, Intel, have good compatibility and should be compared mostly on price. Before you purchase any coprocessor, make sure that your software will benefit from it; a look through the documentation or a call to the vendor's technical support line should be enough to get this information. Any multitasking environment (Windows, OS/2, Macintosh) benefits from a coprocessor.

If you are buying a new system and think you will need math coprocessing capability, consider a true 80486, as described in the following section; it includes a very fast, built-in math coprocessor. If you're shopping on price, be sure to include the cost of a math coprocessor when comparing an 80386-based system against an 80486-based one.

80486SX and 80486

The 80486 is the current middle-of-the-road microprocessor in the Intel family. The 80486 has 32-bit internal and external data buses and very fast internal processing. Like the RISC chips that power UNIX workstations, the 80486 completes most operations in a single clock cycle. Unlike earlier microprocessors, the 80486 includes a built-in math coprocessor that runs much faster than the add-on units used with earlier chips. This coprocessor makes the 80486 ideal for running heavily graphical programs and numerically intensive programs, such as spreadsheets. The 80486 also has a small on-chip cache to store the most recently used instructions and data, making it fast for repetitive operations. Most 80486s can be clock-doubled and -tripled to increase their internal performance even further. All these features, as well as complete compatibility with the 80386, make the 80486 worth considering for any PC purchase.

80486-based systems are more expensive than 80386-based ones, but the premium is dropping fast. To lessen the price shock associated with 80486 computers, Intel released the 80486SX, a cheaper version of the 80486 processor with the math coprocessor circuitry disabled. (This strategy was successful enough that Intel created a new 486SX with the offending circuits removed rather than just disabled.) If you later buy an 80487SX *math coprocessor*, you get a slightly modified true 80486 that completely disables the 80486SX and runs the system itself.

Until recently, Intel had a monopoly on the 486 chip, but now other companies have begun creating Intel-compatible 486 chips. AMD's 486 microprocessors get consistently high marks in performance tests (equal to or surpassing Intel's in most cases). Cyrix's 486s are not so favorably regarded, though their chip uses less power and enhances floating-point functions.

Because most users today run at least some graphically intensive operations (including Microsoft Windows) as well as some numerically intense ones (such as recalculating a spreadsheet), performance-oriented buyers should get a true 486 system rather than one based on the 80486SX. In most cases, an 80486-based system with clock-doubling potential is the best moderate-performance buy. For desktop systems that are used every day, look for an 80486DX. For infrequently used desktop systems or for portables that are used occasionally, consider an 80486SX.

Pentium

Intel's Pentium chip is the next entry in Intel's line of microprocessors, after the 80486. In terms of what it does, Pentium is just a very fast 80386 or 80486. It has a 32-bit internal data path, but unlike earlier versions, it can process two instructions at once. Pentium also has a 64-bit external data bus. These characteristics make the Pentium run twice as fast, when running the right kind of software, as the 80486. Pentium should also be able to run at higher speeds than the 80486; expect to see speeds of 150 MHz or so as the Pentium reaches maturity.

Building a system that takes full advantage of all this power is difficult. Pentium is a big, hot chip. Software needs to be recompiled to enable Pentium to run two instructions at once more of the time; hardware systems have had to be redesigned to cool the microprocessor and support 64-bit access to memory.

Yet another concern is Intel's PCI bus. A Pentium is so fast that it needs fast access to peripherals, and a PCI bus may be just the ticket. But, as with the Pentium, it will take PCI a while to get tested, debugged, and fully used by new video systems and hard disks.

Unless you need top performance and are willing to pay for it, you should wait to buy a Pentium system. Most Pentium systems will carry a high price; the ones that advertise a lower price will be hard to get. Pentium-based systems with all the performance features in, the bugs out, and selling for a reasonable price, should be available by the middle of the year; until then, buy carefully.

One of the most exciting features of Pentium is support for multiprocessing—the capability to have several Pentium microprocessors in one box. No one knows how popular this capability will become, but it may become very important indeed. You may be able to get a reasonably priced, one-Pentium system that can easily be upgraded to use two or more Pentium chips. If you are a high-end user, look for this capability in the system that you buy.

The same concerns that make it hard to build a Pentium system from scratch also make it problematic to upgrade a 386- or 486-based system to use a Pentium instead. You won't get the full performance benefit of a Pentium unless your current system has a 64-bit memory path (this is unlikely), and you upgrade your software. Cooling might also be a problem, and less reputable manufacturers may be less than careful in supporting a proper Pentium upgrade. Don't be the first on your block to try this upgrade.

Various versions of Pentium may eventually become the mainstream powerhouse of IBM-compatible computers, but it will probably take a little while. Don't be a pioneer unless you're in need of the best possible performance and are willing to go through substantial expense and, possibly, hassle to get it.

80x86-Compatible Microprocessors

The success of the 80*x*86 family has spawned several imitators that produce microprocessors compatible with it. Currently, the two major competitors of this sort are AMD and Cyrix. AMD was originally a licensed second source for the 8086 and 80286 microprocessors and eventually led both markets with faster versions of Intel's chips. The company has fought bitterly, in the courts and in its R&D labs, to produce either licensed or independently developed microprocessors compatible with the 80386, 80486, and Pentium.

Having mostly lost in the courts, AMD has done a great deal of R&D work to produce high-performance and low-power 80386-compatible and 80486-compatible chips. Its 386 chip is faster than any of Intel's 386s and has taken a lot of that market; the company can be expected to offer solid 486s also. AMD has provided a real alternative to Intel and has benefited users by providing products that are cheaper, faster, or lower in power consumption than comparable Intel parts. AMD has also benefited Intel's customers by forcing Intel to come out with new chips faster and keep prices more reasonable than otherwise. Don't hesitate to consider purchasing a system that meets your needs in other ways and is based on an AMD microprocessor.

Cyrix came into the game later. Cyrix developed a chip compatible with the 80386—you can remove an 80386 and plug in a Cyrix chip to replace it—and sporting the added benefit of a 1K on-chip cache that noticeably improves performance. But Cyrix has called this chip an 80486 on the dubious basis that its high performance—actually between an 80386 and an 80486—entitles it to the higher number. However, a real 486 has an 8K on-chip cache, not 1K, and a few additional instructions.

Some third-tier system manufacturers are using the Cyrix chip for 486 systems. Although some (Wyse and Zeos, for example) use the Cyrix name prominently so that savvy buyers can be aware of what they're getting, others bury the Cyrix name as deep in their press releases and advertisements as possible (Leading Edge, for example). Do not consider the purchase of a Cyrix-based system unless you are aware of and comfortable with the trade-offs involved.

Low-Power Microprocessors

Microprocessors are now being designed with low power consumption as a prime consideration. Specific microprocessors designated for use in portable computers have low-power features now; all may have it in the future.

AMD took the lead in this market by introducing a low-power, 3.3V 386 microprocessor. Running at 3.3V, rather than the Intel-standard 5V, reduces power consumption; so do other features of the chip's design. Power consumption will be even less when other parts of the computer also become available in 3.3V models.

Intel has come back strong with its 386SL and 486SL microprocessors. These chips also draw less power and run at 3.3V. They also integrate a cache controller and voltage management to make it easy to use them with 5V as well as 3.3V peripherals. The 486SL uses even less power than the 386SL and will be found in more and more notebooks.

Neither Intel nor AMD will sit still in this race, and buyers will only benefit. Use the 486SL as a price/performance/power management standard, and look for systems that use 3.3V peripherals and a 486SL or something newer and even better as a microprocessor.

Motorola 68000 Microprocessors and the Macintosh

The Motorola microprocessors numbered 68000, 68020, 68030, and 68040 have been used in Macintosh personal computers. Like the Intel microprocessors, each new Motorola microprocessor improves on the speed, capability to handle information, and special features of previous versions. The 68000 has a 16-bit external and 32-bit internal data path, twice the comparable numbers for the 8088. Higher-numbered chips in the family are 32 bits both externally and internally and feature increasing amounts of on-board cache RAM.

Current Macintosh desktop and portable systems use either the 68030, 68040, or the PowerPC chip (a joint venture between Apple, IBM, and Motorola). Motorola will introduce a 68060 at some point; they have cynically skipped the name 68050 in order to give the appearance of being ahead of Intel.

The Macintosh is different from other systems not only by its use of the 68000 family, in which it is not alone, but in having highly complex software stored in read-only memory (ROM). Macintosh ROMs are copyrighted in such a way that it has been very difficult for competitors to legally produce a compatible machine. Apple also includes the highly complex Finder and System files on each of its computers, further obscuring the hardware capabilities of the microprocessor. The specific microprocessor inside a Macintosh makes less difference to the user than specific Intel chips do to IBM PC-compatible users. System 7.1, the current version of the Finder and System, works best on the 68030 and up.

Like Intel and Intel-compatible microprocessors, the earlier chips in Motorola's line are slower handling mathematical functions. The 68882 is the most commonly used math coprocessor for the Macintosh. As with Intel-based machines, you should match the clock speed of the math coprocessor you buy to the speed of the system's microprocessor. Like the 80486DX, the 68040 has on-chip math coprocessing capability and doesn't need a coprocessor.

Intel's much greater success with the 80*x*86 family and the failure of Motorola to get new versions out in a timely fashion is leading to the demise of 68000 microprocessors in the personal computer market. IBM, Apple, and Motorola created the PowerPC family, to succeed the 68000 family and hopefully gain a competitive advantage over Intel.

If you buy a 68000-based Macintosh system today, it can probably be upgraded with any of a variety of performance enhancement products to meet the needs of tomorrow. But as Apple moves its customer base to the PowerPC family, be aware that you might have to upgrade the Mac's system board to keep pace with peripheral and software manufacturers.

The PowerPC Family

IBM, Apple, and Motorola have worked together to produce a new family of compatible microprocessors called the PowerPC family. The first versions of this microprocessor are remarkably faster than existing 80*x*86- and 68000-family chips. The first PowerPC-based

Macintosh computers have been a hit with users, not only for their low prices (rare with new technology) but also for their performance and features.

Because of the flexibility of the microprocessor and the up-front development efforts of IBM, Microsoft, Apple, and many other large companies, Power Macs are already able to run Windows and Macintosh programs, as well as a growing base of native PowerPC applications. Even non-Macintosh machines based on the PowerPC should be able to run the Macintosh operating system, Windows, UNIX, DOS, NT, and several other operating systems.

The first Power Macs are based on the PowerPC 601 chip running at 60, 66, or 80 MHz. Future machines will use the PowerPC 603 or 604 chips, which will allow lower power consumption and higher speeds. If you're wary of new technology, you might want to wait for the newer chips before purchasing a PowerPC-based system.

The Motherboard

A computer system's motherboard is the heart of the computer. It is a highly complex mix of plastics and metal traces measuring from a few square inches (for portable computers) to 8 inches by 11 inches or larger for big desktop or deskside systems. The motherboard provides attachment points for, and communications between, different parts of the computer system implemented on it. It houses the microprocessor, read-only memory (ROM), timing chips, support for expansion slots, and support for input/output ports, (*I/O ports*) such as serial and parallel ports. It was once a real accomplishment to handle these basic functions on a single board about the size of a piece of paper; any other functionality had to be handled by cards plugged into the expansion slots.

Now the computer's basic functions can be handled by one or two chips, leaving room on the motherboard for a number of other functions, such as a microprocessor cache, a math coprocessor, random-access memory (RAM), a floppy disk controller, a video adapter, and more.

Computer system manufacturers move functions on and off a system's motherboard as needed to support basic or advanced functionality, small or large system sizes, greater or lesser customizability of the system, and other considerations. Having more functionality on the motherboard means that a moderate level of performance is assured at a reasonable price; having less functionality on the motherboard means that the system has a lower base price, and its eventual price and level of functionality depend greatly on what controllers and adapters are plugged into the expansion slots.

The sections that follow describe parts of the system that are usually found on the motherboard. Less highly integrated motherboards have only these functions. The most highly integrated ones, such as small portables, have everything on the motherboard. Most systems fall somewhere in between.

System Clock

One of the most difficult things about designing a computer system is getting the timing coordinated between all its parts. The *system clock* sends out a pulse of electricity several million times per second to provide a timing base for the rest of the system. The faster this pulse is, the trickier it is to design the core parts of the system, and the more radio interference the system tends to generate. Preventing or shielding this interference, which can prevent radios, portable telephones, and other electronic devices from working properly, is one of the most expensive and difficult parts of building a system.

The system clock's speed is usually the same as the operating speed of the microprocessor. Standard expansion slots run at some fraction of the system clock's speed; for instance, a 40 MHz system may have circuits that divide its clock speed by four and use the resulting pulse to drive the slots at 10 MHz. Local bus slots run at the same speed as the system clock, so they are much faster than standard slots. The microprocessor, on the other hand, runs at either the same speed as the system clock or, for clock-doubled or clock-tripled chips, at two or three times the speed.

Microprocessor Cache

Computers based on the 80386 and 80486 microprocessors often have an external cache, a chunk of high-speed memory placed between the microprocessor and regular RAM. It holds instructions and data that the microprocessor is most likely to need next. The larger the cache, the higher the system's performance and the higher its price. If you are concerned enough about performance to be looking at systems with caches, you may want to investigate systems based on the 80486SX and 80486, which have a built-in cache and other performance-enhancing features. These systems usually have external caches as well.

ROM

ROM (read-only memory) permanently holds programs needed by the computer to perform its most basic operations. When a computer is first starting up, it doesn't know how to access its disk drives, RAM, or other components. Code permanently stored in the computer's ROM chips give it the initial instructions it needs to get started. The ROM is also used to hold other code that needs to be quickly available to different parts of the system.

> Software that is stored in the system's ROM is called *firmware*.

On IBM-compatibles, ROM is used to hold the BIOS (Basic Input/Output System), software that handles communication between the microprocessor and components such as disk drives and printers. You usually don't need to worry about what kind of ROM BIOS a system has except in the case of systems from obscure makers who may use incompatible ones. Some ROMs, called Flash ROMs, can be updated from a floppy disk, easing worries about incompatibility. Snap-in ROMs are installed in such a way that they can be easily taken out and replaced if needed. Some portable systems have DOS, Windows, and even applications in ROM.

For the Macintosh, all newly purchased systems have snap-in ROMs that are easy to upgrade. You will require the assistance of a dealer if you are trying to upgrade the ROMs of an older system, such as a Macintosh 512K or Macintosh Plus. After you purchase any computer, try to keep abreast of major changes to its ROM software and replace ROMs with updated versions when needed.

RAM

RAM (random-access memory) is the computer's working memory. It responds quickly to requests from the microprocessor to send or store information and is relatively cheap. But anything stored in RAM—your latest budget figures, the first chapter of your novel—is lost when you turn off power. Unless you have saved the information to a disk, the data is lost forever.

RAM used to be relatively expensive—hundreds of dollars per megabyte—and systems had sharp limits on the amount of RAM they could take advantage of. Early IBM-compatibles running DOS could only use 640K of RAM (about two-thirds of a megabyte); the Macintosh could use all the RAM you could afford, up to 13M or so. Now RAM is cheap ($40-$50 per megabyte at this writing), and both the Macintosh and systems running Windows can use all the RAM they can get. 4M is a reasonable minimum amount of RAM for a system running a graphical user interface, and 8M is better. (This amount may sound like a lot to some computer buyers, but 8M today is cheaper than 2M a few years ago.) Demanding systems like Microsoft Windows NT or UNIX and powerful programs like AutoCAD require, or can benefit from, 16M of RAM or more.

The dynamic RAM that you buy by the megabyte is cheaper and slower than static RAM, which is used for cache memory. In computers with high-performance microprocessors, you should look for some static RAM; many 80486 or better computers have 256K of static RAM. A static-RAM cache is most important for computers based on the 80386 or 68030 or better.

When you purchase a computer, the motherboard has the capacity to hold a certain amount of RAM. Make sure that there's room for at least 16M; power users should look for a system that can support 32M or even 64M on the motherboard. Portable systems suffer some power drain from the presence of RAM, which must be constantly refreshed, but benefit a great deal if enough RAM is present to keep the system from spinning its hard disk too often.

To increase the memory in your computer, you must know what kind of memory chips it uses. Older systems used DIP (dual-in-line package) chips, which are shown in figure 3.3, or SIP (single-in-line package) chips; almost all today's systems use SIMMs, which are cheaper and more reliable. Figure 3.4 shows a SIMM.

Before you buy a computer, find out the type and capacity of RAM chips it uses and find out how you can get additional RAM if you want to expand the memory at a later date. Also check whether you can do the upgrade yourself or have to bring the system in to have it done.

Figure 3.3 *A standard dual-in-line-package (DIP) RAM chip.*

Figure 3.4 *A single-in-line memory module (SIMM).*

Conventional, Extended, and Expanded Memory

Macintosh users have long had the ability to easily use several megabytes of RAM in their systems without changes to software. But DOS users were for many years greatly hampered in their ability to access more than 640K—less than a single megabyte—of RAM. This limit is because the 8088 microprocessor had a 1M limit on the amount of RAM it could use; DOS claimed the first two-thirds or so of this and left the rest for use in accessing hardware devices. DOS and programs written for it were stuck with the limitation even when more powerful Intel microprocessors that could access much more memory became available.

Conventional memory is memory up to 640K, or about two thirds of a megabyte. DOS can only access 640K of memory directly. This quality has become a real limitation on today's powerful software. *Expanded memory* is a clever scheme that allows DOS and DOS programs to access memory beyond the 640K limit. It originally required special hardware and modifications to software programs. Access to expanded memory is slow. *Extended memory* is just plain old memory in quantities greater than 640K. For a while, expanded memory was the most important way to get above 640K. Then drivers appeared that allowed extended memory to be used as if it were expanded memory.

Now Windows has this capability built into it, as do many DOS programs, and the 640K limit is almost history. However, users running DOS programs that require substantial memory below 640K while running drivers, such as network drivers, that also want to be in the first 640K are among those who might still run into problems. If you're concerned about these sorts of problems, avoid DOS; run Windows and Windows programs whenever possible, and you can mostly or entirely avoid these problems.

Virtual Memory

Virtual memory capability allows the computer to use a hard disk as overflow storage when RAM becomes full. This convenient feature is available only on systems that combine an advanced microprocessor, such as an 80386 or 68030 or higher, with advanced operating software like Microsoft Windows or Macintosh System 7.1. You must have several megabytes of free hard disk space for use as virtual memory. Also, virtual memory is much slower than RAM, so watch your disk light; if your system is frequently going to disk during normal operations, it's being forced to depend too much on virtual memory, and performance (and your hard drive) will suffer until you add RAM to your system.

Expansion Slots and the Computer Bus

Expansion slots for computers have gotten a degree of attention that's out of proportion to their effect on performance. A set of electrical channels called a *bus* connects the microprocessor to several expansion slots that can hold cards with circuitry on them. The expansion cards can do any number of things. In early PCs, key system functions were supported by add-in cards. Additional serial and parallel ports, memory, the hard disk controller, and the video adapter were all found on add-in cards.

Now, to lower costs and system size and improve performance, more and more functionality is being integrated onto the motherboard. Portable systems are the extreme examples of this because they don't have room for traditional ports or expansion slots. You only need expansion slots for functions that you want a choice in, such as network adapters, or to override or supplement the built-in video or hard disk subsystems. The issue of which bus to use to get higher performance is becoming less important; just don't make a choice that leaves you unable to buy the expansion cards you need.

Different kinds of buses do a better or poorer job of supporting fast communications between the microprocessor and expansion cards and between the cards themselves. The ISA, EISA, MCA, and PCI buses are all solutions to this problem for IBM-compatibles.

Because ISA has the most expansion cards built for it and EISA supports ISA cards as well as higher performance, EISA-specific cards, you can't go too far wrong with ISA or EISA. Most users will do fine with a small-footprint desktop or mini-tower system that has three ISA or EISA expansion slots. The MCA bus introduced by IBM and used in some of its PS/2 systems supports a smaller collection of expansion cards and should be avoided. The newest PC bus on the scene is the PCI bus, used in Pentium machines. Motherboards with PCI features typically offer ISA slots as well, so if you're buying a Pentium you won't have to worry about finding peripherals for it.

All Macintosh systems support SCSI, which is kind of a hybrid between a device interface (such as a parallel port) and an expansion bus (such as ISA, EISA, and MCA). Apple's consistent implementation of SCSI across all Macs makes it easy to connect external hard disks, CD-ROM drives, tape drives, and so on to a Mac system, and to carry devices around and use them on one system after another. The expansion slots inside a Mac are mostly NuBus slots, which are fast and smart in their capability to support device configuration. Some Macs have a fast PDS (Processor Direct Slot) in addition to or instead of NuBus slots. Make sure that the expansion cards you need are available for the specific Macintosh you're considering buying, and get a system with NuBus slots if you are unsure of your future needs.

Makers of video cards for IBM-compatibles have taken the PDS idea and run with it. They have come up with a standard called the VESA local bus standard that has established a strong foothold in the video card market. The local bus is represented by one or more very fast slots on the computer's motherboard, next to regular ISA or EISA slots.

Local bus slots are so far used mostly for video support, but local bus hard disk controllers, video adapters, and even network adapters are in the offing. Video built into a system's motherboard can be just as fast as local bus, but there are no choices and no upgradability with built-in video as there are with standard local bus slots. Local bus video does a good job of speeding up Windows and heavily graphical programs, and is dropping fast in price; look for it in the systems you are considering.

Portable systems need device expansion too, for memory, communications, networking, and other uses. A standard called PCMCIA (Personal Computer Memory Card International Association) is becoming very popular, offering a consistent way to expand portables with a high-speed connection to any device that can fit on a credit card-sized PCMCIA card. If you plan to get a lot of use out of your portable, and especially if you plan to use it in place of a desktop system at home or work, consider a system with a PCMCIA connector. You can get network cards, modems, and even hard drives that plug into your portable's PCMCIA slots.

Disk Drives

Disk drives are the slowest form of storage used by a computer during normal operations. Main memory is faster; a system's built-in cache is faster still; and the microprocessor's registers and on-chip cache, if any, are the fastest of all. However, hard disk drives have gotten fast enough, and the software advanced enough, that they can be used as auxiliary main memory. CD-ROM drives are an increasingly popular way to distribute large amounts of data, especially sound and graphics data as used in multimedia. So the demands on the various kinds of disk storage that can be used in, or connected to, your system are growing fast.

Getting all the different kinds of disk drives connected to your system without conflicts between them and without undue expense can be the biggest hassle a computer user faces. The following sections discuss each type of disk drive and how it's connected to your system, building a coherent picture of what's available and how to manage your options.

Floppy Drives

Floppy disk support takes just a couple of chips that can be integrated onto your system's motherboard or attached to a hard disk controller. The method doesn't matter much, as long as your system can support at least two floppy drives. For most users of desktop IBM-compatibles, it's still a good idea to get both 3.5- and 5.25-inch floppy drives. More people are using the 3.5-inch drive, but you never know when some old 5.25-inch game or file storage floppy disk will turn up.

Macintosh users can get by with a single floppy disk drive as long as it's a SuperDrive (found on all current Macs). The SuperDrive can read and write any type of floppy disk formatted for the Macintosh and 1.44M, 3.5-inch disks formatted for IBM-compatibles.

Hard Disk Drives

Many IBM-compatible systems come with an IDE hard drive interface integrated onto the motherboard, but most sold today use an IDE controller card. IDE is a fast, dumb interface (which means it leaves most of the work of responding to read and write requests to the disk drive itself). You can also get ESDI, SCSI, or SCSI-2 hard disk controllers. MFM and RLL are outdated technologies you should avoid in new systems. High-end controllers have caching built into them, but how much benefit you get from this feature depends on how you use your system. Software-based disk caches deliver similar performance gains.

An IDE interface with no or little caching will do the job for most users, though SCSI has real advantages for users who will be expanding their systems a lot. Just be sure to get a big enough disk drive; Windows applications are so large that 80M fills up very fast, and 120M to 200M is reasonable for a middle-of-the-road system. Bigger hard disks tend to be faster, too, so there's a double benefit from getting a large drive.

Getting information from the hard drive takes much more time than getting information from RAM. Caching controllers speed up some of the process by drawing some of the drive's information into RAM. Disk-intensive operations (such as working with multimedia) benefit greatly from this technology, but you won't see much improvement in non-disk-intensive operations (such as word processing).

Upgrading an IBM-compatible system's hard disk can be a real pain. Before spending the money on a new hard disk, try buying more RAM to increase your system's speed and using disk-doubling software to increase capacity. You may be able to use your existing IDE interface or hard disk controller, or you may decide to buy a new one. Keep in mind that changing can cause configuration problems.

If there's an empty drive bay in your system, you can add the new drive to the existing one; otherwise, you have to remove your current drive and find some use for it elsewhere. If you run into problems in converting to a new controller or swapping drives, you can be left diskless; if you don't have experience or in-house support, consider buying your new hard disk from a dealer or store that will install it and transfer your data and programs for you.

Apple has historically charged top dollar for small, slow hard disks, so be willing to consider a third-party hard disk when you buy a Macintosh system.

Expanding or upgrading hard disk drives is much easier with a Mac. You can always connect a SCSI disk drive to your system to expand capacity or for quick backup while upgrading the internal drive. Because the internal device interface is consistent between Macs, it's quite likely that you can purchase and install an additional or replacement internal drive yourself. If you do have a dealer do it, you shouldn't have to pay much.

CD-ROM Drives

CD-ROM drives are growing in popularity and usefulness. Faster units (double- and triple-speed) are coming out. Many new systems come with CD-ROM drives built in, eliminating the installation hassle. More and more programs and databases are being published on CD-ROM; access to a CD-ROM drive is becoming a necessity for many.

Apple is currently having the greatest success with CD-ROM drives. The built-in SCSI interface on all Macs makes it easy to hook up an external CD-ROM drive, even to a portable, and to share a drive among several computers. The Mac's built-in sound and graphics support make playing back multimedia data easy. Now Apple has come out with new, fast external drives, as well as systems with optional CD-ROM drives that are being ordered for about half the systems sold.

If you decide to add a CD-ROM drive to your system, the adapter card that supports it will take up a slot in your system. Several sound cards double as CD-ROM controllers, so if you know you will want CD-ROM and a sound card, you can use a single expansion slot for both functions. You might also consider getting a drive with a SCSI interface; you can use the same SCSI controller for up to seven devices including external hard disks, tape drives, and additional CD-ROM drives. (If you want a specific CD available at all times, you need a second drive for other CDs that you access occasionally.)

Be aware that SCSI implementations on IBM-compatibles are sometimes (though rarely) incompatible, so you may have to buy your SCSI controller, CD-ROM drive, tape drive, and external disk drive all from the same manufacturer.

Tape Drives

A tape drive is a good thing to have for backup and for exchanging data with others who have tape drives, but they haven't really caught on. Although a tape drive is a good thing to share among systems, many require internal adapter cards, which make them tough to share without disassembling multiple machines or using a network. If you know you will want to share a tape drive among several systems, you can get one with a parallel interface (which can be temporarily connected to any computer's parallel port). Parallel drives are typically slower than internally controlled or SCSI drives, which can take time away from other work if you do backups often.

SCSI tape drives are another good idea because they can share the SCSI controller with other devices. If you think tape backup is a good idea for you or your workgroup, and you don't want to do backups over the network or use a parallel drive, consider standardizing on systems with SCSI interfaces.

System Unit

The computer's power supply and all the parts already mentioned—motherboard, expansion slots, adapters and controllers, and internal disk drives—fit inside a case sometimes called the system unit. The system unit is what many people consider to be the computer.

Viewed externally, the system unit has a specific size and shape (its *form factor*), connectors (that are actually connected to the back of the motherboard or the back edge of an expansion card), one or more openings of floppy drives, a hard disk light, a power cord, a power-on light, and an on-off switch. The system unit may also have a reset button, an LED display, a key lock, a speaker grille, and other features. The following sections take a closer look at the elements that make up the system unit and that have not been discussed previously.

Ports

Connectors on an IBM-compatible desktop system should include at least one parallel port, two serial ports, a keyboard port, a mouse port (so the mouse doesn't take up a serial port or require its own expansion card), a video output port, a power outlet for the monitor (so turning on the system turns on the monitor), and possibly sound in and out connectors if you want to use sound. A portable system needs the same set of connectors except for the power plug for the monitor. You have to check carefully to make sure that the system has the connectors you want because some manufacturers try to save a few cents in manufacturing costs by leaving off things you need. A SCSI port is a bonus; if you get one, make sure it's from one of the top few manufacturers so you can get compatible devices to hook to it.

Macintosh systems have a similar complement of ports and are less likely to leave off something you need, but if you're looking at used Macs, you should know the original

PowerBook portables—the 100, 140, and 170, which were otherwise excellent machines—lacked a video output port. Users who wanted to hook up an external monitor at home or in the office had to buy a SCSI video adapter, a strange idea that worked well enough but was slow.

Power Supply

The system's power supply may become very important if you want to use several expansion cards, each of which draws some power, or if you want to use internal devices, such as an additional hard disk drive. If you want to plug your monitor into the back of the system unit, the power supply needs to accommodate this as well. Some Macintosh models and a number of IBM-compatible systems have had inadequate power supplies that tended to burn out when even moderately loaded; ask detailed questions about the capacity of the power supply if you plan to expand your system. External devices, such as those that connect to a SCSI port, generally have their own power cord and do not draw from the system's power supply.

Drive Bays

A drive bay is an empty area inside the system unit for storage devices such as floppy disks, hard disks, CD-ROM drives, or even a tape drive. The more such devices you order for your system or plan to add later, the more drive bays (and the larger the power supply) you need. Most desktop systems are limited in the number of drive bays they have. Mini-tower systems with room for two full-height and two half-height devices, give or take a device, offer enough room for most expansion needs; power users should consider a floor-standing tower system. If you run out of room inside your system unit, you can use external devices instead, but if you have an IBM-compatible without a SCSI port, you will quickly use up your computer's expansion slots.

Form Factors

The system unit of a desktop computer can come in any number of sizes and shapes, also known as form factors. These are generally designed in response to two conflicting needs. For expandability and cooling, you want a big system unit with several slots and several drive bays. For convenience, you want a small system unit that fits comfortably under the monitor or even, as with the Macintosh Classic line, has the monitor built-in. Mini-tower systems that stand next to the monitor are a popular alternative; power users favor full tower systems that stand under or beside the desk. There are two problems to be aware of before you buy. Because floor-standing tower systems are further away from your keyboard, monitor, and other peripherals, you sometimes have power cords and cables that are shorter than you need, forcing awkward setups (though you can get extensions for monitor, keyboard, and most other cables). It's also all too easy to knock a tower system over.

Portable computers are a whole other ball game. In trying to make systems smaller and lighter, designers have tried leaving out floppy drives, making keyboards too small, using cheap and easily damaged materials for the system's case, and every other trick in the book. Until recently, portables did not have slots in a traditional sense, and every system was different in how, if at all, it could support internal devices such as a modem. These differences led to needed devices being late to market, expensive, or even completely unavailable. (An example is the lack of a viable video-out option for the early models of the PowerBook.) Now the PCMCIA standard solves all that. With it, portable computer owners can enjoy some of the same expandability long taken for granted by owners of desktop systems.

Software

There is a variety of software available. Later sections of this book describe your choices in operating systems and environments, and utilities. The following sections describe all the software that goes into your system, what each type does, and how it all works together.

ROM Firmware

As described previously, ROM holds firmware that helps the computer start up and handles basic I/O functions. On the Macintosh, ROM also holds Quickdraw, a set of very fast routines for drawing on-screen, and other code used by the System and Finder. Some portables have DOS and Windows or even application software in ROM.

Operating System Software

The operating system (OS) takes over operation of the computer after it has started up. It provides basic functionality for communicating with the keyboard and disk drives, and enables the user to execute system functions, such as copying files. Advanced operating systems do much more. Some, like the Macintosh operating system, provide a graphical interface for system functions and application programs; others, such as OS/2, work with the intrinsic capabilities of the microprocessor to provide system capabilities such as true multitasking and memory protection between applications.

Operating Environments

An operating environment adds advanced capabilities to the operating system that hosts it. A simple operating system coupled with an advanced operating environment can deliver almost as much functionality as a complete, advanced operating system, though limitations imposed by the underlying OS may peek through. Microsoft Windows, the best-known operating environment, adds a graphical user interface and much more sophisticated memory management, among other capabilities, to DOS. An example of the limitations that an OS can impose on the operating environment is the short file names that DOS and Windows use; these names are a feature of DOS that Windows has not yet overcome. Current versions of Windows only use DOS to start up the computer and for a few I/O functions; future versions will not need DOS at all.

Drivers

A driver is a piece of software that allows the system to control or access a new device. On the Macintosh, a driver is called a system extension. The driver performs this function by translating commands that the system makes to known devices into a format understandable by the new device. For instance, a network driver allows the DOS COPY command to access disk drives on a network in the same way that it can access drives that are an intrinsic part of the computer. Drivers often need to be installed in special places in a system to be recognized. On a DOS system, you need to install drivers in CONFIG.SYS and/or AUTOEXEC.BAT files for them to work right; on a Macintosh, you need to store drivers in the Extensions subfolder of the System folder. Bad, missing, buggy, and out-of-date drivers can make your personal computing life miserable.

Utilities

Utility programs extend or replace parts of the operating system to alter the way it works or to provide additional functionality. Programs that replace the Windows user interface are utilities; so are programs that increase the apparent capacity of your hard disk or put a scene from Star Trek on your screen when your computer isn't in use. In theory, you shouldn't need utilities because the operating system should provide all the functionality you need; in reality, many users find that utilities are vital for making their computing experience more productive and more enjoyable.

Applications

Applications are the first thing people usually mean when they talk about software. Application programs are software that make it possible to do productive work on the computer. For instance, a word-processing application makes it possible to use your computer as a replacement for your typewriter; a desktop publishing application allows the computer to replace any number of tools including scissors, paste-pots, and stick-on letters. Most applications available today are fairly direct replacements for tools and ways of working that existed before personal computers were available; others, such as multimedia and groupware, allow new ways of working that were not only impossible, but difficult to imagine before people had experience using computers and trying to get them to do more and more.

How Hardware and Software Work Together

You walk into your office in the morning and turn on your computer; what happens? The following roughly describes the events that take place on a Mac running System 7.1, with notes to describe how DOS and Windows do things where differences exist.

With most Macs, you start the computer by pressing a special key on the keyboard. (IBM compatible users reach for the power switch.) Power flows into the computer, and it begins its startup sequence. The microprocessor automatically runs a routine in ROM, which finishes, and then passes control to another routine, then another. Under the control of these routines, the system checks memory to see if it's functioning correctly and starts checking its disk drives in an attempt to find more code to execute. When the hard disk is read, the computer finds the operating system and starts to load it into memory; on the Macintosh, an icon of a smiling Macintosh (the "happy Mac") appears on-screen at this point. DOS and Windows systems just keep going.

Before the operating system is fully loaded, the computer looks in its Extensions file—on a DOS system, it looks in CONFIG.SYS—and installs any and all device drivers it needs, including network and video drivers. Then the operating system finishes loading. The computer is ready to run.

Once ready, the first thing the system does is look for any instructions as to what programs it should run first. The Macintosh system looks in its Startup Items folder; a DOS system executes AUTOEXEC.BAT. One of the many things that instructions in the AUTOEXEC file can do is start Windows. Windows may in turn automatically run other programs, such as any of several utilities that change the appearance of the Windows desktop.

At this point, the system finally stops working and starts waiting for user input. Much of the operating system, probably several drivers, and possibly one or more programs, are already in memory.

Chapter Summary

This chapter describes the components of a typical personal computer system—the many different kinds and versions of microprocessors used in key personal computer systems, the motherboard and the many things found on it, the various kinds of disk drives, the remaining parts of the system unit, and the software that makes the computer come to life. It explains how the different pieces work together and some of the key considerations you need to take into account in order to buy a system that will meet your needs today and tomorrow.

IN THE NEXT CHAPTER

The next chapter offers guidelines for picking the kind of computer you want. These guidelines include deciding what underlying hardware and which operating system and graphical user interface, if any, you want. It also includes choosing between a desktop and a portable computer.

PART II

Choosing a System

Includes

Deciding What Kind of Computer You Want

Choosing a Computer System Manufacturer

Listing of Computers

Deciding What Kind of Video System You Need

Listing of Monitors and Adapters

Deciding What Kind of Printer You Need

Listing of Printers

CHAPTER FOUR

Deciding What Kind of Computer You Want

This chapter helps you decide whether you want a Macintosh system, an IBM-compatible that runs Windows, or some other option. It makes the case for portable computers as a one-system solution to many of your needs, and then tells you when a desktop system is a better buy.

There are many shades of opinion on each of the issues discussed in this chapter. Compare what you read here to your own impressions and experiences and those of coworkers and friends whose judgment you trust. Gathering this kind of information will help you make a good buying decision.

How To Choose an Operating Environment

If you want to buy a mainstream computer system, you should choose from among the most popular kinds of systems: an IBM-compatible running DOS, Windows, or OS/2; or a Macintosh with its operating system.

Each of these choices is an *operating environment*. An operating environment is made up of three main elements:

- *Type of Computer.* The two main choices are Macintosh and IBM-compatibles, but the limits on which operating systems run on each type are rapidly disappearing. PowerPC-based computers, for example, can use Macintosh, Windows, UNIX, DOS, and several other operating environments.

- *Operating System.* This low-level software provides the user and programs with an interface to the computer's hardware and peripherals.

- *Graphical User Interface.* The GUI (pronounced "gooey") is the higher level software that provides the user with a consistent, easy-to-use interface for the system and its applications.

Different computer systems provide different numbers of choices in these areas. For a Macintosh computer, there are maybe ten to twenty different models available at any one time. The low-level operating system is hidden from you if you only use the Macintosh user interface, the first popular GUI. On cross-platform Macs (based on the PowerPC), you can use several operating systems with varying levels of "insulation" between you and the low-level functions.

For an IBM-compatible system, there are dozens of major manufacturers with hundreds of models available at any one time. For any given IBM-compatible computer model, you can choose among the DOS operating system, Microsoft Windows (with DOS underneath), IBM's OS/2, or Microsoft's Windows NT.

Most entry-level or intermediate users end up choosing between Macintosh and an IBM-compatible running DOS or Microsoft Windows. If another operating environment seems to suit your needs better, that's fine; this book describes how to make an appropriate buying decision for almost any user. But most of the material concentrates on the most popular products that can work with the Macintosh, DOS, or Microsoft Windows. Whatever kind of system you choose, these environments will dictate most of the choices that will be available to you over the next few years.

The next few paragraphs describe some of the major factors that go into deciding what operating environment to use. These factors may lead you to lean heavily in one direction or another or even make up your mind completely without the need to consider the individual merits of each of the major contenders.

Your Budget

If you're on a tight budget, you may be limited to considering DOS or the Macintosh. The least expensive choice is an IBM-compatible desktop system from a less-well-known manufacturer running DOS. For only a little more money, you can get a compact Macintosh, such as a Classic, that will be slower but easier to use.

Watch out, though; although the base price of a computer may be as low as $700-$800, by the time you buy the computer system, monitor, printer, one productivity-related software package, and an add-on or two, such as a modem or a game program, you end up spending around $2,000. For a few hundred dollars more, your choices broaden to include more reputable manufacturers of IBM-compatibles, including systems that can run Windows, and mid-range Macintosh systems.

Many people make successful computer purchases on a tight budget, but most end up spending more than they had planned. If you're short on money, invest the time to learn about your options and how to make choices that you will be happy with.

What You and Your Coworkers Use at the Office

If you're choosing a system for use at work, or you want to bring work home from the office, give the utmost consideration to buying a system that can run the same operating environment used by your coworkers and others with whom you need to exchange information and computer data. There is a huge difference between being able to tap your coworkers for help and having to dig through the manual or call a vendor every time you have a question or problem. If your coworkers use a variety of environments (Macs and Windows-based PCs, for example), you may want to choose a cross-platform solution.

If you are the only one in your workgroup who uses a specific kind of computer or operating environment, you will need to spend more time in preparation and learning in order to get your work done. Even users who make a relatively common choice, such as buying a Macintosh portable for use on the road while operating a Windows system at work, run into problems that are only solved with generous applications of time and/or money.

Unless you work with users experienced in cross-platform data transfer, you shouldn't try to save a few bucks by buying a PC-compatible running DOS or Windows if you need to interact with Macintosh users at work. The safest and easiest choice is to buy a system that can run the same operating environment that your closest coworkers use.

Specific Programs You May Need

Usually, you need a specific program in order to share data and get help from friends and coworkers who use the same program. In this case, buy into the same environment they use. But if you are making a really independent choice, you need to think about what kinds of things you will do with the computer and whether specific programs that you need are only available for a certain system.

There are a few programs that are only available for the Macintosh, largely concentrated in high-end desktop publishing and color graphics work. (The number of things that are *easier* to do on the Mac is high, but the number of things you can *only* do on the Mac is low.)

A number of programs are only available for Windows, and thousands and thousands of programs exist on DOS and nowhere else. You might never need any of these programs, but if you do, you will be happy if you bought a DOS-capable machine and less happy if you bought a Macintosh-only machine. (Don't panic if you are determined to get a non-PowerPC Mac; you can buy DOS-emulation software that enables you to run most DOS programs on most Macintoshes.)

Before you buy, check with others who share your work needs and personal interests to find out what specific programs they use and in what operating environment(s) those programs run.

How and Where You Plan To Use Your Computer

If you plan to use your computer at home and don't need to communicate with systems in your own or someone else's office, you have a great deal of freedom of choice. Even if you do work on your computer at home, you can choose programs that allow you to use the same data in both environments. (Most Macintoshes can read and write data on the 3.5-inch floppy disks used by IBM-compatibles. If you have programs on each end that can use or convert data from the other system, you're all set.) Getting the easiest-to-use system for your children, for instance, may outweigh the consideration of compatibility with your coworkers.

You have almost as much freedom in buying a portable computer, even for work use, as you do in buying a home system (a fact that has contributed greatly to the sales of Apple PowerBooks) because the portable system is used as a stand-alone unit. If there is any file transfer or converting to be done, you do it in one step when you get back to the office. You can even use your portable's modem to exchange mail with your office's e-mail system, provided you have a version of the e-mail program that runs on your operating system. Almost all e-mail companies (cc:Mail, for example) offer programs that run under DOS, Windows (and, therefore, OS/2), and Macintosh operating systems.

If you plan to use your computer system in an office, compatibility with your coworkers is very important. You will be shut out of a lot of informal and formal support options if you use a different operating environment than the majority of your coworkers. If you decide to go your own way, proceed with caution.

Macintosh, DOS, Windows, or ?

For each of the major operating environments, you will encounter proponents and opponents. Listen to each of them; they're valuable sources of information.

But as you listen, remember that all of the hardware and software products described in this book are now being used by many people to do productive work. The most one can really say is that some products have proved to be better for most of the people who share a common background, approach to computing, or type of job that they want to do. Remember that it's your money and time and that you, not a friend, coworker, or book author, are the one who has to be comfortable with the decisions you make.

Run DOS if You Can

DOS is the operating system that's used on most of the world's personal computers. It is well known for two things. The first is its command-line interface. This term means that the user interacts with DOS by typing commands; the user must remember what commands to type in order to do anything. (Recent versions of DOS have added an optional menu-driven interface.) The second is the 640K memory limit. This means that DOS can only directly use 640K of memory. As users have tried to do more and more with their

PCs, the combination of networking software, utilities, and application programs running at any one time has often totaled more than 640K. This situation has triggered no end of clever workarounds, some of which have been built into recent versions of DOS.

Despite these problems, good old DOS is still the most popular operating system on personal computers. If you buy an IBM-compatible, it will have some version of DOS loaded on it.

Here are a few reasons to consider using DOS as your operating system:

- *Tight budget.* If you're on a tight budget, an IBM-compatible that can run DOS is quite a bit cheaper than a similar model bulked up to run Windows. Application programs are often less expensive and take up less memory and disk space.
- *1 or 2 programs.* Although Windows is better at running multiple programs, DOS does just fine at running one program at a time. If you only want to use one or two programs total, running them one at a time may not be a big limitation.
- *DOS in the office.* If DOS is still commonly used in your office, it may also be a good choice for you. There will be people around who will know how to get most tasks accomplished under DOS and who will be able to recommend the right hardware and software solutions.
- *Not shut out.* DOS users are not totally shut out of the brave new world of Windows. If you use DOS, you can probably share data with Windows users. If you later move to Windows, you can probably upgrade your machine to it. You will certainly be able to run your old programs and use or convert your existing data.

To run today's DOS programs well, you should look for a computer system with the following minimum specifications:

- 386 microprocessor
- 1M-2M of RAM
- 40M-80M hard disk
- VGA or Super VGA graphics
- 13- or 14-inch monitor

This is very much a low-end system by today's standards; you should be able to find such a system from a reputable manufacturer for a very low price.

Don't assume that PC-compatibles are the only computers that are "DOS-capable," though. Macintosh users have been using DOS emulators to tap into DOS's wealth of available software for years, and the new Power Macs are able to run both DOS and Windows programs in addition to Macintosh programs.

The Case for Windows

Windows is an operating environment that runs on top of the DOS operating system. Its status as an operating environment means that Windows has many capabilities of its own, such as a graphical user interface and memory management for Windows applications, but it inherits certain limitations from DOS, such as short (11-letter) file names and the 640K limit for drivers and DOS applications. Although Windows is only an add-on to DOS, its memory and disk requirements have caused many DOS users to upgrade or even replace their systems to run Windows well.

Despite the limitations of Windows on top of DOS, Windows 3.1 has been a tremendous success. This success is largely due to Windows graphical user interface, which makes IBM-compatibles much easier to use than with DOS alone. DOS programs still run under Windows, sharing the machine with Windows programs.

The following list describes the key things in favor of choosing Windows-on-DOS as your operating environment:

- *Hardware base.* Windows runs on IBM-compatible machines, the most popular type of computer of all time. It uses all the hardware that was developed for the DOS world.

- *Software base.* As an operating environment that runs on top of DOS, Windows benefits in two ways. It can run DOS software with good performance and few compatibility problems, and Windows software is relatively easy for DOS developers to create.

- *New features.* Windows can take advantage of much more memory than DOS, and it adds a graphical user interface to make operating the computer and running software easier to learn.

- *Popularity.* Once Windows became somewhat popular, it attracted a great deal of attention from DOS developers eager for new markets. They created Windows software that in turn has made Windows itself even more popular. This snowball effect is creating a great number of hardware and software choices for Windows users.

- *Growth path.* Windows NT has already made a great contribution to the success of Windows even before it sells many copies. NT lets serious software developers and corporate developers know that the Windows applications they develop have a growth path to a more powerful environment.

To run Windows and several Windows programs well on a PC-compatible, you need a system with at least the following specifications:

- 486 or 486SX microprocessor
- 4M-8M of RAM

- 120M or greater hard disk
- VGA or Super VGA graphics (local bus if possible)
- 14- or 15-inch monitor (17-inch for desktop publishing)

This is a mainstream computer system by today's standards. Although you probably won't find such a system cheap, especially if you go for the 17" monitor, you won't be on the high end of the price/performance curve either.

The Windows environment does have some problems. Windows-ready machines are more expensive than those that run DOS, and troubleshooting in a DOS-plus-Windows environment can be difficult. But the popularity of Windows and its position between DOS and NT make it an attractive option.

The Case for Macintosh and Power Macs

The Macintosh is the only broadly successful alternative to IBM-compatibles running DOS and, more recently, Windows. The term Macintosh includes several elements. Macintosh computer hardware is based on Motorola's 68000 microprocessor family or the PowerPC family and includes a ROM chip with core software embedded on it. The Macintosh operating system includes the System, which roughly corresponds to DOS, and the Finder, which handles about the same functions as Windows. The System and the Finder are much more closely integrated with one another and with the hardware than DOS and Windows are. Macintosh applications are famous for a consistent "look and feel" that helps make the overall experience of using a Macintosh easier than using any other popular computer.

Macintosh systems were for a long time much more expensive than IBM-compatibles with similar performance. But the Macintosh interface was so much better than DOS that Apple maintained its premium prices and high profit margins throughout the late 1980s. When Windows 3.0 appeared in 1989, narrowing the gap in ease-of-use, Apple responded rapidly by dropping prices and making aggressive efforts to reach new users. The company also launched the highly successful PowerBook line of portable computers. These efforts have helped Apple grow, and it is still a viable competitor in the race with IBM as the leading seller of personal computers.

Despite the tremendous success of Windows, Macintosh remains the favorite of a large and growing group of users. The following list details some of the reasons.

- *Ease of setup.* Any Macintosh is easier to set up and get running than any IBM-compatible of similar capabilities. Apple builds in a few more capabilities, such as sound output, than most PCs have, and all the parts are well-integrated. This design makes both setting up the system and adding new hardware to it easy, which makes a tremendous difference to users.

- *Ease of use.* Basic computer operations such as copying files and installing software programs are easier to accomplish on the Mac than on an IBM compatible. Macintosh software applications are more like one another, and therefore easier to use together, than Windows software applications. (DOS applications vary even more than Windows applications.)

- *Ease of purchase.* Like ease of setup, this feature is an oft-ignored factor in the Mac's success. When you go to buy a Macintosh, there are many fewer decisions to make. You don't have to choose between DOS and Windows, and there are fewer monitors, disk drives, printers, and so on. New users especially tend to buy all-Apple systems that may not be the cheapest but are a very safe and simple choice.

- *Intangibles.* Apple as a company and the Macintosh as a product have a mystique about them that is hard to describe but that somehow communicates itself to new and experienced users alike. Macintosh users buy a lot of software and are willing to experiment with new kinds of programs. Software developers, inspired by the Macintosh's easy-to-use, elegant graphical user interface, have done much of their best work on the Mac. All this works together to create an experience that's hard for the more fragmented IBM-compatible world to match.

To run today's Macintosh programs well takes a fairly capable system. However, Apple has discontinued its low-muscle models to the point that almost any Macintosh can capably run most Macintosh software. Be sure to look at the high end if you want to run multimedia or use voice recognition or other sophisticated applications.

The Macintosh is still the best choice for many individual users and for educational users and institutions, all of whom find the ease of setup, use, and purchase to be compelling advantages. The PowerBook line is hard for portable buyers to ignore.

Business users are starting to take a second look at Macintosh, with the company's new focus on cross-platform computers. In the early days of the Mac vs. PC debate, PCs were easier to justify in business because of their lower price and the popularity of PC-based business software like Lotus 1-2-3 and WordPerfect. The Macintosh's lead in publishing and graphics software led to the classic stereotype of "Business Macs" appearing only in the art and advertising departments. Throughout those years, businesses have faced problems transferring data and sharing peripherals between Mac and DOS/Windows users.

The Mac/PC climate is much different today, though. Almost all popular business *and* graphics applications have both PC (Windows) and Macintosh versions. All popular networking products support both platforms, enabling them to share networked printers, modems, and file servers. Now, with reasonably priced Power Macs, you can run DOS, Windows, and Macintosh software on the same computer, virtually eliminating the need to use more than one type of personal computer in any business setting.

Give the Macintosh full consideration as a choice for personal or home use, but make sure to get answers to all your questions before making a big investment in it for use in a business setting.

Run OS/2 or NT if You Have to

OS/2 and Microsoft Windows NT are advanced operating systems that do a lot and require a lot—in terms of time, energy, and money. OS/2 was developed by IBM and Microsoft in the mid-80s, and then abandoned by Microsoft shortly after its introduction. With OS/2 2.0 and the latest version, 2.1, IBM has taken up the cause of OS/2 on its own. OS/2 2.1 can multitask DOS programs, Windows programs, and the relatively small number of OS/2-specific programs that have been written. It runs a capable interface called the Workplace Shell. OS/2 requires at least 8M of memory and a large hard disk.

Windows NT is a complete operating system written largely by the team that wrote the widely admired VMS operating system for DEC minicomputers many years ago. NT has built-in capabilities for security, multitasking, multithreading (a sophisticated form of multitasking, also used in OS/2), and other high-end needs. It has the same user interface as Windows. NT requires 16M or more of memory, an even larger hard disk than OS/2, and a CD-ROM drive.

If you are an experienced Windows user and you are running up against severe limitations in terms of multitasking capability, system reliability, or speed for high-performance applications, consider one of these systems as an option. Otherwise, wait.

Most people who move to OS/2 will do so because their companies develop their own in-house OS/2 applications that they need to run. Although in-house custom applications will also be developed for NT, there will probably also be many mass-market applications that will be worth having. As they develop, each of these environments will offer a reliable, less crash-prone way of multitasking DOS and Windows applications.

To run OS/2 or NT, you need a highly capable system. The low end of the following specifications is sufficient to run OS/2 well; look at the high end if you want to run NT.

- 486DX 50MHz-plus or Pentium microprocessor
- 8M-16M or more of RAM
- 200M or greater hard disk
- Super VGA local bus graphics
- 14-inch or larger monitor

This is a high-end computer system, and the demands of sophisticated OS/2 or NT applications may take you even further out on the price/performance curve. Such systems are much more expensive than a slightly less powerful system that can run Windows or DOS at top speed. You're also likely to have problems getting peripherals to work, a problem that will go away if you wait a bit. Unless you have a lot of support or really know what you're doing, stay clear of these operating systems for now.

Making a Safe Choice

There is a widespread belief that success in PC buying means getting the "hottest" system, the fastest computer of its kind. This belief conflicts with the widespread desire to pay the lowest possible price. But these factors are not the only, or even the most important, factors in making a good choice of a personal computer system.

When most people buy a car, the highest performance isn't the most important factor, or everyone would be driving Ferraris. Price isn't the sole determinant either. Most car buyers decide on a price range, identify the performance and features they want, and then look for cars that are solidly built, backed by a brand name manufacturer, and that meet or somewhat exceed their needs in performance, price, and features.

Although there are important differences between buying a computer and buying a car, the PC business is becoming more like the car business. Most PC buyers today are users rather than true enthusiasts. The business itself is consolidating; the reassurance of a solid brand name and solid service and support policies equal or exceed the importance of high speed and low price. Although there will always be savvy buyers who are willing and able to focus more on performance or price/performance ratios, most people need to take a number of factors into account when making a purchase.

The idea for most buyers, then, is to make a safe choice. That is, get a computer that you can learn to use without too much trouble and without giving up the whole effort in frustration. Get a system that you know is backed by a company you can trust, unless you're willing to take your chances on the company going under during the period you own your machine. Consider the manufacturer's reputation for service and support when making a buying decision.

For novice users who don't have knowledgeable coworkers or friends to help with learning and troubleshooting the system, the safest choice is probably the Macintosh. You get a system and a company you can count on. You're almost certain to be able to master the computer with reasonable effort and get it to do the things you want.

If you are already an IBM-compatible user or have knowledgeable friends or coworkers who can help, consider an IBM-compatible PC. The less you know, the more you should consider paying extra for excellent service and support policies. Look for a vendor who can deliver a system with the applications and peripherals you need already installed.

If you want to do a lot of different things with your IBM-compatible system, Windows is the best choice. Windows makes it easier to learn and use several applications at once, and there are more and more Windows-knowledgeable users who can help. Be ready to spend more to get a powerful machine that can run Windows and several applications at once with acceptable performance.

Desktop or Portable?

For years, portable PCs were poor relations of their desktop cousins. A "real" PC was a desktop machine; a portable was something you used when you had to (while you were on the road) and was abandoned as soon as you got home from your trip. Now portable machines are getting more and more capable. Many users are doing most or all of their work on portable machines.

The next section discusses various uses for a portable computer, including some that might surprise you.

Who Can Use a Portable

If you already have a computer in the office, and are traveling on business, you no doubt feel the need for a portable. Go ahead and buy one, but don't automatically get a cheap system that barely meets your needs. You will want a system that can run the software you use in the office and that can connect to the office network, which means that you need to consider a machine about as expensive as your desktop system, if not more so.

How to get the most out of your investment? Consider using your portable machine as your desktop machine as well. You will need a system with a docking bay that can connect your portable system to the network in your office and to a "real" monitor, keyboard, and mouse. You use the portable machine's built-in screen and keyboard on the road and the add-on peripherals back in the office. You can also use the portable machine for working at home. If you do a lot of work at home, use a docking bay to extend the machine just as you do at work.

You should also consider buying a portable if you're getting your first machine. The enhanced capabilities of today's portables mean that you may not have to compromise much on system capabilities. You can directly connect a standard monitor, keyboard, and mouse to most machines; for others, you have to use a docking bay to get this kind of access.

Portables Take Center Stage

Increasingly, both new and experienced users are turning to portables for most or all of their computing needs. Consider using a portable as your first or main machine if some or all of the following apply to you:

- *Novice user*. If you're a new user, you need a simple machine that you will get a lot of use out of. Portables are great for these needs. You can use them anywhere, and you don't have to deal with the file transfer headaches between your separate desktop and portable systems.

- *Work on the road*. If you work while traveling, you need a portable machine anyway. Why not buy the portable first and try to use it for all your needs? If it works, great; if not, adding a desktop machine later is just spending money you were going to spend anyway.

- *Work at home.* Many experienced users have a computer at home, a computer for the office, and one for the road. Such users spend a lot of time trying to remember which system had that memo to the boss and transferring files from one machine to another. If you have this problem, or are facing it in the near future, try using a portable for at least two of these needs, if not all three.

- *Student use.* If you're a student, a portable machine can be perfect. Although few people go so far as to use a computer in class, you can take it with you on breaks from school, to the library, and so on. Just be careful that no one steals it.

Super-Portables: Subnotebooks, Palmtops, and PDAs

The next step down in size from a portable is a subnotebook, palmtop, or Personal Digital Assistant (PDA). These machines are typically under three pounds and quite a bit smaller than even notebooks. They are designed to fit in your briefcase, purse, or even in your coat pocket, but some pack as much punch as larger systems. You will see some tradeoffs for the sake of portability—many super-portables don't have floppy drives or backlit screens.

When considering a super-portable, its capability to communicate with other PCs is very important. Most of these small systems include built-in software that lets you transfer data back and forth with your desktop PC, but a few require add-ons for data transfer. This function is a necessity, so make sure that you know what you're buying when you get a super-portable.

Industry analysts predict the super-portable market will boom very soon, so many computer companies are introducing models with a huge variety of capabilities. A major complaint of super-portable users is the unusable size of some keyboards, so some machines abandon keyboards altogether and let you write on their screens with special pens. Your handwriting is then translated into letters and numbers by special software within the computer. Other capabilities you might find include built-in application software (you will almost always find a built-in day planner/calendar, but you may also find more advanced functions, such as word processing and spreadsheets), infrared (wireless) communication, a built-in trackball, and many others.

If you plan to do serious work on a super-portable, try its keyboard first. Writing even a few sentences on some of the smaller machines requires a lot of patience and good aim with a pencil eraser. Some super-portables, PDAs in particular, are ideal for day planning and keeping track of addresses and phone numbers, but they're not designed for heavy computing work. Others (subnotebooks) are full-fledged PCs that run Windows and DOS and all your business applications.

When a Desktop System Is a Better Buy

Although portables are becoming more and more popular, there will still be a need for desktop systems for a long time to come. Here are some of the factors that may make you want to stick with a desktop system for now:

- *Low price.* The cheapest systems are all desktop machines, and in the mid-range prices, you can get a lot more for your money with a desktop system.

- *Expandability.* Although most portable systems can handle some peripherals, desktop systems are much more expandable. You can add more peripherals, more easily, to a desktop system than to a portable one.

- *Upgradability.* It's also much easier to upgrade a desktop system than a portable one. You can replace anything from the keyboard to the monitor to the hard disk much more easily, cheaply, and with many more choices than with a portable system.

- *Fungibility.* A *fungible* is a low-priced, interchangeable commodity such as salt, steel, or sprockets. Desktop computers are moving in this direction, so it's becoming easier to justify the purchase of one and to make a safe choice. Portable computers are still more expensive, more specialized, harder to select, and harder to justify the purchase of.

Chapter Summary

This chapter describes the major choices you will make in deciding what kind of a computer to buy—an IBM-compatible running DOS, Windows, OS/2, or NT, or a Macintosh system. It lists important considerations in choosing the right operating environment and in deciding between a desktop or a portable computer system.

IN THE NEXT CHAPTER

The next chapter offers detailed information about the major manufacturers of PCs and their product lines. It helps you decide whether to buy retail or from a direct marketer and which vendors to consider.

CHAPTER FIVE

Choosing a Computer System Manufacturer

Everyone makes buying decisions in a different way. For some people, a computer manufacturer is the first thing to consider in buying a system; for others, it's the last. Most people take a mainstream approach and choose from among a small group of manufacturers that they or people they know have had experience with or whose names they recognize from computer magazine articles and ads.

Choosing a manufacturer is, however, becoming more important. As prices drop, differences in manufacturers' service and support policies become just as important as differences in price. Some manufacturers are facing bankruptcy as system prices drop and the cost of doing business rises.

This chapter lists the major differences between manufacturers and describes several of the top computer vendors. Read this chapter before you start shopping for a system to familiarize yourself with the major players. Later, as you get closer to a buying decision, refer to it again to make sure that you're choosing a company, and not just a computer, that you feel comfortable with.

Important Factors in Choosing a Manufacturer

Choosing a manufacturer, or coming up with a list of manufacturers you will consider, is a difficult decision. Many users don't feel that they have a good way to choose either a computer system manufacturer or a particular system. So choices tend to be made based on a particular magazine review or even on the effectiveness of one manufacturer's ads over another's.

This section helps you make informed decisions by discussing the most important factors in choosing a manufacturer. Read through the descriptions of these factors and decide which are most important to you. Then look at the descriptions of manufacturers later in the chapter. Compare the manufacturer descriptions to your key factors and come up with a list of vendors whose products are worth your consideration. Through this process, you should be able to consider a wide range of manufacturers and systems and come up with the one choice that best meets your needs.

Name Recognition

This is a key deciding factor for many people, but it's an unreliable one. Many of the computer companies whose names you would quickly recognize are in financial trouble. IBM's subsidiary Ambra has been trying to overcome early delivery and quality complaints; Zeos and several other mid-range manufacturers have serious financial problems. Smaller companies that you may be familiar with through local advertising are quickly falling by the wayside.

Use name recognition in a more conscious way. Use this book, computer magazine articles, and your own experiences and contacts to build up your own approved list. Then use the listings in this book, computer magazine articles, and even ads to keep track of the latest products from among your chosen manufacturers. When it comes time to make a purchasing decision or recommendation, you will be well on your way to making a good choice.

Price and Performance

The three related factors that seem to get the most attention from the computer trade press are price, performance, and price/performance. None of these factors should be the sole determinant of your buying decisions.

Price is important, but the least expensive PCs are from small or even medium-sized manufacturers who, in many cases, lack the staying power of their larger (and slightly more expensive) competition. Since the dramatic price drops that have occurred in the last few years, systems with more extras, better service and support policies, and from more solid vendors are likely to be available for only a little bit more money.

Performance gets a tremendous amount of attention from the computer press. But the highest performance systems are often from smaller vendors without much else to offer. These systems are a good buy for those who know their way around the inside of a PC and are willing to risk incompatibilities or difficulties getting service. For the rest of the world, the highest performance systems serve a useful purpose in pressuring other vendors to increase the performance of their own systems.

Price/performance is the combination of these factors into one benchmark. Vendors can get a good mark on price/performance by offering a system at a less-than-average price with better-than-average performance. You should look for a system with good price/performance, but also look beyond this single factor to other things that matter to you.

There is no single characteristic that determines what the best computer buy is. Don't let the industry's focus on price, performance, and price/performance fool you into ignoring the other important factors in making a computer purchase.

Compatibility

Shortly after the IBM PC came out, many vendors introduced systems that were somewhat but not completely compatible. Mass-market software and add-on hardware sometimes ran on such systems and sometimes didn't. The computer trade press performed a very useful function in identifying systems that were highly compatible and recommending them strongly to users.

Now compatibility has increased to the point that most hardware and software works most of the time. But the steady weakening of IBM's leadership position means that there is no longer a single standard of compatibility for others to measure against. Instead, each user is likely to run into one or more difficult-to-solve compatibility problems in the course of their computing career.

Some tasks are more likely to cause problems than others. Simple things like connecting an external modem to a PC are likely, but not guaranteed, to work with no problems. Complicated things like adding multimedia hardware to a middle-of-the-road PC are very likely to run into problems. The more reputable your system vendor and the vendor of the add-on hardware are, the more likely the two products are to work together.

In the IBM-compatible world, many users restrict their buying to name brands to avoid compatibility problems. And more and more users buy preconfigured machines, with software and add-on hardware installed and at least somewhat tested, to improve the chances that all the parts will work together. The trade press has lessened its focus on compatibility, ease-of-installation, and related issues as vendors (prompted by end-users) iron out those problems. But all the problems aren't over—you still need to watch out for compatibility problems in your buying decisions and solve them when they occur.

Compatibility is much less of a problem in the Macintosh world. Macintosh is famous for making upgrades easy. Macs have fewer obstacles, such as the DOS 640K limit, to work around. Third-party developers only have to worry about one manufacturer's machines. All these factors combine to make expanding your Mac system easy.

Service and Support Policies

As the price wars that have raged for the last few years start to settle down, vendors are competing on other fronts. One of the key competitive weapons in this area is service and support policies. These policies vary widely by manufacturer and even by model within a manufacturer's offerings. Service and support policies for each system are found in this book's listings. Check for current information before buying, however; like price, service and support policies are adjusted frequently to meet competitive pressures.

Support can take several forms. The most popular is phone support. The top support services cover software that you buy bundled with the machine as well as the hardware.

Your vendor should include a period of free phone support after you buy your system, and then offer it for a reasonable price thereafter. Enough phone lines and trained personnel need to be available so that you can get through to someone quickly. Vendors also offer support by fax and by bulletin board service, which are great for less urgent problems, but phone support is the key element.

Service policies differ widely. On-site service within 24 hours or less of experiencing a problem is the best, but is expensive for a manufacturer to provide; you may pay extra for a system that has this kind of service "for free." Make sure that you can continue the policy for a reasonable price after the free period ends. If you buy from a dealer, fast carry-in service through the dealer can be a good alternative. But if computer dealers had done a good job with this kind of service, more of them would still be in business; try to get to know a dealer's reputation before counting on them for service.

Compaq and IBM are leaders in service and support, especially for their expensive network file server products, and other vendors are trying to match or exceed them. Find a vendor that offers the service and support options you want at a price you can afford.

Sales Channel

The microcomputer revolution largely happened in computer stores. Thousands of dealerships, many of which were mom-and-pop operations with poorly trained personnel, opened all over the world. Buyers flocked in to get the latest systems from vendors big and small.

Many dealerships improved, but buyers began to complain more and more about unknowledgeable salespeople, high prices, poor selection, and poor service and support. Many small dealers fell prey to large ones like Businessland, Computerland, and Entre Computer Centers. Then the big dealer chains faltered too. Although dealers still sell many computers, they are becoming less dominant as the most important places to buy computers.

The failures of the dealer channel and the increasing savvy of buyers has led to new ways of buying computers. Superstores have gathered together thousands of products in warehouse-like shopping floors and offer low prices and decent service. Mail-order sales have exploded, going from almost nothing a few years ago to become one of the most important ways of buying computers today.

Until recently, some manufacturers only sold through dealers and, in some cases, superstores, and others only sold through mail order. If you wanted to buy a specific system, there was just one channel through which you could buy it. As the computer business begins to consolidate, however, vendors established in one channel are selling through the others as well. You can now buy a certain system from two or more different kinds of sources.

All of the mainly mail-order vendors described in this chapter are an equally good choice anywhere in the U.S. Other vendors may be a better or worse choice depending on how close to you a dealer that carries their PCs is. Many experienced and novice buyers are strongly recommending mail order as an excellent way to buy a system. If you do buy at a dealer or superstore, make sure that the service and support options are comparable to the best offered through mail order.

Financial Viability

This is one of the most important factors in choosing a vendor and one of the most difficult to assess. With the increasing competitiveness of the microcomputer business, it is likely that more small and mid-size PC vendors will close their doors. (In fact, some of the larger companies have made it a goal to keep lowering prices until at least some of the small fry close up shop.) Some of the companies that go out of business, or continue selling other merchandise but not PCs, behave responsibly and pay a third-party provider to take over their service and support obligations. Others just pack up and shut down, leaving no forwarding address. Although few vendors go out of business, it's problematic for that vendor's customers when one does.

It is very hard to assess the risk that a given PC vendor will go out of business. At the safe end, all the companies described in this chapter are top sellers who can be counted on to stay in the business for at least the next few years. At the risky end, many of the smallest, least-known companies are likely to abandon their obligations at some point. The great number of companies in the middle, neither huge nor tiny, represent the biggest unknown. Many are solid and will continue offering good value for years to come. Others are hiding serious financial problems.

If the company you bought your computer from goes out of business, it's not a complete disaster. Most PCs today are made from name-brand components that a local computer store can easily replace. But no one wants to be an orphan—a buyer whose vendor goes out of business—if they can help it. Consider the size and solvency of the manufacturer before you make a computer buying decision.

Top PC Manufacturers

When you are deciding which manufacturer to buy your computer from, start by considering companies that have a healthy share of the market and that are growing in sales. These companies have the highest likelihood of being around in years to come, no matter how brutally competitive the PC business gets. These are the companies that are covered in the following sections. All of them are among the top sellers of PCs; almost all of them have had large increases in their unit sales over the last two years. Together, the companies covered in this chapter have about two-thirds of the U.S. PC market.

This chapter does not cover either small companies or mid-size companies that have had relatively flat or declining sales during the recent PC sales boom. You should consider buying from such companies only when they offer a noticeable advantage in an area that is important to you, whether this means the lowest price, highest performance, strong local presence in your area, or some other factor. Then assure yourself that the company meets your standards in terms of other factors, such as compatibility, service and support, and staying power. If the lesser-known company meets your criteria, consider its offerings seriously.

This approach seems to tilt the field against the little guys. It actually just reflects the harsh realities of today's consolidating PC market. Look hard at products from all the currently successful companies, and consider those from other companies only if they have features or functionality that you need.

Identifying the top PC manufacturers is difficult. Not all manufacturers report unit sales and/or dollar sales. The question of whether to look at U.S. sales or worldwide sales also complicates things. Finally, relative sales positions change depending on how long a time period you examine.

This book uses U.S. unit sales estimates from the major market research firms to identify leading companies. These firms are all solid and look to be in business for the long term. Many companies not listed in this chapter are also worth looking at, but some are more likely than the top companies to experience extreme competitive pressures if the market continues to consolidate.

The description of each company includes generally agreed-on information about its success and strategies, plus some opinions of the author. Get information from a variety of sources before deciding whether to consider products from a given manufacturer. However, you probably won't go wrong if you start your list with some or all of the companies described here.

The Top Three Manufacturers

Apple and IBM have each defined major standards for personal computing. They continue to be the market leaders. In recent years, Apple's market share has steadily risen while IBM's has bounced up and down, and the two companies are now in a neck-and-neck race for sales leadership. Compaq is the company that successfully cloned the IBM PC, and it has gone on to become a market and technology leader in its own right. Compaq is growing rapidly and may eventually challenge Apple and IBM for sales leadership.

Because these companies are the biggest sellers of personal computers worldwide, and likely to remain so for the foreseeable future, most buyers give their products extra consideration. Also, the markup for a top brand over a no-name clone has dropped from 100 percent or more to 25 percent or even less, making these companies a much more attractive choice for a wide range of buyers.

The following sections provide in-depth descriptions of each of these companies and its prospects for continued leadership.

Apple

Apple Computer, Inc. (Cupertino, CA) has enjoyed a renaissance and is once again closing in on being the leading maker of personal computers, a distinction it lost to IBM in the early 1980s. The Macintosh, whose original developers flew a pirate's flag over their building to signal rebellion, is now one of the best-selling personal computers in the U.S. and does well around the world.

Apple has excellent name recognition. The company has been more profitable than other personal computer vendors and is experiencing steady growth, although it's had some recent bumps. The Macintosh tends to be somewhat higher priced than IBM-compatible PCs, but its ease of use and other features make the price differential acceptable for many users. The Macintosh line, famous for its innovative graphical user interface, has now been extended to the highly popular PowerBook line of portable computers.

The Mac has not been compatible, in the usual sense, with IBM-compatible PCs, but it could read and write data files from their floppy disks. Many Macintosh programs, however, share data easily with IBM-compatible machines and emulation software allows Mac users to run DOS and Windows software (significantly slower than on PC-compatibles). The new Power Macs have blurred the difference considerably, running either Macintosh- or Windows-based software at very respectable performance levels.

The Macintosh is sold through dealers, superstores, Sears, and some other stores. The company is flirting with mail order, but sells few systems this way. Service and support have been provided through dealers until recently, but the company is improving its policies in this area and is backing more and more of its systems directly.

Because of its built-in graphics support and graphical user interface, the Macintosh is excellent for graphics applications like desktop publishing. As a high-performance business computer, the Macintosh is also a fine choice for word processing, spreadsheets, databases, and many other applications. The ease of use and reliability of Macintosh computers, offset somewhat by the "problem" of incompatibility with the IBM-compatible standard, have made them a leading choice for home, educational, and portable use, and the Power Macintosh's Windows integration is making them an attractive choice as desktop machines for use in business.

Compaq

Compaq Computer (Houston, TX) now competes with IBM for technical leadership of the IBM-compatible industry. It has excellent name recognition and is the third-largest seller of personal computers, though still well behind IBM and Apple. Compaq has returned to profitability after some recent problems and is well-positioned for the long term.

The company has accomplished several firsts, such as building one of the first widely popular IBM-compatible portable computers and building the first personal computer with an 80386 CPU. Compaq also was a driving force behind the development of the EISA bus standard. Compaq specializes in high-performance servers, desktop computers, and portable computers that are well-designed and solidly built. Its QVision video accelerator is currently a leading product.

In the last few years, Compaq has abandoned its former high-price strategy and dropped prices dramatically. Other vendors have matched or even exceeded the price cuts, but where a Compaq system once cost thousands of dollars more than a comparable system from a less-known manufacturer, the difference is now down to hundreds of dollars or less. Because Compaq has high performance and high user satisfaction ratings, especially for its portable machines, the difference is often worth it.

Like Apple, which also used to sell exclusively through dealers, Compaq is broadening its sales options. The company now backs more of its systems directly and offers phone support and on-site service. Compaq's systems get mixed reviews for compatibility. The company makes many of its own components, rather than depending heavily on external suppliers like other IBM-compatible vendors, which can cause compatibility problems. Yet any software or add-on hardware vendor worth its salt tests its products on Compaq systems and is ready to help with any problems users experience.

Compaq's competitive goals are to drive some of the smaller vendors out of the PC market, to steadily close the sales gap between itself and IBM, and to increase its current technical leadership in the IBM-compatible industry while keeping costs and prices down. The company's recent agreement with Microsoft to establish standards for integration and ease of use is the basis for further steps in this direction. The company has successfully restructured itself to the extent that it can credibly pursue all of these ambitious goals. If you had to commit today to a single vendor to meet your desktop and portable computer needs for the next several years, Compaq would be a good choice.

IBM

IBM (International Business Machines) Corporation has been a standard setter in the microcomputer industry since the introduction of the IBM PC in 1981. Recently, however, IBM has lost huge amounts of money and faces serious problems. IBM established the IBM-compatible standard in the early '80s and still is the leading seller of IBM-compatible machines, but its market share has dropped almost every year. Microcomputer product development and decision-making have been almost entirely spun off into the IBM Personal Computer Company, a unit that is largely separate from the rest of IBM. Once clearly dominant, IBM is now trying to stave off challenges by Apple for unit sales leadership and Compaq for technical leadership.

The IBM Personal Computer Company lost some of its advantages in the attempt to defend its position. The company once had a top network of dealers. The MCA (Micro

Channel Architecture) bus found in almost all its PS/2 line of PCs made adding peripherals easy, and IBM built most of its own components. IBM sold conservatively configured systems for high prices, but it was always a safe choice.

Now IBM has added new lines of personal computers to its flagship PS/2 lines. More and more of its sales come from the Valuepoint and PS/1 lines, which use the ISA bus instead of the MCA bus. These products contain greater and greater proportions of non-IBM components and are sold through the same channels as other PCs. This strategy should allow IBM to get right down there in the price/performance trenches with its competitors, but its systems still tend to be high-priced for what they offer.

One path IBM has taken to regain its profitability is creating a spin off: Ambra, the world's most successful "virtual corporation"—one made up almost entirely of outside contractors. Formed in August of 1993, Ambra originally had very few employees, contracting out the sales, manufacturing, and shipping duties. Coordinating this somewhat experimental effort led to some delivery and quality problems early on, but customer satisfaction has risen dramatically recently. Ambra is positioned as "small and entrepreneurial enough to be nimble, with the strength of IBM."

No matter what happens to the parent company, the IBM Personal Computer Company is a valuable property that won't disappear. Its systems are increasingly competitive and its service and support are solid. IBM is making daring moves in a volatile industry, which scares some analysts and potential buyers. Don't eliminate IBM from your buying list, but don't buy it simply based on its past reputation—make sure that the current company and system can offer what you need.

The Second Tier

A second-tier PC company is a solid, dependable company that is one of the top 10 to 15 in PC sales volume. Unlike the leaders, second-tier companies buy nearly all of their components rather than making them. For example, the top three often make the motherboards of their computers themselves, and the companies on the second tier usually buy them from third-party suppliers. As a result, the second-tier companies exercise less technical leadership and differentiate themselves by optimized combinations of existing components, addition of features such as external caches or multimedia hardware add-ons, domination of specific new or existing sales channels, and solid service and support.

The following sections identify some leading second-tier companies that have managed to grow and maintain profitability during the difficult market conditions of the last two years. These conditions included a year or so of declining overall PC sales, followed by a wave of intense price cutting and exploding overall sales. Companies that have been able to come out ahead in these demanding conditions are the most likely to be around for the long term.

The companies are divided into two groups: those that sell entirely or primarily through dealers, superstores, or other retail outlets, and those that get most of their sales through mail-order. Some of the companies described here may be more or less interesting to you depending on whether their strength is in desktop or portable machines, your own experiences and those of people you know, and whether their products are available in your area. Each is worth your consideration.

Buying Retail

Buying a computer retail once meant going to a computer dealer. But as desktop computers have moved toward being commodities that compete largely on price, distribution channels have expanded to include computer superstores, electronics stores large and small, mass-market merchandisers such as Sears, and even discount and warehouse outlets that do much of their business in clothing and food.

Computer dealers on the whole have done a mediocre job of supporting their customers, which contributed to the explosion of other channels for buying PCs. This problem continues in other retail channels. Salespeople are generally not highly knowledgeable about what they're selling. This problem makes the high-quality support and service offered by the most successful manufacturers increasingly important. Start your shopping list with these top vendors, and then consider others to the extent that they offer specific advantages that better meet your needs.

AST

AST Research is one of the survivors from the early garage era of PCs. Founded by three immigrants to America whose first names start with A, S, and T, AST is now one of the top PC companies in the world.

AST sells both desktop and laptop machines. Its basic strategy is to sell systems that are above-average in performance at a below-average price. It has consistently followed through on this strategy and achieved solid customer satisfaction. Like its Los Angeles neighbor and rival ALR, AST sells through dealers; but, unlike ALR, it has maintained consistent profitability and growth.

The company has been a leading exponent of upgradable PCs and was an early adopter of PCMCIA slots for its notebook systems. These small slots greatly improve the expandability of portable computers.

AST offers a wide range of service and support options, but most customers get support from the company's highly regarded dealers. If you want to buy a system from a dealer, put AST at or near the top of your buying list.

Packard Bell

Packard Bell (Chatsworth, CA) has a name made famous by top-quality radios in the 1920s and TV sets in the 1950s, but Packard Bell today is a new company that purchased the name from its predecessor. Its systems are also found under other names such as Axcel, Executive, Force, Legend, and Packmate.

Packard Bell sells desktop systems and some portables. It sells through superstores, price clubs, dealers, and other retail outlets. Its strategy is saturation—the company has achieved a huge share of the retail market with low-priced machines that give middle-of-the-road performance. Its machines are very popular among home users, much less so in business.

Packard Bell has achieved a few noteworthy innovations. It includes how-to-use-it software called Navigator on its systems and bundles applications from Lotus. It has upgradable CPUs in many of its computers and has made a real effort to meet user needs by offering bigger monitors and hard disks than competitors. However, many of the company's machines are made by others and resold under its name, and Packard Bell is not a technical leader.

The company has recently improved service and support that had been rated as mediocre by users. Options include on-site service and carry-in support. Packard Bell is a good choice for a low-priced system with a few extra features from a vendor who will be around for a while.

Tandy/Grid

Tandy (Fort Worth, TX) sells its computers through a large chain of Radio Shack stores, through its Computer City and Incredible Universe superstores, and (in its Grid division) through direct sales to the Fortune 500. Although it has sold many PCs, the company's PCs do not consistently excel in any of the important areas—performance, price, or customer satisfaction. As a result, the company is one of the few market leaders to have poor recent financial results.

Tandy-labeled PCs are a mixed bag. They tend to be middle-of-the-road systems at higher-than-average prices. They also tend to lack features. Some Tandy systems are very highly priced or come in odd configurations. An exception is in multimedia, where Tandy has been a real leader, but its multimedia offerings have been slow to catch on. Exercise some care before buying a Tandy system, especially a used one—early Tandy PCs suffered severe compatibility problems with PC-compatible components and software.

Grid is another story. The company is an innovator in pen-based computing and sells high-performance, high-priced systems to the Fortune 500, largely through direct sales.

Tandy has sold its manufacturing operations to AST. It's probable that Grid's product lines will be kept, but the future support for the Tandy nameplate is in doubt. Although the Tandy-owned Computer City is a good place to buy a computer, you may want to buy a different kind of system.

Toshiba

Toshiba America Information Systems is a division of the Japanese electronics giant Toshiba Inc. It sells portable and, less successfully, desktop systems through a large number of dealers and distributors. Toshiba has been a consistent innovator in portable computing, with its most recent success being in top-quality color portables.

Toshiba's portable machines rate high in reliability and customer satisfaction. However, the company has been slow to cut prices, and the success of other vendors has cut into Toshiba's U.S. market share. Toshiba is now innovating in higher end areas, such as machines based on the SPARC microprocessor and UNIX servers.

This company is still a good choice for portable systems, but it does not seem to be making a strong commitment to long-term success with IBM-compatible desktop machines. If you are looking at portable computers at a dealer or superstore, Toshiba's systems are a good place to start.

Buying Direct

Buying a computer "direct," or mail-order, once meant risking your money on a system that was likely to offer poor performance and be backed by little in the way of service and support. This is still true for the smallest and least-known mail-order vendors. But Dell Computer, followed by other vendors, has led the creation of a higher tier of mail-order vendors who have turned this perception around almost completely. If you buy direct from one of the top-rated vendors listed in the following sections, you are likely to get low prices, high quality, and top-rated service and support.

Even novice computer users, who tend to appreciate the presence of a local vendor, have learned that buying direct can be the best way to go. Some mail-order vendors are experiencing financial problems in the increasingly competitive PC market, but all of those described here are winners who will be around for the long haul. Unless you have a local dealer who you have heard especially good things about, buying direct may be your best choice.

Dell

Michael Dell started selling PCs from his dorm room at age 19. His company, Dell Computer (Austin, TX), has led the development of mail-order sales as a credible way to buy PCs. The company consistently earns top honors for user satisfaction with innovations such as a pre-loading operating system and application software on the hard disk. Dell's growth has been incredible, with some recent quarters seeing 100 percent revenue increases over the previous year. The company is now one of the few top sellers of PCs worldwide.

Dell's systems have been largely Dell-built, and the company has often been a leader in performance and, to a slightly lesser extent, in price. Dell has done extremely well with both desktop and notebook machines. However, the company has lost just a little bit of its golden glow recently. Dell's machines are more and more built from third-party components, with Dell adding only a few custom-built pieces. The company is not always a price leader and sometimes slips to middle-of-the-road performance. Like other companies, Dell has experienced delays in filling orders. Also, its notebook systems have had some technical flaws.

Dell continues to be both a rapidly growing company and one that offers very good value with almost all its systems. The company now sells software and peripherals from other companies and is becoming a more complete marketer even as its innovation slips somewhat. Systems include a free one-year, on-site service plan, a one-day turnaround policy, and top-rated phone support. Dell is the leader among mail-order sellers and also offers its systems through retail outlets. If you buy from Dell, you are likely to get a good deal on a well-made, tested system.

DEC

Digital Equipment Corporation (Maynard, MA), widely known as DEC, has tried many times to achieve success in PCs. Like other companies large and small, its early efforts focused on almost-IBM-compatible systems that met with poor customer acceptance. After other mediocre attempts, the company has finally managed to get past its big-system focus to become a success selling computers through DEC Direct, a mail-order service selling desktop and portable systems along the same lines as Dell and Gateway 2000.

Although DEC's systems tend to be solid and achieve relatively high performance, they are made following a high-cost strategy that makes it difficult for the company to keep prices low. Many of DEC's desktop systems are made by Intel; many of its portables come from Grid. By the time everyone involved makes some money, the customer is stuck with a higher price. Higher prices may be the reason that DEC is not known for the highest customer satisfaction with its computers.

Despite its fast growth in the PC arena, DEC has a lot of challenges before it can achieve long-term success. First, it has to make its own PCs or be stuck with charging high prices. Second, it has to keep itself isolated from the financial problems of its parent company, which is only now achieving stability after huge losses and severe layoffs. Finally, it has to figure out how its highly anticipated, high-performance Alpha microprocessor fits into its PC plans.

DEC's name has attracted a lot of buyers, and it's a solid, conservative choice for either a desktop or a portable system. Service and support are solid, even by the high standards set by competing direct vendors. However, carefully compare the price, performance, and configuration of the DEC machine you are considering to other direct and retail vendors before making a final purchase decision.

Gateway 2000

Gateway 2000 (N. Sioux City, SD) has followed Dell's formula for mail-order success and grown very quickly to the point where it is an equal with Dell in the U.S. The company has lagged behind Dell only in selling to larger businesses and in cracking markets in other countries. Gateway 2000 has focused somewhat less on technical innovation and somewhat more on low price, leading it to do very well in the home and small-business markets. Its systems, packed in white boxes with black spots known as "cow cubes," reflect what the company calls a Midwestern emphasis on values and value.

Gateway 2000 has won many Best Buy awards and battles Dell for top honors in customer satisfaction. Computer industry insiders talk a lot about the leading-edge performance offered by other companies, but often buy Gateway 2000 when they're spending their own money. The company is now becoming more of an innovator as well. Though still built from third-party components, its desktop systems include technical advances like local bus video. The company also offers a popular extra-small notebook system.

The company's growth has led to some widely publicized problems in its otherwise top-rated phone support, but Gateway 2000 continues to develop. The company is expected to continue as a leader in attractively priced mail-order systems while adding more technical savvy as well. Gateway 2000 is a good choice for home use and is becoming a good choice for business as well.

The Best of the Rest

The companies described previously are not the only ones worth buying from; they are just the standard-setters that are almost guaranteed to be around for the long haul. You can consider a huge variety of vendors before making your purchase decision.

Companies that have not yet achieved market-leading success, at least in the U.S. market, but that are worth serious consideration, include the following:

- *Acer.* Acer America (San Jose, CA) has recently shed its low profile. It has come out with new lines of both desktop and network file server systems and has been rewarded with sharp sales increases. Service and support policies have improved, going from "call the dealer" to "call us, anytime." Some recent offerings have received high ratings for performance. An Acer system that meets your price and performance criteria may be a good choice.

- *HP.* Hewlett-Packard (Cupertino, CA), widely known as HP, is starting to add computer systems success to its market leadership in laser printers. The company's systems have long been tops in performance and in quality; now its prices are dropping. HP is a strong player in the "super-portable" market with its three-pound OmniBook, which includes DOS, Windows, and applications (like Microsoft Excel and Word) in ROM. With customers paying more attention to brand names in today's more competitive computer market, HP may further improve its position. If the price offered isn't too much higher than competing systems, and if the dealer's service and support seem solid, an HP computer may be a good buy.

- *NEC.* NEC Technologies (Foxborough, MA), an affiliate of Japan-based NEC, sells desktop and portable systems through dealers. It's a large seller but has lost some market position to the competition recently. Users don't express undue unhappiness or great joy with either its desktop or portable systems. Although NEC CD-ROM drives and monitors are often the best of their kind, the company's PCs are not as outstanding; consider your options carefully before laying your money down.

- *ZEOS*. Another mail-order success story, ZEOS (Minneapolis, MN) has begun a strong push on the portable and subnotebook market. Its desktop systems are still the company's bread and butter, but innovations like 24-hour phone support and the tilt/swivel screen on the Freestyle laptop have made it an attractive choice. The low-priced, high-powered Contenda subnotebook (starting at $995) is another feather in the sometimes-troubled company's cap.

Buying from a local computer maker is another option that is increasingly popular. These very small companies do well by offering customized collections of well-known components to knowledgeable buyers, and then following up with personalized service and support. Buying from a local vendor is likely to get you a good deal price-wise, but may be risky. You won't know how good the system's performance is unless you run your own tests, and getting a satisfactory resolution to a service or compatibility problem may depend to a great extent on the individual who picks up the phone or comes out on a service call. Make sure that you know what you're doing before buying from a local computer maker.

Chapter Summary

This chapter describes the major manufacturers of PCs—Apple for the Macintosh, and IBM, Compaq, and many others for IBM-compatibles. It describes key differences between the top vendors, the best of the second tier, and others. It also gives detailed information about each of the top manufacturers—how buyers and the trade press perceive their machines, who they sell to, how they sell, and whether their offerings have recently been successful in the market. Use this chapter to help develop a list of manufacturers to consider in buying a PC.

IN THE NEXT CHAPTER

The next chapter consists of listings of PCs from major manufacturers. Use it to help you decide which personal computer to buy.

…

CHAPTER SIX

Listing of Computers

Buying a computer system is an important and difficult decision. There are a great number of models with different price/performance characteristics and features available from many sources. The information in previous chapters should help you decide what the important factors are in getting the right system for you. For instance, you need to decide whether you need a desktop or portable system, a Macintosh or an IBM-compatible, a high-performance system or a low-cost one. The tables in this chapter will help you match your needs against the systems that are out there.

The tables cover desktop IBM-compatibles, desktop Macintoshes, portable IBM-compatibles, and portable Macintoshes. Because they are so large, tables for desktop and portable IBM-compatibles are separated into several tables by CPU type. This organization allows you to look at groups of systems that are similar in performance and price. Each of the IBM-compatible tables is further sorted by CPU type, speed, and cache size. This organization allows you to look, within a table, at lower performance and lower priced systems first. You can then keep reading your way down the list until the price starts to get to, or beyond, your comfort range. You can then focus your attention on that area of the table for a system that meets your needs.

The Macintosh tables are shorter, so they are arranged differently. For desktop systems, the overall power of a given family of Macs (Classic, Centris, Quadra, and so forth) determines the order, followed by the CPU type and speed of a given model. Power Macintosh systems are listed the same way. Portable systems are listed by family name, and then by model number.

These tables are an attempt to capture a very fast-changing situation because computer manufacturers are constantly introducing new models and changing prices and feature mixes on existing ones. Remember, however, that the main goals of the major manufacturers tend to remain fairly constant. Some concentrate on low price, others on higher performance. Use these tables to hone in on systems and manufacturers that meet your price/performance needs, and then call around for the current pricing and configuration data from your top few choices. Also, keep an eye on trade magazines like *PC Magazine* and *PC World* for up-to-date information about new models and performance comparisons.

Most of the fields for all the tables are described in the first section; only different fields or additional considerations are described in the specific sections for each table.

Fields for Computer Tables

The following descriptions mostly apply to all the tables, though a few are desktop-specific, and a few are IBM-compatible specific. Look in the descriptions of each table for information specific to that table.

- *Company, Model.* Use the company and model to help find out more about a system by calling the company or a dealer. Refer to Appendix B for manufacturer contact information.

- *CPU, Speed, Cache.* This is the field by which the IBM-compatible tables are sorted. AMD and IBM CPUs, which tend to be faster than Intel CPUs with similar numbers and speed ratings, appear in the later, higher performance part of their respective tables. Cyrix CPUs, which are lower in performance, appear earlier, among the lower performance systems.

- *Unit Size.* The system's height, width, and depth. A system taller than it is wide is a mini-tower or tower arrangement.

- *RAM Incl., Max.* The amount of RAM included in the base price is listed, as is the maximum amount of RAM you can put in the system. You can add even more RAM on add-in cards, but performance will be unacceptably slow. *M'board* indicates the amount of memory you can put on the motherboard, the fastest and most convenient arrangement.

- *Hard Disk.* The hard disk size included in the price is listed. You can often order a system with no hard disk for less and add one of your own choice instead. Alternatively, you can often order a larger hard disk than the one listed for only a small increase in price.

- *Floppy Drive.* The number of floppy disk drives included in the system is listed. Most systems include only a single 3.5-inch, 1.44M floppy drive. Some vendors, starting with IBM, are moving to 3.5-inch, 2.88M floppy drives. Ask whether an additional 5.25-inch, 1.2M drive can be added and what the price for this upgrade is; it's valuable for interchanging data between newer and older systems.

- *Drive Bays.* Where available, this is the number of additional drives you can add. Most expansion devices can fit in a half-height slot, but the largest tape drives and disk drives still require a full-height slot. (Most systems with two half-height slots can accept a single full-height device in its place.) Few devices other than 3.5-inch floppy drives fit in a 3.5-inch bay.

- *Adapters.* The standard setup of 2 serial, 1 parallel, and 1 mouse port is adequate for most needs. A SCSI port is a valuable addition.

- *Slots.* Look for several ISA and, in high-performance systems, EISA slots. A VESA or PCI local-bus slot for video is a key consideration in mid-range systems; high-end systems may have more than one. MCA slots don't have as many adapter cards available as ISA or EISA.

- *Bus.* IBM is the only major computer maker to use MCA, and it uses ISA in some systems. Other manufacturers use ISA or EISA. For fast video and, in some cases, hard disk access, look for a VESA local bus or Intel PCI slot or two. Apple currently uses NuBus and proprietary Processor Direct Slots, but will use PCI in future systems.

- *Power Supply.* Most systems have adequate power supplies for the number of slots they have; Macs are known for having inadequate power supplies in some systems. Keep track of the power demands of add-in cards if you add more than one card.

- *Warranty.* One year is now standard, but some makers, such as Compaq, are moving to three years. A longer warranty is a valuable bonus and says something about the manufacturer's confidence in its systems.

- *Price.* Mail-order vendors usually sell at well below list price. With other vendors, you can usually get a system for at least slightly less than list. Also, prices are adjusted constantly. This situation makes comparing your true cost difficult. Check newspaper and magazine ads and other sources for exact, current information—or check with the manufacturer for a list of local vendors.

- *Graphics Adapter.* For a lower end system, look for an integrated adapter (SVGA for IBM-compatibles). For a higher end system, look for a local bus or PDS card.

- *Monitor.* Getting a monitor included is nice, but buyer beware—some vendors include cheap monitors. Dell includes high-quality monitors with its systems.

- *Upgradability.* For low-end systems without math capability, make sure that there's a math coprocessor socket. For higher end systems, make sure that there's some kind of CPU upgrade available.

- *Software.* For IBM-compatibles, DOS and Windows should be preinstalled with the appropriate drivers for your video system. Macs come with System 7.1 on the hard disk. Otherwise, bundled software is nice, but only if it's something you really need and don't already own; otherwise, it just takes up space on the hard disk.

- *Other.* Built-in modems are nice extras, but look for a CD-ROM drive as a real bonus.

Table 6.1 386DX-Based Desktop Computers

This table includes IBM-compatible, 386DX-based desktop computers. They are a little bit faster than SX-based systems. The table is sorted by ascending CPU type, speed, and cache size, so the least powerful, least expensive systems come first. When two or more systems have the same CPU type, speed, and cache size, the one with the company and model name that comes first alphabetically appears first.

For inexpensive, decent performance, look at an IBM 386SLC or AMD386-based system. But watch out, some IBM systems are price/performance disasters, and the MCA bus has fewer cards available for it than ISA or EISA systems. If you can find an AMD-based system from a top manufacturer, it's probably a good buy. Otherwise, look at a 486SX-based system unless you find a real bargain that you're confident can meet your needs for at least a year or two. As with 386SXs, don't worry too much about expandability; if you need more power, you'll probably want to move to a whole new system with higher overall performance.

Table 6.1 486SX-Based Desktop Computers

Company, Model	CPU, Speed, Cache	RAM Incl. Max	Hard Disk	Floppy Drive	Drive Bays	Adapters	Slots
AMBRA D433SXA	486SX, 33MHz, 128K	4M, 36M	240M	3.5" 1.44M	5		5 16-bit ISA
Canon Innova 486e	486SX, 33MHz	4M, 36M	210M	3.5" 1.44M	2	2 ser., 1 par. 1 PS/2	4 16-bit ISA
Canon Innova 486s	486SX, 33MHz	4M, 68M	240M	3.5" 1.44M	2	2 ser., 1 par. 1 PS/2	4 16-bit ISA
Packed!							
Canon Innova VisionL33/210	486SX, 33MHz	4M, 36M	210M	3.5" 1.44M	1	2 ser., 1 par. 1 PS/2	2 16-bit ISA

Listing of Computers

Specific differences in the fields for this kind of system are pointed out here:

- *Company, Model.* As with 386SX-based systems, check that the model is still offered before going out to buy.
- *CPU, Speed, Cache.* A 33 or 40 MHz system with cache or an Intel or AMD-based system may put you into the low-end 486 performance range at 386 prices.
- *Price.* Don't pay much for any 386-based system—it will be considered obsolete at resale time.
- *Graphics Adapter.* Integrated SVGA is probably your best bet.
- *Upgradability.* A math coprocessor socket is worth having.

Warranty	Price	Graphics Adapter	Monitor	Upgradability	Software	Other
30 day MBG, 1 year	$1,399	VESA local bus SVGA, 1MB	14" SVGA color	processor	DOS 6.2, Windows 3.1	
1 year on-site	$1,399	VESA local bus	14" SVGA	processor	DOS 6.2, Windows 3.1, MS Works 3.0	Energy Star
1 year on-site	$1,599	VESA local bus (2 are VESA/ISA)	14" SVGA	processor	DOS 6.2, Windows 3.1, MS Works 3.0, MicroFax	24/96 faxmodem, Energy Star
1 year on-site	$1,979	VESA local bus	14" SVGA	processor	DOS 6.2, Windows 3.1, MS Multimedia Works 2.0, MicroFax, MS Encarta, MS Golf, MS Cinema, MS Soundbits	96/24 faxmodem, 2X CD-ROM drive, Sound Blaster 16, speakers, Energy Star

continues

Table 6.1 Continued

Company, Model	CPU, Speed, Cache	RAM Incl. Max	Hard Disk	Floppy Drive	Drive Bays	Adapters	Slots
Compaq ProLinea MT	486SX, 33MHz	4M, 64M	340M	3.5"	5	2 ser., 1 par.	5 ISA
Compaq ProLinea 4/33s	486SX, 33MHz	4M, 32M	240M	3.5"	3	2 ser., 1 par.	3 ISA
Compaq ProLinea Net1/25s	486SX, 25MHz	4M, 32M	100M	3.5"	3	2 ser., 1 par.	3 ISA
DEC, DECpc LPv+ 425sx	486SX, 25MHz	4M, 64M	170M	3.5"	3-4	2 ser., 1 par.	3 ISA
DEC, DECpc LPv+ 433sx	486SX, 33MHz	4M, 64M	170M	3.5"	3-4	2 ser., 1 par.	3 ISA
DEC, DECpc LPv+ 450sx2	486SX2, 50MHz	4M, 64M	170M	3.5"	3-4	2 ser., 1 par.	3 ISA
DEC, DECpc LPx+ 433sx	486SX, 33MHz	4M, 64M	170M	3.5"	4-5	2 ser., 1 par.	6 ISA (2 w/ VESA)
DEC, DECpc LPx+ 450s2	486SX2, 50MHz	4M, 64M	170M	3.5"	4-5	2 ser., 1 par.	6 ISA (2 w/ VESA)
Dell Dimension XPS 433SV	486SX, 33MHz	4M, 64M	210M	3.5"	1	2 ser., 1 par. mouse	5 ISA (2 of which are VESA/ISA)

Value Leader

| Gateway 2000 4SX-33 | 486SX, 33MHz | 4M, 32M | 340M | 3.5" | 3 | 2 ser., 1 par. | 5 16-bit ISA |
| Gateway 2000 4SX-33 VESA | 486SX, 33MHz | 4M, 64M | 340M | 3.5"/5.25" combination drive | 5 | 2 ser., 1 par. | 7 16-bit ISA (2 w/ VESA) |

Warranty	Price	Graphics Adapter	Monitor	Upgradability	Software	Other
3 years	$1,849	local bus SVGA	14" SVGA	processor	DOS, Windows, TabWorks	
3 years	$1,625	local bus SVGA	14" SVGA	processor	DOS, Windows, TabWorks	
3 years	$1,249	local bus SVGA	Built-in 14" SVGA	processor	DOS, Windows, Tabworks	Energy Star
3 years, 30-day MBG	$1,348	S3 local bus SVGA	14" SVGA	processor	DOS, Windows for Workgroups	
3 years, 30-day MBG	$1,398	S3 local bus SVGA	14" SVGA	processor	DOS, Windows for Workgroups	
3 years, 30-day MBG	$1,548	S3 local bus SVGA	14" SVGA	processor	DOS, Windows for Workgroups	
3 years, 30-day MBG	$1,527	S3 local bus SVGA	14" SVGA	processor	DOS, Windows for Workgroups	
3 years, 30-day MBG	$1,677	S3 local bus SVGA	14" SVGA	processor	DOS, Windows for Workgroups	
1 year on-site	$1,299	VESA local bus	14" SVGA	processor	DOS, Windows	
3 years parts, 1 year labor (on-site)	$1,295	integrated local bus SVGA, 1 MB	14" SVGA	processor	DOS, Windows for Workgroups, QA Plus, Works for Windows	Microsoft mouse, Energy Star
3 years parts, 1 year labor (on-site)	$1,495	local bus SVGA, 1 MB	14" SVGA	processor	DOS, Windows for Workgroups, QAPlus, choice of several software packs	Microsoft mouse, 124-key programmable keyboard, Energy Star

continues

Table 6.1 Continued							
Company, Model	CPU, Speed, Cache	RAM Incl. Max	Hard Disk	Floppy Drive	Drive Bays	Adapters	Slots
Packed!							
Gateway 2000 Family PC	486SX, 33MHz	4M, 32M	340M	3.5"	3	2 ser., 1 par.	5 16-bit ISA
IBM, ValuePoint 425SX/Si	486SX, 25MHz	4M, 64M	212M	3.5"	1	2 ser., 1 par.	2 ISA, 1 VESA
IBM, ValuePoint Performance 433DX	486SX, 33MHz	4M, 128M	270M	3.5"	1	2 ser., 1 par.	2 ISA, 1 VESA 30 day MBG
ZEOS Ambra 486SX-25	486SX, 25MHz	4M, 128M	214M	3.5"	4	2 ser., 1 par.	2 VESA, 3 16-bit ISA
ZEOS Ambra 486SX-33	486SX, 33MHz	4M, 128M	214M	3.5"	4	2 ser., 1 par.	2 VESA, 3 16-bit ISA
ZEOS Pantera 486SX-33	486SX, 33MHz	4M, 128M	214M	3.5"	6	2 ser., 1 par.	3 PCI, 5 ISA

Table 6.2 486SX-Based Desktop Computers

This table includes IBM-compatible, 486SX-based desktop computers. The table is sorted by ascending CPU type, speed, and cache size, so the least powerful, least expensive systems come first. When two or more systems have the same CPU type, speed, and cache size, the one with the company and model name that comes first in the alphabet appears first.

Warranty	Price	Graphics Adapter	Monitor	Upgradability	Software	Other
3 years parts, 1 year labor (on-site)	$1,495	integrated SVGA, 1 MB		processor	DOS, Windows for Workgroups, QAPlus, choice of several software packs (games, programs encyclopedias, etc.)	2X CD-ROM drive 96/24 faxmodem, 16-bit Sound Blaster compatible sound card, speakers, Microsoft mouse
1 year, 30 day MBG	$949	N/A	N/A	processor	DOS, Windows	
3 years	$1,599	VESA local bus, 1M	N/A	processor	DOS, Windows	
1 year	$1,195	VESA local bus, 1M	14" SVGA	processor	DOS, Windows for Workgroups	Microsoft mouse
1 year	$1,245	VESA local bus, 1M	14" SVGA	processor	DOS, Windows for Workgroups	Microsoft mouse
1 year	$1,495	PCI local bus, 1M	14" SVGA	processor	DOS, Windows	

A 486SX-based system is mostly used as a cheap Windows system. This approach is good for price/performance, but make sure that you don't need math coprocessing capability; if you do, you're better off buying a 486DX to start. You should be somewhat concerned about expandability, but by the time you are ready to expand this kind of system much, Pentium or PowerPC-based systems may be looking really good.

Specific differences in the table fields for this kind of system are pointed out here:

- *CPU, Speed, Cache.* For Windows, look for a 33 MHz system with 128K or more of cache.
- *Hard Disk.* If you're going to splurge on anything in a 486SX-based system, get a little more hard disk; 150M is a good size.

Table 6.2 486DX-Based Desktop Computers

Company, Model	CPU, Speed, Cache	RAM Incl., Max	Hard Disk	Floppy Drive	Drive Bays	Adapters	Slots
DEC, DECpc LPv+ 433dx	486DX, 33MHz	4M, 64M	170M	3.5"	3-4	2 ser., 1 par.	3 ISA
DEC, DECpc LPx+ 433dx	486DX, 33MHz	4M, 64M	170M	3.5"	4-5	2 ser., 1 par.	6 ISA (2 w/ VESA)
DEC, DECpc XL 433dx	486DX, 33MHz	8M, 128M	340M	3.5"	4-5	2 ser., 1 par., 1 SCSI II	2 PCI, 3 ISA, 1 ISA/PCI
Value Leader							
Gateway 2000 4DX-33	486DX, 33MHz	4M, 32M	340M	3.5"	3	2 ser., 1 par.	5 16-bit ISA
IBM, ValuePoint 433DX/Si	486DX, 33MHz	4M, 64M	212M	3.5"	1	2 ser., 1 par.	2 ISA, 1 VESA
IBM, Value-Point Performance 433DX	486DX, 33MHz	4M, 128M	270M	3.5"	1	2 ser., 1 par.	2 ISA, 1 VESA

- *Price.* A 486SX-based system will keep some resale value, but if extras start sending the price up, look at a 486DX-based system.
- *Graphics Adapter.* A VESA local bus slot and graphics adapter will really boost Windows.
- *Upgradability.* A math coprocessor socket is worth having, but if you know you'll need it, buy a 486DX-based system.

Warranty	Price	Graphics Adapter	Monitor	Upgradability	Software	Other
3 years, 30-day MBG	$1,648	S3 local bus SVGA	14" SVGA	processor	DOS, Windows for Workgroups	
3 years, 30-day MBG	$1,777	S3 local bus SVGA	14" SVGA	processor	DOS, Windows for Workgroups	
3 years, 30-day MBG	$2,948	S3 local bus SVGA	14" SVGA	processor	DOS, Windows for Workgroups	
3 years parts, 1 year labor (on-site)	$1,495	integrated local bus SVGA, 1 MB	14" SVGA	processor	DOS, Windows for Workgroups, QAPlus, Works for Windows	Microsoft mouse, Energy Star
1 year, 30 day MBG	$1,319	N/A	N/A	processor	DOS, Windows	
3 years, 30 day MBG	$1,769	VESA local bus, 1M	N/A	processor	DOS, Windows	

continues

Table 6.2 Continued

Company, Model	CPU, Speed, Cache	RAM Incl., Max	Hard Disk	Floppy Drive	Drive Bays	Adapters	Slots
ZEOS Ambra 486DX-33 mouse	486DX, 33MHz	4M, 128M	214M	3.5"	4	2 ser., 1 par.	2 VESA, 3 16-bit ISA
ZEOS Pantera 486DX-33	486DX, 33MHz	4M, 128M	214M	3.5"	6	2 ser., 1 par.	3 PCI, 5 ISA

Table 6.3 486DX-Based Desktop Computers

This table includes IBM-compatible, 486DX-based desktop computers. The table is sorted by ascending CPU type, speed, and cache size, so the least powerful, least expensive systems come first. When two or more systems have the same CPU type, speed, and cache size, the one with the company and model name that comes first alphabetically appears first.

A 486DX-based system is a mainstream Windows system. (It is also capable of running OS/2 well and Windows NT less well.) The price and performance differences between a Cyrix "486" on the low end and a 33 MHz or faster system on the high end are very great. If you have some money to spend and want flexibility, a 33 MHz 486 system that can have a clock-doubling upgrade added later is a great buy. Otherwise, find the system that best meets your price and performance needs. Look for upgradability and add-on slots; a 486DX-based system can meet your needs for quite a while.

Table 6.3 486DX2-Based Desktop Computers

Company, Model	CPU, Speed, Cache	RAM Incl., Max	Hard Disk	Floppy Drive	Drive Bays	Adapters	Slots
AMBRA D46	486DX2, 66MHz, 256K	8M, 64M	440M (12ms IDE)	3.5" 1.44M	5		1 32-bit VESA, 4 16-bit ISA

Warranty	Price	Graphics Adapter	Monitor	Upgradability	Software	Other
1 year	$1,395	VESA local bus, 1M	14" SVGA	processor	DOS, Windows	Microsoft for Workgroups
1 year	$1,645	PCI local bus, 1M	14" SVGA	processor	DOS, Windows	

Specific differences in the table fields for this kind of system are pointed out here:

- *CPU, Speed, Cache.* Look for 128K or more of cache.
- *Adapters.* Look for a SCSI port for external expandability.
- *Slots.* Make sure that there are several open slots for expandability. You may, for instance, want to add multimedia capabilities later.
- *Price.* You can spend almost as much or as little as you want on a 486DX-based system by trading off brand name, upgradability, expandability, and features.
- *Graphics Adapter.* A VESA local bus slot and graphics adapter are nearly a necessity for getting the full performance that this kind of system can give to Windows.
- *Upgradability.* Look for expandability and the capability to upgrade to a clock-doubled chip or a Pentium. Check the trade press for up-to-date information about possible problems in upgrading specific models to Pentium. Intel points to Dell as a model of how to build in Pentium upgradability.

Warranty	Price	Graphics Adapter	Monitor	Upgradability	Software	Other
	$2,219	VESA local bus graphics accelerator, 1MB	15" FST-NI color	bus, processor	DOS 6.2, Windows 3.1	

continues

Table 6.3 Continued

Company, Model	CPU, Speed, Cache	RAM Incl., Max	Hard Disk	Floppy Drive	Drive Bays	Adapters	Slots
AMBRA D466I/VL (alternate configuration)	486DX2, 66MHz, 256K	16M, 64M	540M (12ms IDE)	3.5" 1.44M	6		1 32-bit VESA, 7 16-bit ISA
AMBRA D466I/VL (alternate configuration)	486DX2, 66MHz, 256K	8M, 64M	440M (12ms IDE)	3.5" 1.44M	5		1 32-bit VESA, 4 16-bit ISA
Canon Innova 486v L50/210	486DX2, 50MHz	4M, 36M	210M	3.5" 1.44M, 5.25" 1.2M	1	2 ser., 1 par., 1 PS/2	4 16-bit ISA
Canon Innova 486v L50/340	486DX2, 50MHz	4M, 36M	340M	3.5" 1.44M, 5.25" 1.2M	1	2 ser., 1 par., 1 PS/2	3 16-bit ISA
Canon Innova 486v L66/210	486DX2, 66MHz	4M, 36M	210M	3.5" 1.44M, 5.25" 1.2M	1	2 ser., 1 par., 1 PS/2	4 16-bit ISA
Canon Innova 486v L66/340	486DX2, 66MHz	4M, 36M	340M	3.5" 1.44M, 5.25" 1.2M	1	2 ser., 1 par., 1 PS/2	3 16-bit ISA
Canon Innova Vision L50/340	486DX2, 50MHz	4M, 36M	340M	3.5" 1.44M	1	2 ser., 1 par., 1 PS/2	2 16-bit ISA
Compaq ProLinea MT	486DX2, 66MHz	4M, 64M	340M	3.5"	5	2 ser., 1 par.	5 ISA
DEC, DECpc LPv+ 466d2	486DX2, 66MHz	4M, 64M	170M	3.5"	3-4	2 ser., 1 par.	3 ISA

Listing of Computers

Warranty	Price	Graphics Adapter	Monitor	Upgradability	Software	Other
	$2,798	VESA local bus graphics accelerator, 1MB	14" SVGA color	bus, processor	DOS 6.2, Windows 3.1	2X multisession CD-ROM
	$2,399	VESA local bus graphics accelerator, 1MB	15" FST-NI color	bus, processor	PFS: Window Works, DOS 6.2, Windows 3.1	24/96 faxmodem, 2X multisession CD-ROM
1 year on-site	$1,749	VESA local bus	14" SVGA	processor	DOS 6.2, Windows 3.1, MS Works 3.0	Energy Star
1 year on-site	$1,879	VESA local bus	14" SVGA	processor	DOS 6.2, Windows 3.1, MS Works 3.0, MicroFax	96/24 faxmodem, Energy Star
1 year on-site	$2,049	VESA local bus	14" SVGA	processor	DOS 6.2, Windows 3.1, MS Works 3.0	Energy Star
1 year on-site	$2,199	VESA local bus	14" SVGA	processor	DOS 6.2, Windows 3.1, MS Works 3.0, MicroFax	96/24 faxmodem, Energy Star
1 year on-site	$2,499	VESA local bus	14" SVGA	processor	DOS 6.2, Windows 3.1, MS Multimedia Works 2.0, MicroFax, MS Encarta, MS Golf, MS Cinema, MS Soundbits	96/24 faxmodem, 2X CD-ROM drive, Sound Blaster 16, speakers, Energy Star
3 years	$2,494	local bus SVGA	14" SVGA	processor	DOS, Windows, TabWorks	
3 years, 30-day MBG	$1,998	S3 local bus SVGA	14" SVGA	processor	DOS, Windows for Workgroups	

continues

Table 6.3 Continued

Company, Model	CPU, Speed, Cache	RAM Incl., Max	Hard Disk	Floppy Drive	Drive Bays	Adapters	Slots
DEC, DECpc LPv+ 450d2	486DX2, 50MHz	4M, 64M	170M	3.5"	3-4	2 ser., 1 par.	3 ISA
DEC, DECpc L Px+ 450d2	486DX2, 50MHz	4M, 64M	170M	3.5"	4-5	2 ser., 1 par.	6 ISA (2 w/ VESA)
DEC, DECpc L Px+ 466d2	486DX2, 66MHz	4M, 64M	170M	3.5"	4-5	2 ser., 1 par.	6 ISA (2 w/ VESA)
DEC, DECpc XL 466d2	486DX2, 66MHz	8M, 128M	340M	3.5"	4-5	2 ser., 1 par., 1 SCSI II	2 PCI, 3 ISA, 1 ISA/PCI
Gateway 2000 4DX2-66	486DX2, 66MHz	8M, 32M	340M	3.5"	3	2 ser., 1 par.	5 16-bit ISA
Gateway 2000 4DX2-66V	486DX2, 66MHz	8M, 64M	540M	3.5"	5	2 ser., 1 par. (2 w/ VESA)	7 16-bit ISA
Gateway 2000 Family PC	486DX2, 66MHz	4M, 32M	340M	3.5"	3	2 ser., 1 par.	5 16-bit ISA

Value Leader

Company, Model	CPU, Speed, Cache	RAM Incl., Max	Hard Disk	Floppy Drive	Drive Bays	Adapters	Slots
Gateway 2000 P4D-33	486DX2, 33MHz, 128K	8M, 128M	540M	3.5"	5	2 ser., 1 par.	5 16-bit ISA (1 w/ PCI), 2 PCI

Listing of Computers

Warranty	Price	Graphics Adapter	Monitor	Upgradability	Software	Other
3 years, 30-day MBG	$1,698	S3 local bus SVGA	14" SVGA	processor	DOS, Windows for Workgroups	
3 years, 30-day MBG	$1,827	S3 local bus SVGA	14" SVGA	processor	DOS, Windows for Workgroups	
3 years, 30-day MBG	$2,127	S3 local bus SVGA	14" SVGA	processor	DOS, Windows for Workgroups	
3 years, 30-day MBG	$3,048	S3 local bus SVGA	14" SVGA	processor	DOS, Windows for Workgroups	
3 years parts, 1 year labor (on-site)	$1,795	integrated local bus SVGA, 1 MB	14" SVGA	processor	DOS, Windows for Workgroups, QA-Plus, Works for Windows	Microsoft mouse
3 years parts, 1 year labor (on-site)	$2,295	local bus SVGA, 1 MB	15" SVGA	processor	DOS, Windows for Workgroups, QA-Plus, choice of several software packs	2X CD-ROM drive, Microsoft mouse, 124-key programmable keyboard, Energy Star
3 years parts, 1 year labor (on-site)	$1,995	integrated SVGA, 1 MB	14" SVGA	processor	DOS, Windows for Workgroups, QA-Plus, choice of several software packs (games, programs, encyclopedias, etc.)	2X CD-ROM drive, 96/24 faxmodem, 16-bit Sound-Blaster-compatible sound card, speakers, Microsoft mouse
3 years parts, 1 year labor (on-site)	$1,995	local bus SVGA, 1 MB	14" SVGA	processor	DOS, Windows for Workgroups, QA-Plus, MS Works Multimedia Edition	2X CD-ROM drive, Microsoft mouse, 124-key programmable keyboard, Energy Star

continues

Table 6.3 Continued

Company, Model	CPU, Speed, Cache	RAM Incl., Max	Hard Disk	Floppy Drive	Drive Bays	Adapters	Slots
Gateway 2000 P4D-66	486DX2, 66MHz, 128K	8M, 128M	540M	3.5"	5	2 ser., 1 par.	5 16-bit ISA (1 w/ PCI), 2 PCI
IBM, ValuePoint 466DX2/Si	486DX2, 66MHz	4M, 64M	212M	3.5"	1	2 ser., 1 par.	2 ISA, 1 VESA
IBM, ValuePoint Performance 466DX2	486DX2, 66MHz	8M, 128M	270M	3.5"	5	2 ser., 1 par.	5
IBM, PS/2 E	486SLC2 50/25MHz	8M	120M	3.5"	3	2 ser., 1 par.	3
IBM, PS/2 E (w/ TFT Monitor)	486SLC2 50/25MHz	8M	120M	3.5"	3	2 ser., 1 par.	3
ZEOS Ambra 486DX2-50	486DX2, 50MHz	4M, 128M	214M	3.5"	4	2 ser., 1 par.	2 VESA, 3 16-bit ISA
ZEOS Ambra 486DX2-66	486DX2, 66MHz	4M, 128M	214M	3.5"	4	2 ser., 1 par.	2 VESA, 3 16-bit ISA
ZEOS Pantera 486DX2-50	486DX2, 50MHz	4M, 128M	214M	3.5"	6	2 ser., 1 par.	3 PCI, 5 ISA
ZEOS Pantera 486DX2-66	486DX2, 66MHz	4M, 128M	214M	3.5"	6	2 ser., 1 par.	3 PCI, 5 ISA

Table 6.4 486DX2-Based Desktop Computers

This table includes IBM-compatible, 486DX2-based desktop computers. The table is sorted by ascending CPU type, speed, and cache size, so the least powerful, least expensive systems come first. When two or more systems have the same CPU type, speed, and cache size, the one with the company and model name that comes first in the alphabet appears first.

486DX2 computers are clock-doubled, which makes the microprocessor run twice as fast but doesn't affect the other components in the system. A 486DX2-based system is a

Warranty	Price	Graphics Adapter	Monitor	Upgradability	Software	Other
3 years parts, 1 year labor (on-site)	$2,295	local bus SVGA, 1 MB	15" SVGA	processor	DOS, Windows for Workgroups, QA-Plus, choice of software apps	2X CD-ROM drive, Microsoft mouse, 124-key programmable keyboard, Energy Star
1 year, 30-day MBG	$1,729	N/A	N/A	processor	DOS, Windows	
3 years, 30-day MBG	$2,449	VESA local bus, 1M	N/A	processor	DOS, Windows	
1 year onsite, 30-day MBG	$2,474	XGA-2	14" energy-saving color	processor	DOS, Windows	Energy Star
1 year onsite, 30-day MBG	$5,314	XGA-2	10.36" flat-panel energy-saving color	processor	DOS, Windows	Energy Star
1 year	$1,445	VESA local bus, 1M	14" SVGA	processor	DOS, Windows for Workgroups	Microsoft mouse
1 year	$1,545	VESA local bus, 1M	14" SVGA	processor	DOS, Windows for Workgroups	Microsoft mouse
1 year	$1,695	PCI local bus, 1M	14" SVGA	processor	DOS, Windows	
1 year	$1,795	PCI local bus, 1M	14" SVGA	processor	DOS, Windows	

powerful Windows, NT, or OS/2 system. It can also be a light-duty file server for a small office.

Specific differences in the table fields for this kind of system are pointed out here:

- *CPU, Speed, Cache.* Look for 128K or more of cache.
- *Adapters.* Look for a SCSI port for external expandability.
- *Slots.* Make sure that there are several open slots for expandability. You may, for instance, want to add multimedia capabilities later.

- *Price.* You can spend almost as much or as little as you want on a 486DX2-based system by trading off brand name, upgradability, expandability, and features.
- *Graphics Adapter.* A VESA local bus slot and graphics adapter are nearly a necessity for getting the full performance that this kind of system can give to multitasking environments.

Table 6.4 486DX4-Based Desktop Computers							
Company, Model	CPU, Speed, Cache	RAM Incl., Max	Hard Disk	Floppy Drive	Drive Bays	Adapters	Slots
AMBRA, D4100I/VL	486DX4, 100MHz, 256K	8M, 64M	540M (12ms IDE)	3.5" 1.44M	5		1 32-bit VESA, 4 16-bit ISA
AMBRA Lightning 100	Blue Lightning, 100MHz, 128K	8M, 64M	540M (12ms IDE)	3.5" 1.44M	5		1 32-bit VESA, 4 16-bit
Value Leader							
AMBRA Lightning 100 (with multimedia)	Blue Lightning 100MHZ, 128K	8M, 64M	540M (12ms IDE)	3.5" 1.44M	5		1 32-bit VESA, 4 16-bit ISA
DEC, DECpc LPv+ 4100	486DX4, 100MHz	4M, 64M	170M	3.5"	3-4	2 ser., 1 par.	3 ISA
DEC, DECpc XL 4100	486DX4, 100MHz	8M, 128M	340M	3.5"	4-5	2 ser., 1 par., 1 SCSI II	2 PCI, 3 ISA, 1 ISA/PCI
Dell Dimension XPS 4100V	486DX4, 100MHz, 256K	8M, 128M	450M	3.5"	1	2 ser., 1 par., mouse	5 ISA (2 of which are VESA/ISA)
Dell Dimension XPS 466V w/CD-ROM	486DX4, 66MHz, 256K	8M, 128M	450M	3.5"	1	2 ser., 1 par., mouse	5 ISA (2 of which are VESA/ISA)

- *Upgradability.* Look for expandability and the capability to upgrade to Pentium. Check the trade press for up-to-date information about possible problems in upgrading specific models to Pentium. Intel points to Dell as a model of how to build in Pentium upgradability.

Warranty	Price	Graphics Adapter	Monitor	Upgradability	Software	Other
	$2,489	VESA local bus SVGA, 1MB	14" SVGA color	bus, processor	DOS 6.2, Windows 3.1	
	$2,160	VESA local bus graphics accelerator	14" SVGA color	processor	DOS 6.2, Windows 3.1	
	$2,599	VESA local bus graphics accelerator	15" FST color	processor	DOS 6.2, Windows 3.1	2X Multi-session CD-ROM drive, 16-bit stereo sound card w/speakers
3 years, 30-day MBG	$2,498	S3 local bus SVGA	14" SVGA	processor	DOS, Windows for Workgroups	
3 years, 30-day MBG	$3,398	S3 local bus SVGA	14" SVGA	processor	DOS, Windows for Workgroups	
1 year on-site	$2,499	VESA local bus	15" SVGA	processor	DOS, Windows	2X CD-ROM drive
1 year on-site	$2,399	VESA local bus	15" SVGA	processor	DOS, Windows, MS Office, Quicken, MS Bookshelf CD	2X CD-ROM drive SoundBlaster 16 w/Peavey speakers

continues

Table 6.4 Continued

Company, Model	CPU, Speed, Cache	RAM Incl., Max	Hard Disk	Floppy Drive	Drive Bays	Adapters	Slots
Gateway 2000 P4D-100	486DX4, 100MHz, 128K	8M, 128M	540M	3.5"	5	2 ser., 1 par.	5 16-bit ISA (1 w/ PCI), 2 PCI
IBM, Value Pointer Performance 100 DX4	486 DX4, 100 MHz	8M, 128M	360M	3.5"	5	2 ser., 1 par.	5
ZEOS Pantera	486DX4, 100MHz	4M, 128M	214M	3.5"	6	2 ser., 1 par.	3 PCI, 5 ISA

Table 6.5 486DX4-Based Desktop Computers

This table includes IBM-compatible, 486DX4-based desktop computers. The table is sorted by ascending CPU type, speed, and cache size, so the least powerful, least expensive systems come first. When two or more systems have the same CPU type, speed, and cache size, the one with the company and model name that comes first in the alphabet appears first.

486DX4 computers are clock-tripled, which makes the microprocessor run three times as fast but doesn't affect the other components in the system. These PCs are very new, and some vendors are having trouble with the naming scheme. Some advertise 486DX4s as 486DX3s, and Intel itself drops the "486" from the beginning of the name, calling the chip simply "DX4." 486DX4/100s deliver roughly the same performance as a 60MHz Pentium at a slightly lower price point. A 486DX4-based system is a powerful Windows, NT, or OS/2 system. It can also be a file server for a small-to-medium office.

Specific differences in the table fields for this kind of system are pointed out here:

- *CPU, Speed, Cache.* Look for 128K or more of cache.

Warranty	Price	Graphics Adapter	Monitor	Upgradability	Software	Other
3 years parts, 1 year labor (on-site)	$2,495	local bus SVGA, 1MB	15" SVGA	processor	DOS, Windows for Workgroups QAPlus, choice of software apps	2X CD-ROM drive, Microsoft mouse, 124-key programmable keyboard, Energy Star
3 years, 30-day MBG	$2,949	VESA local bus, 1M	N/A	processor	DOS, Windows	
1 year	$2,095	PCI local bus, 1M	14" SVGA	processor	DOS, Windows	

- *Adapters.* Look for a SCSI port for external expandability.
- *Slots.* Make sure that there are several open slots for expandability. You may, for instance, want to add multimedia capabilities later.
- *Price.* 486DX4s are new, so you might have to wait a while before they reach reasonable prices.
- *Graphics Adapter.* A VESA local bus slot and graphics adapter are nearly a necessity for getting the full performance that this kind of system can give to multi-tasking environments.
- *Upgradability.* Look for expandability and the capability to upgrade to Pentium. Check the trade press for up-to-date information about possible problems in upgrading specific models to Pentium. Intel points to Dell as a model of how to build in Pentium upgradability.

Table 6.5 Pentium Desktop Computers

Company, Model	CPU, Speed, Cache	RAM Incl., Max	Hard Disk	Floppy Drive	Drive Bays	Adapters	Slots
AMBRA, DP9 OPCI	Pentium, 90MHZ, 256K	8M, 128M	540M (12ms IDE)	3.5" 1.44M	6		2 32-bit PCI, 1 PCI/ISA, 4 16-bit ISA
AMBRA, DP60/PCI	Pentium, 60MHz	8M, 128M	540M (12ms IDE)	3.5" 1.44	varies		2 32-bit PCI, 1 PCI/ISA, 4 16-bit ISA
AMBRA, DP60/PCI (alternate configuration)	Pentium, 60MHz, 256K	16M, 128M	540M (12ms IDE)	3.5" 1.44M	varies		2 32-bit PCI, 1 PCI/ISA, 4 16-bit ISA
AMBRA, DP60/PCI (alternate configuration)	Pentium, 60MHz	16M, 128M	1G (8.5ms IDE)	3.5" 1.44M	varies		2 32-bit PCI, 1 PCI/ISA, 4 16-bit ISA
DEC, DECpc XL 560	Pentium, 60MHz	8M, 128M	340M	3.5"	4-5	2 ser., 1 par., 1 SCSI II	2 PCI, 3 ISA, 1 ISA/PCI
DEC, DECpc XL 566	Pentium, 66MHz	8M, 128M	340M	3.5"	4-5	2 ser., 1 par., 1 SCSI II	2 PCI, 3 ISA, 1 ISA/PCI
DEC, DECpc XL 590	Pentium, 90MHz	8M, 128M	340M	3.5"	4-5	2 ser., 1 par., 1 SCSI II	2 PCI, 3 ISA, 1 ISA/PCI
Dell Dimension XPS	Pentium, 90MHz	8M, 128M	528M	3.5"	1	2 ser., 1 par., mouse	7 ISA (2 of which are VESA/ISA)
Value Leader							
Dell Dimension XPS (alternate configuration)	Pentium, 90MHz	8M, 128M	450M	3.5"	1	2 ser., 1 par., mouse	7 ISA (2 of which are VESA/ISA)

Warranty	Price	Graphics Adapter	Monitor	Upgradability	Software	Other
30-day MBG, 1 year	$3,597	PCI local bus graphics accelerator, 2MB	15" FST-NI color		DOS 6.2, Windows 3.1	Multimedia kit (2X CD-ROM drive, sound card, speakers)
30-day MBG, 1 year	$2,669	PCI local bus graphics accelerator, 2MB	14" SVGA color		DOS 6.2, Windows 3.1	
30-day MBG, 1 year	$3,449	PCI Diamond Viper graphics accelerator	15" FST-NI color		DOS 6.2, Windows 3.1	
30-day MBG, 1 year	$4,370	PCI Matrox MGA II+ graphics accelerator	15" FST-NI		DOS 6.2, Windows 3.1	2X CD-ROM
3 years, 30-day MBG	$3,598	S3 local bus SVGA	14" SVGA	processor	DOS, Windows for Workgroups	
3 years, 30-day MBG	$3,848	S3 local bus SVGA	14" SVGA	processor	DOS, Windows for Workgroups	
3 years, 30-day MBG	$4,048	S3 local bus SVGA	14" SVGA	processor	DOS, Windows for Workgroups	
1 year on-site	$2,999	PCI local bus	15" SVGA	processor	DOS, Windows	2X CD-ROM drive
1 year on-site	$2,599	PCI local bus	14" SVGA	processor	DOS, Windows	

continues

Table 6.5 Continued							
Company, Model	CPU, Speed, Cache	RAM Incl., Max	Hard Disk	Floppy Drive	Drive Bays	Adapters	Slots
Gateway 2000 P560	Pentium, 60MHz	8M, 128M	340M	3.5"	5	2 ser. 1 par.	5 16-bit ISA (1 w/PCI), 2 PCI
Value Leader							
Gateway 2000 P566	Pentium, 66MHz	16M, 128M	540M	3.5"	5	2 ser., 1 par. 1 par.	5 16-bit ISA (1 w/PCI), 2 PCI
Gateway 2000 P5-90	Pentium 90MHz, 256K	16M, 128M	540M	3.5"	5	2 ser. 1 par.	5 16-bit ISA (1 w/PCI), 2 PCI
IBM, ValuePoint Pentium	Pentium 60MHz	8M, 128M	527M	3.5"	5	2 ser., 1 par.	5
ZEOS Pantera Pentium-66	Pentium 66MHz	4M, 192M	214M	3.5"	6	2 ser., 1 par.	3 PCI, 5 ISA
ZEOS Pantera Pentium-90	Pentium 90MHz	4M, 192M	214M	3.5"	6	2 ser., 1 par.	3 PCI, 5 ISA

Table 6.6 Pentium Desktop Computers

This table includes IBM-compatible, Pentium-based desktop computers. The table is sorted by ascending CPU type, speed, and cache size, so the least powerful, least expensive systems come first. When two or more systems have the same CPU type, speed, and cache size, the one with the company and model name that comes first in the alphabet appears first.

Warranty	Price	Graphics Adapter	Monitor	Upgradability	Software	Other
3 years	$2,495	local bus SVGA, 1MB	15" SVGA	processor	DOS, Windows for Workgroups, QAPlus, MS Works Multimedia Edition	2X CD-ROM drive, Microsoft mouse, 124-key programmable keyboard
3 years parts, 1 year labor (on-site)	$3,295	local bus SVGA, 2MB	15" SVGA	processor	DOS, Windows for Workgroups, QAPlus, Choice of software apps	2X CD-ROM drive, 16-bit Soundblaster-compatible soundcard, speakers, Microsoft mouse, 124-key programmable key board
3 years parts, 1 year labor (on-site)	$3,995	local bus SVGA 2MB	17" SVGA	processor	DOS, Windows for Workgroups QAPlus, Choice of software apps	2X CD-ROM drive, Microsoft mouse, 124-key programmable keyboard
1 year, 30 day MBG	$2,860	PCI local bus, 1M	N/A	processor	DOS, Windows	
1 year	$2,395	PCI local bus, 1M	14" SVGA	processor	DOS, Windows for Workgroups	Microsoft mouse
1 year	$2,595	PCI local bus, 1M	14" SVGA	processor	DOS, Windows for Workgroups	Microsoft mouse

Pentium computers offer greatly improved performance over their PC-compatible predecessors. They are based on a PCI bus, which is much faster than EISA and ISA buses used in earlier PC's. Pentiums are also designed for symmetric multiprocessing (SMP), which means you can use multiple Pentium processors simultaneously on the same motherboard. A Pentium system is a powerful Windows, NT, or OS/2 system. Programmers and multimedia users benefit from the Pentium's speed, and it can act as a file server for a small-to-medium office.

Specific differences in the table fields for this kind of system are pointed out here:

- *CPU, Speed, Cache.* Look for 128K or more of cache.
- *Adapters.* Look for a SCSI port for external expandability.
- *Slots.* Make sure that there are several open slots for expandability. You may, for instance, want to add multimedia capabilities later.

Table 6.6	486- and Pentium-Based Portable Computers					
Company, Model	CPU, Speed, Cache	Keyboard	Weight	RAM Incl., Max	Hard Disk, Floppy Drive	Adapters
AMBRA, NC425SL	486SL 25MHz	85-key w/integrated trackball	6.8 lbs. w/battery	4M, 12M	120M removable 3.5" internal	
Value Leader						
AMBRA, N433C	486SX, 33MHz	86-key w/integrated trackball	6.7 lbs. w/battery	4M, 12M	120M, 3.5" internal	2 PCMCIA Type II
AMBRA, N450C	486DX2 66MHz	86-key w/integrated trackball	6.7 lbs. w/battery	4M, 12M	200M, 3.5" 3.5" internal	1 par., 1 ser., VGA keybd.
AMBRA, N100-450	486DX4, 100MHz	85-key with centered trackball	6.7 lbs. w/battery	4M, 20M	450M, 3.5" internal	1 par., 1 ser., VGA, PS/2 keyboard or mouse, Audio in/out, docking station

- *Price.* Manufacturer's suggested retail price.
- *Graphics Adapter.* A VESA local bus slot and graphics adapter are nearly a necessity for getting the full performance that this kind of system can give to multitasking environments.
- *Upgradability.* Look for expandability and the capability to upgrade multiple Pentium processors.

Slots	Warranty	Price	Screen	Power, Battery Life Recharge	Software	Other
		$1,799	9.5" DSTN dual-scan color		Borland Office 2.0 (WordPerfect for Windows, Paradox, Quattro Pro), Sidekick for Windows, DOS 6.2 Windows 3.1	Integrated fax modem
		$1,799	9.5" DSTN dual-scan color		Borland Office 2.0 (WordPerfect for Windows, Paradox, Quattro Pro), Sidekick for Windows, DOS 6.2, Windows 3.1	
1 PCMCIA III (can hold 2 PCMCIA type II)		$2,599	9.5" DSTN dual-scan color		DOS 6.2, Windows 3.1	case
1 PCMCIA III (holds 2 PCMCIA II devices)		$5,299	9.5" TFT color (local bus)	NiMH battery, AC adapter	DOS 6.2, Windows for Workgroups 3.11, Audio Clip library	case, MIDI and Wave audio support, SoundBlaster II support, integrated microphone

continues

Table 6.6 Continued

Company, Model	CPU, Speed, Cache	Keyboard	Weight	RAM Incl., Max	Hard Disk, Floppy Drive	Adapters
AMBRA, N75T-340	486DX4, 75MHz	85-key w/centered trackball	6.7 lbs. w/battery	4M, 20M	340M, 3.5" 3.5" internal	1 par., 1 ser., VGA, PS/2 keyboard or mouse, Audio in/out, docking station
AMBRA, N75D-340	486DX4, 75MHz	85-key w/ centered trackball	6.7 lbs w/battery	4M, 20M	340M, 3.5" internal	1 par., 1 ser., VGA PS/2 keyboard or mouse, Audio in/out, docking
AUSTIN, Monochrome Notebook	486SX, 25MHz	85-key w/ centered trackball	6.3 lbs. w/battery	4M, 32M	127M, 3.5" internal	1 par., 2 ser., VGA, keyboard
AUSTIN, Dual Scan Color Notebook	486SX, 25MHz	85-key w/ centered trackball	6.3 lbs. w/battery	4M, 32M	127M, 3.5" internal	1 par., 2 ser., VGA, keyboard
AUSTIN, DX2-66 Dual Scan Color Notebook	486DX2, 66MHz	85-key w/ centered trackball	6.3 lbs. w/battery	8M, 32M	262M, 3.5" internal	1 par., 2 ser., VGA, keyboard
AUSTIN, DX2-66 Active Matrix Color Notebook	486DX2, 66MHz	85-key w/ centered trackball	6.3 lbs. w/battery	8M, 32M	340M, 3.5" internal	1 par., 2 ser., VGA, keyboard
AUSTIN, DX4-75 Active Matrix Color Notebook	486DX4, 75MHz	85-key w/ centered trackball	6.3 lbs. w/battery	8M, 32M	542M, 3.5" internal	1 par., 2 ser., VGA, keyboard

Slots	Warranty	Price	Screen	Power, Battery Life Recharge	Software	Other
1 PCMCIA III (holds 2 PCMCIA II devices)		$4,299	9.5" TFT color (local bus)	NiMH battery AC adapter	DOS 6.2, Windows for Workgroups 3.11, Audio Clip library	case, MIDI and Wave audio support, SoundBlaster II support, integrated microphone
1 PCMCIA III (holds 2 PCMCIA II devices)		$3,199	10.3" dual-scan DSTN color (local bus)	NiMH battery, AC adapter	DOS 6.2, Windows for Workgroups 3.11, Audio Clip library	case, MIDI and Wave audio support, SoundBlaster II support, integrated microphone
1 PCMCIA III (hold 2 PCMCIA II devices)	1 year	$1,599	Backlit mono LCD (local bus), 9.5"	AC, Auto, NimH or NiCad (2-5 hours)	DOS 6.2, Windows 3.1	
1 PCMCIA III (hold 2 PCMCIA II devices)	1 year	$2,199	Dual Scan Color (local bus), 9.5"	AC, Auto, NimH or NiCad (2-5 hours)	DOS 6.2, Windows 3.1	
1 PCMCIA III (hold 2 PCMCIA II devices)	1 year	$2,999	Dual Scan Color (local bus), 9.5"	AC, Auto, NimH or NiCad (2-5 hours)	DOS 6.2 Windows 3.1	
1 PCMCIA III (hold 2 PCMCIA II devices)	1 year	$4,199	TFT Active Matrix Color (local bus), 9.5"	AC, Auto, NimH or NiCad (2-5 hours)	DOS 6.2 Windows 3.1	
1 PCMCIA III (hold 2 PCMCIA II devices)	1 year	$4,999	TFT Active Matrix Color (local bus), 9.5"	AC, Auto, NimH or NiCad (2-5 hours)	DOS 6.2 Windows 3.1	

continues

Table 6.6 Continued

Company, Model	CPU, Speed, Cache	Keyboard	Weight	RAM Incl., Max	Hard Disk, Floppy Drive	Adapters
AUSTIN, P5E, Multimedia Notebook	P5E, 75MHz	85-key w/ centered trackball	6.5 lbs. w/battery	8M, 32M	340M, 3.5" internal	1 par., 2 ser., VGA, keyboard
Canon Innova Book 10	486SX, 33MHz	85-key w/ built-in trackball	4.0 lbs. w/ battery	4M, 20M	120M, 3.5" 1.44M external	1 par., 1 ser., 1 PS/2, VGA
Canon Innova Book 10c	486SX, 33MHz	85-key w/ built-in trackball	4.0 lbs. w/ battery	4M, 20M	170M, 3.5" 1.44M external	1 par., 1 ser., 1 PS/2, VGA
Canon Notejet 486	486SX, 33MHz	85-key w/ handheld trackball	8.8 lbs. w/ battery	4M, 12M	120M, 3.5" 1.44M	1 par., 1 ser., 1 PS/2, VGA
Canon Notejet 486c	486SX, 33MHz	85-key w/ handheld trackball	8.8 lbs. w/ battery	4M, 12M	120M, 3.5" 1.44M	1 par., 1 ser., 1 PS/2, VGA
Canon NotejetII 486c	486SLC2, 50MHz, 16K	85-key w/ handheld trackball	8.6 lbs. w/ battery	4M, 12M	130M, 3.5" 1.44M	1 par., 1 ser., 1 PS/2, VGA
Compaq Contura (mono)	486SL(DX), 25MHz	84-key, w/ integrated trackball	6.2 lbs.	4M, 20M	120M, 3.5" 1.44M	1 ser., 1 par., 1 VGA, 1 PS/2
Compaq Contura (color)	486SL(DX), 25MHz	84-key, w/ integrated trackball	6.2 lbs.	4M, 20M	120M, 3.5" 1.44M	1 ser., 1 par., 1 VGA, 1 PS/2
DECpc 425 SE Color	486SX, 25MHz	82-key w/ integrated trackball	6.2 lbs.	4M, 20M	120M, 3.5" 1.44M	1 ser., 1 par., VGA, keyboard, mouse
DECpc 425 SE Monochrome	486SX, 25MHz	82-key w/ integrated trackball	5.5 lbs.	4M, 20M	120M, 3.5" 1.44M	1 ser., 1 par., VGA, keyboard, mouse

Slots	Warranty	Price	Screen	Power, Battery Life Recharge	Software	Other
1 PCMCIA III (hold 2 PCMCIA II devices)	1 year	$2,849	Dual Scan Color (local bus), 9.5"	AC, Auto, NimH or NiCad (2-5 hours)	DOS 6.2 Windows 3.1	16-bit sound-card w/speaker jacks and integrated microphone
1 PCMCIA II	1 year roadside or mail-in	$1,530	8.5" DSTN mono, 640x480	NiCad (2.5 hours avg.), AC	DOS 6.2, Windows 3.11	
1 PCMCIA II	1 year roadside or mail-in	$1,982	7.8" DSTN color, 640x480	NiMH (2.5 hours avg.), AC	DOS 6.2, Windows 3.11	
1 PCMCIA III (hold 2 PCMCIA II devices)	1 year on-site	$1,790	9.5" DSTN mono, 640x480	NiCad (2.5 hours avg.), AC	DOS 6.2, Windows 3.11	built-in Bubblejet 360 dpi printer
1 PCMCIA III (hold 2 PCMCIA II devices)	1 year on-site	$2,321	9.5" DSTN color, 640x480	NiCad (2.5 hours avg.), AC	DOS 6.2, Windows 3.11	built-in Bubblejet 360 dpi printer
1 PCMCIA III (hold 2 PCMCIA II devices)	1 year on-site	$2,724	10.3" DSTN color, 640x480	NiCad (2.5 hours avg.), AC	DOS 6.2, Windows 3.11	built-in Bubblejet 360 dpi printer
	3 years	$1,799	9.5" mono VGA	NiCad	DOS, Windows, TabWorks	
	3 years	$2,099	9.5" color VGA	NiCad	DOS, Windows, TabWorks	
1 PCMCIA I, II, or III	3 years	$2,229	9.5" STN color	NiMH	DOS, Windows, Card and Socket Services	LED battery gauge
1 PCMCIA I, II, or III	3 years	$1,549	9.5" STN grayscale	NiMH	DOS, Windows, Card and Socket Services	LED battery gauge

continues

Table 6.6	Continued					
Company, Model	CPU, Speed, Cache	Keyboard	Weight	RAM Incl., Max	Hard Disk, Floppy Drive	Adapters
DECpc 433 SE Color	486SX, 33MHz	82-key w/ integrated trackball	6.2 lbs.	4M, 20M	120M, 3.5" 1.44M	1 ser., 1 par., VGA, keyboard, mouse
DECpc 433 SE Monochrome	486SX, 33MHz	82-key w/ integrated trackball	5.5 lbs.	4M, 20M	120M, 3.5" 1.44M	1 ser., 1 par., VGA, keyboard, mouse
DECpc 433 SLC Premium	486SX, 33MHz	83-key w/ snap-on trackball	6.8 lbs.	4M, 20M	200M, 3.5" 1.44M	1 ser., 1 par., VGA, keyboard, mouse
Dell Latitude 425	486SL, 25MHz	82-key w/ built-in trackball	5.75 lbs.	4M, 20M	120M, 3.5"	N/A
Dell Latitude 433c attache	486SL, 33MHz	82-key w/ built-in trackball	6.4 lbs.	8M, 20M	170M, 3.5"	N/A
Dell Latitude 433c (alt. config.)	486SL, 33MHz	82-key w/ built-in trackball	6.4 lbs.	8M, 20M	170M, 3.5"	N/A
Dell Latitude 433c (alt. config.)	486SL, 33MHz	82-key w/ built-in trackball	6.4 lbs.	4M, 20M	170M, 3.5"	N/A
Gateway 2000 Color-Book 486DX2-40	486DX2, 40MHz	85-key w/ slide-out trackball	5.6 lbs.	4M, 20M	200M, 3.5" 1.44M	1 ser., 1 par., VGA, PS/2
Gateway 2000 Color-Book 486DX2-50	486DX2, 50MHz	85-key w/ slide-out trackball	5.6 lbs.	8M, 20M	250M, 3.5" 1.44M	1 ser., 1 par., VGA, PS/2

Slots	Warranty	Price	Screen	Power, Battery Life Recharge	Software	Other
1 PCMCIA I, II, or III	3 years	$2,399	9.5" STN color	NiMH	DOS, Windows, Card and Socket Services	LED battery gauge
1 PCMCIA I, II, or III	3 years	$1,699	9.5" STN grayscale	NiMH	DOS, Windows, Card and Socket Services	LED battery gauge
1 PCMCIA III (2 I or II)	3 years	$4,199	9.5" Active Matrix color	NiMH	DOS, Windows, BitFax, BitCom	
1 PCMCIA III	1 year	$1,449	9.5" mono, local bus	NiMH, 2-4 hrs.	DOS, Windows, CommWorks for Windows, America Online, RadioMail	
1 PCMCIA III	1 year	$2,649	9.5" DSTN color, local bus	NiMH, 2-4 hrs.	DOS, Windows, CommWorks for Windows, America Online, RadioMail	PCMCIA 14.4K faxmodem, case
1 PCMCIA III	1 year	$2,649	9.5" DSTN color, local bus	NiMH, 2-4 hrs.	DOS, Windows, CommWorks for Windows, MS Office, America Online, RadioMail	attache case
1 PCMCIA III	1 year	$2,449	9.5" DSTN color, local bus	NiMH, 2-4 hrs.	DOS, Windows, CommWorks for Windows, MS Works, PowerPoint, Act!, America Online, RadioMail	96/24 faxmodem, attache case
1 PCMCIA III (2 type II's)	3 years parts, 1 year labor	$2,495	10.3" LCD color	NiMH	DOS, Windows for Workgroups, Works for Windows	
1 PCMCIA III (2 type II's)	3 years parts, 1 year labor	$2,995	10.3" LCD color	NiMH	DOS, Windows for Workgroups, Works for Windows	

continues

Table 6.6	Continued						
Company, Model	CPU, Speed, Cache	Keyboard	Weight	RAM Incl., Max	Hard Disk, Floppy Drive	Adapters
Gateway 2000 Color-Book 486DX4-75	486DX4, 75MHz	85-key w/ slide-out trackball	5.6 lbs.	8M, 20M	250M, 3.5" 1.44M	1 ser., 1 par., VGA, PS/2
Gateway 2000 Color-Book 486SX-33	486SX, 33MHz	85-key w/ slide-out trackball	5.6 lbs.	4M, 20M	120M, 3.5" 1.44M	1 ser., 1 par., VGA, PS/2
IBM ThinkPad 360	486SL, 33MHz	85-key w/ Trackpoint II	5.6 lbs.	4M, 20M	170M, 3.5" 1.44M (both removable)	N/A
IBM ThinkPad 360 (alt. config.)	486SL, 33MHz	85-key w/ Trackpoint II	5.6 lbs.	4M, 20M	340M, 3.5" 1.44M (both removable)	N/A
IBM ThinkPad 360C	486SL, 33MHz	85-key w/ Trackpoint II	6.1 lbs.	4M, 20M	170M, 3.5" 1.44M (both removable)	N/A

Slots	Warranty	Price	Screen	Power, Battery Life Recharge	Software	Other
1 PCMCIA III (2 type II's)	3 years parts, 1 year labor	$3,495	10.3" LCD color	NiMH	DOS, Windows for Workgroups, Works for Windows	
1 PCMCIA III (2 type II's)	3 years parts, 1 year labor	$1,995	9.4" LCD color	NiMH	DOS, Windows for Workgroups, Works for Windows	
1 PCMCIA III	1 year, 30-day MBG	$2,099	9.5" mono	NiMH, 2-4 hrs./charge	DOS, Windows, cc: Mail, Advantis mail, Lotus Organizer, Lotus Screencam, Triton CoSession Host, FaxWorks, PRODIGY, America Online, Official Airline Guide	audio in/out, microphone, speakers, AC adapter
1 PCMCIA III	1 year, 30-day MBG	$2,599	9.5" mono	NiMH, 2-4 hrs./charge	DOS, Windows, cc: Mail, Advantis mail, Lotus Organizer, Lotus Screencam, Triton CoSession Host, FaxWorks, PRODIGY, America Online, Official Airline Guide	audio in/out, microphone, speakers, AC adapter
1 PCMCIA III	1 year, 30-day MBG	$2,699	8.4" TFT color	NiMH, 2-4 hrs./charge	DOS, Windows, cc: Mail, Advantis mail, Lotus Organizer, Lotus Screencam, Triton CoSession Host, FaxWorks, PRODIGY, America Online, Official Airline Guide	audio in/out, microphone, speakers, AC adapter

continues

Table 6.6 Continued						
Company, Model	CPU, Speed, Cache	Keyboard	Weight	RAM Incl., Max	Hard Disk, Floppy Drive	Adapters
IBM ThinkPad 360C (alt. config.)	486SL, 33MHz	85-key w/ Trackpoint II	6.1 lbs.	4M, 20M	340M, 3.5" 1.44M (both removable)	N/A
IBM ThinkPad 360Cs	486SL, 33MHz	85-key w/ Trackpoint II	6.1 lbs.	4M, 20M	170M, 3.5" 1.44M (both removable)	N/A
IBM ThinkPad 360Cs (alt. config.)	486SL, 33MHz	85-key w/ Trackpoint II	6.1 lbs.	4M, 20M	340M, 3.5" 1.44M (both removable)	N/A
IBM ThinkPad 755Cs	486SL2, 50MHz	85-key w/ Trackpoint II	6.1 lbs.	4M, 36M	170M, 3.5" 1.44M (both removable)	N/A

Slots	Warranty	Price	Screen	Power, Battery Life Recharge	Software	Other
1 PCMCIA III	1 year, 30-day MBG	$3,199	8.4" TFT color	NiMH, 2-4 hrs./charge	DOS, Windows, cc: Mail, Advantis mail, Lotus Organizer, Lotus Screencam, Triton CoSession Host, FaxWorks, PRODIGY, America Online, Official Airline Guide	audio in/out, microphone, speakers, AC adapter
1 PCMCIA III	1 year, 30-day MBG	$2,999	9.5" dual scan color	NiMH, 2-4 hrs./charge	DOS, Windows, cc: Mail, Advantis mail, Lotus Organizer, Lotus Screencam, Triton CoSession Host, FaxWorks, PRODIGY, America Online, Official Airline Guide	audio in/out, microphone, speakers, AC adapter
1 PCMCIA III	1 year, 30-day MBG	$3,199	9.5" dual scan color	NiMH, 2-4 hrs./charge	DOS, Windows, cc: Mail, Advantis mail, Lotus Organizer, Lotus Screencam, Triton CoSession Host, FaxWorks, PRODIGY, America Online, Official Airline Guide	audio in/out, microphone, speakers, AC adapter
1 PCMCIA III	1 year, 30-day MBG	$3,999	9.5" DSTN color	NiMH, 2-4 hrs./charge	DOS, Windows, cc: Mail, Advantis mail, Lotus Organizer, Lotus Screencam, Triton CoSession Host, FaxWorks, PRODIGY, America Online, Official Airline Guide	audio in/out, microphone, speakers, AC adapter

continues

Table 6.6 Continued

Company, Model	CPU, Speed, Cache	Keyboard	Weight	RAM Incl., Max	Hard Disk, Floppy Drive	Adapters
Toshiba T4800CT	486DX4, 75MHz	82-key w/ Microsoft Ballpoint	6.9 lbs. w/ battery	8M, 24M	500M, 3.5" 1.44M	1 ser., 1 par., VGA, PS/2
Toshiba Satellite T1910	486SX, 33MHz	82-key w/ Microsoft Ballpoint	6.5 lbs. w/ battery	4M, 20M	120M, 3.5" 1.44M	1 ser., 1 par., VGA, PS/2
Toshiba Satellite T1910CS	486SX, 33MHz	82-key w/ Microsoft Ballpoint	6.5 lbs. w/ battery	4M, 20M	120M, 3.5" 1.44M	1 ser., 1 par., VGA, PS/2
Toshiba T4700CS	486DX2, 50MHz	82-key w/ Microsoft Ballpoint	6.9 lbs. w/ battery	8M, 24M	200M, 3.5" 1.44M	1 ser., 1 par., VGA, PS/2
Toshiba T4700CT	486DX2, 50MHz	82-key w/ Microsoft Ballpoint	6.9 lbs. w/ battery	8M, 24M	200M, 3.5" 1.44M	1 ser., 1 par., VGA, PS/2

Most Expandable

Company, Model	CPU, Speed, Cache	Keyboard	Weight	RAM Incl., Max	Hard Disk, Floppy Drive	Adapters
Toshiba T6600C Mobile Multimedia Computers	486DX2, 66MHz	101-key (detach-able) w/ Logitech TrackMan	17.1 lbs. w/ battery	8M, 40M	510M, 3.5" 1.44M	1 ser., 1 par., VGA, PS/2, SCSI
Toshiba T6600C/CD Mobile Multimedia Computer	486DX2, 66MHz	101-key (detach-able) w/ Logitech TrackMan	17.1 lbs. w/ battery	8M, 40M	510M, 3.5" 1.44M	1 ser., 1 par., VGA, PS/2, SCSI

Slots	Warranty	Price	Screen	Power, Battery Life Recharge	Software	Other
1 PCMCIA II, 1 PCMCIA I, II, or III	3 years	$6,499	9.5" active matrix color, SVGA	NiMH	Microsoft Windows Sound System 2.0 (16-bit .WAV audio), microphone and speakers, audio in/out	
1 PCMCIA I, II, or III	1 year	~$1,499-$1,599	9.5" STN - gray scale VGA	NiMH		
1 PCMCIA I, II, or III	1 year	~$2,099	9.5" DSTN color VGA	NiMH	DOS, Windows, UltraFont	
1 PCMCIA II, 1 PCMCIA I, II, or III	3 years	$3,699	9.5" Dynamic-STN color LCD VGA	NiMH	DOS, Windows, UltraFont, Microsoft Sound System, Indeo 3.0, Run Time Video for Windows	internal microphone, headphone speaker jack, microphone jack
1 PCMCIA II, 1 PCMCIA I, II, or III	3 years	$5,299	9.5" TFT-LCD active matrix color VGA	NiMH	DOS, Windows, UltraFont, Microsoft Sound System, Indeo 3.0, Run Time Video for Windows	internal microphone, headphone/speaker jack, microphone jack
2 full-length 16-bit ISA slots, 1 PCMCIA II	1 year	$7,699	10.4" TFT-LCD active matrix color VGA	NiMH	DOS, Windows, UltraFont, Asymetrix COMPEL, Asymetrix MediaBlitz, EZ-SCSI	Microsoft Microphone
2 full-length 16-bit ISA slots, 1 PCMCIA II	1 year	$8,299	10.4" TFT-LCD active matrix color VGA	NiMH	DOS, Windows, UltraFont, Asymetrix COMPEL, Asymetrix MediaBlitz, EZ-SCSI	2X CD-ROM drive, Microsoft Microphone

continues

Table 6.6	Continued					
Company, Model	CPU, Speed, Cache	Keyboard	Weight	RAM Incl., Max	Hard Disk, Floppy Drive	Adapters
ZEOS ColorNote	486SX, 33MHz	81-key w/ trackball	5.6 lbs.	4M, 20M	80M, 3.5" 1.44M	1 ser., 1 par., VGA
ZEOS ColorNote (alt. config.)	486SX, 33MHz	81-key w/ trackball	5.6 lbs.	4M, 20M	120M, 3.5" 1.44M	1 ser., 1 par., VGA
ZEOS Freestyle	486SL, 33MHz	81-key w/ mouse key	5.6 lbs.	4M, 20M	120M, 3.5" 1.44M	1 ser., 1 par., VGA
ZEOS Freestyle (alt. config.)	486SL, 33MHz	81-key w/ mouse key	5.6 lbs.	4M, 20M	180M, 3.5" 1.44M	1 ser., 1 par., VGA

Table 6.7 Macintosh 680X0-Based Desktop Computers

This table includes Apple Macintosh desktop computers. Only systems based on the 68000 family, not the newer PowerPC chip, are included. This table is sorted by product family, and then CPU speed and cache size within product family. Because there are relatively few Macintosh desktop systems, it's easy to compare all the available models and focus on one or two product families, and then examine a specific model that meets your needs.

Macintosh systems have better-integrated hardware and software than IBM-compatibles running Windows, so you can do more with a little less computer than in the IBM world. The ubiquity of SCSI ports makes even humble systems very expandable. A 68030-based system may meet your needs, but a 68040-based system is now considered mainstream and is a better choice for running multimedia or driving a large monitor.

Specific differences in table fields for the Macintosh are pointed out here:

- *Model.* The company name isn't listed because all Macs are made by Apple.

Slots	Warranty	Price	Screen	Power, Battery Life Recharge	Software	Other
PCMCIA III	1 year	$2,195	9.5" dual scan LCD color, backlit	NiMH	DOS, Windows, UltraFont	
PCMCIA III	1 year	$2,395	9.5" dual scan LCD color, backlit	NiMH	DOS 6.2, Windows for Workgroups, Lotus Organizer	
N/A	1 year	$1,695	9.4" LCD gray scale, backlit	NiCad		tilt/swivel display
N/A	1 year	$1,995	9.4" LCD gray scale, backlit	NiCad	DOS, Windows for Workgroups	tilt/swivel display, case

- *CPU, Speed, Cache.* 68040 microprocessors have a small built-in cache, and Apple tends to use fast memory chips. However, an add-on cache unit will improve system performance.
- *Unit Size.* The Classic systems are all-in-one units that have a built-in monitor. The Performa 200 and some Quadras are tower-type units.
- *Floppy.* The Mac uses a SuperDrive floppy drive that can read and write MS-DOS formatted floppy disks as well as Macintosh floppy disks. Many Macintosh applications can save in DOS- and Windows-compatible file formats.
- *Drive Bays.* The need for additional drive bays is reduced by the fact that Macs have built-in SCSI ports for external expandability.
- *Adapters.* The Mac's ADB ports are useful for keyboards, mice, and trackballs.
- *Graphics Adapter.* Most Macs have built-in graphics adapters; there are also many choices of add-in cards.

Table 6.7 Macintosh 680X0-Based Desktop Computers

Macintosh offers a budget line of 680X0-based systems geared toward the home user called the Performa. They are available in department stores and superstores in a huge variety of configurations, usually including modems, CD-ROM drives, and bundled software. Check dealers for locally available Performa configurations. Call 1-800-538-9696 for the names of dealers in your area.

Model	CPU, Speed, Cache	Unit Size	RAM Incl., Max	Hard Disk	Floppy Drive	Drive Bays	Adapters
LC 475	68040, 25MHz	3.2 x 12.2 x 15	4M, 36M	160M	SuperDrive		2 ser, 1 ADB, video out, SCSI, sound in/out, LocalTalk
LC 550	68030, 33MHz	17.9 x 13.5 x 16.5	4M, 36M	160M	SuperDrive	1 half-ht. 5.25" bay	2 ser, 2 ADB, SCSI, sound in/out, LocalTalk, built-in mic.
LC 575	68LC040, 33MHz	17.9 x 13.5 x 16.5	4M, 36M	160M	SuperDrive	1 half-ht. 5.25" bay	2 ser, 1 ADB, SCSI, sound in/out, LocalTalk, built-in mic.
Quadra 605	68LC040, 25MHz	2.9 x 12.2 x 15.3	4M, 36M	80M	SuperDrive		2 ser, 1 ADB, video out, SCSI, sound in/out, LocalTalk

Listing of Computers **137**

Slots	Warranty	Price	Graphics Adapter	Monitor (if included in price)	Software	Other
1	1 year	(offered through education channels only, contact Apple or your local college or university)	512K Apple		System 7	Energy Star
1	1 year	(offered through education channels only, contact Apple or your local college or university)	512K Apple	14" Sony Trinitron RGB (built-in)	System 7	Stereo speakers
1	1 year	(offered through education channels only, contact Apple or your local college or university)	512K Apple	14" Sony Trinitron RGB (built-in)	System 7	Stereo speakers, Energy Star
1	1 year	$899	512K Apple		System 7	Energy Star

continues

Table 6.7	Continued						
Model	CPU, Speed, Cache	Unit Size	RAM Incl., Max	Hard Disk	Floppy Drive	Drive Bays	Adapters
Quadra 610	68040, 25MHz, 8K	3.4 x 16.3 x 15.6	8M, 68M	230M	SuperDrive	1 half-ht. 5.25" bay	2 ser, 2 ADB, video out, SCSI, sound in/out, LocalTalk, Ethernet
Quadra 950	68040, 33MHz, 8K	16.8 x 8.9 x 20.6	8M, 256M	230M	SuperDrive	3 half-ht. 5.25" bays	2 ser, 1 ADB, video out, dual-channel SCSI, sound in/out, LocalTalk, Ethernet
Quadra 660AV	68040, 25MHz, 8K	3.0 x 16.1 x 15.2	8M, 68M	230M	SuperDrive	1 half-ht. 5.25" bay	2 ser, 1 ADB, 2 video in, 2 video out, SCSI, stereo sound in/out, Local Talk, Ethernet
Quadra 840AV	68040, 40MHz, 8K	14.2 x 7.8 x 16.0	8M, 128M	230M	SuperDrive	2 half-ht. 5.25" bays	2 ser, 1 ADB, 2 video in, 2 video out, SCSI, stereo sound in/out, LocalTalk, Ethernet

Table 6.8 Power Macintosh Computers

Specific differences in table fields for the Macintosh are pointed out here:

- *Model.* The company name isn't listed because all Macs are made by Apple.
- *CPU, Speed, Cache.* PowerPC microprocessors have a built-in cache, and Apple tends to use fast memory chips. However, an add-on cache unit will improve system performance.
- *Unit Size.* Dimensions can be important if desk space is at a premium.

Slots	Warranty	Price	Graphics Adapter	Monitor (if included in price)	Software	Other
	1 year	$1,899	512K VGA/SVGA		System 7	Can include an Intel 486 processor
5 NuBus, 1 PDS	1 year	$3,899	512K VGA/SVGA		System 7	Energy Star, 24-bit graphics
	1 year	$2,200	1M VGA/SVGA		System 7, Plain-Talk speech recognition/ text-to-speech	Onboard AT&T 3210 55MHz DSP, 16-bit stereo sound
3 NuBus, 1 DAV (digital audio/ video)	1 year	$3,399	1M VGA/SVGA		System 7, Plain-Talk speech recognition/ text-to-speech	Onboard AT&T 3210 66MHz DSP, 16-bit stereo sound

- *Floppy.* The Power Macintosh uses a SuperDrive floppy drive that can read and write MS-DOS formatted floppy disks as well as Macintosh floppy disks. Many Macintosh applications can save in DOS- and Windows-compatible file formats.
- *Drive Bays.* The need for additional drive bays is reduced by the fact that Macs have built-in SCSI ports for external expandability.
- *Adapters.* The Mac's ADB ports are useful for keyboards, mice, and trackballs.
- *Graphics Adapter.* Most Macs have built-in graphics adapters; there are also many choices of add-in cards.

Table 6.8 Power Macintosh Computers

Model	CPU, Speed, Cache	Unit Size	RAM Incl. Max	Hard Disk	Floppy Drive	Drive Bays
6100/60	PowerPC 601, 60 MHz, 32K	3.4 x 16.3 x 15.6	8M, 72M	160M	SuperDrive	1 half-ht. 5.25" bay
6100/60AV	PowerPC 601, 60 MHz, 32K	3.4 x 16.3 x 15.6	8M, 72M	250M	SuperDrive	1 half-ht. 5.25" bay
7100/66	PowerPC 601, 66 MHz, 32K	6.0 x 13.0 x 16.5	8M, 136M	250M	SuperDrive	1 half-ht. 5.25" bay
7100/66AV	PowerPC 601, 66 MHz, 32K	6.0 x 13.0 x 16.5	8M, 136M	5000M	SuperDrive	1 half-ht. 5.25" bay
8100/80	PowerPC 601, 80 MHz, 32K w/ 256K memory cache	14.2 x 8.9 x 16.0	8M, 264M	250M	SuperDrive	2 half-ht. 5.25" bays, 2 3.5" bays
8100/80AV	PowerPC 601, 80 MHz, 32K w/ 256K memory cache	14.2 x 8.9 x 16.0	16M, 264M	500M	SuperDrive	2 half-ht. 5.25" bays, 2 3.5" bays

Table 6.9 Macintosh Portable Computers

This table includes Apple Macintosh portable computers. This table is sorted by product family, then model number. Because there are relatively few Macintosh portable systems, it's easy to compare all the available models to focus on the one that meets your needs.

Macintosh portables are extremely popular. They are widely used by people who don't have a desktop system and also by those whose desktop system is an IBM-compatible. These users find that the problems generated by the incompatibilities of the systems are outweighed by the ease of use and quality engineering for which Macintosh systems are well known. The PowerBook's center-mounted, built-in trackball is the best around, and

Listing of Computers

Adapters	Slots	Warranty	Price	Graphics Adapter	Software	Other
2 ser, 1 ADB, monitor port, SCSI, stereo sound in/out, LocalTalk, Ethernet		1 year	$1,950	Apple	System 7	16-bit CD-Quality sound
2 ser, 1 ADB, monitor port, SCSI, stereo sound in/out, LocalTalk, Ethernet		1 year	$2,799	Apple	System 7	16-bit CD-Quality sound, 2X CD-ROM, AV capabilities
2 ser, 1 ADB, 2 monitor ports, SCSI, stereo sound in/out, LocalTalk, Ethernet	3 NuBus	1 year	$3,125	1M Apple	System 7	Energy Star, 16-bit CD-Quality sound
2 ser, 1 ADB, 2 monitor ports, SCSI, stereo sound in/out, LocalTalk, Ethernet	3 NuBus	1 year	$4,299	1M Apple	System 7	Energy Star, 16-bit CD-Quality sound, 2X CD-ROM, AV capabilities
2 ser, 1 ADB, 2 monitor ports, SCSI, stereo sound in/out, LocalTalk, Ethernet	3 NuBus	1 year	$4,499	Apple	System 7	Energy Star, 16-bit CD-Quality sound
2 ser, 1 ADB, 2 monitor ports, SCSI, stereo sound in/out, LocalTalk, Ethernet	3 NuBus	1 year	$5,999	Apple	System 7	Energy Star, 16-bit CD-Quality sound, 2X CD-ROM, AV capabilities

the built-in SCSI port is great for expandability and mixing and matching external devices with desktop units. Because of the tight integration of hardware and software, a 68030-based portable is powerful enough to run most Macintosh software well.

The Duo is a different kind of system than most portables. It's designed to be used with a dock in the office so that you only have one computer that you use at home, in the office, or on the road. It doesn't have a built-in floppy drive and is very light for an otherwise full-function portable.

The fields in the table are described in general in the first section above; specific differences for this kind of system are pointed out here. Some considerations are repeated from the preceding sections on 386-based portables and on Macintosh desktop systems.

- *CPU, Speed, Cache.* If you're going to be using your portable much, and especially if you'll be hooking up an external monitor, get the fastest CPU you can.

- *Weight.* This is very important if you travel much. The nearly 3-pound reduction in weight for a Duo makes it much easier to carry around.

- *Hard Disk, Floppy Disk.* Get the biggest hard disk you can; even 80M is smallish. The Mac uses a SuperDrive floppy drive that can read and write MS-DOS formatted floppy disks as well as Macintosh floppy disks. Many Macintosh applications can save in DOS- and Windows-compatible file formats.

Table 6.9 Macintosh Portable Computers

Model	CPU, Speed, Cache	Unit Size	Weight	RAM Incl. Max	Hard Disk	Floppy Drive	Adapters
PowerBook 145	68030, 25MHz	2.3 x 11.3 x 9.3	6.8 lb.	4M, 8M	80M	SuperDrive	2 ser, 1 ADB, sound in/out, SCSI, LocalTalk
PowerBook 165	68030, 33MHz	2.3 x 11.3 x 9.3	6.8 lb.	4M, 14M	80M	SuperDrive	2 ser, 1 ADB, video out, sound-in/out, integrated microphone, SCSI, LocalTalk
PowerBook 520	68LC040, 50/25MHz	2.3 x 11.5 x 9.7	6.3 lb.	4M, 36M	160M	SuperDrive	1 ser, 1 ADB, video out, power adapter, stereo sound in/out, integrated microphone,SCSI, LocalTalk, Ethernet
PowerBook 520c	68LC040, 50/25MHz	2.3 x 11.5 x 9.7	6.4 lb.	4M, 36M	160M	SuperDrive	1 ser, 1 ADB, video out, power adapter, stereo sound in/out, integrated microphone, SCSI, LocalTalk, Ethernet

- *Adapters.* The ADB port is used for keyboards, mice, and trackballs. You can also get a SCSI-based video adapter for a system that doesn't have a video port, but get the video port if you'll be driving an external monitor. Duos have their adapters on their docks.
- *Price.* Get the price of an external floppy and a docking station, and add it in before making a purchase decision on a Duo.
- *Power, Battery Life.* The battery life of color systems is just too short—look for a monochrome screen if you'll be running from a battery much.

Warranty	Price	Screen	Pointing Device	Battery, Avg. Life	Software	Other
1 year	$1,399	10" monochrome supertwist, backlit (640x400)	Integrated trackball	Nicad, 2.5-3 hrs.	System 7	Energy Star
1 year	$1,599	10" grayscale supertwist, backlit (640x400) and/or external Apple or VGA/SVGA	Integrated trackball	Nicad, 2.5-3 hrs.	System 7	Energy Star
1 year	$2,449	9.5" FSTN grayscale, passive matrix (640x480) and/or external Apple	Trackpad	NiMH, 2-4 hrs. on one battery, 4-7 hours on 2 batteries	System 7, PowerBook Mobility Pack	Energy Star
1 year	$3,099	9.5" dual-scan, 256 color passive matrix 640x480) and/or external Apple	Trackpad	NiMH, 2-4 hrs. on one battery, 4-7 hours on 2 batteries	System 7, PowerBook Mobility Pack	Energy Star

continues

Table 6.9	Continued						
Model	CPU, Speed, Cache	Unit Size	Weight	RAM Incl. Max	Hard Disk	Floppy Drive	Adapters
PowerBook 540	68LC040, 66/33MHz	2.3 x 11.5 x 9.7	7.1 lb.	4M, 36M	240M	SuperDrive	1 ser, 1 ADB, video out, power adapter, stereo sound in/out, integrated microphone, SCSI, LocalTalk, Ethernet
PowerBook 540c	68LC040, 66/33MHz	2.3 x 11.5 x 9.7	7.3 lb.	12M, 36M	320M	SuperDrive	1 ser, 1 ADB, video out, power adapter, stereo sound in/out, integrated microphone, SCSI, LocalTalk, Ethernet
PowerBook Duo 230	68LC040, 33MHz	1.4 x 10.9 x 8.5	4.2 lb.	4M, 24M	120M		1 ser, docking connector, power adapter, integrated speakers, integrated microphone, modem port, LocalTalk
PowerBook Duo 280	68LC040, 66/33MHz	1.4 x 10.9 x 8.5	4.2 lb.	4M, 40M	240M		1 ser, docking connector, power adapter, integrated speakers, integrated microphone, modem port, LocalTalk

Warranty	Price	Screen	Pointing Device	Battery, Avg. Life	Software	Other
1 year	$3399	9.5" active-matrix, 64 grayscale (640x480) and/or external Apple	Trackpad	NiMH, 1.5-3 hrs. on one battery, 3-6 hours on 2 batteries	System 7, PowerBook Mobility Pack	Energy Star
1 year	$5850	9.5" active-matrix, 256 color at 640x480 or thousands of colorsat 640x400 and/or external Apple	Trackpad	Type II NiMH, 1.5-3 hrs. on one battery, 3-6 hours on 2 batteries	System 7, PowerBook Mobility Pack	Energy Star, Global Village Mercury modem
1 year	$1698	9" backlit supertwist, 16 grays (640x400)	Trackball	NiMH, 2-4 hrs.	System 7	Energy Star
1 year	$3110	9" backlit active-matrix, 16 grays (640x400)	Trackball	Type II NiMH, 2-4 hrs.	System 7, PowerBook Mobility Bundle	Energy Star

continues

Table 6.9	Continued						
Model	CPU, Speed, Cache	Unit Size	Weight	RAM Incl. Max	Hard Disk	Floppy Drive	Adapters
PowerBook Duo 280c	68LC040, 66/33MHz	2.3 x 11.5 x 9.7	4.8 lb.	4M, 40M	320M		1 ser, docking connector, power adapter, integrated speakers, integrated microphone, modem port, LocalTalk

Table 6.10 Subnotebooks and PDAs

The final table in this chapter lists subnotebooks and PDAs (personal digital assistants). These computers are smaller than notebooks (they are typically under 4 pounds, whereas a typical notebook is around 6 or 7 pounds), but some are very powerful. The major problem with subnotebooks and PDAs has always been finding a usable keyboard. If at all possible, try before you buy.

The fields in this table are very similar to the fields for other portable computers:

- *CPU, Speed, Cache.* Some subnotebooks are built around high-powered CPUs like their desktop cousins.

- *Keyboard.* Try the keyboard before buying (or deciding to keep) a subnotebook or PDA. If the system uses a pen for input, this field is N/A.

- *Weight.* This factor is very important if you travel much; one pound feels more like 10 pounds if you have to carry it very far.

- *RAM, Max.* The amount of on-board memory and the maximum expansion, in megabytes.

- *Hard Disk.* Some subnotebooks and PDAs use other storage schemes (like special cards), but most have hard disks. Look for the capability to replace the hard disk or add a PCMCIA hard disk.

Warranty	Price	Screen	Pointing Device	Battery, Avg. Life	Software	Other
1 year	$4,344	8.4" backlit active-matrix, 256 colors at 640x480, thousands at 640x400	Trackball	Type III NiMH, 2-4 hrs.	System 7, PowerBook Mobility Bundle	Energy Star

- *Adapters.* Many subnotebooks and PDAs skimp on ports for lack of real estate on the small case. Pay close attention to the availability of *at least* a communications port if you want to share data with a desktop PC.
- *Price.* Manufacturer's suggested retail price.
- *Screen.* As with regular laptops, the bigger the better. Get a look at it in use before committing to a purchase.
- *Power, Battery Life, Recharge.* The information here is provided by the manufacturer. Try and check reviews or talk to other users before buying if you'll be depending on batteries much.
- *Included Software*. Almost all of the computers in this ultra-portable class include day planners, but some also include word processors and spreadsheets. To see if you're really saving money, compare the bundle's price with the price of a similar system and off-the-shelf software.
- *Other.* The field is so wide open, many subnotebook and PDA manufacturers add unique features to their machines. Some features are "padding," which means they look neat but don't really add much functionality. Pay attention to what you *need*, especially if bonuses are pricey.

Table 6.10 Subnotebooks and PDAs

Company, Model	CPU, Speed, Cache	Unit Size	Keyboard	Weight	RAM Incl., Max	Hard Disk, Floppy Drive	Adapters
Value Leader							
AMBRA, SN425-80	486SL, 25MHz		86-key w/ integrated trackball	4.0 lbs. w/ battery	4M, 20M	80M Removable, 3.5" ext.	
AMBRA, SN425-170	486SL, 25MHz		86-key w/ integrated trackball	4.0 lbs. w/ battery	4M, 20M	170M Removable, 3.5" ext.	
Solid Value, with Color							
AMBRA, SN425C-170	486SL, 25MHz		86-key w/ integrated trackball	4.0 lbs. w/ battery	4M, 20M	170M Removable, 3.5" ext.	
Apple Newton Messagepad	ARM610 RISC, 20MHz	1.2" x 4.2" x 7.9"	pen-based	1.3 lbs.	1M, 5M	none	LocalTalk
Compaq Contura Aero	486SX, 25MHz	7.5" x 10.25" x 1.5"	76-key, w/ integrated trackball	3.5 lbs.	4M, 12M	84M	1 ser., 1 par.
Gateway 2000 Handbook	486SL, 25MHz	9.75" x 5.9" x 1.6"	78-key keyboard, 92% scale, w/ built-in pointing device	2.94 lbs. w/ battery	4M, 20M	80M	1 par., 1 ser., PS/2

Listing of Computers

Slots	Warranty	Price	Screen	Power, Battery Life, Recharge	Software	Other
1 PCM CIA II		$899	8.2" LCD		Borland Office 2.0 (WordPerfect for Windows, Quattro Pro, Paradox), Sidekick for Windows, Windows 3.1, DOS 6.2	Carrying case
1 PCM CIA II		$1,199	8.2" LCD		Borland Office 2.0 (WordPerfect for Windows, Quattro Pro, Paradox), Sidekick for Windows, Windows 3.1, DOS 6.2	Carrying case
1 PCM CIA II		$1,599	7.8" STN Color		Borland Office 2.0 (WordPerfect for Windows, Quattro Pro, Paradox), Sidekick for Windows, Windows 3.1, DOS 6.2	Carrying case
1 PCM CIA II	1 year	~$600	3"x4" LCD	4 AA alkaline, or NiCad pack	advanced system software with apps, games, comm., handwriting recognition, etc.	
1 PCM CIA II	3 year	$1,399	8" monochrome VGA, backlit	NiMH, AC	DOS, Windows, TabWorks	
1 PCM CIA II	3 years parts, 1 year labor	$1,495	7.9" backlit black negative FSTN	NiMH	DOS, Windows for Workgroups, MS Works for Windows	Interlink software and serial download cable

continues

Table 6.10 Continued

Company, Model	CPU, Speed, Cache	Unit Size	Keyboard	Weight	RAM Incl., Max	Hard Disk, Floppy Drive	Adapters
Gateway 2000 Handbook 486DX2-40	486DX2, 40MHz	9.75" x 5.9" x 1.6"	78-key keyboard, 92% scale, w/ built-in pointing device	2.94 lbs. w/ battery	8M, 20M	130M	1 par., 1 ser., PS/2
HP Omni-Book 425	486SL	11.1" x 6.4" x 1.4"	85-key keyboard, w/ pop-up mouse	<4 lbs.	2M, 6M	40M	1 par., 1 ser., infrared
HP Omni-Book 430	486SL	11.1" x 6.4" x 1.4"	85-key keyboard, w/ pop-up mouse	<4 lbs.	2M, 6M	40M	1 par., 1 ser., infrared
Most Portable							
HP Palm-top PC	80C186, 8 MHz.	6.3" x 3.4" x 1"	QWERTY-style	11 oz.	1M, 64M		1 ser., infrared
IBM ThinkPad 500	486SL2, 50/25MHz	7.23" x 10.11" x 1.67"	81-key w/ Trackpoint II	3.5 lbs.	4M, 12M	85M, 3.5" 1.44M external	
Toshiba Portege T3400	486SX, 33MHz	7.9" x 9.9" x 1.7"	82-key w/ AccuPoint pointing device	4.1 lbs. w/ battery	4M, 20M	120M, 3.5" 1.44M external	1 par., 1 ser., VGA
Toshiba Portege T3400CT	486SX, 33MHz	7.9" x 9.9" x 1.7"	82-key w/ AccuPoint pointing device	4.4 lbs. w/ battery	4M, 20M	120M, 3.5" 1.44M external	1 par., 1 ser., VGA
ZEOS Contenda 386SL	386SL, 25MHz	9.7" x 6.1"	80-key w/ trackball	3.9 lbs.	2M, 10M	80M	1 ser., 1 par., VGA

Slots	Warranty	Price	Screen	Power, Battery Life, Recharge	Software	Other
1 PCMCIA II	3 years parts, 1 year labor	$2,295	7.9" backlit black negative FSTN	NiMH	DOS, Windows for Workgroups, MS Works for Windows	Interlink software and serial download cable, extra battery, leather case
1 PCMCIA II	1 year		9" grayscale 640x480	AA alkaline	DOS, Windows, Word, Excel, LapLink, organizer software, HP Calculator	
1 PCMCIA II	1 year		9" grayscale 640x480	AA alkaline	DOS, Windows, Word, Excel, LapLink, organizer software, HP Calculator	
1 PCMCIA II	1 year		80 column 25 row CGA-compatible LCD mono	2 AA alkaline	DOS, Lotus 1-2-3, cc:Mail Mobile, organizer software	
1 PCMCIA II		$1,599	7.8" STN mono	NiMH (2-4 hrs.)		
1 PCMCIA II		$2,299	8.4" STN LCD grayscale VGA	Li-Ion (4-8 hrs)	DOS, Windows, UltraFont, CommWorks for Windows	
1 PCMCIA II		$3,999	7.8" TFT-LCD color VGA, local bus	Li-Ion (3-6 hrs.)	DOS, Windows, UltraFont, CommWorks for Windows	
	1 year	$995	7.4" 640x480 grayscale	NiMH (2-4 hrs.)	DOS, Windows	Energy Star

continues

Table 6.10 Continued

Company, Model	CPU, Speed, Cache	Unit Size	Keyboard	Weight	RAM Incl., Max	Hard Disk, Floppy Drive	Adapters
ZEOS Contenda 386SL (alt. config.)	386SL, 25MHz	9.7" x 6.1"	80-key w/ trackball	3.9 lbs.	4M, 10M	80M, 3.5" 1.44M external	1 ser., 1 par., VGA
ZEOS Contenda 486SL	486SL, 25MHz	9.7" x 6.1"	80-key w/ trackball	3.9 lbs.	4M, 10M	80M	1 ser., 1 par., VGA
ZEOS Contenda 486SL (alt. config.)	486SL, 25MHz	9.7" x 6.1"	80-key w/ trackball	3.9 lbs.	4M, 10M	80M, 3.5" 1.44M external	1 ser., 1 par., VGA

Slots	Warranty	Price	Screen	Power, Battery Life, Recharge	Software	Other
	1 year	$1295	7.4" 640x480 grayscale	NiMH (2-4 hrs.)	DOS, Windows for Workgroups, Lotus Organizer	Energy Star
	1 year	$1395	7.4" 640x480 grayscale	NiMH (2-4 hrs.)	DOS, Windows	Energy Star
	1 year	$1695	7.4" 640x480 grayscale	NiMH (2-4 hrs.)	DOS, Windows for Workgroups, Lotus Organizer	Energy Star

CHAPTER SEVEN

Deciding What Kind of Video System You Need

Getting the right display system is one of the toughest choices you will make in computer-related buying. Your display system needs have a great deal of influence on the computer you buy. For portable systems, the type of display you want has a great effect on the price of the computer. For desktop computers, the display size, resolution, and number of colors displayed are all things you can choose when you buy a system, and then upgrade later. In either case, you may end up spending a great deal of time and money trying to get a display that works for your needs.

To make the right choices, you need to understand the basics of display technology and how they relate to the way you use your computer. This chapter contains information about display standards, monitor features, and how software choices determine monitor needs. Understanding the information in this chapter will make you a competent shopper for computer display systems.

The Video Display System

A few years ago, choosing a monitor for an IBM-compatible computer was relatively easy. You chose monochrome or color. If you were buying a Macintosh, the choice was even easier. You used the (monochrome) monitor built into the computer.

More recently, however, video display technology has experienced vast growth in entry-level and high-end products. The computer buyer must give more than passing consideration to the purchase of a display adapter and monitor because the number of choices has increased dramatically. You are also likely to revisit this choice as you get more experience with your system; everything from the monitor to the computer's microprocessor can be upgraded as a way to improve the video display.

As an added twist, many IBM-compatible computer manufacturers are now integrating the display adapter into the computer's main logic board and, at least to some degree, dictating what type of display you must purchase with the system. Most

Macintosh computers come with built-in video as a standard feature; in both cases, you can upgrade video by adding video memory or installing a different adapter.

There are also complicated interdependencies between the amount of video memory you have, the monitor's size and resolution, and the resolution and number of colors you can see on-screen. To make an informed decision as to what type of monitor to buy, you must keep these factors and others, including cost, in mind.

Before you can make a decision about what type of monitor you should purchase, you need to understand the two components that make up the video display portion of the personal computer system. The first of these components is the video adapter to which the monitor connects at the system unit. The second component is the monitor itself. The sections that follow discuss these components in detail.

The Video Adapter

The video adapter translates the video data produced by the CPU into electronic signals that are painted onto individual dots on the monitor. The physical design of the video adapter can vary greatly from one computer system to the next. Some of these adapters are cards that are installed in an expansion slot, but other adapters are integrated into the main logic board of the computer. More and more systems have one or more local bus slots, fast connectors that can run specially designed adapters at high speed. In any case, the adapter performs the same function; it acts as a channel of communication between the computer and the monitor.

With any monitor, the quality of the image displayed depends partly on the resolution of the video adapter to which it's connected. Today's video adapter is likely to support high-resolution text and color graphics and to be dedicated solely to the video interface function. If the adapter is built into the main logic board, you need only connect the monitor to the proper port on the system unit to activate your video display. If, however, the computer has no integrated video support, or if you want higher quality video than the integrated adapter provides, you must install an add-on video adapter in a standard or local-bus expansion slot before you connect a monitor.

Built-In vs. Add-On

More and more systems, both Macintoshes and IBM-compatibles, come with built-in video. Built-in video means that support for VGA or, more likely, Super VGA video—or, for the Mac, 13- or 16-inch monitors—is integrated into the motherboard. Built-in video tends to run slightly faster and be more reliable than an add-in video card of the same capabilities. Built-in video also adds a little bit to the cost of a system, but it's a good way to get started even if you upgrade later.

Built-in video should have 512K of RAM, which allows it to support 256 colors at the Super VGA resolution of 800 x 600. Being able to upgrade the video to 1M of RAM later is desirable, but don't forget that you usually can get a faster, add-in display adapter if you want to use more colors or higher resolutions later. Some systems don't allow you to disable the built-in video and add your own card, so if you might upgrade in the future, check with the manufacturer before you buy.

Some higher end systems may have video acceleration built in along with Super VGA support. This feature is great if it's cheap, but if it adds substantially to the cost of your system, you may have a problem. If you really need fast video, you will probably want to choose your own adapter and plug it into a local-bus slot, bypassing the built-in video support. If you have already paid extra for accelerated built-in video, and then bypassed it with a faster adapter, you are to some extent paying for the same functionality twice. Don't pay extra for accelerated built-in video unless you're sure that you won't need a further upgrade for awhile.

Portable systems have two kinds of video that you have to worry about. The first is support for the built-in screen; this video may be built-in motherboard video or local bus video. The second is support for an attached external monitor. If you're using the built-in screen exclusively, built-in video with as little as 256K of RAM may be sufficient. But if you plan to use an external monitor, you need the same 512K of RAM that a desktop system needs. Because it's hard or impossible to upgrade a portable's video adapter later, built-in acceleration and the capacity to upgrade to 1M of video RAM on the motherboard are very valuable features.

Local Bus

Local bus video is an offspring of built-in motherboard video. It uses a special controller chip to support extremely fast communications between the microprocessor and add-ons. These add-ons are mainly graphics cards, but they also include hard disk and even networking controllers.

The graphics card may be integrated into the motherboard, a small daughtercard, or a full-size add-in card plugged into an extra-long local bus slot. The first two options reduce the amount of space needed within your system for video support and are common in small footprint systems and portables. The third option, a full-size local bus add-in card, takes up a lot of space but also gives you a great deal of flexibility. The large amount of free space on the card makes it possible for the manufacturer to include advanced functionality, such as large amounts of video memory and support for multimedia.

For a portable system, consider local bus if you will have your portable hooked up to an external monitor a good part of the time. For a desktop system, the non-upgradable local bus options are probably fine for most users as long as they support up to 1M of RAM for video. Insist on a free local bus slot for a local bus video card if you anticipate that you will need very fast video, a very large screen (17 inches or more), or advanced functionality, such as multimedia.

Windows Accelerators

If you already own a desktop system and are frustrated by slow Windows performance, you may want to consider a Windows accelerator card. If your existing system is more than a year or so old, it's unlikely to have local bus support, so you will probably be looking for an ISA (Industry Standard Architecture) card to fit in a standard 16-bit slot.

You may, however, want to consider a few other options instead of, or in addition to, accelerated video. From least expensive to most expensive (and effective), your options for Windows acceleration include:

- *New drivers.* Most graphics card manufacturers have come out with new, faster Windows drivers to meet competitive demands. If your graphics card is more than a few months old, contact the manufacturer to see whether new drivers and utilities are available. These drivers and utilities are free, so make this step the first step in upgrading.

- *More memory.* If your computer has less than 8M of RAM, you may benefit from getting more system memory. Portable users can especially benefit because additional memory can help keep the hard disk from being accessed, saving battery life.

- *Windows accelerator card.* For desktop systems, especially those with slow video subsystems, a Windows accelerator card may provide a relatively cheap speed boost.

- *Faster hard disk.* If your hard disk light comes on frequently and you have sufficient RAM, you probably need a faster hard disk. For desktop system owners, this upgrade is expensive, but may be necessary. For portable users, upgrading may be too expensive to consider; check prices carefully before buying.

- *Microprocessor upgrade.* A microprocessor upgrade improves computation speed and directly benefits video performance, unless you have a graphics processor card. Intel Overdrive upgrades are a good idea; the effectiveness of other microprocessor upgrades depends on your system's overall configuration. If you're handy with the inner workings of your PC, you often can save money by replacing the entire motherboard with one that is more powerful, rather than just upgrading the processor.

- *New system.* The most effective way to accelerate Windows is to buy a new system with plenty of memory, a faster microprocessor and hard disk, and accelerated video. If you need a lot more performance than you're currently getting and your base system is less than a 486, consider trading up.

The Windows accelerator card market is currently kind of a mess. It's hard to predict how well a given accelerator card will work in a given system; it may not work at all, or it may do little to speed up the system. The most expensive card may be the one that does the least for your computer.

Video Adapter Memory

A video adapter must have built-in memory to remember how the image on-screen looks. The greater the complexity of the image you display, the more memory is required. More colors require more memory, and more resolution also requires more memory.

The basic video adapter today contains 256K of memory. This amount is enough to display 640 x 480 resolution with 16 colors (the original VGA standard) or even 800 x 600 (middle-of-the-road Super VGA resolution) with 16 colors. These resolutions are adequate if you only work with text.

If, however, you want to run graphics programs, you need at least 512K of video memory, which is just enough to display 800 x 600 resolution with 256 colors. Almost all current monitors can handle this resolution and number of colors. Higher resolution adapters that display more than 256 colors require even more memory, such as 1M or even 2M; such adapters usually include acceleration as well.

If you are considering buying a video system that uses special, fast video memory (VRAM) instead of the same slower, standard DRAM used by the computer as a whole, watch out for the terms "video memory" and "video RAM." These terms are often used to describe display adapters that actually use DRAMs. Ask if you're unsure what's in a specific product; because it's faster, true VRAM usually means higher performance and a higher price.

Video Memory Math

If you want to be able to determine what resolution and number of colors can be supported by a given amount of video memory, read this section; otherwise, you can skip it. The numbers in tables 7.1 and 7.2 contain the information that most people need to know, but knowing the math behind them is interesting and sometimes helpful.

To determine the number of bytes of video memory needed to support a given monitor resolution and number of colors, follow these steps:

1. Multiply the horizontal resolution by the vertical resolution to get the number of pixels on-screen. For instance, 800 x 600 resolution equals 480,000 pixels.

2. Adjust for the number of colors to be displayed. Monochrome displays require one bit per pixel; 16 colors or grays require 4 bits per pixel; 256 colors require 8 bits per pixel; 32,768 colors require 15 bits per pixel; 65,536 colors require 16 bits per pixel; 16,777,216 colors (true color) require 24 bits per pixel. For instance, 800 x 600 resolution with 256 colors requires 3,840,000 bits.

3. Divide the number of bits by 8 to get the number of bytes of video memory to support the given resolution and number of colors. For instance, a 256-color 800 x 600 display requires 480,000 bytes of memory.

4. Divide the number of bytes by 1,024 to get the number of kilobytes, or K, of memory required. For example, a 256-color, 800 x 600 display requires about 469K.

5. Round up to the nearest multiple of 256K. If the result is less than 256K, then a 256K card can support the desired resolution and number of colors. Otherwise, you will need 512K, 1,024K, or a larger amount of memory on your card to support the display quality you desire.

When you become more familiar with the math, a shorthand way of doing the same thing is to think in terms of bytes. Multiply the horizontal by the vertical resolution to get the number of pixels. This amount is the number of bytes of video memory you need to display 256 colors. Divide by 8 to get the number of bytes needed to display in monochrome; divide by 2 for 16 colors. Multiply by 2 for high color, either 32K or 64K colors; multiply by 3 for 24-bit true color.

The Monitor

The second component of the video system on your personal computer is the display, or monitor. This device evolved from the cathode ray tube (CRT) technology commonly used in televisions. It hasn't evolved all that much, however. Because TV makers have already wrung all the price/performance they can out of video technology, the price/performance ratio for monitors improves much more slowly than that for other components of the computer. For instance, an 80486 microprocessor is over 30 times faster than the ancient 8086, but a current 13-inch display monitor has only about double the resolution of the same monitor from 10 years ago, and its weight and power consumption are about the same.

Desktop computer displays vary in size from 9 to 21 inches, which is a diagonal measurement of the screen—not necessarily the size of its image. The same-size screen may be called 13-inch by one vendor and 14-inch by another; don't be afraid to check with your own ruler. A measurement of 13 or 14 inches is typical for a color monitor that comes with a basic computer system. 15- to 17-inch screens, though large and heavy, are becoming common for use with graphical user interfaces, and 20- or 21-inch screens, often gray-scale rather than color, are used for programming, non-color desktop publishing, and other demanding work.

Portable computers typically have a smaller screen size and lower resolution. 9- or 10-inch screens are most common. A smaller screen doesn't work well for general personal computing, though it may be useful for task-specific work such as personal information management. A larger screen imposes too much size, weight, and power consumption overhead.

Features common to most desktop systems' monitors include a tilt-swivel base that enables the user to adjust the viewing angle and a screen that is either etched or coated to reduce glare. A 9- or 15-pin data cable connects the monitor to the video adapter at the rear of the CPU. Power for the monitor comes from either the power supply on the system unit or from the monitor's own power cord that plugs into the wall or a surge protector.

Controls on the monitor usually include a power switch and adjustments for brightness, contrast, horizontal and vertical size, and horizontal and vertical positioning. Controls for adjusting the horizontal and vertical size and position of the picture are especially important because the picture may need to be centered or increased in size when you switch from text to graphics mode or from one resolution to another.

Monitors come in one of three general types: monochrome, gray-scale, or color. Monochrome means one color, generally white, green, or amber, with a black background. (Paper-white monitors, such as those used with the Macintosh, display black on a white background.) Monochrome monitors are now rare except on some portables. Gray-scale monitors use various intensities of a single color to give the appearance of shades on the monitor (typically 16 shades of gray). VGA gray-scale monitors are popular for non-color desktop publishing, mostly because they are less expensive than unnecessary color monitors. Color monitors enable you to display at least 16 colors on-screen. Higher capability adapters enable you to display from 256 colors into the millions.

Resolution

High resolution on a small screen means a crisp picture but smaller text characters. Although many video systems now come with larger fonts that look good at 800 x 600 resolution on a small (13- or 14-inch) monitor, consider buying a larger monitor for higher resolutions. Table 7.1 shows the most comfortable screen sizes for working with text at various resolutions.

Table 7.1	Recommended Screen Size vs. Resolution	
Resolution	*Screen Size*	*Comments*
640 x 480	13 or 14 inches	You can run higher resolutions on most of these monitors, but you will squint to read text in standard font sizes.
800 x 600	15 to 17 inches	These monitors are big, heavy, and power-hungry, but this size is the new standard for Windows or Macintosh work.
1,024 x 768	17 to 21 inches	For CAD graphics and desktop publishing, bigger and faster are better. If you do much writing, there's nothing like a 20- or 21-inch two-page gray-scale display.

Some specialized monitors have different resolutions than those listed here. *Full-page* or *portrait* monitors are taller than they are wide, so they may use resolutions like 640 x 870. *Two-page* monitors are designed to show a much larger work space, so they may have resolutions like 1,360 x 1,024.

Portable computer displays sometimes have a 640 x 400 display, which is slightly smaller than the base VGA standard of 640 x 480. This resolution allows them to support up to 16 gray scales or colors with only 128K of video memory, or 256 colors with only 256K. However, a full 640 x 480 screen looks more normal, especially when working with text in a graphical user interface environment. Also, a portable that can support 640 x 480 on its internal screen can probably support 640 x 480, or even 800 x 600, on an externally attached monitor—an important consideration if you want to use this kind of setup some of the time. Ask carefully about both the resolution of the built-in screen and external video support capabilities before buying a portable.

Dot Pitch

An important unit of measurement is the size of the pixel, which is called the *dot pitch*. A pixel is measured in millimeters. You may see advertised a monitor with a dot pitch of 0.31, or you may see another advertisement for a monitor with a dot pitch of 0.28. These numbers may seem small, but you can see a world of difference between their respective monitors. For the sharpest quality, select the smallest dot pitch. Remember, however, that a smaller dot pitch comes with a higher price. You have to weigh the two factors and come up with the best solution for your needs. For most purposes, however, select a monitor that has a dot pitch no greater than 0.28.

Following are dot pitch recommendations for different purposes:

- For VGA text resolution of 640 x 480, a dot pitch of 0.31 or smaller is acceptable.
- For Super VGA graphics (800 x 600) or 1,024 x 768, use a dot pitch of 0.28 or smaller.
- For precise resolutions of 1,024 x 768 or greater, use a dot pitch of 0.26 or smaller.

Scan Rate

A more technical specification of a monitor is the *scan rate*. Scanning is done to update, or *refresh*, the monitor. (If the displayed image is not refreshed, the screen quickly goes blank, as you see when you turn off your television.) Each line on-screen is scanned and refreshed, from top to bottom, several times a second. If, for example, your monitor has 480 lines (640 x 480 resolution), each of the 480 lines is scanned.

Scan rates are measured in hertz (Hz), or cycles per second. At 60 Hz, a common scan rate, the monitor reads video memory and updates the display 60 times a second. 60 Hz is the minimum scan rate that you should accept for a monitor. Lower scan rates cause the monitor to flicker, which leads to a great deal of eye fatigue. Most people experience only moderate eye fatigue at 60 Hz, and little eye fatigue at higher scan rates. Although the 60 Hz speed is common, better monitors now have a scan rate of 70 Hz or more.

Higher resolution means more work to support a given scan rate. In order to cut costs, some high-resolution monitors are manufactured using a method called *interlaced* scanning. This term means that only every other line is scanned on one complete pass. On the next pass, the lines that were missed are updated. This method makes a monitor cheaper to manufacture because it can do only half of the work and maintain its scan rate.

This technology works, but interlaced scanning also causes a noticeable flickering effect. Although the flickering does not bother some people, many people are sensitive to it. You can avoid this flickering by purchasing a more expensive *noninterlaced* monitor. On a noninterlaced monitor, the scanning is very fast, and the screen is updated in the usual manner.

Most monitors today are *multiscanning* or *multisynchronous* monitors. These monitors generally support video display adapters of several different resolution ratings. A multi-scanning monitor can detect when a resolution changes and adjust the scan rate accordingly. A multi-scanning monitor is more of a multipurpose monitor because of its capability to accommodate multiple scan rates. As usual, the price reflects this extra capability.

Some multiscanning monitors offer a 72 Hz scan rate at all resolutions; others offer high scan rates at lower resolutions and fall back to lower scan rates at higher ones. For your eyes' sake, make sure that the monitor you buy supports 70 Hz scanning or better at all the resolutions you plan to use frequently.

Types of Portable Screens

Displays for portable computers are limited by the need to draw less power than desktop screens and the need to use LCD (liquid crystal display) rather than CRT (cathode ray tube) technology. The flatness of LCD screens makes them a necessity for portable use.

The most important features in portable screens are described briefly in the following list. Note that all the features that increase quality also increase price and decrease battery life, so a better screen hits you with a double whammy.

- *Size.* A 9-inch screen is standard for portables; 10 inches or a little more is a big help. Anything smaller than 9 inches isn't really suitable for general computer-type use.

- *Resolution.* 640 x 480, the base VGA standard, is a necessity if you want to be able to run your office software acceptably on the road or hook up an external monitor with good results.

- *Passive vs. Active Matrix.* Despite its higher price and power consumption, look for an active-matrix screen, which is brighter than a passive-matrix screen. Even the best passive-matrix screen is just too hard on your eyes, and active-matrix screens have become affordable.

- *Monochrome vs. Gray-scale.* Look for a unit with 16 gray scales; Windows can look surprisingly good on a top-notch gray-scale screen. Consider monochrome only for a single, text-heavy DOS or Windows application.
- *Color.* Color is still very expensive and limited in portables. Compromises to get affordable color with acceptable battery life include small screens (8 inches or so), passive-matrix instead of active-matrix screens, and only 16 (rather than 256) colors.

> **Portable Display Standards: Under the Hood**
>
> As you look at advertisements for portable computers, you will see the entire alphabet soup of portable display technology—LCD, STN, PMLCD, AMLCD, and more. Take heart. They're simple to decode once you know the language.
>
> Desktop computers, for the most part, use cathode ray tube-based monitors. Because laptop, notebook and subnotebook computers cannot use a CRT without drastically increasing their size and weight, they have to use FPDs (flat panel displays). Both FPDs and CRTs use electronics to light up the individual pixels on the screen, but FPDs use several different methods. LCD is by far the most common, with several variations; and gas plasma is in the running.
>
> Whenever you see *LCD* as part of the display's name, it means the display uses liquid crystal technology, like a digital watch. LCD displays are quite common, and relatively inexpensive. Two variations you see are *AMLCD* (active matrix LCD) and *PMLCD* (passive matrix LCD). With *passive matrix* LCD, the horizontal lines on the screen are each electrically charged on every *pass* (one pass means each line on the screen has been charged once, in sequence from top to bottom, and a new pass can begin). To light up individual pixels within the horizontal line, charges are applied to corresponding vertical lines. Wherever the charged lines intersect, a pixel lights up for a very short time. Because the pixel stays lit for such a short period and cannot be re-lit until the next pass, passive matrix screens tend to flicker a little. *Active matrix* LCD, on the other hand, makes each pixel addressable, using much less power and eliminating the flicker effect found in passive matrix screens.
>
> *STN* stands for "Supertwist-nematic," which is usually shortened to just "Supertwist." Displays with Supertwist technology are able to illuminate each pixel for a longer time than normal, which reduces flicker.
>
> *Gas plasma* displays are able to electronically change the state of gases at each pixel location, which makes the gases light up. Unlike LCD, gas plasma pixels stay lit until they are turned off, which makes them ideal for large screens like presentation panels. Early gas plasma screens gave off a distinctive red-orange glow, but some companies are developing color and grayscale versions.

You can probably get a sharp, bright gray-scale screen with VGA resolution at a reasonable price. Color is what's going to cost you; expect to pay top dollar for a system with a decent color screen. Unless you can pay the big bucks for an active-matrix color screen, stick with an active-matrix gray-scale screen over passive-matrix color; your eyes will thank you.

Display Standards

Makers of video adapters and monitors have a great number of choices to make in designing video subsystems that are affordable and compatible while meeting buyers' demands for ever-greater performance. The fact that video adapter makers are usually not the same companies that manufacture monitors makes this wide range of possibilities even more complicated. To bridge this gap, a series of progressively more capable video standards have evolved. These standards are described in the following sections.

Obsolete IBM-Compatible Standards

For many years, monitor standards in the IBM-compatible market were set almost single-handedly by IBM. (The Hercules graphics standard is one important exception.) If you are using an older system or considering buying a used one, you may need to know about these standards. Here are capsule descriptions of the important standards that shaped the evolution of IBM-compatible display technology:

- *MDA.* IBM developed the MDA (Monochrome Display Adapter) standard for the first generation IBM PC. It supports high-resolution text, with each character cell being 9 x 14 pixels in size (720 x 350, a better horizontal resolution than VGA), but it does not support graphics.

- *Hercules graphics.* A third-party manufacturer, Hercules Computer, recognized the shortcomings of the MDA and developed an improved monochrome adapter that supported high-resolution graphics (720 x 348) as well as text. The adapter, known as the Hercules Graphics Card, soon became the monochrome standard.

- *CGA.* The CGA (Color Graphics Adapter) standard was the first color standard developed by IBM for the PC. CGA supports 25 lines by 80 columns and up to 8 colors in text mode. The graphics mode can display a mere 4 colors simultaneously from a palette of 16 colors at a resolution of 320 x 200. Some 640 x 400 portable screens can only handle CGA graphics, which are shown at double resolution.

- *EGA.* The EGA (Enhanced Graphics Adapter) standard was the second-generation color standard developed for the PC. In text mode, EGA supports 80 columns and up to 16 colors simultaneously. The graphics mode is capable of displaying up to 16 colors simultaneously from a palette of 64 at a maximum resolution of 640 x 350. EGA is also downwardly compatible, so EGA supports software written for CGA and MDA.

- *MCGA.* IBM developed another color standard, MCGA (Multi-Color Graphics Array) for the first entry-level PS/2 systems. MCGA draws features from both CGA and EGA, supporting software drivers for both and switching automatically to the one currently in use. MCGA never caught on outside the PS/2 line.

Current IBM-Compatible Display Standards

Today, the IBM-compatible standard is a somewhat of a misnomer for graphics. Although IBM developed today's base-level display standard, VGA, for use in its PS/2 line, the succeeding graphics standards have been developed by others.

The Super VGA standard, which has come to encompass several resolutions, was put together by VESA, the Video Electronics Standards Association. This group of display adapter makers, monitor manufacturers, and others was formed to address the many incompatible enhancements that were being made to the VGA standard, and it has succeeded admirably.

Today's major display standards are described in the following list:

- *VGA.* IBM originally developed the VGA (Video Graphics Array) standard for the PS/2 line, but many other manufacturers have improved upon it. The base VGA standard supports graphics in 16 colors at a resolution of 640 x 480. The text mode has a resolution of 720 x 400, but most text today is displayed in graphics mode for a more accurate display. VGA is now the mainstream standard for portable machines.

- *Super VGA.* A new standard, Super VGA, has resulted from improvements to VGA standardized by VESA. Super VGA can display images at two resolutions greater than standard VGA (sometimes called the extended VGA standard): 800 x 600 and 1,024 x 768. Super VGA is now the mainstream standard for desktop machines.

- *8514/A.* Technically, Super VGA has only the 800 x 600 resolution. Resolution of 1,024 x 768, according to IBM, is specific to the 8514/A standard. Most vendors, however, call both resolutions "Super VGA."

- *XGA.* IBM's XGA (Extended Graphics Array) standard is an extension of VGA that supports resolutions up to 1,280 x 1,024. What is even more impressive is XGA's capability to display as many as 32,768 colors on-screen at once. Neither XGA nor the faster XGA/2 have caught on yet, and their success doesn't look likely. The failure of these standards to become widely accepted marks the end of IBM's capability to single-handedly set graphics standards.

Table 7.2 lists the modes that usually are supported by VGA and Super VGA cards with different amounts of memory. (In the table, 640 x 480/16 means that the resolution is 640 x 480, with 16 colors supported.)

Table 7.2 Resolutions and Colors Supported by VGA and Super VGA Cards with Varying Amounts of Memory

Resolution/Color	VGA 256K	Super VGA 512K	Super VGA 1,024 K
640 x 480/16	✔	✔	✔
640 x 480/256	✔	✔	✔
800 x 600/16	✔	✔	✔
800 x 600/256	–	✔	✔
800 x 600/32,768	–	✔	✔
1,024 x 768/16	–	✔	✔
1,024 x 768/256	–	–	✔
1,280 x 1,024/16	–	–	✔
1,280 x 1,024/256	–	–	–

For companies to remain compatible with video standards, video *chip sets* have been developed. A chip set is a custom set of integrated circuit chips that emulates a standard, most commonly VGA or Super VGA. Many companies make video adapters, but fewer manufacturers make chip sets. You may find, therefore, that several manufacturers' boards use the same chip set. Different adapters using the same chip set often have similar performance.

Macintosh Display Standards

Because Apple has much more control over the Macintosh than any one company has over IBM-compatibles, it does not have display standards in the same way. Macintosh video is classified by display resolution in pixels and the number of colors that can be displayed. The original Macintosh had built-in adapter circuitry and a 9-inch monochrome monitor. This size monitor is still standard on the Macintosh Classic line of computers and is also used in the PowerBook line of Macintosh portables.

The rest of the Macintosh line, however, is modular in design, meaning that the monitor is separate from the computer. These computers can support different resolutions and types of monitors, including monochrome, gray-scale, and 4-, 8-, 16-, and 24-bit color (refer to the section "Video Memory Math" earlier in this chapter for details). Some Macintosh users favor a portrait monitor, which is taller than it is wide. Most portrait screens are about the size of a single sheet of paper. Table 7.3 lists the major Macintosh video resolutions and color depths and the amount of memory needed to support each. (In the table, 640 x 480/16 means that the resolution is 640 x 480, with 16 colors supported.)

Table 7.3 Resolutions and Colors Supported by Macintosh Video Cards and On-Board Video with Varying Amounts of Memory

Resolution	Apple monitor	Minimum memory
512 x 384/mono	Classic II built-in	32K
512 x 384/256	Color Classic II built-in	128K
640 x 480/16	14-inch monitor	256K
640 x 480/256	14-inch monitor	512K
640 x 480/millions	14-inch monitor	1M
640 x 870/16	Portrait monitor	256K (with compression)
640 x 870/256	Portrait monitor	1M
832 x 624/256	16-inch monitor	512K
832 x 624/millions	16-inch monitor	2M
1,152 x 870/16	2-page display	512K
1,152 x 870/256	2-page display	1M
1,152 x 870/millions	2-page display	2M

Most desktop Macs now come with built-in video support and 512K of video memory to support 256 colors at resolutions up to 832 x 624, the base resolution of Apple's 10-inch monitor. This resolution and number of colors can just barely be supported by 512K of video memory. Because the Mac is popular for high-end graphics applications, you can add additional memory, up to 1M or even 2M worth, to the built-in video in higher-end Macs. (2M is enough to support 24-bit true color on a 21-inch, two-page display.) There is also a wide variety of add-on graphics adapters to choose from, but there is not at this time anything like a unified local bus standard in the Macintosh world.

Apple usually sells monitors that support only one resolution. The standard Apple 14-inch monitor supports only 640 x 480 resolution, whereas most IBM-compatibles also can display 800 x 600 resolution. When this chapter refers to needing Super VGA graphics for a specific task, you need a 16-inch Apple monitor, not the more common 14-inch Apple monitor, or a third-party solution to get this higher resolution.

Portable Macs usually have top-quality screens. The newer PowerBooks support video-out as well as sharp built-in screens. Watch out for PowerBooks with passive-matrix color screens, though; they don't live up to what Macintosh users are used to. Stick with monochrome or gray-scale, or go whole-hog and buy a PowerBook with a sharp active-matrix color screen.

Software Drivers

One of the most difficult issues in using various screen resolutions and color depths is the issue of software drivers. Under DOS, each software program needs its own driver to support a specific resolution. (The driver may be built into the program or be separate from the program.)

Using Windows or the Mac, a single driver suffices for all programs because the individual programs send their graphics commands to the system software, and the system software handles all writing to the screen. This two-step process slows performance but greatly increases flexibility. The Macintosh offers the ultimate in such flexibility: you can easily set up a Mac to support two monitors at once. With such a setup (and with no special software for the system, let alone for individual programs), you can easily move program windows from one screen to another or even allow them to rest partly on one screen and partly on the other.

Getting the right drivers can make a big difference in performance and compatibility. On a DOS or Windows system, users often have to reboot to get from one resolution or color depth to another. Mac systems can change color depth without a reboot, but they need a reboot to change resolutions.

DOS and Windows systems also impose difficulties in getting drivers to work together correctly. Successive software installations change the CONFIG.SYS, AUTOEXEC.BAT, Windows setup files (SYSTEM.INI, WIN.INI, and so on), and other system files in different and contradictory ways. Windows users in particular have grown accustomed to re-installing Windows, software drivers, and applications when things get too confusing. This kind of problem is just a fact of Windows life that is unavoidable at this point.

What To Look for in a Monitor

In discussing the differences between adapters and monitors, this chapter has touched on many of the most important differences between monitors. The following list summarizes some key tips:

- *Size*. The bigger the monitor, the more you can get out of your system, but balance size against resolution, cost, weight, and the amount of desk space the monitor takes up.

- *Dot pitch.* Look for a dot pitch of .28 for middle-of-the-road monitors. A smaller dot pitch is necessary for demanding applications and the highest resolutions.

- *Resolutions.* Most monitors today support several resolutions. In the IBM-compatible world, 640 x 480 and 800 x 600 are a necessity; 1,024 x 768 is nice for some uses. Apple's Macintosh monitors are often single-resolution; consider a competitor that may offer multiple resolutions for the same price.

- *Image quality.* There are a lot of highly technical ways to measure image quality, but the best method is to trust your eyes. Put several images on-screen and look for bending, warping, differences in color, and so on. Make sure that you can return the monitor for a full refund when you buy it so that you can test it before committing.

- *Refresh rate.* Although 60 Hz is acceptable, look for a 70 Hz refresh rate at the resolutions you will use frequently. (A 60 Hz refresh rate at 1,024 x 768 is adequate if you don't use that resolution much.)

- *Low-frequency emissions.* There is a lot of concern about possible health problems resulting from color screen radiation, especially when used by pregnant women. Though there is not yet solid proof of problems, many monitors now meet tough Swedish standards for low emissions. Look for conformance to these standards if you're concerned.

- *Controls.* Look for a monitor with controls on the front of the display. These controls should include a power switch and controls for brightness, contrast, and horizontal and vertical size and positioning.

- *Price.* Different manufacturers may sell the same monitor for substantially different prices. Start by looking at a top-notch monitor that meets your size and resolution criteria, such as one in the NEC Multisync line, to set a starting price. Then see whether you can get the comparable quality at a lower price.

The Right Video System for You

When determining which monitor is right for you, start by evaluating your software needs. After you have selected the software, match the hardware components to the program requirements to achieve the maximum performance that your budget allows. For an IBM-compatible desktop system, a local bus Super VGA display adapter and a monitor that can support an 800 x 600 resolution and at least 256 colors are fast becoming the accepted minimum. For the Macintosh, 640 x 480 resolution and 256 colors are a reasonable starting point. For a portable system, 640 x 480 resolution and 16 gray scales or colors are adequate.

Selecting the proper display adapter and monitor for the task can increase productivity greatly and enhance the perceived value of owning a computer. The following sections offer information about various types of software to help you see which factors you need to consider for each software type. Keep in mind that the quality of the display system may affect how happy you are with your computer more than any other single factor.

- *GUIs.* Using a graphical user interface makes you want a larger screen. A monitor with a 15- to 17-inch screen, though large, heavy, and expensive, enables you to use 800 x 600 resolution with good text readability or even 1,024 x 768 resolution with so-so readability. You need local bus or some other form of video acceleration if you go beyond 800 x 600 resolution with 16 colors. For the Macintosh, look for built-in fast video and a 16-inch screen.

- *Word processing.* For serious word processing or desktop publishing, you want a full-page display or a two-page display. Although you may have to settle for gray-scale instead of color in order to be able to afford the larger screen size, it's worth it.

- *Desktop publishing.* Much of what used to be called desktop publishing has been absorbed by word processing. Desktop publishing now refers to highly demanding publications with lots of graphics and color. Most professional desktop publishers use 17- to 21-inch monitors. For color desktop publishing, you need a big, expensive monitor with color matching. Consult with other experienced desktop publishers before making a purchase decision.

- *Spreadsheets.* For spreadsheets, you want as big a screen as possible to display lots of rows and columns, but you also want color for graphs. A good tradeoff is the Radius Pivot and similar monitors which are full-page displays that can be flipped horizontally to display more columns of a spreadsheet. Another good tradeoff is a color screen in the 15- to 17-inch range.

- *Databases.* Database software can be used for so many things now that its monitor needs are hard to pin down. For simple database queries, a small screen is fine. For forms design, you may want a full-page or two-page display with 16 gray scales. If you also generate charts, you want color.

- *Communications.* The best and easiest-to-use communications programs on IBM-compatibles are Windows programs. Macintosh communications programs are also good. In either case, a standard-size monitor should be sufficient.

- *Multimedia.* A small screen may be OK for multimedia because most motion video and animation shows up in small screens anyway, but be sure to get local bus or other accelerated video.

- *Graphics.* You need a big screen, lots of colors, and acceleration for graphics work.

- *Games and education.* Games can be among the most demanding computer programs. Give serious consideration to a Sega or Super Nintendo system, possibly with a CD-ROM drive, for game playing before you spend thousands on a computer that can handle the newest games. A basic Super VGA color system should be enough to handle many games and most education programs.

Chapter Summary

This chapter introduces the most important technical considerations that differentiate display systems. It also describes the various video standards available for both IBM-compatible and Macintosh computers. Additionally, the chapter discusses what monitors work best within specific software environments.

IN THE NEXT CHAPTER

The next chapter consists of listings of display adapters, monitors, and adapter-monitor combinations from major manufacturers. Use it to help you make purchasing decisions relating to the monitor.

CHAPTER EIGHT

Listing of Monitors and Adapters

Buying a monitor or a video adapter is becoming more complicated. With the growing popularity of Windows and the Macintosh, video performance is becoming a greater and greater priority. Multitasking systems and demanding applications like desktop publishing make larger screens a necessity. System vendors are increasingly building in faster video and including a monitor in the price of a system, but there is also growing interest in add-on purchases for existing systems.

The information in the previous chapter should help you focus on what you want, need, and can afford in a video system. For instance, you need to find out whether the video adapter that's already built into your system's motherboard or plugged into an expansion slot is fast enough and capable enough to drive the kind of monitor you want. Then you need to decide on the size of the monitor and the resolutions you want it to support. Finally, you need to look at some monitors to see which ones look good to you. Then use the tables in this chapter to help identify the monitor and/or adapter that you need.

The tables cover small monitors (up to 14 inches), mid-size monitors (15 to 17 inches), and large monitors (19 inches and above), plus graphics adapters for IBM-compatibles and for the Macintosh. The division of monitors by size allows you to quickly move to the size of monitor that you want to learn more about. Macintosh and IBM-compatible monitors are mixed in together because some Macs now have VGA adapters, and many monitors can work with both standard Mac adapters and IBM-compatibles. The monitor tables are sorted by screen size, monochrome vs. color, and price. The smaller, bare-bones monitors are listed first; move down into the table until you reach the area where the combination of screen size, price, and features matches your needs.

The graphics adapter tables are sorted by maximum resolution and by company name. This method of organization allows you to look at the adapter with the resolution you need, and then compare models within and between manufacturers to find the right one for you. Adapters with multimedia capabilities are a specialized area and are not included in the table.

As with all the tables in this book, the monitor and adapter tables cover a mix of products that is rapidly changing as new models are introduced and old ones pulled from the market. Prices are adjusted continuously. Use these tables to identify several products that meet your needs, and then call around for availability and current pricing for these products. The trade magazines regularly review video-related products, so keep an eye on them for comparative performance information.

Each of the tables is introduced in the following sections. The first section describes most of the fields for all the tables. The specific sections for each table describe different fields or additional considerations.

Fields for Monitor Tables

The following descriptions apply to all the monitor tables. Look in the descriptions of each table for information specific to that table.

- *Company, Model.* Use this information to find out more about the product by calling the company or a dealer. NEC monitors are probably the highest rated overall, but Sony is also well-regarded. Monitor makers often put their own names on products from other manufacturers, however, so don't count too much on a brand name.

- *Size (Diagonal); Color/Mono.* The same screen may be called a 13-inch monitor by one manufacturer and a 14-inch monitor by another. Ignore small differences in diagonal size until you get to see the monitor.

- *Resolution.* Working at 1,024 x 768 resolution on a 14-inch or smaller monitor makes it very difficult to read text, but you may want this resolution for preview modes or graphics work. If you plan to use this resolution, get a monitor that can display it without interlacing.

- *Dot Pitch.* Try to stick with monitors that have a dot pitch of .28mm or smaller; this size gives a denser, easier to read display.

- *Max Vert. Refresh Rate.* This number is becoming important; a refresh rate of 70 Hz or more is said to be easier on the eyes. Check whether the monitor you want has a high refresh rate at the resolutions you plan to use most.

- *Compatibility.* Monitors that are IBM PC-compatible work with SuperVGA adapters and VGA adapters, which are the standard for IBM-compatible systems and even some Macintoshes.

- *Warranty.* If you buy your monitor mail-order, make sure to check who's responsible for shipping costs in the event of a problem; monitors are big, heavy, and expensive to ship.

- *Price.* As noted previously, prices are being adjusted constantly. Call the manufacturer or a dealer for current pricing.

- *Other.* Flat screens are preferred by many users; the picture seems sharper. Paper-white phosphors on monochrome monitors produce a reversed image that looks like black type on white paper. A tilt-swivel base is a nice extra to get with your monitor if you don't already own a suitable one.

Table 8.1 Small Monitors Sorted by Screen Size, Resolution, and Manufacturer

This table includes small (up to 14 inches) monochrome and color monitors. It's sorted by ascending screen size, with smaller monitors first and monochrome monitors preceding color ones.

These monitors are big enough for using DOS, or for focusing on one Windows or Mac application at a time, but are uncomfortably small for general use with Windows or the Macintosh. Despite this limitation, these inexpensive, less-bulky monitors are very popular. However, unless price or small overall size is your primary criterion, look for a medium-sized monitor for use with Windows or the Mac.

Here are some things to remember when choosing a small monitor:

- *Size (Diagonal); Color/Mono.* Many 14-inch monitors are no larger than 13-inch ones; look at the resolution and dot pitch to decide what's best for you.

- *Resolution.* You may be able to save a few bucks by getting a monitor that has to use interlacing to display at 1,024 x 768 if you won't use this very dense resolution much. Otherwise, look for a non-interlaced monitor. Don't spend the extra money for 1,280 x 1,024 resolution in this size monitor unless you plan to do CAD or graphics work.

- *Dot Pitch.* Many small monitors have large dot sizes, but try to stick with monitors that have a dot pitch of .28mm or smaller; this size allows a denser, easier-to-read display.

- *Price.* If you can spend more than $600, consider a 15- or 16-inch monitor.

Table 8.1 Small Monitors Sorted by Screen Size, Resolution, and Manufacturer

Company, Model	Size (Diagonal); Color/Mono.	Resolution	Dot Pitch
Amdek AM/432E	14"; mono	640x480	N/A
Amdek AM/732E	14"; color	800x600 (1024x768 interlaced)	.28mm
Amdek AM/732NI	14"; color	1024x768 (non-interlaced)	.28mm
Amdek AM/815E	15"; color	1280x1024 (non-interlaced)	.28mm
Apple AudioVision 14 Display	14"; color	640x480	.26mm
Apple Color Plus	14"; color	640x480	.28mm
Macintosh Color Display	14"; color	640x480	.26mm
Value Leader			
MAG DX15F	15"; color	up to 1280x1024 (non-interlaced)	.28mm
MAG LineaXync	14"; color	up to 1024x768 (non-interlaced)	.28mm
MAG MXE15F	15"; color	up to 1280x1024 (non-interlaced)	.28mm
Value Leader			
Mitsubishi Diamond Pro SVGA	14"; color	800x600 (non-interlaced)	
Mitsubishi Diamond Scan 15FS	15"; color	1024x768 (non-interlaced)	
NEC MultiSync 3FGE	15"; color	up to 1024x768 (non-interlaced)	.28mm

Max Vert. Refresh Rate	Compatibility	Warranty	Price	Other
60-70Hz	PC-compatibles or Macs with VGA	1 year, parts and labor	$199	Flat square, non-glare screen
56, 60, 70Hz	PC-compatibles or Macs with VGA	1 year, parts and labor	$359	Non-glare screen
50-70Hz	PC-compatibles or Macs with VGA	1 year, parts and labor	$379	Non-glare screen
55-90Hz	PC-compatibles or Macs with VGA	1 year, parts and labor	$499	Flat square, non-glare screen
66.7Hz	Mac (specifically Quadra 660AV and 840AV)	1 year	$729	Two built-in speakers, built-in microphone, two ADB ports, sound input, head-phone and microphone ports, Energy Star
67Hz	Mac	1 year	$315	Energy Star
66.7Hz	Mac	1 year	$539	Energy Star
50-100Hz	PC, Mac	1 year (2 on CRT)	$449	Energy Star
50-100Hz	PC	1 year (2 on CRT)	$379	Energy Star
50-100Hz	PC, Mac	1 year (2 on CRT)	$699	Flat square, Energy Star
60Hz	PC, Mac	3 years	$360	
60Hz	PC, Mac	3 years	$469	
90Hz	PC, Mac	3 years	$595	Flat square screen

continues

Table 8.1 Continued

Company, Model	Size (Diagonal); Color/Mono.	Resolution	Dot Pitch
NEC MultiSync 3V	15"; color	up to 1024x768 (non-interlaced)	.28mm
NEC MultiSync 4FGE	15"; color	up to 1024x768 (non-interlaced)	.28mm
Radius Full Page Display/gs	15"; gray-scale	640x870 (non-interlaced)	
Radius Precision-Color Pivot	15"; color	up to 1024x768 (non-interlaced)	.28mm
RasterOps ClearVue /15 Portrait Display	15"; gray-scale	640x480 (non-interlaced)	.28mm
ViewSonic 15	15"; color	1280x1024 (non-interlaced)	.27mm

Table 8.2 Medium Monitors Sorted by Screen Size, Resolution, and Manufacturer

This table includes medium-size (15, 16, and 17 inches) monochrome and color monitors. It's sorted by ascending screen size, with smaller monitors first and monochrome monitors preceding color ones.

These monitors are a very comfortable size for general use of Windows or the Mac (although you may have to rearrange your workspace—they're too heavy to sit on top of the computer). They show text well at 800 x 600 resolution, but are somewhat cramped at 1,024 x 768. You need a video adapter with at least 512K of memory to get 16 colors at 1,024 x 768 and 256 colors at 800 x 600.

It's a good idea to spend the extra money for this size monitor over a small one. If you do a lot of writing or desktop publishing, however, consider a large monitor, 19" and up; you may need to get a monochrome or grayscale monitor rather than a color monitor to keep the price down.

Max Vert. Refresh Rate	Compatibility	Warranty	Price	Other
90Hz	PC, Mac	3 years	$495	Flat square screen
90Hz	PC, Mac	3 years	$655	Flat square screen
75Hz	Mac		$599	Full-page portrait display, Energy Star
50-90Hz	Mac		$999	Pivots to portrait or 2-page landscape orientation
75Hz	PC, Mac	3 years	$489	
50-90Hz	PC, Mac		$549	Flat square, non-glare screen with radiation filtering, Energy Star

Specific considerations for medium-sized monitors are pointed out here:

- *Size (Diagonal); Color/Mono.* The distinction between a 15-inch and a 16-inch monitor often has more to do with marketing than with measurements; look at the maximum resolution and dot pitch to decide which is the right one for you.

- *Resolution.* Look for a monitor that can display 1,024 x 768 resolution without interlacing. You probably don't need 1,280 x 1,024 resolution with this size of monitor unless you plan to do CAD or graphics work.

- *Dot Pitch.* Some medium-size monitors have larger dot sizes, but try to stick with monitors that have a dot pitch of .28mm or smaller; this size allows a denser, easier-to-read display.

- *Other.* Look for flat screen monitors in this size range.

Table 8.2 Medium Monitors Sorted by Screen Size, Resolution, and Manufacturer

Company, Model	Size (Diagonal); Color/Mono.	Resolution	Dot Pitch
Value Leader			
Amdek AM/817E	17"; color	1600x1280 (non-interlaced)	.26mm
Apple Multiple Scan 17	17"; color	640x480 through 1024x768, software switchable	.26mm
E-Machines T16 II	16"; color	1024x768 (non-interlaced)	
Value Leader			
MAG DX17F	17"; color	up to 1280x1024 (non-interlaced)	.28mm
MAG MXP17F	17"; color	up to 1600x1280 (non-interlaced)	.26mm
Mitsubishi Diamond Pro 17	17"; color	1280x1024 (non-interlaced)	
Mitsubishi Diamond Scan 16	16"; color	1280x1024 (non-interlaced)	
Mitsubishi Diamond Scan 17F	17"; color	1280x1024 (non-interlaced)	
NEC MultiSync 5FGE	17"; color	up to 1024x768 (non-interlaced)	.28mm
NEC MultiSync 5FGP	17"; color	up to 1024x768 (non-interlaced)	.28mm
RasterOps Sweet 16 Color Display	16"; color	832x624 (non-interlaced)	.28mm
SuperMac SuperMatch 17T	17"; color	1024x768 (non-interlaced)	.26mm
SuperMac SuperMatch 17XL	17"; color	1024x768 (non-interlaced)	.28mm

Max Vert. Refresh Rate	Compatibility	Warranty	Price	Other
47-105Hz	PC-compatibles, Mac II, Mac with VGA	1 year, parts and labor	$999	Flat square, non-glare screen
75Hz	Mac	1 year	$1125	Automatic degaussing, Energy Star
75Hz	PC, Mac	1 year	$1399	Trinitron-based
50-100Hz	PC, Mac	1 year (2 on CRT)	$799	
50-120Hz	PC, Mac	1 year (2 on CRT)	$1299	Energy Star
60-74Hz	PC, Mac	3 years	$1199	
60Hz	PC, Mac	3 years	$939	
60-74Hz	PC, Mac	3 years	$1069	
90Hz	PC, Mac	3 years	$1045	Flat square screen
90Hz	PC, Mac	3 years	$1175	Flat square screen
75Hz	Mac	3 years	$1099	
75Hz	Mac	1 year	$1249	
75Hz	PC, Mac	1 year	$1199	Energy Star

continues

Table 8.2	Continued		
Company, Model	Size (Diagonal); Color/Mono.	Resolution	Dot Pitch
ViewSonic 17	17"; color	1280x1024 (non-interlaced)	.27mm
ViewSonic 17E	17"; color	1024x768 (non-interlaced)	.28mm
ViewSonic 17G	17"; color	1280x1024 (non-interlaced)	.28mm

Table 8.3 Large Monitors Sorted by Screen Size, Resolution, and Manufacturer

This table includes large (19, 20, and 21 inches) monochrome and color monitors. It's sorted by ascending screen size, with smaller monitors first and monochrome monitors preceding color ones.

These monitors take up lots of space on your desk. They're too large and heavy for a lot of desks, and they leave a big hole in your wallet. For serious work, however, they're very much worthwhile. For desktop publishing, a large monitor that can display a two-page spread at high resolution is just about a must. For many uses, you can save money by forgoing color. If you plan to do color matching, though, you'll need specialized products that aren't covered in this book.

Problems that are tolerable on smaller screens are a real problem with a big monitor. For instance, a low refresh rate or interlacing will produce flickering that will tire out your eyes quickly. A slow computer system or non-accelerated graphics adapter will slow video updating, causing eye fatigue and frustration. Look for a high-quality monitor and make sure that you have the system and graphics adapter to drive it.

Table 8.3	Large Monitors Sorted by Screen Size, Resolution, and Manufacturer		
Company, Model	Size (Diagonal); Color/Mono.	Resolution	Dot Pitch
Apple Multiple Scan 20	20"; color	640x480 through 1152x870, software switchable	.31mm

Max Vert. Refresh Rate	Compatibility	Warranty	Price	Other
50-120Hz	PC, Mac		$1199	Flat square, non-glare screen with radiation filtering, enhanced focus, Energy Star
50-90Hz	PC, Mac		$899	Flat square, Energy Star
50-160Hz	PC, Mac		$999	Flat square, non-glare screen with radiation filtering, Energy Star

Specific differences for this kind of monitor are pointed out here:

- *Size (Diagonal); Color/Mono.* The size difference between one manufacturer's 20-inch model and another's 21-inch may be negligible; use the dot pitch and maximum resolution to decide which one to buy.

- *Resolution.* 1,024 x 768, non-interlaced display is fine for most work; 1,280 x 1,024 is helpful for CAD or graphics, or for desktop publishing if your program has a zoom mode so you can adjust display size.

- *Dot Pitch.* Look for .28mm if you can get it, .31mm otherwise.

- *Max. Vert. Refresh Rate.* Look for at least 70 Hz to avoid eye fatigue.

- *Warranty.* Look for a long warranty because the cost of replacing a large monitor is high. If you buy mail order, make extra sure that you know who pays for shipping if you have to send the monitor to the manufacturer for repairs.

Max Vert. Refresh Rate	Compatibility	Warranty	Price	Other
75Hz	Mac	1 year	$2200	Antiglare/antistatic screen coating, Energy Star

continues

Table 8.3 Continued

Company, Model	Size (Diagonal); Color/Mono.	Resolution	Dot Pitch
E-Machines E20	20"; color	1152x870 (non-interlaced)	.31mm
MAG MX21F	21"; color	up to 1600x1280 (non-interlaced)	.28mm
Mitsubishi Diamond Pro 21FS	21"; color	up to 1280x1024 (non-interlaced)	
Mitsubishi Diamond Pro 21T	21"; color	up to 1600x1200 (non-interlaced)	.31mm
Mitsubishi Diamond Scan 20 Plus	20"; color	up to 1280x1024 (non-interlaced)	
Mitsubishi Diamond Scan 20LP/20M	20"; color	up to 800x600 (non-interlaced)	
NEC MultiSync 6FGP	21"; color	up to 1280x1024 (non-interlaced)	.28mm
Radius IntelliColor Display/20	20"; color	up to 1600x1200 (non-interlaced)	.30mm
Radius Precision-Color Display/20v	20"; color	up to 1152x870 (non-interlaced)	.31mm
Radius Precision-Color Display/21	21"; color	up to 1360x1024 (non-interlaced)	.28mm
Radius TPD/20gs	20"; grayscale	up to 1152x870 (non-interlaced)	

Value Leader

Company, Model	Size (Diagonal); Color/Mono.	Resolution	Dot Pitch
Radius TPD/21gs	21"; grayscale	up to 1152x870 (non-interlaced)	
RasterOps 20/20 Multimode Color Display	20"; color	up to 1152x870 (non-interlaced)	.31mm
RasterOps 20T MultiScan Color Display	20"; color	up to 1280x1024 (non-interlaced)	.31mm

Listing of Monitors and Adapters

Max Vert. Refresh Rate	Compatibility	Warranty	Price	Other
75Hz	PC	1 year	$1899	
50-120Hz	PC, Mac	1 year (2 on CRT)	$2499	Energy Star
60-74Hz	PC, Mac	3 years	$2335	
	PC, Mac	3 years	$2525	Energy Star, vertically flat, anti-static and anti-glare coating
60-74Hz	PC, Mac	3 years	$2075	
60-76Hz	PC, Mac	3 years	$1825	
90Hz	PC, Mac	3 years	$2125	Flat square screen
50-160Hz	Mac	1 year	$2299	
50-90Hz	PC, Mac	1 year	$1999	Two-page display
60-120Hz	PC, Mac	1 year	$2499	Two-page display
75Hz	Mac		$999	Two-page display
75Hz	Mac		$1199	Two-page display
60-76Hz	Mac	3 years	$1869	Anti-static, anti-reflectvie coating
60-160Hz	Mac	3 years	$2349	Anti-glare coating

continues

Table 8.3 Continued

Company, Model	Size (Diagonal); Color/Mono.	Resolution	Dot Pitch
RasterOps 21" Color Display	21"; color	1152x870 (non-interlaced)	.28mm
RasterOps 21" Monochrome/Gray-Scale Display	21"; grayscale	1152x870 (non-interlaced)	
SuperMac Platinum 20	20"; grayscale	1024x768 (non-interlaced)	
Value Leader			
SuperMac Platinum 21	21"; grayscale	1152x870 (non-interlaced)	
SuperMac PressView 21	21"; color	1600x1200 (non-interlaced)	.28MM
SuperMac SuperMatch 20 Plus	20"; color	1152x870 (non-interlaced)	.31MM
SuperMac SuperMatch 20-TXL Trinitron	20"; color	1152x870 (non-interlaced)	.31MM
SuperMac SuperMatch 21	21"; color	1152x870 (non-interlaced)	.31MM
SuperMac SuperMatch 21-TXL	21"; color	1600x1200 (non-interlaced)	.31MM
ViewSonic 20	20"; color	1600x1280 (non-interlaced)	.28mm
Value Leader			
ViewSonic 21	21"; color	1600x1280 (non-interlaced)	.25mm

Max Vert. Refresh Rate	Compatibility	Warranty	Price	Other
75.08Hz	Mac	3 years	$2749	Anti-glare coating
75.08Hz	Mac	3 years	$1299	
75Hz	Mac	1 year	$999	
75Hz	Mac	1 year	$1199	
75Hz	Mac	1 year	$3999	Anti-glare hood, high-end color calibration
75Hz	Mac	1 year	$1949	
75Hz	PC, Mac	1 year	$2399	High-end color calibration
75Hz	Mac	1 year	$2599	Two-page
75Hz	PC, Mac	1 year	$2599	High-end color calibration, Energy Star
50-90Hz	PC, Mac	1 year	$1899	Flat square, non-glare screen with radiation filtering, enhanced focus
50-152Hz	PC, Mac	1 year	$2199	Flat square, non-glare screen with radiation filtering, enhanced focus, Energy Star

Fields for Graphics Adapter Tables

The following fields appear in both of the graphics adapter tables. Look in the descriptions of each table in the following sections for information specific to that table.

- *Manufacturer, Model.* Use this information to find out more about the product by calling the company or a dealer.

- *Number Of Colors.* The amount of RAM you have installed and the resolution at which you're running the monitor determine the actual number of colors you can see on-screen.

- *Resolutions.* Because most monitors now support 1,024 x 768 or higher resolution, look for a graphics adapter that also supports at least this resolution.

- *RAM: Base/Max.* You can get a small amount of RAM on the card initially if your needs are modest, but make sure that you can put in more if needed; 1M is a reasonable maximum for many users.

- *Graphics Coprocessor.* This chip makes fast calculations for graphics. It significantly improves graphics performance while reducing the workload of the main system CPU.

- *Compatibility.* This field tells what kind of slot the adapter fits in.

- *Adapter Size.* A half-length card is a good idea if you have an empty half-length slot in your system; this size leaves the full-length slots free for other uses.

- *Warranty.* A long warranty (more than one year) is nice, but not essential for the lower priced products.

Table 8.4 PC-Compatible Graphics Adapters

Manufacturer, Model	Number of Colors	Resolutions
ATI Graphics Pro Turbo	16.8 million	up to 1280x1024 (65,536 colors, 800x600 @ 16.8 million colors)
ATI Graphics Wonder	16.8 million	up to 1280x1024 (16 colors, 640x480 @ 16.8 million colors)
Value Leader		
ATI Graphics XPression	16.8 million	up to 1280x1024 (256 colors, 800x600 @ 16.8 million colors)

- *Price.* A higher price may not necessarily get you much. Check trade magazines for competitive reviews before paying top dollar for a card.

- *Other.* This field describes other considerations that may be important in your purchase.

Table 8.4 PC-Compatible Graphics Adapters

This table includes a variety of PC-compatible graphics adapters. It's sorted by compatibility (the type of slot the adapter fits in), maximum resolution, and then price. You can look in the area of the table that has the right type of card for you, and then scan downward to the specific products that fit your price range.

Some things to consider in choosing a PC-compatible graphics adapter are pointed out here:

- *Graphics Coprocesor.* This chip is very important if you're driving a big screen or need fast graphics performance. The TI 34020 is a very fast coprocessor with lots of support from high-end graphics programs. However, a VESA Local Bus Super VGA adapter driven by a fast 486 or a Pentium provides all the performance most people need.

- *Compatibility.* ISA slots give good performance, especially for cards with built-in coprocessors. These cards don't need the wide bandwidth to the system's microprocessor that's the key feature of local-bus adapters. "Dumb" VGA and SVGA cards benefit more from local bus. For performance, local bus is still better than ISA.

- *Other.* If you run DOS programs that don't have high-end graphics drivers and buy a card that does not support VGA as a native mode, a VGA pass-through allows an existing VGA or SVGA adapter to be used part of the time.

RAM: Base/Max	Compatibility	Adapter Size	Warranty	Price	Other
2M	PCI, VL, ISA		5 years	$599	64-bit processing, accelerated, panning
1M	VL, ISA		5 years	$199	32-bit processing, accelerated
2M	PCI, VL, ISA		5 years	$299	64-bit processing, accelerated, panning

continues

Table 8.4 Continued		
Manufacturer, Model	Number of Colors	Resolutions
Diamond SpeedStar 64	16.8 million	up to 1280x1024 (16 colors, 640x480 @ 16.8 million colors)
Diamond SpeedStar Pro	16.8 million	up to 1024x768 (16 colors, 640x480 @ 16.8 million colors)
Diamond Stealth 24	16.8 million	up to 1280x1024 (16 colors, 640x480 @ 16.8 million colors)
Diamond Stealth 32	16.8 million	up to 1280x1024 (16 colors, 640x480 @ 16.8 million colors)
Diamond Stealth 64	16.8 million	up to 1280x1024 (65,536 colors, 800x600 @ 16.8 million colors)
Diamond Stealth Pro	16.8 million	up to 1280x1024 (16 colors, 640x480 @ 16.8 million colors)
Diamond Viper	16.8 million	up to 1280x1024 (65,536 colors, 800x600 @ 16.8 million colors)
Diamond Viper Pro	16.8 million	up to 1600x1200 (65,536 colors, 800x600 @ 16.8 million colors)
Orchid Fahrenheit 1280 Plus/ISA	16.8 million	up to 1280x1024 (16 colors, 640x480 @ 16.8 million colors)
Orchid Fahrenheit 1280 Plus/VLB	16.8 million	up to 1280x1024 (16 colors, 640x480 @ 16.8 million colors)
Orchid Kelvin 64/VLB	16.8 million	up to 1280x1024 (16 colors, 640x480 @ 16.8 million colors)
RasterOps PaintBoard PC	16.8 million	up to 1024x768
SuperMac Spectrum/24 for Windows	16.8 million	up to 1152x910
SuperMac Thunder/24 for Windows	16.8 million	up to 1152x910
Western Digital, Paradise Accelerator Pro	16.8 million	up to 1280x1024
Western Digital, Paradise Accelerator Value Card	65,536	up to 1280x1024 (16 colors, 800x600 @ 65,536 colors)

RAM: Base/Max	Compatibility	Adapter Size	Warranty	Price	Other
1M	ISA, PCI			$179-$195	64-bit processing, accelerated
1M	VL, ISA			$169-$179	Accelerated
1M	ISA, VL			$249	32-bit processing, accelerated
1M	PCI, VL			$199	64-bit processing (32-bit interleaved), accelerated
2M	PCI, VL			$399	64-bit processing, accelerated
1M	ISA, VL			$299	32-bit processing, accelerated
2M	PCI, VL			$399	32-bit processing, accelerated
2M	PCI, VL			$479	64-bit processing (32-bit interleaved), accelerated
1M	ISA		4 years	$185	Hardware-based zoom and panning
1M	VL		4 years	$205	Hardware-based zoom and panning
1M	VL, PCI, ISA		4 years	$250	64-bit memory path for quicker access
3M	ISA			$399	
	ISA, EISA, or VL		1 year	$799	
	ISA, EISA, or VL		1 year	$1499	Includes color calibrator
1M, 2M	ISA, EISA	8" long	3 years	$349	
1M	ISA	6.22" long	3 years	$139.95	

continues

Table 8.4 Continued		
Manufacturer, Model	Number of Colors	Resolutions
Western Digital, Paradise Accelerator 24	16.8 million	up to 1280x1024 (16 colors, 640x480 @ 16.8 million colors)
Western Digital, Paradise Accelerator VL Plus	16.8 million	up to 1280x1024 (16 colors, 640x480 @ 16.8 million colors)
Western Digital, Paradise Accelerator Ports O' Call	16.8 million	up to 1280x1024 (16 colors, 640x480 @ 16.8 milion colors)

Table 8.5 Macintosh-Compatible Graphics Adapters

This table includes several Macintosh-compatible graphics adapters. It's sorted by maximum resolution and price. You can scan downward to the area of the table that fits your price range.

Specific differences for this kind of monitor are pointed out here:

- *Number Of Colors.* The Macintosh has some fantastic graphics programs that benefit from 16.8 million colors.

Table 8.5 Macintosh-Compatible Graphics Adapters		
Manufacturer, Model	Number of Colors	Resolutions
E-Machines Futura II LX	16.8 million	up to 1152x870
E-Machines Futura II SX	16.8 million	up to 832x624
E-Machines Ultura LX	16.8 million	up to 1152x870
Radius LeMans GT	16.8 million	up to 1152x870
Radius PrecisionColor 8XJ	256 colors or grays	up to 1152x870
Radius PrecisionColor PRO 24X	16.8 million	up to 1152x870
Radius PrecisionColor PRO 24XK	16.8 million	up to 1024x768
Radius PrecisionColor PRO 24XP	16.8 million	up to 832x624

RAM: Base/Max	Compatibility	Adapter Size	Warranty	Price	Other
1M	ISA	6.19" long	3 years	$199	
1M, 2M	VESA	10.48" long	3 years	$249	
1M, 2M	VESA	9.63" long	3 years	$299	Includes parallel port, 2 serial ports, game port, floppy and IDE hard drive interfaces

- *Compatibility.* NuBus cards work in all the Mac IIs and the Quadra series, but some of the newer Macs use VGA cards instead. Check for compatibility with your system before buying.

- *Other.* QuickDraw acceleration can make a big difference in screen updating speed. Make sure that the accelerator you're buying will work with QuickDraw GX as well.

RAM: Base/Max	Compatibility	Warranty	Price	Other
	NuBus	1 year	$899	
	NuBus	1 year	$499	
	NuBus	1 year	$1299	Includes acceleration, up to 23X
3M	NuBus	lifetime	$2499	32-bit color, accelerated
	NuBus	lifetime	$599	
	NuBus	lifetime	$1799	
	NuBus	lifetime	$999	
	NuBus	lifetime	$599	

continues

Table 8.5 Continued

Maufacturer, Model	Number of Colors	Resolutions
RasterOps 24 X Li	16.8 million	up to 1152x870
RasterOps 24Mx	16.8 million	up to 832x624
RasterOps 8XL	256	up to 1152x870
RasterOps 8XLi	256	up to 1152x870
Value Leader		
RasterOps ClearVue/GSXL	256 gray levels	up to 1152x870
RasterOps ClearVue/XL	256 gray levels	up to 1152x870
RasterOps Horizon 24	16.8 million	up to 1152x870
RasterOps PaintBoard 8Li	256	up to 1024x768
Value Leader		
RasterOps PaintBoard Li	16.8 million	up to 1024x768
RasterOps PaintBoard Professional	16.8 million	up to 1152x870
RasterOps PaintBoard Turbo	16.8 million	up to 1024x768
RasterOps PaintBoard Turbo XL	16.8 million	up to 1152x870
RasterOps ProColor 32	virtually limitless	up to 1152x870
SuperMac Futura II SX	16.8 million	up to 832x624
SuperMac Spectrum Power-1152	16.8 million	up to 1152x870
SuperMac Spectrum/24	16.8 million	up to 1024x768
SuperMac Thunder IIGX-1152	16.8 million	up to 1152x870
SuperMac Thunder IIGX-1360	16.8 million	up to 1360x1024
SuperMac Thunder IIGX-1600	16.8 million	up to 1600x1200
SuperMac Thunder/24	16.8 million	up to 1152x870

Listing of Monitors and Adapters

RAM: Base/Max	Compatibility	Warranty	Price	Other
3M, 16M	NuBus		$1999	Hardware-based zoom and panning, 6X acceleration
2M, 16M	NuBus		$599	Hardware-based zoom and panning, 6X acceleration
1M	NuBus		$549	Hardware-based zoom and panning
1M, 16M	NuBus		$599	Hardware-based zoom and panning, upgradeable to 24-bit
1M	NuBus		$399	Hardware-based zoom and panning
1M	NuBus		$199	
8M	NuBus		$2799	Hardware-based zoom and panning
1M	NuBus		$399	
3M	NuBus		$999	Hardware-based zoom and panning, 6X acceleration
8M	NuBus		$2199	Hardware-based zoom and panning
4M	NuBus		$1199	Hardware-based zoom and panning
4M	NuBus		$1399	Hardware-based zoom and panning
4M, 16M	NuBus		$1999	32-bit color, hardware-based zoom and panning, 6X acceleration
	NuBus	1 year	$499	
	NuBus	1 year	$1399	
	NuBus	1 year	$999	
	NuBus	1 year	$2599	Dual 80MHz DSP chips
	NuBus	1 year	$3299	Dual 80MHz DSP chips
	NuBus	1 year	$3999	Dual 80MHz DSP chips
up to 8M	NuBus	1 year	$1999	

CHAPTER NINE

Deciding What Kind of Printer You Need

Buying considerations are different for printers that will be used by an individual or a very small number of users and those that are designed to be used by large workgroups or for large print jobs. This chapter deals with printers that are used by individuals or small groups for a relatively small number of pages per month, from a few pages a week up to as many as 2,500 or so a month. Prices for such printers tend to fall between $200 on the low end to $1,000 on the high end. Color printers are considerably more expensive, but they're included later in the chapter.

This chapter explains the major kinds of technologies and features for these low-end to mid-range printers, and then describes how to match up the available kinds and models of printers with your needs.

Introduction to Personal Printers

The main things that determine what kind of printer you choose to buy are the quality of print a printer produces, the speed at which it can put out pages, and the price of the printer. The three most popular kinds of printers offer you a clear choice in these areas.

- *Dot matrix.* So-so speed and the lowest quality for the lowest price, as low as $150 or so. Although dot-matrix printouts are practically unsuitable for business correspondence, a dot-matrix printer is much better than no printer at all.

- *Inkjet.* So-so speed (same range as dot matrix) and quality approaching that of lasers for $300 and up. Printouts are suitable for business correspondence if you pick your fonts carefully and don't get the page wet. A good choice for home use.

- *Laser.* A personal laser printer for around $500 and up has better print quality and is faster than a dot-matrix or inkjet printer. Stretch for a low-end laser printer if you're setting up a home office.

The ease of setup and ease of use of a Macintosh are nowhere more evident than in printing. You are much more likely to be able to "plug and play" with a Macintosh and a printer than with an IBM-compatible, either DOS or Windows, and a printer. Software and hardware manufacturers are trying to resolve some of the difficulties with printer drivers, font compatibility, graphics languages, and so on that arise in the IBM-compatible world, but they have quite a way to go before catching up to the Mac. If you are an IBM-compatible user, be aware of these potential difficulties and be sure that service and support are available for resolving them.

The following sections describe the features and characteristics of the major types of printers. You may need a specific feature of a lower end product, such as the capability of dot-matrix printers to print multipart forms, or the easy transportability of lightweight inkjet or thermal printers. But if not, go for the higher quality printers when possible. For instance, don't decide to buy dot matrix for price reasons, and then add features until you end up in the $400 range; buy a cheap inkjet printer instead. The same goes for inkjet printers—if you need more than the base models offer, buy a low-end laser printer.

You're likely to end up living with your printer decision for quite a while. Unlike other choices you make in computer buying, many others (the people who receive things you print out) will have to live with your decision too. A well-chosen printer may well outlast your computer system—buy the best one you can afford.

Dot-Matrix Printers

Dot-matrix printers were popular for a long time because of their flexibility in printing text and graphics and their low price. Now inkjet printers for as little as $300 and personal laser printers costing $500 and up have emerged, relegating dot-matrix printers to the low end.

You can get a good dot-matrix printer that can handle anything short of business correspondence for just a few hundred dollars, making it a great price/performance choice for many individual needs. However, dot-matrix printers can be a pain to operate; it can be very difficult to get paper fed into some models. Models that are easier to use also come at a higher price, negating the only real advantage dot-matrix printers have for most users. Think carefully about your needs before buying a dot-matrix printer.

The next few sections explore considerations for purchasing a dot-matrix printer. Important aspects include speed, resolution, paper handling, and printing in color.

How It Works

Dot-matrix printers produce alphanumeric characters and graphic images by striking an inked ribbon with tiny metal rods called *pins*. Each time a pin strikes the ribbon, a dot is left on the page; look closely at a print sample and you can see the dots. The pins are located in a *print head*, which moves back and forth to create one line of text or graphics (see fig. 9.1). A tension arm keeps the paper in place, and a roller bar exerts pressure directly on the paper without jamming it. Dot-matrix printers usually use 24 pins to put dots on the page, but may use 18 pins or some other number (older dot-matrix printers used 9 pins). The more pins a printer has, the faster the printer can produce a high-resolution image. Because dot-matrix printers use an impact technology, they are noisy (often they produce an unpleasant, high-pitched whine) and relatively slow.

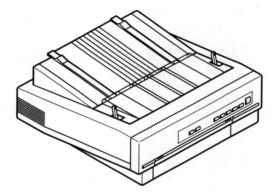

Figure 9.1 *A dot-matrix printer.*

A dot-matrix printer usually connects to your computer through a Centronics parallel port or a serial port. A cable usually comes with the printer and is easily connected to the computer. You probably will have to tell the application program (under DOS) or the operating environment (using Windows or the Macintosh) which printer port to print to.

Price and Costs

The price of the dot-matrix printer and the per-page costs are as low as you can get. A low-end dot-matrix printer costs $300 or less. If your print needs are great enough to require a more robust, higher capacity model, start looking at inkjet or personal laser printers instead.

The cost of operating a dot-matrix printer is minimal. Typically, the only recurring expense during the lifetime of the printer is replacing the ribbon, which can cost less than $5, and buying paper. Print heads do wear out, but only with constant use. The total cost per page of paper and consumables is about 1¢ per page.

Speed

Most dot-matrix printers have two speeds: draft and letter-quality. (Dot-matrix letter-quality used to be called near-letter-quality or NLQ, but the "near" has been dropped recently.) For example, the speed of draft print may be 240 characters per second (cps), whereas letter-quality speed may be 120 cps. (In laser printer terms, the draft speed is about four pages per minute, and the letter-quality speed is about two pages per minute.) At letter-quality precision, mid-range dot-matrix printer speeds are about the same as inkjet printer speeds and about half as fast as a typical four-page-per-minute laser printer.

A dot-matrix printer runs faster in draft mode because it puts fewer dots on the page to produce a rougher image; it goes slower in letter-quality mode because it puts more dots down for each character. On some printers, the print head moves more slowly in letter-quality mode; on others, the print head makes two passes per line of text in letter-quality mode instead of one.

Resolution and Print Quality

The resolution of a dot-matrix printer depends on the number of pins in the print head, how they are spaced, and how many passes the print head makes over the paper in letter-quality mode. The typical resolution of a 24-pin printer is 360 by 360; the typical resolution of a 9-pin printer is 240 by 216. These numbers refer to the horizontal resolution and vertical resolution in dots per inch. Notice that dot-matrix printers can have different horizontal and vertical resolutions. These resolutions compare favorably to inkjet and personal laser printers, but there is a noticeable quality improvement with inkjet and laser technology.

There are two problems with dot-matrix print quality. The first is that you have to sacrifice speed, by putting the printer in its slower letter-quality setting, to get decent quality. The second is that dot-matrix printing, no matter how good it looks, is seen as below business quality by many people. The widespread availability of better printers has raised people's standards; text and graphics printing that is quite legible now seems visibly lacking in quality.

Let your own eyes be the judge of one printer's quality compared with another's. You can get surprisingly good results from dot-matrix printers. For instance, look at the samples of letter-quality type from different dot-matrix printer manufacturers shown in figure 9.2. Notice the differences in the quality and sharpness of the images. Don't buy a dot-matrix printer without seeing print samples or at least seeing quality ratings in a magazine review.

```
I went to the woods because I          I went to the woods because I
wished to live deliberately,            wished to live deliberately,
to front only the essential             to front only the essential
facts of life. - H. D. Thoreau          facts of life. - H. D. Thoreau
```

Figure 9.2 *Samples of letter-quality print from different dot-matrix printers.*

Fonts

Most dot-matrix printers do not support more than one or two fonts. They do print in different sizes and support printing in boldface and italics. Dot-matrix printers used with a Macintosh or Windows can print TrueType fonts. You can buy a dot-matrix printer that takes an add-on font cartridge, but if you have extra money to spend on this type of thing, you should use it to buy a better kind of printer instead.

Graphics

Nearly all dot-matrix printers can print graphics. Some dot-matrix printers may even print high-resolution or color graphics.

Although graphics printed by a 24-pin printer may be of high resolution, they also may be less than desirable in other ways. The print head may have to make many passes over a piece of paper to print the graphic. Each pass makes a stripe on the page. These stripes are most noticeable when you print a great deal of black on the paper. If you print only outlines, as in some charts or graphs, the stripes may be hardly noticeable.

Drivers

Most programs can print to an Epson dot-matrix printer, and most dot-matrix printers can emulate a low-end Epson model, so you can print from almost any program to almost any dot-matrix printer. To take advantage of printer-specific features such as higher resolution or color requires other emulations or a driver specific to your printer. Ask a salesperson what it will take to make a dot-matrix printer work with your software before you buy the printer.

Size

Dot-matrix printers come in two standard sizes: narrow carriage and wide carriage. The narrow-carriage printer accepts standard 8 1/2- by-11-inch paper. The wide-carriage printer accepts 11- by-17-inch paper.

The narrow-carriage printer is adequate for most printing. You can print as many as 80 characters per line using the standard font (10 cpi) on a narrow-carriage printer. Using a condensed font (17 cpi), you can print up to 144 characters per line.

If you print financial reports and spreadsheets, however, the wide-carriage printer may be more useful. Using the condensed mode on wide paper enables you to print large amounts of information on one page.

Paper Handling

One reason for the quick decline of dot-matrix printers is their problematic paper handling. Most dot-matrix printers use a tractor-feed mechanism and continuous tractor-feed paper. (Continuous means that the pages are attached to one another at top and bottom, making them into one long stream of paper.) This paper is regular 8 1/2- by-11-inch or larger paper attached to paper strips with holes in them. Tearing off each sheet of paper from the others, and from the line of holes running along the edge, leaves a slight but noticeable bumpiness along the paper's edges.

The trouble usually comes in getting the paper started in the printer. Aligning the holes with the sprockets that pull the paper through the printer and aligning the paper to the top of a page can be difficult. Many hours have been wasted trying to get paper to go into badly designed dot-matrix printers, and many pages of tractor-feed paper have been wasted because they were not aligned correctly and consistently with the top of a page. Try to test the paper loading and alignment of a dot-matrix printer before buying it, or ask a friend or colleague about his or her experiences with different models.

Epson has (finally) introduced a dot-matrix printer that draws sheets of paper from a paper tray, like a laser printer, virtually eliminating the problems discussed here. It is difficult to predict whether other companies will follow suit, as the dot-matrix printer market is dwindling rapidly.

Dot-matrix printers are the only printers that can print on multipart forms, which require an impact on the top form to force carbon or other material onto the sheets below. If you need a printer for this kind of work, buy a nine-pin dot-matrix printer that feeds forms from the bottom of the printer. This kind of printer helps you to keep the forms straight and avoid waste because you can tear off the form exactly where you want.

Controls

Look for controls that make it easy to switch print quality and print type from the front of the printer. Try to visit a store or dealer and see some of these features in operation before buying. Be aware that making these changes can interfere with correct page breaks; ask how to get them to work correctly when you switch modes. If the printer does not have controls to make these changes or if the procedure is confusing, consider a different printer.

Memory

When you print, your application program sends information to the printer. Without any kind of buffering, the program and your computer are forced to wait until the entire print operation is complete before they can do anything else. There are several ways around this problem. Some computer systems have built-in print buffers that send the print information to a disk file, release the application from waiting, and then send the print information from the disk file to the printer. Another option is to have RAM in the printer to accept the print information; once the information is transferred into the printer's RAM, your application is finished with its part in the print job and returns control to you.

If your system doesn't have print buffering built into its operating software or as an add-on, either buy a utility program to support this feature or get a printer with a moderate amount of RAM in it. A full page of text takes up about 2K of RAM; a full page of graphics takes as much as 1M. Either option prevents you from having to wait until a print job is complete before you can use your computer again.

Portability

Most narrow-carriage dot-matrix printers are transportable; they're pretty easy to carry around and may even fit in your luggage on a trip. Only a very few dot-matrix printers, however, are truly portable—very light, very small, and able to run from batteries. If you need transportability and a low price, dot-matrix is a good choice. If you need true portability, consider inkjet printers for lower weight and higher quality or small thermal-fusion printers for the lowest possible weight.

Color

Many dot-matrix printers have the physical capability to print in color because you can just put in a color ribbon to replace the usual black one. However, if you want to use more than one color in the same document, the printer also must come with drivers that support color printing from your applications, or must emulate a kind of printer that your application can already print to in color. Check out this feature carefully before buying.

Dot-matrix color printouts are fun but are not suitable for business uses. If you need better-quality color at a relatively affordable price, look at a color inkjet printer instead. For true business color, look to the "Color Printers" section, later in this chapter.

Manufacturers

Starting your search for a dot-matrix printer with Epson is a good idea. Epson has set the dot-matrix printing standards for many years. For this reason, almost all software programs for IBM and compatible computers support Epson printers. This fact does not mean that you must buy a dot-matrix printer from Epson, but you should purchase a dot-matrix printer that offers Epson emulation.

After years of watching its market share erode, Epson has taken action on several fronts. It has introduced dot-matrix printers that use cut sheet paper from a paper tray, like laser printers, and produce good quality at very low prices.

Other manufacturers with highly rated dot-matrix printer models are Panasonic, Star Micronics, and Citizen. Printers often need service during their lifetimes, so make sure that you buy from a reliable manufacturer and that you have good service and support available throughout the life of the printer.

Inkjet Printers

Inkjet printers are the new printer of choice for mid-range uses. A good inkjet printout doesn't have the dotty look of most dot-matrix printers. For medium-size text and simple graphics, inkjet quality approaches laser printers for many hundreds of dollars less. Inkjet prices cluster around $300 to $500, though you can easily pay more for one that supports sophisticated features like color.

These printers are also light, quiet, and easy to use. The per-page cost can be high, around 5¢ or so per page, and printing is no faster than a middle-of-the-road dot-matrix printer. But for most users who don't do volume printing, the higher quality results are worth the premium per-page and purchase cost. You can send off a report or business letter printed on an inkjet printer with pride.

As with dot-matrix printers, you should think carefully before buying a more expensive inkjet printer; if you get much above the $500 range for a non-color inkjet printer, think about a personal laser printer instead. The next few sections describe key considerations in buying an inkjet printer; important among them are speed, resolution, drivers, and portability.

How It Works

An inkjet printer has a mechanism that squirts dots of ink onto the page to form characters, so it runs quietly and has good type quality. The print head is a key component; the accuracy with which it deposits ink drops determines the quality of the print. The ink used by most inkjet printers is water-soluble, meaning that it smears easily until it dries. Even after it's dry, a small amount of moisture can make the ink smear again.

You cannot use these printers for tasks like printing on multipart forms because inkjet technology does not use an impact method to create characters. You can, however, expect high-quality output at a reasonable price.

Prices and Costs

The list prices of inkjet printers run from about $350 to $550 and up. Street prices are usually heavily discounted and can run from just under $300 on up. If you're looking at a model with greater features that costs more than these amounts, compare it carefully to a low-end personal laser printer before you buy.

The per-page costs of inkjet printers are high. Most of these printers use a combination print head/ink cartridge unit that must be replaced every time the ink runs out. This quality makes it easy to change the ink and ensures that you always have a fresh print head, but raises costs to about 5¢ per page. If you buy an inkjet printer, look for someplace to get the ink cartridges cheap.

Speed

Inkjet printers run at speeds of up to two pages per minute, about the same as a mid-range dot-matrix printer. Even this relatively high speed is frustratingly slow for printing more than 10 pages or so. Use the on-screen preview features of your application programs to make sure that the document is perfect before printing it, so you don't have to make corrections based on one printout and wait for a second printout.

Laser printers start at four pages per minute for low-end models and go up from there; think about a laser printer if you will be printing high volumes or are frequently in a hurry for a printout.

Resolution and Print Quality

The resolution of an inkjet printer is usually 300 dots per inch (dpi) for HP printers or 360 dpi for most competitors (as good as or better than a low-range 300 dpi laser printer). HP's new DeskJet and DeskWriter 520 and 560C offer 600 x 300 dpi, which is almost indistinguishable from laser output. However, the ink used in inkjet printers tends to spread after it's sprayed onto the page, producing a large, imprecise dot. The control mechanism of an inkjet printer also lacks the fancy resolution enhancement features of most laser printers, so text and graphics are not quite as good as laser-printed copy.

For most uses, the quality of an inkjet printer is just fine; the problems are subtle rather than obvious. Some fonts look better than others when printed by an inkjet printer; try a couple sample pages before printing a big job with a new font or combination of fonts.

One problem may occur if the ink used by the printer is water soluble, as most such inks are. If a page printed with water-soluble ink gets wet, the printing smears on the paper. To combat this problem, manufacturers also sell water-resistant ink for inkjet printers. These inks are solvent-based rather than water-based so that the print does not smear if it gets wet—but think twice before paying extra for such inks because they cause your per-page cost to be even higher. Whichever kind of ink you're using, avoid touching the ink until a few seconds after the page is printed to avoid smearing. Paper can be a factor as well. Glossy papers prevent the ink from adhering properly, and very absorbent papers (like cotton bond) can make the ink appear to spread. Some inkjets (especially color inkjets) require a special paper that keeps the ink from blurring.

Fonts

You can get an inkjet printer with a font cartridge slot, but you may not need it. TrueType font technology (used in Mac and Windows) generates fonts on the computer, not the printer, and sends the result as a bit-map to the printer. Although this technique is slower than having built-in or plug-in fonts on the printer, its quality is good, it's cheap, and you don't have to limit your range of fonts.

If you can get the built-in fonts you need at a small premium, pay it; if someone gives you a useful font cartridge, use it. You will get good quality at faster speed. Before you spend big bucks for fancy font handling on an inkjet printer, however, consider buying a personal laser printer. Speed and quality will both be better no matter what kind of fonts you use.

Graphics

You can run into a problem with an inkjet printer when you print graphics. Because an inkjet printer sprays ink onto the page, large black areas of a graphic are wet with ink as the page comes out of the printer, and the page may curl or wrinkle as it dries.

Otherwise, inkjet printers do a fine job with graphics. For occasional high-resolution or half-tone graphics, you may want to use your inkjet printer as a preview printer, and then print the final version on a laser printer at your work place or a copy shop that rents computer and laser printing services.

Drivers

Inkjet drivers have improved greatly since the printers were first developed. If you use DOS, you must make sure that your application programs support the printer you want to use, through a custom driver or through emulation. For Windows, you only need a Windows driver to make the printer accessible to all your applications. Macintosh users usually benefit from high standards for drivers for any printer sold into the Macintosh market.

When buying an inkjet printer, get a look at print samples from it and one or two competitors running your software with the fonts and types of graphics that you normally use. The quality of the driver has a big impact on the final output quality.

Size

An inkjet printer is likely to be small and easily transportable. The Apple StyleWriter II, for instance, is designed to be used on a desktop, but it folds into a shape about the size of a hardback dictionary for travel. If you remove the sheet feeder, the thickness drops in half. Look for this kind of clever design if you plan to transport your printer much.

Paper Handling

Paper handling for inkjet printers is easy because they're designed to feed regular cut sheets. Most also allow you to hand-feed single sheets and envelopes, bypassing the sheet feeder that is used for regular paper.

Inkjet printers generally use only 8 1/2-inch wide paper, but most allow you to use either standard-size (11 inches long) or legal-size (14 inches long) paper. Some inkjet printers or their controlling software enable you to rotate the printed output. This rotation of print, called *landscape mode*, makes the printer treat the length of the paper as the width and the width of the paper as the length.

Because inkjet printers use a non-impact technology, you cannot use them to print forms that have carbon paper or other pressure-sensitive material between the pages to make multiple copies.

Controls

Especially if you use Windows or the Macintosh, software should handle most of the controlling functions. Front-panel controls for inkjet printers range from the simple to the complicated. Too many controls may hurt, rather than help, ease of use.

Memory

Affordable inkjet printers leave font and graphics generation and print buffering, if any, to the software that controls them. Therefore, they tend not to come with memory of their own. If you spend much time waiting for control of your machine to return to you after you start a print job, consider buying print buffering software.

Portability

Most inkjet printers are transportable, if a little heavy. Models designed for portability are light (four to five pounds) and very small. Some can even run off batteries if you need to print while you're away from an outlet. For the ultimate in portability, consider a thermal-fusion printer; it's about half the weight and half the quality for the same amount of money as an inkjet. Also consider buying a notebook computer with a built-in printer.

Color

Color inkjet printers are rapidly becoming the main choice for affordable color. Although they cost about twice as much as monochrome inkjet printers, the quality can be quite good for the price. You get better results if you also use expensive, glossy paper for output. Some models print in black at no cost or quality penalty over a monochrome printer, and you only pay for color when you need it.

There are a lot of issues you may need to consider in buying a color printer, such as software drivers, color matching, and quality. For business graphics and presentations, the medium-quality color offered by color inkjet printers is a huge improvement over monochrome printouts at a relatively small difference in price.

Manufacturers

HP is the leader in the low- to mid-range inkjet market with the DeskJet (for PC) and DeskWriter (for Mac) models 520 for monochrome and the DeskJet 560C for color. Epson and Apple have highly rated monochrome offerings as well. Start your shopping with one or more of these manufacturers. Before buying a less popular model, check that quality, price, performance, available drivers, and service and support all add up to a package that meets your needs better than the market leaders.

Laser Printers

Laser printers run a gamut of price and performance from personal laser printers up to monster machines costing tens of thousands of dollars. This section concentrates on low-price, high-quality laser printers that cost around $2,000 or less.

Until recently, laser printers cost $2,000 or more and were used almost exclusively by workgroups in business settings. However, several recent developments have combined to reduce prices of the least expensive laser printers to under $500, placing them within the reach of individuals and small businesses. Even inexpensive laser printers can do high-quality output and some fancy effects; see figure 9.3 for an example.

The most important factor is the development of slower, less expensive print engines that operate at 4 pages per minute (ppm) rather than the standard 8 ppm. Printers that run at 4 ppm have been steadily dropping in price at about 10 percent per year.

The other important factor is the introduction of mid-price (under $2,000) 600- and 800-dot-per-inch (dpi) printers by market leaders like HP. With the mid-range now occupied by 600 dpi (and better) machines, the formerly top-quality 300 dpi printers have to be reduced in price to find buyers. As a result, 4 ppm, 300 dpi printers hover around the $500 price range, down from nearly $2,000 only a couple of years ago. Some printers under $1,000 will start to get faster print speeds or higher end features like resolution enhancement for better quality results from the basic 300 dpi engine.

Figure 9.3 *Special effects produced by a Hewlett-Packard LaserJet IV printer.*

If you intend to do much printing, seriously consider the purchase of a laser printer. The attractive quality of 600 dpi laser printouts and the relatively high speed of even the slowest laser print engines makes them a real pleasure to use as compared to dot-matrix or even inkjet printers. Look to inkjet printers for affordability, transportability, and color; try to stretch for a laser printer for moderate to large quantities of monochrome output, especially for business use. If you are buying a PC and a printer simultaneously, consider getting a less-expensive PC in order to get a better printer. You may also be able to talk a dealer into giving you a price break on the pair.

Buying a laser printer can be fairly complex, so read the following sections with care. Pay special attention to the sections on resolution, fonts, and printer control languages.

How It Works

Laser printers form characters in a fairly complex way. The printer points a laser beam at a rotating hexagonal mirror. The light is reflected off the mirror onto a rotating cylinder called a *drum*. This reflection creates an electronic image on the drum. The image on the drum attracts a fine black powdery ink, called *toner*, which adheres to the drum. When paper passes under the drum, the toner is attracted to the paper by static electricity, forming the image. Finally, the toner is fused to the paper by a combination of heat and pressure.

The internal parts of a laser printer, the *printer engine*, can differ from printer to printer. Knowing which engine a laser printer uses is important because the toner cartridge and other parts that may need to be replaced fairly often differ from engine to engine. Canon, IBM, Kyocera Unison, Ricoh, Sharp, and other companies make the engines.

If you are thinking of buying a laser printer, make sure that you find out how to replace the toner and parts that wear out, such as the OPC (optical photo coupler). Also, make sure that these items are readily available.

High-end laser printers may have two or more ports for connecting to different computers or to a network. You will not usually find this feature in personal laser printers; look for a model that works with your computer setup.

Some printers that look like laser printers have basic technological differences. A laser printer can be more broadly classified as a *page printer*. Other kinds of page printers are *liquid-crystal shutter (LCS) printers* and *light-emitting diode (LED) array printers*. These printers look and act like laser printers but do not use a laser beam as part of their operation. The differences among the print outputs of LCS printers, LED printers, and lower-end laser printers are slight.

Price and Costs

The purchase price of laser printers varies depending on several factors. You can pay as little as $600 for a low-end model, and up to many thousands of dollars for a high-capacity unit. The main things to consider for personal laser printers are a resolution of 300 dpi or more, a print speed of 4 ppm or more, the availability of an HP-compatible font cartridge slot (unless you use Windows or Macintosh), and brand name, with HP and Apple getting a slight premium for their products. Most laser printers support HP PCL IV (Hewlett-Packard emulation) and can be upgraded to support PostScript; don't consider printers that can't be upgraded to have these capabilities unless you are very sure you won't need them.

Per-page costs are about 2¢ to 4¢ per page—less than an inkjet printer and more than dot matrix. Printers that allow you to conveniently replace the drum and toner as one integrated unit (the vast majority) cost more to operate than those that allow you to refill the toner and replace the drum as separate operations.

Speed

Laser printer speeds are measured in pages per minute (ppm). Most laser printers are rated at 4 to 8 ppm; some may be as high as 20 ppm. Laser printers run at close to their rated speed for text, but are much slower for graphics. The more complex a graphic is, the longer it takes to print.

Resolution and Print Quality

In determining the print quality of a laser printer, you need to consider both the rated resolution of the print engine, usually either 300 or 600 dpi, and whether any enhancement technologies are included. Most personal laser printers are 300 dpi with no resolution enhancement. If you can get resolution enhancement technology and software drivers that take advantage of it with your printer, your effective resolution will improve to almost double the rated resolution. Laser-quality output is just about the best that you can buy.

Fonts and Printer Control Languages

Most laser printers have a number of fonts built into them. These built-in fonts print faster than fonts that are generated on the computer and downloaded to the printer. You can add more fonts easily with a font cartridge; make sure that the printer you buy can accept HP LaserJet-compatible cartridges (unless you use Macintosh or Windows, where font cartridges are unnecessary).

The printer may also use a page-description language that allows it to accept high-level commands from the computer and translate them into characters and graphics on the page. Using this language means that your computer does all the font work, and the printer is only responsible for printing. Although this process can be slow, the quality of the result is excellent. Buy a printer that supports HP's Printer Control Language (PCL) and the TrueType standard from Apple and Microsoft. You should also be able to upgrade it to use PostScript if you decide to add that feature later.

Many printers that use HP's PCL or Adobe's PostScript need some memory so that a page image can be stored in the printer after it's generated by the built-in language. To print a full page of graphics, you need 1M of printer memory. 4M or more of memory are recommended for decent performance with PostScript. Printer memory often is more expensive than regular PC memory (though some laser printers use regular SIMMs), so be prepared to shell out extra money if you want to upgrade your printer's memory. LaserMaster's WINPrinter uses no memory at all—at least not in the printer. It works with Windows to use the memory in your computer to process PostScript or PCL pages, relying on special software to minimize the impact on system performance. If you have a powerful computer and use Windows, you may want to consider this option.

You are not shut out from PostScript if you do not have PostScript built into your printer. (Although the price of PostScript is dropping, upgrading your printer to use it costs $600 or so, plus expensive add-on memory for the printer.) Print utility software exists that can convert PostScript fonts and graphics to other printer control languages on your computer. This process is slower than PostScript, but it's also a lot less expensive.

Graphics

Laser printers produce wonderful graphics. Although you can do a lot with HP's PCL and HPGL (HP Graphics Language), the industry standard for graphics printing is PostScript. If you very rarely use PostScript, get a utility program to generate page images using your computer system's microprocessor and memory. If you use PostScript a lot, buy a printer that can handle it for you in order to get decent performance.

Few users who don't already use PostScript need it right off the bat. The best strategy is to buy a printer that you can upgrade to use PostScript, and then try to avoid doing the upgrade until you really have to. At that point, you will have proven your need for it, rather than spending $500 or more extra for a capability that you may not need.

Drivers

Good drivers for your printer are very important in order to get the most out of it. For instance, a laser printer can produce half-tones and other complex, shaded graphics through a process called *dithering*—making patterns of dots that look like shades of gray. A good driver gives you high-quality dithering and excellent images; a poor one produces ugly, muddy images.

Drivers for the Macintosh and, to an increasing extent, Microsoft Windows are growing in quality. If you use a graphical environment and HP PCL or PostScript, you will probably get good results. However, stay in touch with your printer's manufacturer; new drivers that improve performance or use less memory may become available during the time you own your printer. Some manufacturers make updated drivers available regularly through CompuServe or some other on-line service.

Size

Laser printers are usually big and heavy—too heavy and clumsy to move easily. Unless you get a personal laser printer, which is only about as big as a bread box, you will need to set aside a good part of a typical desktop to have space for the laser printer and room to change the paper.

Paper Handling

Laser printers use both letter- and legal-size paper. Get both letter- and legal-size paper trays if you use legal paper much at all. Laser printers also offer landscape and portrait modes (portrait mode being normal, or vertical, printing). The number of characters you can print on a page varies by the size and type style of the characters.

Keep in mind that each letter you print usually needs an envelope. A laser printer should have a way to feed one envelope or a stack of envelopes into the printer. This feature may be standard or optional. You also can purchase sheets of labels to use with your laser printer.

Controls

The control panel of a laser printer helps you control the printer directly and identify problems. Many printers use an LCD panel to convey information to the user. Be wary of purchasing a printer that forces you to learn cryptic codes rather than plain English for performing normal operations.

Most PostScript printers do not have a complicated control panel on the front. The PostScript printer operations are controlled through software. Printers that handle multiple input ports often have control panels to assist in switching between modes.

Memory

Many laser printers are actually high-powered computers. These printers contain high-performance microprocessors and several megabytes of memory. Laser printer memory is used mainly to store image data. To print a page, the laser printer must have enough memory to store all the information about the page, including text and formatting codes. Pages with more white space and fewer graphics require less memory.

A laser printer cannot print part of a page, receive more information, and then print the rest of the page. If a laser printer runs out of RAM in the middle of a page, the printer prints half the page and either halts or ejects the paper, and then prints the other half of the page on another sheet of paper.

The standard amount of printer memory varies with the manufacturer. For example, the standard Hewlett-Packard LaserJet 4 printer has 1M of RAM, enough to store an entire page of graphics, whereas many other printers have .5M (512 kilobytes) of memory and can only print half a page of graphics. If you choose the minimum amount of memory for a laser printer, you may find that it cannot print pages that contain both text and graphics. Make sure that the printer can print the kinds of documents you want. If not, you will have to order additional memory.

If you add PostScript to your printer, you will probably need 4M or more of memory. The more complex the graphic, the more memory it needs to print at all. Graphics print faster if more memory is available for the printer to use while it generates the graphic. If you have PostScript on your printer, you need to treat the printer as a separate computer that has its own memory, processor, and possibly even hard disk requirements. Purchasing a large amount of memory is worthwhile in multiple-user environments but not in most single-user situations.

At any time, you can add RAM in amounts up to the printer's maximum capacity. Generally, adding RAM is not a difficult procedure. For example, the Hewlett-Packard LaserJet IV contains a slot on the side of the printer where a memory-expansion board slides into the printer. Some printers use regular SIMMs; however, many printers use specialized memory boards that are more expensive than standard SIMMs; third parties offer memory upgrades much more cheaply than the manufacturers of such printers.

Portability

Don't plan to take a laser printer on a trip; instead, find a print shop or copy shop at the other end that will let you print. (Watch it, though; some of these places charge 40¢ to 50¢ per page.) If you need to print on the road much, get a portable inkjet printer for that purpose.

Color

Personal laser printers don't handle color; look for an inkjet model for an affordable color printer. If you need professional color printing, see the section "Color Printers" later in this chapter.

Manufacturers

The most popular laser printer brand for IBM and compatible computers is Hewlett-Packard. If you are considering a PCL printer other than the HP LaserJet series 4, make sure that the printer can emulate one of these models. The most popular laser printer brand for Apple Macintosh computers is Apple, with HP in second place. If you are considering a PostScript printer other than one of the Apple LaserWriters, make sure that the printer can emulate one of the LaserWriter models. Some Apple LaserWriters work not only with Macintosh computers but also with IBM and compatible computers; some models even have multiple input ports and support both PostScript and HP's PCL.

Competing manufacturers offer more than HP and Apple in order to try and grab a piece of the market. One highly rated, low-price laser printer is the Epson ActionLaser 1000. Although its quality is not top-of-the-line, a bare-bones version may be available for around $600 for a fast 6 ppm laser printer. Other manufacturers offer even faster speeds, additional built-in fonts, and low prices. Start your shopping process by identifying the name-brand printer that best fits your needs, and then see whether you can find a compatible model with better price/performance or more features that has solid service and support.

Color Printers

High-end color printers are relatively new to the scene, so they're still relatively expensive. The printers listed in the next chapter start at about $5,000 and go up well over $10,000. Still, if you want good-quality color without waiting for a professional print shop, they're the only way to go.

The main use for these printers is for presentations. Studies by advertising and sales organizations have long shown that color adds impact and increases sales. These printers let you use those advantages in your daily work. With most of them, you can create color transparencies for overhead projectors, and all help you make impressive documents, graphs, and charts.

These color printers vary widely in quality, not necessarily according to price. The technology and market are still so new, you don't yet "get what you pay for" in color printers. Fortunately, in some cases this means you can find real bargains on top-quality machines.

How It Works

You will find four technologies competing in the color printer arena: solid ink, color laser, dye sublimation, and thermal wax-transfer. Each produces an acceptable full-color image (including output of color photographs), but color lasers produce a slightly more grainy output. Dye sublimation is popular for its smooth color transitions. Each technology has distinct advantages and disadvantages, as shown in table 9.1.

Table 9.1 Color Printer Technologies

Description	Advantages	Disadvantages	Cost/Page
Color Laser			
The page makes one pass by each of four colored toner cartridges	Relatively fast (about one hour per page, compared to two or more for other types)	Grainy images	About $1
Dye Sublimation			
The page makes one pass by each of four "dye rolls"	Very popular, high-quality images	High cost per page	About $2
Solid Ink			
Much like an inkjet, passing a four-color printhead over the page once for each horizontal line	Low cost per page, good quality output	Slower than other types	50¢ to $1
Thermal Wax Transfer			
Much like dye sublimation, but using wax-based dye rolls	A good mix of quality output and low cost per page	Wide quality variation between vendors	50¢ to $1

Price and Costs

Unless you do a lot of color work, a color printer probably won't pay for itself (at least not at current price levels). If you output a few color pages a month, you would be better off using a professional print shop and possibly buying an inexpensive color inkjet for proofing. Up-front investment in even the least expensive color printer is around $5,000, with more expensive models topping out at nearly three times that much.

High-end color printers are also expensive to feed. Where black-and-white laser printers average about 3¢ to 5¢ per page, color printers cost from 50¢ to over two dollars per page. Some require special paper, and in most cases supplies like color toner or dye rolls are available only through mail order.

Speed

Don't wait up. The fastest color printers can output a page in about an hour. Very complex images take two to two-and-a-half hours for each page, so your best bet is to spool them to a network and print four or five overnight.

Resolution and Print Quality

"Resolution" doesn't mean as much in a color printer as it does in a standard laser printer. A less-than-300 dpi (dot per inch) color printer (almost all of them are) can produce clear photographic images, whereas a 600 dpi black-and-white printer can't. Some color printers with lower resolutions produce higher quality images than those with higher resolutions. The differences between color technology and standard single-color laser technology are huge, so don't be fooled by a claim of high resolution in a color printer. The proof is in the output—get several output samples, including some of your own work, from several companies before you buy a color printer.

Fonts and Printer Control Languages

All of these color printers use PostScript. Its combination of color vector graphics and color bit-maps makes it the only solution for color. In some cases, you can use a color printer as a (slow, expensive) monochrome printer by sending it regular black-and-white jobs. Because they all support PostScript, all your PostScript and TrueType fonts will work.

Graphics and Text

Color printers are built for graphics. The human eye forgives much more variation in graphics than in text, so while resolution for photographs isn't an issue (see "Resolution and Print Quality," above), resolution in text is very important. If possible, use a standard laser printer for large blocks of text and reserve the color printer for graphics alone. If you want text in a single color other than black, you may still be able to take advantage of a standard laser printer's resolution for your text—just get a color toner cartridge. Several toner suppliers sell red, green, blue, orange, brown, and every other color, and these cartridges fit right into your regular laser printer.

Drivers
You can be sure a color printer will work with Windows or Macintosh, but if your work is primarily DOS-based, check with the company to see whether drivers are available for each of your applications.

Size
These printers are large, in some cases twice as large as standard laser printers. The special color transfer equipment inside takes up considerably more space than a regular laser printer's single toner cartridge. Some accept larger-than-normal paper (11 by 17 inches for example), which increases their size further. Set aside a table just for your color printer and supplies—it won't fit on the corner of your desk.

Paper Handling
Color printers aren't designed for high-output jobs, so don't look for high-capacity paper trays or double trays. Make sure that you can get paper trays with the appropriate dimensions, however (having a printer that can use 11- by-17-inch paper is useless if you can only get an 8 1/2- by-11-inch tray).

Memory
Color printers need a lot of RAM—16M to 64M is not uncommon—to process complex images. If you have a specific use in mind for a color printer (like printing color photographs), contact the manufacturer to find out whether the standard amount of RAM can do the job or whether you will need more.

Portability
In the days of larger, heavier laser printers, some were dubbed "boat anchors" (not to name names). Color printers carry on the boat anchor tradition, staying wherever you install them until you have two strong people to move them. If you have to go on the road with a color printer, investigate the lower quality inkjets, which are slightly more mobile.

Manufacturers
Tektronix, a mainstay of professional high-resolution printing, and Eastman Kodak are the quality leaders in color printers. Their printers are not as expensive as those of some competitors, but both supply strong warranties and excellent output. QMS (another

leader in professional printing) makes some very popular, speedy color printers, and Dataproducts sells a remarkably high-quality printer at a very low price.

The Right Printer for You

This section helps you identify your needs and find the kind of printer that makes sense for you. After you read this section, you can look again at the preceding detailed descriptions to help identify features that are important to you with the kind of printer you have chosen.

How To Pick a Printer

For the most part, printers fall into a few different kinds that have relatively clear price, speed, and quality differences. These kinds are dot-matrix printers in the range of $150 to $300 and up, inkjet printers for $300 to $500 and up, and personal laser printers for $500 and up.

After you pick a kind of printer, start shopping by looking at the market leaders. (There are clear market leaders in printing to a greater extent than in other major kinds of computing equipment.) For IBM-compatibles, the leaders are any of several Epson models for dot-matrix printers, the HP DeskJets for inkjet printers, and the HP LaserJet for laser printers. For the Macintosh, the market leader in each case is Apple—the ImageWriter for dot-matrix, the StyleWriter II for inkjet, and the LaserWriter for laser printers. HP gives Apple a run for its money in the inkjet and laser printer categories.

After you look at the features and performance of the leading models, try to find a competing printer that costs less, runs faster, or is otherwise better that also meets your needs. The preceding sections that describe the characteristics of each kind of printer will help you identify what to look for. Find out whether the trade-offs you will make by buying the competing printer in terms of quality, service and support, availability of drivers, and other important areas make sense for your situation. If the competing printer is a better overall choice for you, that's the one you should buy.

What Kind of Printer?

Picking a type of printer depends on your overall needs for print quality, speed, price, and a few other important areas. You can then refine the decision based on the detailed needs of the software you will be using.

Print Quality

If you need a printer for personal use or for student work, a dot-matrix printer gives adequate quality at a very affordable price. A dot-matrix printer is also useful for drafts of documents whose final version is printed out on a better quality printer.

An inkjet printer is the best of both worlds, quality-wise. It gives almost laser-quality output for a mid-range price.

A laser printer is the ultimate in quality. You can get a 300 dpi printer for a reasonable price or, for more money, add resolution enhancement or higher base resolutions.

Print Speed

Print speed is something you might give little thought to at purchase time, and then become more concerned about as print times drag on (and on, and on). Both dot-matrix printers and inkjet printers cluster around 240 cps or 2 ppm in high-quality mode, noticeably faster in draft mode.

Laser printers offer a wide range of speeds, from 4 ppm on up. Though they run slower when printing graphics, the overall speed of even a slow laser printer is fine for most uses.

Price

Dot-matrix printers cost $150 to $300 and up; inkjet printers cost $300 to $500 and up; and laser printers cost $500 and up (way up). If you find yourself looking at a higher price model within a given type of printer—a dot-matrix printer over $300, or a monochrome inkjet printer over $500—consider buying the next higher kind of printer whose price range you are moving into.

Portability

Dot-matrix printers are, for the most part, transportable rather than truly portable. Inkjet printers are among the most portable. Laser printers are not portable or even easily transportable.

Odd Paper Sizes

Dot-matrix printers are good for multipart forms, and for long strips of large print used as banners. Specific models with wide carriages cost more but are good for reports printed on wide paper. Most inkjet and laser printers handle long paper well but do not support wide paper; the standard 8 1/2 inches is the limit they can use.

Color

Make sure that your application software supports color printing before making a decision in this area. Dot-matrix printers offer low-quality color that can be fun to use, but inkjet printers are the choice for affordable ($700 and up) near-business-quality color. With any other color printing technology besides inkjet, printers cost thousands of dollars and meet high-end needs like color matching.

Your Main Applications

The applications you are using may impose specific needs on your printing setup. This section takes a look at how the applications you use may help determine what kind of printer you buy.

Word Processing

Word processing covers a wide range of tasks, from writing a letter to a friend, to putting together a report for school or work, to writing a business plan to show to investors. You can print your word processing documents on any kind of printer. For most work, you will want to have access to at least a few fonts and symbols, and you will want your document to look the same on the screen as on paper. (This quality is called *WYSIWYG*, pronounced "whizzywig," which stands for What You See Is What You Get.) The best word processing environment is a system running a graphical user interface, either Windows or the Macintosh, with a printer that supports output of fonts and graphics.

This kind of output used to require buying fonts or even upgrading to PostScript, but Apple and Microsoft have cooperated to produce a standard called *TrueType* that can generate fonts on the computer rather than on the printer. With TrueType, you can buy a "dumb" printer, with no on-board processor and little memory, such as an inkjet printer, and still get excellent results.

If you do even a moderate amount of word processing, you need the higher quality of an inkjet printer over a dot-matrix printer. If you produce more than 20 or so pages a day, or have crunch periods in which you print out dozens or hundreds of pages in a day or two, you need a laser printer. Laser printers are built to get pages out fast, and cost less per page than an inkjet printer.

Desktop Publishing

Desktop publishing is high-end word processing with heavy use of columns, graphics, sophisticated layout, and sometimes color. If you are doing desktop publishing work, then you're putting a lot of time and effort into getting your documents to look right. They should be printed on a printer that does them justice, which usually means at least a laser printer. You can do proofs on an inkjet or low-end laser printer, and then print out final copies on a higher-end laser printer with high base resolution and resolution enhancement features.

Most desktop publishing work requires PostScript. PostScript gives you access to the widest range of fonts, and many illustrations are saved in PostScript format. Consider a laser printer that has, or can be upgraded to have, PostScript support.

If you are doing color desktop publishing, you may need to look at an integrated computer and printer system that supports color matching. Such a system may cost many thousands of dollars, but it does the work of color workstations that cost far more.

Spreadsheets and Reports

Spreadsheets often benefit greatly from being printed on wide paper. You can do this in two ways. You can get a wide-carriage dot-matrix printer that can print out the spreadsheet on wider paper. Or you can get an inkjet or laser printer that supports legal-size paper. Use your application software to turn the print image sideways (landscape mode) and possibly shrink it as well, and then print out the spreadsheet on legal-size paper.

If you will be printing out lots of spreadsheets or other reports, especially onto multipart paper, you may want a high-volume, wide-carriage dot-matrix printer. Make sure that the print quality is adequate for the intended use of the reports.

If your needs are more in the direction of spreadsheet publishing—carefully laid-out spreadsheets and reports with fonts, italics, boldface, white space, and even graphics—look at the desktop publishing and presentations sections to see how these concerns are addressed. Keep in mind that color is a great help to business graphics.

Presentations

Presentations need color! You can get mediocre color from a dot-matrix printer, if your graphics or presentation program supports your printer and four-color ribbons are easy to get. But if you're trying to get someone to commit to spending money—the purpose, after all, of most presentations—you need better quality. A color inkjet printer works well for these kinds of uses. In a home office or small office setting, you can buy a mixed-use inkjet printer such as the HP DeskJet 560C that produces equally good results for monochrome or color printing. If your needs are somewhat greater, get a cheap laser printer for text and a color inkjet printer for color graphics. In a larger business setting, you may be able to justify the cost of an even higher quality color laser printer by sharing it among several users or even several departments.

Other Uses

Other uses are for the most part similar to, or combinations of, the needs mentioned previously. Read the descriptions of these other areas and determine how they are similar to yours. Think about what would best meet the needs of the reader of your printed output; if you're in business, think about what your competition uses.

If you don't know yet what your printing needs will be, get an inexpensive dot-matrix printer with color capability. You will be able to print drafts of anything, even color graphics, and use a copy shop or print shop on the occasions when you need higher quality. If you outgrow the dot-matrix printer, you can always make an appropriate buying decision later without having spent too much money in the meantime.

Chapter Summary

Dot-matrix printers are flexible and cheap, but inkjet printers are a more common middle-of-the-road choice. They combine good quality with low price and are transportable or, in many cases, portable. Laser printers are best for the highest quality and high-volume work.

This chapter describes the features of these major types of printers in detail. This chapter also tells you how to choose a printer, lists the differences among the printer types, and describes the needs of different key applications. Give your choice of printer a fair amount of thought before you buy; your printer may outlast your computer.

IN THE NEXT CHAPTER

The next chapter consists of listings of different kinds of printers from major manufacturers. Use it to help you make a printer purchasing decision that you will be happy with over the long term.

CHAPTER TEN

Listing of Printers

The information in the previous chapter should help you decide what kind of printer you want and which features are most important to you. Inkjet printers are popular for home offices and home businesses, but personal laser printers are competitive in this market, too. Dot-matrix and inkjet printers both offer color capability; thermal transfer printers are generally best for going on the road. All of these considerations intersect with the current state of your bank account and how much you want to spend for each page that you print.

The tables in this chapter cover the full range of available products. One table covers thermal transfer printers for portable use; another covers dot-matrix printers; a third covers inkjet devices. Two tables are devoted to laser printers—one for personal printers, running at 4 to 7 pages per minute (ppm), another for office laser printers that run at 8 ppm or more. The final table covers color printers. Each table is sorted by the most important considerations for that type of printer: weight for thermal transfer printers, number of pins and price for dot-matrix, system type for inkjet, and pages per minute for laser printers. The latter tables are also sorted by company name and model so that you can easily look at all the products that meet specific requirements.

Printer makers are steadily modifying their product lines as prices for each kind of technology drop and as buyers move toward higher capability products. Use the tables to identify a few products that meet your needs, and then call vendors for availability and pricing information. The trade magazines regularly do massive reviews of large numbers of printers; *PC Magazine* devotes one issue a year, usually around October, solely to printers. Look for these reviews for comparative pricing and performance information.

Most of the fields for all the tables are described in the following section. The specific sections for each table only describe different fields or additional considerations.

Fields for Printer Tables

The following descriptions apply to all the printer tables. Look in the descriptions of each table for information specific to that table.

- *Company, Model.* Use this information to follow up on a product by calling the company or a dealer. Epson makes the best-known and most imitated dot-matrix printers; HP is the one to beat in laser and inkjet printers; and Canon makes the popular Bubblejet printers.

- *Resolution/Pins.* Thermal transfer printers and 24-pin dot-matrix printers border on being good enough for business use. Inkjet and laser printers easily make the grade, with enhancement features and higher dpi counts putting laser printers on top.

- *Speed.* This factor becomes very important as you use your printer more. Most inkjet printers seem too slow, but a 4 ppm laser printer is fast enough for most uses.

- *Max Width.* This factor is very important to users who need extra-wide printouts. With Windows and the Mac you can scale output; this capability makes the width factor less important to most users than it was under DOS.

- *Paper Size.* Legal size and envelope printing are useful options to have; other sizes may be important if you work outside the U.S. or have specialized needs.

- *Size, Weight.* These factors are crucial if you want transportability or if you have a small office. If these factors are important to you, try to see the printer and, if weight is important, carry it around a bit before making a buying decision.

- *Buffer Size.* A buffer allows a printer to store one or more pages of text (or small graphics), decreasing the time your computer takes to finish its part of the print job. Because Windows and the Mac have background printing, this feature is becoming less important.

- *System Type, Connects To, Ports.* Most printers connect to a serial or parallel port on an IBM-compatible; this feature is important if you only have one or the other free. Drivers and cables exist that allow Macs to drive some IBM-compatible printers.

- *Emulation.* Emulations are very important for DOS, because each application has its own batch of printer drivers; one of them has to match your printer or a printer it can emulate, or you can't print. This feature is less important for Windows, in which all applications can print as long as there's a Windows driver for the printer.

- *Noise Level.* This information is important but the numbers are hard to relate to. Try listening to a printer or two in an office or store to get a feel for what their noise level really means, and then compare these known systems to the numbers in the table.
- *Warranty.* Printers break down frequently, and repairs can be a very large expense if the warranty is too short. If you buy mail-order, check who pays for repairs and shipping.
- *Price.* Look for the "sweet spot" in prices—the point where there are a lot of high-performance products at a similar price. At or a little below this level is where you can find the best buys. Prices for lesser products will not be as cheap as they should be; prices for higher performance products will increase out of proportion to the improved performance.
- *Fonts.* This is an important but confusing topic that is currently in flux as new font and font-independence technologies are developed. Look for a moderate number of built-in fonts. If this is a very important topic to you, get a PostScript printer.

Table 10.1 Thermal Printers Sorted by Weight

This table includes light, relatively low-quality printers that can run from batteries. The listings are sorted by weight because this kind of printer is designed to be carried along with a portable computer.

If you need to print while you're not able to plug into a power outlet, you need this kind of printer. Otherwise, look for a light dot-matrix or inkjet printer that can travel with you but also do some work in the office and at home.

Specific differences for this kind of printer are as follows:

- *Connects To.* This feature is important because you need the printer to work with your portable computer, hopefully without configuration hassles.
- *Power.* For greatest convenience, a portable printer should be able to work from wall current (AC) as well as from batteries.
- *Battery Life.* Longer is better; also, check into the cost and rechargeability of batteries.

Table 10.1 Thermal Printers

Company, Model	Resolution	Speed	Max Width	Size (H, W, D)	Weight
Value Leader					
Citizen PN48	360 dpi	80 cps		8.5"2"x 13.5"x3.5"	6.4 lb.
Citizen Notebook Printer II	360 dpi	210 cps		8.5"2"x 11.7"x4.1"	2.6 lb. w/battery
GCC WriteMove II	360 dpi	.5 ppm		2"x11.7"x 3.5"	2.5 lb. w/battery
Mannesmann Tally Mobile-Writer	300 dpi	6 ppm		2.3"x 11.4"x8.7"	8.3 lb.
Mannesmann Tally Mobile-WriterPS	300 dpi	6 ppm		2.3"x 11.4"x8.7"	8.3 lb.

Table 10.2 Dot-Matrix Printers Sorted by Number of Pins and Price

This table covers dot-matrix printers, once very popular, now increasingly used only for the lowest end applications and jobs where impact is important, like carbonless forms. The table is sorted by number of pins (either 9 or 24) and by price, which is a key consideration for most buyers of this kind of printer.

Dot-matrix printers have low consumable costs—an occasional ribbon, plus paper—as well as low purchase prices, so your savings can continue after you buy the printer. Many dot-matrix printers also offer simple color capability at little additional cost.

One concern that's important but hard to address in a table is durability. Some printers stand up to heavy use better than others. If you intend to print a lot of pages per month, check magazine reviews and ask colleagues to find out more about this characteristic.

Specific differences for this kind of printer are as follows:

- *Company, Model.* The companies listed in the table are all top-line companies that tend to stand behind their products.
- *Pins.* 24-pin printers are higher quality than 9-pin models at little additional cost.

Buffer Size	Connects To	Emulation	Warranty	Price	Power/ Battery Life	Other
	PC	Citizen GSX, Epson LQ, IBM X24	2 years	$279	AC/NiCad	
	PC, Mac	Citizen GSX, Epson LQ, IBM X24, Apple StyleWriter (I and II)	2 years	$399	AC/NiCad	Supports color
	Mac, PC	Citizen, QuickDraw	1 year	$329		
1M	Mac, PC	HP PCL4		$875		
2M	Mac, PC	PostScript, HP PCL4		$999		

- *Speed.* These ratings are supplied by manufacturers; look at reviews for independent speed ratings.
- *Horizontal Characters.* This measurement can be important if you use a fixed font size. Check any reports you plan to produce and see whether you need a wide-carriage printer to fit all the characters on a sheet.
- *Size, Weight.* Some dot-matrix printers are transportable for use in a hotel room or other venue.
- *Emulation.* This factor is especially important if you want to use the printer with DOS programs.
- *Noise Level.* Both the noise level and the type of noise can be important; a steady whir might be much easier to live with than a shrill whine. Try to get a chance to listen to the printer in use before buying.
- *Price.* If you're looking at dot-matrix printers over $500 or so, consider inkjet printers as well.
- *Colors.* This feature is functional for occasional, low-end business graphics or for student use. For more professional color, see table 10.6 for a list of color laser printers.

Table 10.2 Dot Matrix Printers

Company, Model	Pins	Speed	Paper Size	Buffer Size
Apple ImageWriter II		.5ppm-2ppm	3"-10" wide	24K
Brother M-1324	24	72-216 cps	8.5" wide	8K
Brother M-1809	9	75-360 cps	8.5" wide	32K
Brother M-1824L	24	112-270 cps	11" wide	32K
Brother M-1909	9	75-300 cps	11" wide	32K
Brother M-1924	24	112-270 cps	11" wide	64K
Citizen GSX-145	24	64-192 cps	11" wide	8K
Citizen GSX-190	9	40-240 cps	8.5" wide	8K
Citizen GSX-220	24	80-240 cps	8.5" wide	8K
Citizen GSX-230	24	90-270 cps	8.5" wide	8K
Citizen GSX-240	24	99-300 cps	8.5" wide	8K

Value Leader

Company, Model	Pins	Speed	Paper Size	Buffer Size
DEC DECWriter 65	24	53-160 cps	8.5" wide	8K
DEC DECWriter 95	24	99-300 cps	8.5" wide	8K
Epson Action Printer 2250	9	48-240 cps	8.5" wide	4K
Epson Action Printer 3250	24	72-200 cps	8.5" wide	11K
Epson Action Printer 3260	24	66-270 cps	8.5" wide	11K
Epson LQ 1070+	24	90-269 cps	11" wide	8K
IBM 2380 Plus	9	67-270 cps	8.5" wide	11K
IBM 2390 Plus	24	70-210 cps	8.5" wide	32K
Mannesmann Tally MT150/24	24	120-360 cps	11" wide	24K

Listing of Printers

Connects To	Warranty	Price	Fonts/Colors	Other Features
Mac or Apple II	1 year	$439	4 bitmap	(with optional color ribbon)
PC	1 year	$399		
PC	1 year	$549		
PC	1 year	$749		
PC	1 year	$699		
PC	1 year	$949		
PC	2 years	$449 ($528 color)		
PC	2 years	$199		
PC	2 years	$199		
PC	2 years	$299 ($358 color)		
PC	2 years	$349 ($408 color)		
PC	3 years	$229	built-in color	
PC	3 years	$319		
PC	2 years	$239		
PC	2 years	$269		
PC	2 years	$299	built-in 50-sheet paper tray	
PC	2 years	$499		
PC	1 year	$399		
PC	1 year	$429		
PC	1 year	$899		

continues

Table 10.2 Continued				
Company, Model	Pins	Speed	Paper Size	Buffer Size
Mannesmann Tally MT150/9	9	75-300 cps	8.5" wide	10K
Mannesmann Tally MT151/24	24	120-360 cps	11" wide	24K
Mannesmann Tally MT151/9	9	75-300 cps	8.5" wide	10K
Panasonic KX-P1150	9	32-160 cps	8.5" wide	4K
Panasonic KX-P2023	24	53-160 cps	8.5" wide	14K
Value Leader				
Panasonic KX-P2123	24	80-240 cps	8.5" wide	14K
Panasonic KX-P2124	24	106-320 cps	8.5" wide	20K
Star Micronics NX-1001 MultiFont	9	75-180 cps	8.5" wide	4K
Star Micronics NX-1001 Rainbow	9	38-150 cps	8.5" wide	2K
Star Micronics NX-1500 MultiFont	9	45-180 cps	11" wide	16K
Star Micronics NX-2415 II MultiFont	24	67-200 cps	11" wide	40K
Star Micronics NX-2450 Rainbow	24	53-160 cps	11" wide	14.5K
Star Micronics NX-2480 Rainbow	24	67-220 cps	11" wide	47K
Star Micronics XR-1020 MultiFont	9	70-372 cps	8.5" wide	32K

Table 10.3 Inkjet Printers Sorted by System, Company, and Model

This table covers inkjet printers, an increasingly popular type of printer because of their high quality and relatively low cost. The table is sorted by system type, and then by manufacturer and model. The idea is that you can look at all the offerings that work with your machine in deciding the right mix of price, performance, and features for you.

Connects To	Warranty	Price	Fonts/Colors	Other Features
PC	1 year	$699		
PC	1 year	$949		
PC	1 year	$749		
PC	1 year	$169		
PC	1 year	$249		
PC	1 year	$299		
PC	1 year	$369		
PC	1 year	$169		
PC	1 year	$199	color	
PC	1 year	$279		
PC	1 year	$419		
PC	1 year	$279		
PC	1 year	$329		
PC	1 year	$499		

Inkjet printers have low purchase prices but high consumable costs— up to a maximum of about 5¢ a page once ink is paid for. However, they meet a lot of needs; quality is high enough for business use; cost, price, and weight are all low, and many are small enough for you to take on a trip. Also, the best deals in color printing are inkjet printers.

Specific differences for this kind of printer are as follows:

- *Resolution.* Inkjet printers can put down a lot of dots per inch, but their placement of the dots is not as precise as laser printers; 300 dpi output from a laser printer looks better than 360 dpi output from an inkjet. Also, inkjet printers don't use resolution-enhancement technologies, so overall results are not quite as good.
- *Colors.* You can get average-quality color from an inkjet without paying a lot more. This feature is especially valuable for occasional business graphics or student use.

Table 10.3 Inkjet Printers

Company, Model	Resolution	Speed	Max Width	Paper Size	Size (H,W,D)	Weight
Apple StyleWriter II	360 dpi	1-2 ppm	8.5"	Letter, legal, A4, envelopes	7"x13.6"x 7.9"	6.6 lb.
Apple Portable StyleWriter	360 dpi	.5-1 ppm	8.5"	Letter, legal, A4, envelopes	1.9"x 12.2"x 8.7"	4.5 lb. (with battery)
Apple Color StyleWriter Pro	360 dpi	up to 2 ppm (b/w) up to .5 ppm (color)	8.5"	Letter, envelopes	7.2"x16.5"x 10.1"	11 lb.
Brother HJ-400	360 dpi	110 cps		Letter, legal, A4, envelopes		
Canon Bubblejet 100	360 dpi	140 cps		Letter, legal, A4, envelopes	6.8"x 13.7"x 7.6"	6.6 lb.

- *Noise Level.* Inkjets are fairly quiet, and the kind of noise they make is not very irritating.
- *Price.* Laser printers have higher output quality and are better suited for heavy use, so consider a laser printer if the price of a unit that meets your needs starts creeping over the $700 mark and color is not important.
- *Other Features.* Look for a relatively high-capacity input tray to avoid loading in paper all the time.

Buffer Size	Connects To	Emulation	Ports	Color	Warranty	Price	Other Features
128K	Mac	TrueType	serial	no	1 year	$339	Uses GrayShare features, 39 TrueType fonts
16K	Mac		parallel	no	1 year	$439	NiCad battery and charger included, 2-2.5 hours per charge, Energy Star
96K	Mac	N/A	serial	yes	1 year	$629	64 TrueType fonts, supports Color-Share and Color-Sync, Energy Star
64K	PC, Mac	IBM Pro-Printer XL24e, Epson FX-850, QuickDraw	serial, parallel, Mac	no	2 years	$369	
50.4K	PC	Epson LQ IBM X24e	parallel	no	2 years	$359	

Table 10.3 Continued

Company, Model	Resolution	Speed	Max Width	Paper Size	Size (H,W,D)	Weight
Canon Bubblejet 10sx	360 dpi	110 cps		Letter, legal, A4, envelopes	1.9"x 12.2"x8.7"	3.7 lb.
Canon Bubblejet 200e	360 dpi	248 cps		Letter, legal, A4, envelopes	6.8"x 13.7"x7.6"	6.6 lb.
Canon Bubblejet 230	360 dpi	248 cps		Letter, legal, A4, envelopes, Ledger (11"x17"), A3	8.2"x 16.9"x7.9"	7.7 lb.
Canon Bubblejet 600 Color	360 dpi	240 cps		Letter, legal, envelopes	6.8"x 13.7"x7.6"	9.9 lb.
Citizen ProJet II	300 dpi	2-3 ppm		Letter, legal, A4, envelopes	5.5"x 14.5"x 13.5"	8.8 lb.
Epson Stylus 300	360 dpi	165 cps		Letter, legal, A4 envelopes		11 lb.
Epson Stylus 800	360 dpi	225 cps		Letter, legal, A4 envelopes		11 lb.
Epson Stylus 1000	360 dpi	375 cps		Letter, legal, A4 envelopes, Ledger (11"x17")	6"x26"x 20"	19 lb.
Epson Stylus Color	720 dpi	300 cps		Letter, legal, A4 B5	7.5"x 18.5"x20.5"	16.3 lb.

Listing of Printers

Buffer Size	Connects To	Emulation	Ports	Color	Warranty	Price	Other Features
37K	PC	IBM X24e, Epson LQ	parallel	no	2 years	$349	Portable, battery or AC powered
49K	PC	Epson LQ 510, IBM X24e	parallel	no	2 years	$399	Up to 4 ppm in Windows. Includes 20 extra TrueType fonts
41.2K	PC	Epson LQ, IBM X24e	parallel	no	2 years	$549	
60K	PC	Epson LQ, IBM X24e	parallel	yes	2 years	$719	Includes 20 extra TrueType fonts
128K	PC	HP DeskJet	parallel	no	2 years	$349	
24K	PC	ESC/P 2	parallel	no	2 years	$349	
32K	PC	ESC/P 2	parallel	no	2 years	$399	
128K	PC	ESC/P 2	parallel	no	2 years	$599	
64K	PC	ESC/P 2	parallel	yes	2 years	$699	

Table 10.3 Continued						
Company, Model	Resolution	Speed	Max Width	Paper Size	Size (H,W,D)	Weight
IBM ExecJet II 4076	300x600 dpi	300 cps		Letter, legal, A4, envelopes		
Value Leader						
HP DeskJet 520	600x300 dpi	3 ppm		Letter, legal, A4, envelopes		
HP DeskJet 500C	300 dpi	3 ppm		Letter, legal, A4, envelopes		
HP DeskJet 560C	600 x 300 dpi	3 ppm		Letter, legal, A4, envelopes		
HP DeskJet 1200C	600 x 300 dpi	7 ppm		Letter, legal, A4, envelopes		

Table 10.4 Personal Laser Printers Sorted by Speed, Company, and Model

This table covers personal laser printers, roughly defined as laser printers with a print speed of 4 to 7 pages per minute (ppm). It's sorted by speed (number of pages per minute), and then by manufacturer. This setup makes it easy to compare all the printers of a given speed rating.

Most laser printers are based on a couple of different print engines with an 8 ppm speed rating. The print engine manufacturers introduced 4 ppm versions in order to spark the creation of a lower price market. This strategy has worked well for both vendors and users, and prices of these half-speed, high-quality printers continue to drop. Consider a personal laser printer if you plan to print more than a hundred or so pages per month or if laser quality is the minimum you want to consider. Consider an inkjet printer if your needs are more modest or if you need color.

Fields specific to laser printers, and laser-specific considerations for other fields, are as follows:

Buffer Size	Connects To	Emulation	Ports	Color	Warranty	Price	Other Features
	PC		parallel	no	2 years	$335	
	PC		parallel	no	1 year	$399	
	PC		parallel	yes	1 year	$799	
	PC		parallel	yes	1 year	$899	
	PC		parallel	yes	1 year	$2199	Supports PCL5, scalable typefaces

- *Resolution.* The 300 to 600 dpi resolution of most personal laser printers is just fine for standard business use. Office laser printers (see table 10.5) offer higher resolutions and resolution enhancement technologies for even higher quality.
- *Speed.* Unless you print lots of long documents, 4, 5, or 6 ppm is fast enough for most uses.
- *Emulations.* PostScript is a valuable and sometimes expensive extra. If you want PostScript capabilities, you may want to look at a faster, higher quality printer as well.
- *Microprocessor, Speed.* The type and speed of any built-in microprocessor is most important for processing complicated graphics.
- *Memory.* If you print graphics frequently, make sure that you buy a fair amount of memory (4M or more), or that you can add more later inexpensively.
- *In & Out Trays.* The size of these trays can be important for big jobs.
- *Duty Cycle; Toner Cartridge Life; Print Engine Life.* These are important considerations if you print more than a couple hundred pages a month.

Table 10.4 Personal Laser Printers

Company, Model	Resolution	Speed	System Type	Ports	Resident Fonts	Emulation
Apple Personal LaserWriter 300	300 dpi	4 ppm	Mac	serial	39 TrueType	N/A
Apple Personal LaserWriter 320	300 dpi	4 ppm	Mac	LocalTalk, serial	39 scalable	PostScript
Brother HL-6	300 dpi	6 ppm	PC	parallel, serial	48 bitmap, 9 scalable	PCL4, IBM ProPrinter, Epson FX-850
Brother HL-6V	300 dpi	6 ppm	PC	parallel, serial	50 bitmap, 9 scalable	PCL5, PCL4, IBM ProPrinter, Epson FX-850
Canon LBP-430	300 dpi	4 ppm	PC	parallel	2 bitmap, 2 scalable	PCL5
Value Leader DEC DEClaser 1152	300 dpi	4 ppm	PC, Mac	parallel, serial,	17 Post-Script	PostScript, PCL4
DEC DEClaser 1800	300 dpi	6 ppm	PC	parallel, serial	34	PCL5, Epson FX-850, IBM ProPrinter XL-24e
Epson Action-Laser 1500	300 dpi	6 ppm	PC	parallel, serial	27	PCL5, Epson FX/LX, Epson GL/2
Epson Action-Laser 1600	600 dpi	6 ppm	PC	parallel, serial	45	PCL5e, Epson FX/LX, Epson GL/2
HP LaserJet 4L	300 dpi	4 ppm	PC	parallel, serial	34	PCL5, Epson FX-850, IBM ProPrinter XL-24e

Max. Paper Size	CPU Speed	Size (H,W,D)	Weight	In/Out Trays	Warranty	Price	Other Features
8.5"x11"	N/A	6.3"x15.2" x14.9"	15 lb.	100 sheet in	1 year		GrayShare, Energy Star
8.5"x11"	AMD 29205 RISC	6.3"x15.2" x14.9"	15.4 lb.	100 sheet in	1 year		FinePrint, PhotoGrade (optional), Energy Star
8.5"x14"		9.1"x 13.8"x 16.5"	21.5 lb.	150 sheet in	2 years	$895	
8.5"x14"		9.1"x13.8" x16.5"	21.5 lb.	150 sheet in	2 years	$995	
8.5"x14"		6.125"x 14.5"x 14.875"	18 lb.	100 sheet in	2 years	$799	Energy Star
8.5"x11"		8"x13.8"	25 lb.	100	3 years	$699	
8.5"x11"		8.9"x14.1" x17.9"	18.6 lb.	150 sheet in	3 years	$779	
8.5"x14"	Motorola 68000 (16.67 MHz)	8.9"x 14.5"x18"	22 lb.	150 sheet in, 100 sheet out	2 years	$849	
8.5"x14"	SPARClite RISC (17.6 MHz)	9"x14.5" x18"	22 lb.	150 sheet in, 100 sheet out	2 years	$1199	
8.5"x11"		8.9"x14.1" x17.9"	18.6 lb.	150 sheet in	3 years	$779	

continues

Table 10.4 Continued

Company, Model	Resolution	Speed	System Type	Ports	Resident Fonts	Emulation
HP LaserJet 4ML	300 dpi	4 ppm	Mac	parallel, serial, LocalTalk	80	PostScript Level 2, PCL5
HP LaserJet 4MP	600 dpi	4 ppm	Mac	parallel, serial, LocalTalk	80	PostScript Level 2, PCL5
HP LaserJet 4P	600 dpi	4 ppm	PC	parallel, serial	45	PCL5
IBM 4037 5E Page Printer	1500x300	5 ppm	PC	parallel	40	IBM Pro Printer, IBM 4019/4029,PCL
LaserMaster Win-Printer 1000	1000 dpi	4 ppm	PC	proprietary	50	PostScript, PCL, Windows GDI
NEC SilentWriter 610	300 dpi	6 ppm	PC	parallel	34	PCL, Windows GDI
Panasonic KX-P4400	300 dpi	4 ppm	PC	parallel	28	PCL
Panasonic KX-P4410	300 dpi	5 ppm	PC	parallel	28	PCL
Panasonic KX-P4430	300 dpi	5 ppm	PC	parallel, serial	28	PCL5
Panasonic KX-P5400	300 dpi	4 ppm	PC, Mac	parallel, serial, AppleTalk	45	PCL, PostScript
Panasonic KX-P5410	300 dpi	5 ppm	PC, Mac	parallel, serial, AppleTalk	45	PCL, PostScript

Paper Size	CPU Speed	Size (H,W,D)	Weight	In/Out Trays	Warranty	Price	Other Features
8.5"x11"		6.5"x14"x14.5"	15.5 lb.	100 sheet in	1 year	$1279	
8.5"x11"		6.8"x14.7"x15.4"	21 lb.	250 sheet in	1 year	$1729	
8.5"x11"		6.8"x14.7"x15.4"	20 lb.	250 sheet in	1 year	$1229	
8.5"x11"		9.7"x15"x17.6"	30 lb.		1 year	$759	
8.5"x14"	PC-dependent	5.8"x14.3"x13.9"	15.6 lb.	25 sheet in	1 year	$1095	
8.5"x14"	PC-dependent	4.7"x14.6"x14"	16.6 lb.	50 sheet in, 50 out	1 year	$550	
8.5"x11"		11.5"x5"x15"	14.5 lb.	100 sheet in	1 year	$699	
8.5"x14"		9.3"x14.6"x15.5"	30.9 lb.	100 sheet in	1 year	$769	
8.5"x14"		9.3"x14.6"x15.5"	30.9 lb.	200 sheet in, 100 out	1 year	$869	
8.5"x14"		11.5"x5"x15"	14.5 lb.	100 sheet in	1 year	$999	
8.5"x14"		9.3"x14.6"x15.5"	30.9 lb.	200 sheet in, 100 out	1 year	$1399	

Table 10.5 Office Laser Printers Sorted by Speed, Company, and Model

This table covers office laser printers, roughly defined as laser printers with a print speed of 8 pages per minute (ppm) or more. The table is sorted by speed (number of pages per minute), and then by manufacturer and quality. This setup makes it easy to compare all the printers of a given speed rating.

Most laser printers are based on a couple of different print engines with a 4 or 8 ppm speed rating. A few other engines are now becoming available that work at other speeds. The speed rating does not include the amount of time it takes to process complex layouts and graphics; that's dependent on the microprocessor speed and the amount of RAM in the printer. Don't pay for a high speed rating to solve what's really a processing problem.

A key feature of office laser printers is that they can support a number of users over a network. Some of them can also support different kinds of systems. If you are combining Macs and PCs on a network, look for HP emulation, PostScript, and automatic emulation switching.

Table 10.5	Office Laser Printers					
Company, Model	Resolution	Speed	System Type	Ports	Resident Fonts	Emulation
Apple LaserWriter Pro 630	600 dpi	8 ppm	Mac or Windows	EtherTalk, LocalTalk, parallel, serial, 2 SCSI ports (for external hard disks)	64 scalable PostScript and TrueType	PostScript, PCL4+
Apple LaserWriter Pro 810	up to 800 dpi	20 ppm (letter or legal), 10 ppm (tabloid)	Mac, Windows, others	EtherTalk, LocalTalk, parallel, serial	64 scalable TrueType, 35 PostScript	PostScript, PCL4+
Apple LaserWriter Select 360	600 dpi	10 ppm	Mac or Windows	parallel, LocalTalk, serial	64 scalable PostScript and TrueType	PostScript, PCL5

The fields in this table are described in general in the first section and in the personal laser printers section just before this one. Only fields that have specific considerations in relation to office laser printers are covered here:

- *Resolution.* 600 dpi resolution is a mainstream feature of office laser printers. Ask about resolution enhancement technologies as well; they can substitute for or add to the improvement offered by higher resolution.
- *Speed.* 8 ppm is plenty fast enough for any but the most intense use.
- *Emulations.* PostScript is a valuable and sometimes expensive extra. Look for PostScript Level II for greater speed and quality.
- *Duty Cycle; Toner Cartridge Life; Print Engine Life.* If you're going to get an expensive printer, it might as well be inexpensive to operate and last a long time; compare these qualities carefully.

Max. Paper Size	CPU Speed	RAM Max	Size (H,W,D)	Weight	In/Out Trays	Warranty	Price	Other Features
	25MHz	8M, 32M	12"x 16.9"x16.8"	39 lb.	100 and 250 sheet in	1 year	$2172	FinePrint and Photo-Grade
	7.3MHz	8M, 32M	19.5"x 20.5"x21.5"	81 lb.	3 750-sheet universal trays	1 year		
	16MHz	7M, 16M	8"x15" x18.3"	26 lb.	250 sheet in	1 year	$2099	Energy Star

continues

Table 10.5 Continued

Company, Model	Resolution	Speed	System Type	Ports	Resident Fonts	Emulation
Brother HL-10H	600 dpi	10 ppm	PC	parallel, serial	83	PostScript, PCL5e, IBM ProPrinter XL, Epson FX, Diablo 630, HPGL, Brother TwinWriter
Brother HL-10V	300 dpi	10 ppm	PC	parallel, serial	24 bitmap, 12 scalable	PCL5, IBM ProPrinter XL, Epson FX, Diablo 630, Brother TwinWriter
Canon LBP-860	600 dpi	8 ppm	PC, Mac	parallel, serial	35 Intellifont, 10 TrueType	PCL5e
DEC DEClaser 5100	600 dpi	8 ppm	PC, Mac	parallel, serial, AppleTalk	120 resident	PostScript, PCL5e
HP LaserJet 4 Plus	600 dpi	12 ppm	PC	parallel, serial	45 resident	PCL5
HP LaserJet 4M	600 dpi	8 ppm	PC, Mac	parallel, serial, Appletalk	45 resident	PostScript, PCL5
HP LaserJet 4Si	600 dpi	17 ppm	PC	parallel	45 resident	PostScript Level 2, PCL5
HP LaserJet 4Si MX	600 dpi	17 ppm	PC, Mac	parallel, Ethernet, AppleTalk	80 resident	PostScript Level 2, PCL5
IBM 4039 10R	600 dpi	10 ppm	PC	parallel, serial	40	

Max. Paper Size	CPU Speed	RAM Max	Size (H,W,D)	Weight	In/Out Trays	Warranty	Price	Other Features
8.5"x14"		2M, 34M	10.9"x 15.8"x14.6"	37.4 lb.	250 sheet in	2 years	$1695	PCMCIA slot
8.5"x14"		2M, 6M	10.9"x 15.8"x14.6"	37.4 lb.	250 sheet in	2 years	$1295	
8.5"x14"		2M, 34M	12"x17" x16"	37 lb.	250 and 100 sheet in	2 years	$1839	
8.5"x14"		2M, 66M	11.7"x 16.4"x 15.9"	37.4 lb.		3 years	$2199	
8.5"x14"	25MHz	2M, 66M	11.7"x 16.4"x15.9"	37 lb.	250 in	1 year	$1839	
8.5"x14"	25MHz	6M, 66M	11.7"x 16.4"x15.9"	37 lb.	250 in	1 year	$2479	
8.5"x14"		2M, 34M	16.5"x 21.5"x23.5"	94 lb.	dual 500 in	1 year	$3749	
8.5"x14"		10M, 26M	16.5"x 21.5"x23.5"	94 lb.	dual 500 in	1 year	$5499	
8.5"x14"		2M	10.2"x 14.2"x20.6"	33.6 lb.	200 sheet in	1 year	$1479	

Table 10.5 Continued

Company, Model	Resolution	Speed	System Type	Ports	Resident Fonts	Emulation
IBM 4039 12L plus	600 dpi	12 ppm	PC	parallel, serial	39	PCL5, PostScript
IBM 4039 12R plus	600 dpi	12 ppm	PC	parallel, serial	39	PCL5, PostScript
IBM 4039 16L plus	600 dpi	16 ppm	PC	parallel, serial	39	PCL5, PostScript
LaserMaster Win-Printer 600XL	600 dpi	8 ppm	PC	proprietary	50	PostScript, PCL, Windows GDI
LexMark Win-Writer 600	600 dpi	8-10 ppm	PC	proprietary	64	PCL4

Value Leader

Company, Model	Resolution	Speed	System Type	Ports	Resident Fonts	Emulation
Mannesmann Tally MT9008	600 dpi	8 ppm	PC, Mac	parallel, serial	45	PCL5e, HPGL
Mannesmann Tally MT908	300 dpi	8 ppm	PC	parallel, serial	8	PCL5, Epson FX850, IBM Pro-Printer
NEC SilentWriter 1097	600 dpi	10 ppm	PC, Mac	parallel, serial, Appletalk	34	PostScript, PCL5
Panasonic KX-P4440	300 dpi	10 ppm	PC	parallel, serial	8	PCL5
Panasonic KX-P4455	300 dpi	11 ppm	PC, Mac	parallel, serial, AppleTalk	39	PostScript, PCL5

Max. Paper Size	CPU Speed	RAM Max	Size (H,W,D)	Weight	In/Out Trays	Warranty	Price	Other Features
8.5"x14"		4M	16"x14.9"x21"	46 lb.	500 sheet in	1 year	$2765	
8.5"x14"		4M	11.8"x14.9"x21"	40 lb.	200 sheet in	1 year	$1909	
8.5"x14"		4M	16"x14.9"x21"	46 lb.	500 sheet in	1 year	$3239	
11"x17"	host-based	host-based	8.3x19.3"x17.9"	50.6 lb.	250 sheet in	1 year	$2495	
8.5"x14"		2M	12.4"x14.9"x20.9"	35.5 lb.	200 sheet in, 100 out	1 year	$1399	
8.5"x14"	20MHz	2M, 32M	11.2"x15.5"x14.5"	37.8 lb.	250 and 100 sheet in, 250 out	1 year	$1499	Energy Star
8.5"x14"	16MHz	1M, 5M	8.8x15.8"x16.2"	31 lb.	250 sheet in	1 year	$1499	
8.5"x14"		7M, 9M			250 sheet in	1 year	$1499	
8.5"x14"		1M, 5M	11.2"x14.6"x16.7"	35.5 lb.	dual 200-sheet in, 100 out	1 year	$1249	
8.5"x14"		2M, 4M	14.5"x28"x17"	59.6 lb.	dual 250-sheet in, 250 out	1 year	$2249	

Table 10.6 Color Printers Sorted by Company and Model

This table covers color printers other than dot-matrix printers. These printers use a variety of methods, including laser printing, inkjet printing, and dye sublimation printing. All the printers listed in table 10.6 work well for proofing color output, but none comes close to the quality of a professional print shop. Don't buy a color printer to run a thousand copies of a brochure. Instead, have it done professionally—it's worth the trouble.

The fields in this table are described in general in the first section of the chapter. Only fields that have specific considerations in relation to color printers are covered here.

- *Resolution.* Resolution is a tricky issue with color printers. Ask the manufacturer for output samples before assuming that higher resolution equals better output.
- *Speed.* Forget it. Color laser printers can take from one to two hours to finish a single page. In extremely rare circumstances, you can get a page in a few minutes, but you can't rate color printers on a "Page Per Minute" scale like regular printers.

Table 10.6 Color Non-Inkjet Printers

Company, Model	Print Method	Resolution	System Type
CalComp ColorMaster Plus	thermal wax	300	Mac, PC
Dataproducts Jolt PSe	ink	300	Mac, PC
Value Leader			
Fargo Primera	dye sublimation	203	Mac, PC
GCC Technologies ColorTone	dye sublimation	300	Mac, PC
Kodak ColorEase PS	dye sublimation	300	Mac, PC
LaserMaster DisplayMaker	ink	n/a	Mac, PC
QMS ColorScript 1000	color laser	300	Mac, PC

- *Emulations.* PostScript is practically a necessity with color printers. Almost all high-end color applications rely on PostScript's color functions; if you find a color printer that doesn't do PostScript, it won't work with much of your software.
- *Price.* Color costs. If you're serious about getting a color printer, expect to pay from $5,000 to $10,000 (up to $20,000 in some cases) for a good one. Lower quality color printers are not good for much more than printing invitations to a birthday party.
- *Print Method.* These include color laser, dye sublimation, solid ink, or thermal wax-transfer. Dye sublimation printers are expensive to feed (around $2 per page); the other methods average 50¢ to 80¢ a page.

Ports	Resident Fonts	Paper Sizes	CPU Speed	Price	Other Features
serial, parallel	39	letter, tabloid		$8995	
parallel, serial, AppleTalk		letter		$4995	
parallel, serial		letter, A4	host-based	$1445	
Ethernet, LocalTalk, parallel, serial	35	letter, legal, A4	25MHz	$7999	16M RAM included
LocalTalk, parallel, serial	35	letter, A4	40MHz	$7999	
proprietary	35	roll-fed, 24" or 36" wide, up to several feet long	66MHz	$19,995	64M RAM included
serial, parallel, AppleTalk	65	letter	25MHz	$7999	

continues

Table 10.6 Color Non-Inkjet Printers

Company, Model	Print Method	Resolution	System Type
Value Leader			
QMS ColorScript 230	thermal wax	300	Mac, PC
QMS MagiColor	color laser	600	Mac, PC
Seiko Professional ColorPoint	dye sublimation	300	Mac, PC
SuperMac ProofPositive Dual-page	dye sublimation	300	Mac, PC
SuperMac ProofPositive Full-page	dye sublimation	300	Mac, PC
TekTronix Phaser 480	dye sublimation	300	Mac, PC
TekTronix Phaser IISDX	dye sublimation	300	Mac, PC

Chapter Summary

This chapter lists several models of printers, broken out by these categories: dot matrix, thermal, inkjet, personal laser, office laser, and color. Each category has a "Value Leader," which is a subjective rating of the offering with the most features for the least amount of money.

Ports	Resident Fonts	Paper Sizes	CPU Speed	Price	Other Features
serial, parallel, AppleTalk	65	letter, tabloid	25MHz	$7355	
serial, parallel, AppleTalk	65	letter	33MHz	$10,999	
LocalTalk, parallel, serial	104	A3, tabloid	33MHz	$16,495	24M RAM
SCSI	17	letter, A4, tabloid	host-based	$14,999	
SCSI	17	letter, A4	host-based	$7,999	
LocalTalk, parallel, serial	39	letter, legal, A4, tabloid	24MHz	$14,995	32M RAM
LocalTalk, parallel, serial	39	letter, legal, A4	24MHz	$9995	32M RAM

IN THE NEXT CHAPTER

The next chapter explains the importance of creating a healthy and safe computing environment. It lists several ergonomic devices, including special keyboards and sources for ergonomic furniture.

PART III

Deciding What Add-Ons You Need

Includes

Ergonomic Devices

Pointing Devices

Modems and Fax Modems

CD-ROM

Storage

Tape Backup Systems

Sound Devices

Scanners

Feeding Your System

CHAPTER ELEVEN

Ergonomic Devices

Computer users have been slow to believe that using a computer can hurt them, but the increasing number of strains, pains, and even disabling injuries associated with using a computer finally has users, managers, companies, and vendors taking action. Unfortunately, there is no way to definitely identify those at risk and no single surefire technique to prevent a given computer-related injury.

Until this whole topic is better understood, it's up to you to protect yourself. Even if you do all your computer-related work for an employer, you probably will have to spend your own time, and may have to spend some of your own money, to learn how to prevent pain and injury and buy products that help you do so. If you do some or all of your computer-related work at home or on the road, or for your own business, you definitely need to take responsibility for your own well-being.

Few people take action on this issue until they start to experience at least some symptoms. If you're healthy so far, start learning and taking action now to avoid problems later. If you're starting to have problems, tackle them aggressively and immediately before they become more serious.

If you are a manager of computer users, you have a responsibility to take action on behalf of your workgroup and your company. You will see fewer absences and complaints, and your employer will experience fewer disability claims and even lawsuits if you and others in your company take action. If you're balking at the cost of ergonomic equipment, don't—this is one investment that pays off in more ways than one. A Norwegian study showed that when one company equipped their work force with ergonomically designed chairs, desks, and anti-glare screens, they saved a full 10 *times* their investment in medical claims alone. Side benefits included improved productivity, less stress, and better interpersonal relations (due to the decrease in stress).

This chapter is divided into sections discussing the main areas in which people experience problems, with a final section to sum up general rules. Each topic includes some description of what the problems are and identifies products that can prevent or reduce pain and injury. Ergonomics has become a popular issue in the past few years, so many organizations have published guidelines for safe computing. Check your local library for information, or contact your local labor safety organization (in the U.S. contact OSHA).

Easy on the Eyes

The most prevalent problem associated with using a PC is eyestrain. You can reduce eyestrain, headaches, and related problems by taking frequent breaks (about 10 minutes an hour, or 15 minutes every two hours), breathing deeply and regularly, and remembering to blink. Although breathing and blinking may seem to be automatic, many people tend to tense up when using a computer. Forcing yourself to breathe more regularly helps you relax, and blinking more frequently keeps your eyes from drying out.

This section discusses some of the common problems associated with monitors and lists some sources for anti-glare and anti-radiation screens.

Eyestrain

Letters on your computer monitor should be clear—you shouldn't have to squint to read them. If you are a heavy user of word processing, consider a word processing package that enables you to zoom the document to a larger display size. If your current word processor doesn't offer this feature (most do), you can work in a larger font while you're typing, and then change back to a smaller font for printing.

Products that can help reduce eyestrain include larger monitors, higher frequency monitors (at least 70 Hz, as recommended in the monitors chapter), anti-glare screens, and screen shades. Use a monitor stand to get your screen at such a height that the top of the screen is at your eye level—looking down at your monitor, even slightly, causes neck fatigue, which may cause headaches. Make sure that you can look at your monitor square-on instead of at an angle, because focusing on an angled monitor can lead to an imbalance in your eyes' focusing strength (which can cause headaches and vision problems). Portable computer users should look for sharp, backlit screens at least 9 inches in size. Finally, don't run a small monitor, desktop or portable, at high resolutions; text becomes too small to read easily. Some small monitors (or low-capacity video cards) use *interlacing* to achieve higher resolutions—interlacing makes the monitor flicker, which can increase eye strain. If you have to use high-resolution screen displays, invest in a larger monitor (15 to 17 inches or more).

Exposure to Radiation

Radiation from monitors is also a big concern, especially for pregnant women. Some people believe that radiation from monitors may increase the risk of cancer, miscarriage, or birth defects. If you are worried about radiation, consider using a monochrome or grayscale monitor, using a color monitor that meets Sweden's MPR-II guidelines, staying at least 28 inches (about arm's length) from the monitor, and reducing the amount of time you spend using the computer. Turn off the video screen (you can leave the computer on, just turn off the screen) when you're not using the computer for a few minutes.

Radiation from the back of the monitor is almost twice as strong as from the front, so when you arrange your office, make sure that you and others aren't exposed to the back of a monitor. The anti-glare and anti-radiation screens protect only from the front, not the back.

Table 11.1 lists some glare screens with special features like radiation filtering. See Appendix B for information about contacting the manufacturers of these glare screens.

Table 11.1 Anti-Glare and Anti-Radiation Screens

Company, Model	Unit Size	Price	Other
Curtis Glass Filter Plus	Available in several sizes. Cuts glare 99%, improves contrast up to 200%, absorbs 98% of ELF/VLF radiation, grounded to dissipate static, scratch resistant, hinged for easy monitor cleaning.	$99.95	
Global Glare Blocker	Non-reflective coating, absorbs static and some ELF/VLF radiation.	$24.99	
Global Glare Filter	Reduces glare up to 99%, enhances contrast, blocks almost 100% of ELF/VLF radiation, and blocks UVA/UVB radiation. Eliminates static.	$65.99	Many custom fits available for popular NEC, Compaq, and Apple monitors ($65.99-$105.99)
Kantek, SecureView (notebook glare screen)	Fits up to 10" diagonal	$119	Makes the screen viewable only from the front, blurs view from sides or above
Kensington, Anti-Glare Filter	Available in several sizes, including custom. Reduces glare up to 96%, improves contrast up to 20 times, scratch-resistant glass.	14"-15" $69.95	Lifetime warranty
Kensington, 14" Macintosh Color Display Anti-Glare Filter	Custom-fit for Macintosh 14" Color Display. Reduces glare up to 96%, improves contrast up to 20 times, scratch-resistant glass.	$99.95	Lifetime warranty

Value Leader

Polaroid Polarizing Filter	Available in 9"-21" sizes. Cuts glare 99%, improves contrast up to 14 times, absorbs 98% of ELF, eliminates static.	Varies with size, 13"-15" ~$40	

Hurting Hands

Pain in the hands might be the scariest computer-related injury because it can get worse very suddenly. A worker who is experiencing moderate soreness in the hands and wrists one day might become severely disabled the next. Some computer users with carpal tunnel syndrome, tendonitis, and related wrist and hand injuries have been placed on long disability leaves and have found themselves unable to do simple things like drive, button their clothes, or pick up their children. The ultimate result is painful tendon surgery on the hands, followed by years of physical therapy.

You can do a lot of things to reduce soreness and also reduce your chances of serious injury. Learning how to type better may reduce the impact of your fingers on the keyboard and related strain. Your keyboard probably has a height adjustment in the back—lower it, if possible. Elevating the back of your keyboard forces your fingers into an unnatural angle, which causes wrist and tendon problems. Your hands and wrists should be even with your elbows rather than higher or lower. Many software packages on the market, such as Que Software's Typing Tutor, can help you improve your typing, and several of them now include ergonomic tips. Be especially careful if you use a graphical user interface. The combination of keystrokes and mouse clicks required to run Windows programs, for example, has lead to complaints from users, particularly tennis elbow from moving the "mouse hand" back and forth.

As with eyestrain, taking frequent breaks is very important. Reminder programs are available that will watch your work and remind you when it's time to take a break from using the computer. Trying to relax more while working is also a big help.

There are many products that are designed to help with overuse problems. Logitech is one company that makes mice, trackballs, and other products that contribute to improved ergonomics. You may find that switching frequently between a mouse and a trackball prevents soreness that can come from overusing either one. Alternative keyboards are also available (see table 11.2). One inexpensive product that helps is a foam wrist rest for using the keyboard or the mouse. This kind of product is affordable and helps reduce strain and soreness. Wrist rests keep your wrists even with your hands rather than letting them rest below hand-level on the desk. They also provide a cushion around tendons under your forearm—resting your wrists on a bare desk edge causes pressure on those tendons, which can cause them to swell and restrict movement in your fingers.

Portable computer users have much to worry about when it comes to hand injury. You should only buy portable systems that have ports for an add-on keyboard and mouse so that you aren't using the built-in versions all the time. Look for a system with an integrated trackball, but make sure that it's easily accessible. Two leaders in ergonomic laptops are Apple (with its PowerBooks) and IBM (with its ThinkPads).

Table 11.2 Ergonomic Keyboards and Keyboard/Mouse Accessories

Company, Model	Description	Compatibility	Price	Other
ABCOM, Wrist Pad	19.5" wide, 4" deep, several colors		$19.95	
ABCOM, Wrist Pad 2.5	19.5" wide, 2.5" deep, several colors		$12.95	
ABCOM, Wrist Pad and Desk Extension	19.5" wide, 11" deep, supports keyboard and provides wrist rest		$29.95	
ABCOM, PowerBook Pad	Additional padding for built-in wrist rest	Apple PowerBook	$9.95	
ABCOM, Notebook Pad	Wrist rest for notebooks/subnotebooks		$29.95	
Curtis Adjustable Wrist Rest	Easily adjusts to most comfortable height, includes anti-static grounding cord		$24.95	
Curtis Master Deck	Mouse wrist rest with integrated mouse pad and desk organizer		$12.95	
Curtis Wrist Rest	Cushioned support		$14.95	
Global Adapta-Rest	Keyboard wrist rest with adjustable supports, built-in storage and copy holder		$26.95	
Global Deluxe Wrist Rest	Polyurethane wrist rest with keyboard pad		$21.95	
Global Executive Wrist Rest	Black vinyl wrist rest with plexiglass keyboard base		$29.95	
Global Height-adjustable Wrist Rest	Lycra-covered foam wrist rest adjusts to three heights		$18.95	
Global Mini Deluxe Wrist Rest	Mouse/trackball/calculator wrist rest		$16.95	

continues

Table 11.2 Continued

Company, Model	Description	Compatibility	Price	Other
Global Mouse Shadow	Mouse wrist support that moves on your mouse pad like a mouse		$16.95	
Global Operator Wrist Rest	Molded plastic wrist rest with keyboard pad		$14.95	
Global SoftRest	Keyboard rest of softer foam than most others		$24.95	
InfoGrip BAT	7-key keyboard shaped to fit one hand. The fingers never leave their dedicated keys, the thumb moves to any of three keys set within easy reach. Can be used in pairs. The BAT uses a special "chording" method (you press multiple keys simultaneously) to get full keyboard functionality out of 7 keys. Especially useful when one hand must be dedicated to using a pointing device.	PC or Mac	$295 ($495 for dual)	
Jefferson Starpoint-101	101-key keyboard with cursor control, numeric keypad, and Windows menu control integrated into the alphanumeric section. Eliminates the need to move hands out of the "home" position.	PC	$129.99	
KeyTronic FlexPro	Completely adjustable keyboard with "split" design that fits each side of the keyboard to the appropriate hand	PC	$399	Built-in measuring scale to allow multiple users to set customized operating positions

Company, Model	Description	Compatibility	Price	Other
	Each half lifts up at up to 25 degrees to allow more natural hand/wrist position. Includes adjustable hand rests, two-part space bar.			
KeyTronic Pace-Mate	Adjustable wrist pad with integrated work pace monitor. Reminds user when to rest.	PC	$79	
KeyTronic Trak-Mate	Adjustable wrist pad with integrated centered trackball	PC	$149	

Aching Backs

Back pain is a common consequence of all kinds of desk work, including computer use. Taking frequent breaks and stretching can help.

Invest in a good chair, one that is sturdy but allows you good freedom of motion (tilting, swiveling, and so forth). Make sure that your feet are flat on the floor, not dangling or angled. If you want your chair to sit low, get a foot rest so that you can keep your feet out in front of you and perpendicular to your legs. Don't let your knees become elevated too far, as this causes lower-back problems and poor circulation to the feet and legs.

Your desk should also promote healthy computing. It should be adjustable (it shouldn't touch your legs or knees), and should enable you to position your monitor even with your eyes and your keyboard even with your elbows. The best position for your arms, ergonomists say, is straight down from the shoulder, bent at ninety degrees to reach the keyboard.

A good chair and a carefully arranged, comfortable work setup can do a great deal to prevent or minimize back pain. As with hand and wrist injuries, you get much better results if you take steps when the symptoms are moderate than when they have become serious.

Table 11.3 lists ergonomic furniture and accessories that can help you maintain a healthy computing environment.

Table 11.3 Ergonomic Furniture and Accessories

Company, Model	Description	Price	Other
Anthro, AnthroArm GT (compound)	Monitor arm, holds up to 150 lbs., swivels to any position, extends from 6" to 18"	$399-$419 (depending on platform size)	Lifetime warranty, 100 day no-risk trial
Anthro, Anthro-Arm GT (single)	Monitor arm, holds up to 150 lbs., swivels to any position, extends from 6" to 18"	$339-$379 (depending on platform size)	Lifetime warranty, 100 day no-risk trial
Anthro Cart	Adjustable, very durable desks with casters. Huge variety of accessories available, including supports for PCs and printers, completely adustable monitor arms, and keyboard trays.	72" wide- $599-$619 60" wide- $549-$599 48" wide- $399-$429	Lifetime warranty
Curtis Executive Monitor Arm	Lifts monitor up to 6" off of desktop, swivels to any position, tilts up to 25 degrees. Holds up to 65 lbs. Includes keyboard rack to lift keyboard off of desk when not in use.	$139.95	Lifetime warranty
Curtis Professional Monitor Arm	Lifts monitor up to 8" off of desktop, swivels to any position, tilts up to 25 degrees, extends from 22" to 27.5". Holds up to 65 lbs. Includes keyboard rack to lift keyboard off of desk when not in use (tilts up to 30 degrees).	$239.95	Lifetime warranty
Curtis Standard Monitor Arm	Lifts monitor 3" off of desktop, swivels to any position. Holds up to 30 lbs. Includes keyboard rack to lift keyboard off of desk when not in use.	$69.95	Lifetime warranty
Global Anti-Glare CRT Visor	Shields your monitor from overhead light glare	$18.95	
Global CRT Float	Monitor arm lifts monitor 4"-16", tilts 5 degrees, holds up to 35 lbs. Pneumatically-assisted balance for easy adjustment.	$159.95	

Company, Model	Description	Price	Other
Global Dual-Level PC Table	Adjustable desk. Top level adjusts for correct monitor height, bottom for correct typing height.	42" wide- $319 30" wide- $299	
Global EasyTilt Footrest	Adjustable tilt w/ non-skid surface	$23.95	
Global Economy Monitor Arm	Lifts monitor and keyboard off your desk and out of the way. Holds up to 22 lbs.	$49.95	
Global ErgoPro Workstation	Puts monitor just behind keyboard, facing up at an angle (like a book propped up on your desk). Built-in keyboard tray with wrist rest, built-in footrest.	$269.95	
Global Executive Footrest	Adjustable tilt footrest with built-in foot-massaging "relaxer balls"	$39.95	
Global Height Adjustable Footrest	Adjustable height for individuals of different heights. Adjustable tilt w/ non-skid surface.	$37.95	
Global Monitor Riser	Monitor arm lifts monitor 5" to 12.5" above your desk for correct viewing angle	$149.95	
Global Power User Station	Adjustable desk with extra shelves for components. 48" wide.	$469	
Global UltraView Plus	Puts monitor just behind keyboard, facing up at an angle (like a book propped up on your desk). Built-in keyboard tray with wrist rest. Shelves for printer, CPU, and peripherals. Includes slide-out worksheet to let the UltraView Plus function as a small desk.	$299.95	

continues

Table 11.3 Continued			
Company, Model	Description	Price	Other
Global WorkSmart Back Rest	Firm cloth-covered foam rest supports lumbar and upper back. Attaches to your existing office chair.	$29.95	
Global WorkSmart Lumbar Roll	Firm cloth-covered foam rest supports lumbar region. Attaches to your existing office chair.	$18.95	

Overall Ergonomics

Few people know enough about ergonomics to get it right the first time. Every person's reaction to stress on their mind and body is different. You need to take an integrated approach that takes into account physical factors like the computer equipment, the software running on it, your placement in front of the computer, and even emotional factors like the feeling of control over your work and your frustration level.

Here are a few things you can do that can help prevent the problems described in the preceding sections:

- *Improve your work area.* Your chair, desktop height, lighting, and other factors can make your work area your best friend or your worst enemy. Take the time to get your work area set up correctly.

- *Start with a good system.* A well-designed computer system with a sensible keyboard layout, a screen with a high refresh rate (over 70 Hz), and a high-precision mouse or trackball is a good start.

- *Buy ergonomic products.* Get wrist rests for your keyboard and mouse! Upgrade your keyboard and mouse, add a trackball to your peripheral mix, and give some time and attention to your health and comfort.

- *Pick laptops carefully.* If you use a laptop for more than an hour or two at a stretch, be careful. These little wonders are even more likely to hurt you than their desktop cousins. Pick the machine carefully, and then buy add-ons that will help you use it without injury.

- *Take frequent breaks.* Ten minutes per hour or fifteen minutes per two hours are frequently heard recommendations as to how much of a break you need. There are software programs and even some keyboards and wrist rests that remind you to take a break (see table 11.2).

- *Be alert for pain.* If your work setup and computer are causing you pain, pay attention! Today's twinge could become tomorrow's disability leave. Work-related injuries can shorten your career and greatly reduce the overall quality of your life.

- *Get managers involved.* In the workplace, ask your manager to help pick products that work with you rather than against you—it will increase their awareness too. If you are a manager, study the problem; you're either going to be preventing this problem today or dealing with its effects tomorrow.

Chapter Summary

Ergonomics is often dismissed as expensive and unnecessary—don't believe it. Unsafe computer operation causes very serious (and *very* expensive) problems. Pay attention to ergonomic concerns early on so that you don't have to face the problems later.

IN THE NEXT CHAPTER

The next chapter covers different ways you can control your on-screen cursor, with mice, trackballs, and graphics tablets. Several pointing devices are listed along with specifications and prices.

Chapter Twelve

Pointing Devices

Pointing devices, which you use to move a cursor around the screen, are common peripherals that come with many computers. These devices are helpful when you are operating a computer that uses a graphical user interface. The mouse has become a standard pointing device, although there are other types of pointing devices. Laptops and notebooks, for example, increasingly use built-in trackballs. Graphic artists sometimes prefer pen tablets. The table at the end of this chapter lists several input devices for just about any application.

Choosing a Pointing Device

The standard pointing device is a mouse, which is a hand-held device you move around on a mouse pad. In traditional models, a ball on the bottom of the mouse detects the motion and translates it to directional commands that the computer interprets and uses to move the cursor. Some newer models are wireless, transmitting their movements to your PC via infrared signals, like a TV remote control.

If you turn your mouse upside down and move the cursor by rolling the ball directly, you have created a crude trackball. Commercially available trackballs push this idea to new heights of ease of use. Consider a trackball as an alternative if you have very limited desk space or are concerned about repetitive stress injuries—tendonitis, for example—that may result from too much mouse use. Simply switching periodically from one device to the other can go a long way toward reducing such injuries.

Graphics tablets look like little drafting tables. You write on their pressure-sensitive surface with a pen or other special device. Many graphics tablets let you choose different colors as you're drawing, either by pressing different buttons on the input device or choosing different pens. They take up a great deal of desk space, but for artists who are used to working with pen and paper there's no better digital substitute.

Many pointing devices have a feature that enables you to control how quickly the cursor moves across your screen. This feature is especially useful for precise control in paint and drawing programs; however, you may have to switch speeds when you go from detailed drawing work to a word processor. If you frequently move between programs, changing speeds can be a real burden.

Most kinds of pointing devices work with IBM, IBM-compatible, and Macintosh computers. When buying one of these devices, make sure that you indicate which type of computer you have. Also, don't purchase such a device unless you have a chance to try it for a while; people have very different likes and dislikes when it comes to pointing devices.

Reviewing Manufacturers of Pointing Devices

Two major manufacturers of the traditional mouse for IBM and compatible computers are Microsoft and Logitech. There are many other manufacturers, however. Naturally, if the system you are considering comes with a mouse, you likely will choose to use it instead of purchasing another pointing device.

Trackballs are manufactured by a number of companies, including Microsoft. Other manufacturers are Microspeed and Mouse Systems. Trackballs generally cost a bit more than mice.

Kurta has long been the leader in graphics tablets, but some others are gaining market share. Many companies offer color drawing pads and some make tablets designed specifically to sit in your lap.

Table 12.1 Pointing Devices

Manufacturer, Product	Type	Compatibility	Warranty
Kensington Expert Mouse	trackball	PC	5 years
Kensington TurboMouse	trackball	Mac	5 years
KeyTronic ClikMate2	mouse	PC	90 days
Value Leader			
KeyTronic Lifetime Mouse	mouse	PC	lifetime
KeyTronic Trak101	keyboard w/ built-in trackball	PC	3 years
KeyTronic TrakMate	wrist rest w/ built-in trackball	PC, Mac	1 year
KeyTronic TrakPro	keyboard w/ built-in trackball	Mac	lifetime

Pointing Device Listing

Although all pointing devices serve the same basic purpose, each device has a feature that may make a specific pointing device more appealing to you. Table 12.1 gives a listing of many different pointing devices from several manufacturers. Features of each pointing device are listed so that you can make the best selection.

Following are descriptions of each column in the table:

- *Manufacturer, Product.* Use this information to find the maker and model of the pointing device.
- *Type.* Indicates whether the pointing device is a mouse, trackball, or graphics tablet.
- *Compatibility.* This column tells you the computer system(s) with which the pointing device works.
- *Warranty.* Use this information to determine how long the manufacturer warrants the pointing device.
- *Price.* Enables you to make a price vs. feature comparison.
- *Product Description.* This column gives you any additional details about the pointing device.

Price	Product Description
$149.95	2-button trackball with programmable buttons. Optical technology for accuracy.
$169.95	2-button trackball with programmable buttons. Optical technology for accuracy.
$24.95	2-button ergonomically-designed mouse.
$58	User-configurable 2- or 3-button opto-mechanical mouse. Never needs cleaning. 400 dpi.
$224	101 key keyboard with integrated 4-button trackball.
$149	Ergonomic wrist rest with integrated 4-button trackball.
$249	101 key keyboard with integrated 4-button trackball.

continues

Table 12.1 Continued			
Manufacturer, Product	*Type*	*Compatibility*	*Warranty*
Kurta PenMouse	pen-based mouse	PC, Mac	lifetime
Kurta XGT 6" x 8"	graphics tablet	PC, Mac	lifetime
Kurta XGT w/4-button cursor	graphics tablet	PC, Mac	lifetime
Kurta XGT w/pressure-sensitive pen	graphics tablet	PC, Mac	lifetime
Logitech CyberMan	3-D mouse	PC	3 years
Logitech Kidz Mouse	mouse	PC, Mac	3 years
Logitech MouseMan	mouse	PC, Mac	3 years
Logitech MouseMan Cordless II	mouse	PC	3 years
Logitech TrackMan	trackball	PC	3 years
Logitech TrackMan Portable	portable trackball	PC	3 years
Logitech TrackMan Voyager	portable trackball	PC	3 years
Microsoft Ballpoint	portable trackball	PC	lifetime
Microsoft Mouse	mouse	PC	lifetime
Value Leader			
MicroSpeed HyperTrac	trackball	Mac	1 year
MicroSpeed MacTrac 2	trackball	Mac	1 year
MicroSpeed MicroTrac	portable trackball	PC	1 year

Price	Product Description
$348	4" x 5" tablet, simulates mouse movements with cordless pen.
$395 (PC) $425 (Mac)	High-resolution graphics tablet. Pressure-sensitive (256 levels of pressure), 1270 lines per inch, "pen on paper" feel.
12"x12", $445 12"x18", $785	High-resolution graphics tablet. 1270 lines per inch, "pen on paper" feel.
12"x12", $575 12"x18", $915	High-resolution graphics tablet. Pressure-sensitive (256 levels of pressure), 1270 lines per inch, "pen on paper" feel.
$129	3-button mouse designed for 3-D games and virtual reality applications. Includes "pulsating tactile feedback" feature that adjusts resistance and vibrates to simulate game actions (like being shot or thrown to the ground).
$59	2-button mouse, shaped like the real rodent (the ears are buttons). Smaller than most others.
$109	3-button mouse.
$149	3-button cordless mouse, can travel up to 6 feet from sensor unit.
$139	3-button trackball with off-center ball under thumb.
$119	3-button attachable trackball for laptops and notebooks.
$89.95	3-button attachable/detachable trackball for laptops and notebooks. Turns into a hand-held pointer for presentations.
$109	Ergonomically-designed laptop pointing device, designed for right- or left-hand use on a portable PC.
$109	Ergonomically-designed mouse, designed for right- or left-hand use.
$129.50	3-button trackball with "trackwheel" (programmable fingertip roller above the middle button, for scrolling through documents, etc.) and programmable buttons. Ergonomic design. Up to 1000 dpi precision.
$99	3-button trackball with programmable buttons. Ergonomic design. Up to 1200 dpi precision.
$89.95	3-button trackball for portables and desktop PCs. Attaches to portables, or fits in your hand for presentations.

continues

Table 12.1 Continued

Manufacturer, Product	Type	Compatibility	Warranty
MicroSpeed MicroTrac Mac	portable trackball	Mac	1 year
MicroSpeed Mouse Deluxe	mouse	PC	1 year
MicroSpeed Mouse Deluxe Mac	mouse	Mac	1 year
MicroSpeed PC-Trac	trackball	PC	1 year
MicroSpeed Replacement Mouse	mouse	PC	1 year
Value Leader			
MicroSpeed Win-Trac	trackball	PC	1 year
MicroTouch ClearTek TouchScreen	touch-sensitive screen	PC, Mac	

Chapter Summary

This chapter lists several pointing devices, from standard mice to very specialized devices for presentations and remote work.

Price	Product Description
$89.95	3-button trackball for portables and desktop Macs. Attaches to portables, or fits in your hand for presentations.
$49	3-button mouse. Up to 1000 dpi precision. With software and mousepad.
$69	3-button mouse. 500 dpi precision. With mousepad.
$99	3-button trackball. Ergonomic design. Up to 1000 dpi precision.
$24.95	3-button economy mouse. 250 dpi.
$129	3-button trackball with "trackwheel" (programmable fingertip roller above the middle button, for scrolling through documents, etc.) and programmable buttons. Ergonomic design. Up to 1000 dpi precision.
$695	Touch-sensitive screen for existing monitors, includes software drivers.

IN THE NEXT CHAPTER

If you want to start cruising the much-touted information superhighway, check out the next chapter. It lists modems and fax-modems, which let your computer communicate with online services and computerized bulletin board systems.

Chapter Thirteen

Modems and Fax Modems

If you have a PC, you may want a modem. Why? First of all, a lot of the fun of using a computer is in accessing on-line services and bulletin boards. Second, many hardware and software vendors now do their technical support through on-line services such as CompuServe, America Online, and Prodigy.

If you have a portable PC, you really need a modem because you are very likely to need access to files at work while you are on the road. Many workplaces also support the capability to work from home or the road, using a modem that connects to a network in the office.

If you're going to get a modem anyway, you may as well get a fax modem—the fax capability is basically free. Even if you don't send faxes now, you'll want to when you get used to sending things on-line. Even people you can't reach on-line generally have access to a fax machine you can transmit to. Don't buy a non-fax modem unless you are sure that you won't need fax capability.

You can get a very good mid-range fax modem for around $100 or $150 with data compression and bundled software; a more expensive unit from one of the "big name" companies may cost from $200 up to $500 or more. The newest high-speed modems always carry a premium price when they're introduced, and some of the most respected brands (Hayes, Intel, and so on) charge more because of their quality, support, and warranties.

Mainstream modems today are inexpensive, relatively easy to use, and usually include built-in fax capability and control software. Buy a modem when you purchase your computer, or add one as soon as you can afterward. Get a subscription to an on-line service—preferably one that offers support for one or more of your hardware devices or software packages—and spend some time learning to use it. When you first start using on-line services, you'll probably spend a little money exploring and getting lost, but with practice, you can find a wealth of information and software quickly and cheaply. Going on-line can tremendously expand the capabilities of your computer and your own capabilities as a computer user.

What You Need To Know

There are several big books about modems and modem software—get one if you're really interested. If you're not all that interested, the following list of basics should be enough to get you started on the purchase of an inexpensive, useful fax modem.

- *Modem speed.* The modem industry has raised the entry-level speed from 2,400 bits per second (bps) a few years ago to 14,400 bps today. You can get a cheap 14,400 bps modem for just over $100, so 2,400 bps, 4,800 bps, and 9,600 bps are practically extinct. Shop around—modem prices continue to drop quickly as newer and faster modems are introduced.

- *Data compression.* Data compression speeds up your modem even further, squeezing more information into the same number of bits. For example, with some standard compression schemes, a 14,400 bps modem could conceivably transmit 57,600 bits in a second (four times the original transfer rate). All 14,400 bps and above modems come with data compression, so you may see some advertised with a "maximum throughput" of 57,600 bps.

- *Internal/external.* Internal modems are more convenient. External modems are a little more expensive, but they can be carried from machine to machine and have status lights to help you understand what's happening.

- *Control software.* The best modem control software currently available is for Windows. The most expensive such software for Windows or the Mac includes optical character recognition for decoding incoming faxes. The software is nice to have if you plan to receive a lot of faxes; it's unnecessary otherwise. The Terminal program that comes with Windows is fine for simple data communications, but when you connect with on-line services or BBS's, you'll be able to *download* (receive through your modem) much better communications software. You also can buy good communication packages at your software store or through mail order.

- *Shared modems.* Some workplaces have modem pools that you can access from the network. This is a great way to learn how to use on-line communications without spending much of your own money. Just get a starter kit for CompuServe or America Online and sign on—your network administrator may help with any problems. This is an approved use of work time, if kept within reason, in most companies.

This preceding information is really most of what you need to know to make a good fax modem purchase for use with a desktop machine. Buy a major brand that comes with the control software you need, if any; then you only have one place to call for support if there's a problem getting started.

You need to know about a few additional things if you're buying a fax modem for a portable computer:

- *External vs. internal.* Get a built-in fax modem for a portable computer—it should be part of the machine, not something you lose, forget, or break because it's dangling off the back of your machine.

- *PCMCIA slots.* A modem in a PCMCIA slot is supposed to be better than a built-in internal modem because you can replace it with other peripherals as needed. With the industry changing so rapidly, PCMCIA modems are a good bet—when new technology comes along, you can always replace the PCMCIA modem with a new one, as opposed to a built-in modem, which is difficult or impossible to replace.

- *Test before you go.* When you're on the road, you need your fax modem to work. Test your communications setup before you go, during business hours when you can get support if you need it. Then test your setup again anytime you change your communications hardware or software.

Two final notes concerning communications between computers. On-line services, such as CompuServe, can be really expensive. Join the on-line service that has the most vendors on it you want to contact or that most of your friends and colleagues use. Spend some time learning to send and receive mail, download software, and so on, but watch your charges. If you check your bill once each time you sign on, and always log off as soon as possible, you'll avoid the worst surprises.

Logging in to your company's network from home or the road takes a lot more expertise than what is described here, and every network is accessed differently. Luckily, there are probably technical support people at your work who know how to do this procedure. Get them to help you get up and running from the road or home with little hassle on your part. Tell them what you need. If they say "All you have to do is...," have them do it for you, or at least get them to help you through the process step by step. This kind of project can take dozens of hours of your time if you try to do it alone, but may only take an hour or two if you get help.

Making the Purchase

If you're buying a desktop or portable system, get a built-in fax modem with control software as part of the system; then you can get support for any problem, wherever it originates, directly from the vendor. Top mail-order vendors generally understand this and help you get up and running (but you should ask about this before you order); computer dealers may or may not be as helpful. Retail salespeople are not the ones to ask for help.

Modems and fax modems are now so commonplace that not only are lesser known vendors selling them cheaply, the name brand vendors are competing on price as well. You should be able to get a well-regarded unit like those from Intel, Hayes, Global Village, or U.S. Robotics for just a little more than one from a lesser-known manufacturer.

If you already have your system, get a fax modem and control software together, and pick a vendor that uses an on-line service to provide support. That way you can get started with a purpose in mind—getting on the on-line service—and can download software updates and upgrades, such as OCR capability, from the on-line service.

You may experience some difficulties and frustrations in getting connected at first, but hang in there; the fun and education you'll get from being on-line is more than worth it.

Modem Listings

In table 13.1, you see a list of many different modems available for IBM-compatible and Macintosh computers. Many varieties that fit nearly any need are listed. The modems listed range in transmission speeds from 9,600 bps to 28,800 bps (115,200 bps with compression). Most include FAX capabilities.

In table 13.1, the modems are sorted first by baud rate and then alphabetically by company within each baud-rate range. Following are descriptions of each column in the table:

- *Manufacturer, Model.* Use this information to indicate a product you are interested in when you call either the modem manufacturer or a dealer.

- *Type.* Modems come in different varieties. Use this information to determine whether the modem is installed internally in your computer or is attached externally, whether it is a fax/modem, and whether the modem works only with certain types of computers.

- *Speed.* This is the baud rate of the modem.

- *Compression/Error Correction.* Modems can compress information before sending it. Additionally, modems check for errors in transmission. This information tells you the type of compression the modem supports.

- *Fax Modem/Speed.* Use this information to determine whether the modem has fax capabilities, whether it can only send faxes or can send and receive faxes, and the baud rate at which the fax operates.

- *Warranty.* This information indicates how long the manufacturer warrants the modem.

- *Price.* Manufacturer's suggested retail price (expect to pay less through mail order).

- *Software..* Some modems come with communication and fax software. Review this information to determine what software each modem comes with.

- *Other.* If the modem has any other capabilities not disclosed by the previous information, they are listed in this field.

Table 13.1 Modems and Fax Modems

Manufacturer, Model Type	Speed	Compression Error Correction	Fax Modem/Speed
Cardinal MVP144DSP	14.4K	V.42bis, MNP 5/ V.32bis, MNP 2-4	send, receive/14.4K
Cardinal MVP144E	14.4K	V.42bis, MNP 5/ V.32bis, MNP 2-4	send, receive/14.4K
Cardinal MVP144IF	14.4K	V.42bis, MNP 5/ V.32bis, MNP 2-4	send, receive/14.4K
Cardinal MVP144MAC	14.4K	V.42bis, MNP 5/ V.32bis, MNP 2-4	send, receive/14.4K
Cardinal MVP192E	19.2K	V.42bis, MNP 5/ V.32terbo, V.32 bis, MNP 2-4	send, receive/14.4K
Cardinal MVP192I	19.2K	V.42bis, MNP 5/ V.32terbo, V.32 bis, MNP 2-4	send, receive/14.4K
Global Village PowerPort Gold	14.4K	V.42bis, MNP 5/ V.32bis, MNP 2-4	send, receive/14.4K
Global Village PowerPort Mercury	19.2K	V.42bis, MNP 5/ V.32terbo, V.32 bis, MNP 2-4	send, receive/14.4K
Global Village PowerPort Silver	9.6K	V.42bis, MNP 5/ V.32bis, MNP 2-4	send, receive/9.6K
Global Village TelePort Gold	14.4K	V.42bis, MNP 5/ V.32bis, MNP 2-4	send, receive/14.4K
Global Village TelePort Mercury	19.2K	V.42bis, MNP 5/ V.32terbo, V.32 bis, MNP 2-4	send, receive/14.4K
Global Village TelePort Silver	9.6K	V.42bis, MNP 5/ V.32bis, MNP 2-4	send, receive/9.6K
Hayes Accura 144+FAX	14.4K	V.42bis, MNP 5/ V.32bis, MNP 2-4	send, receive/14.4K

Warranty	Price	Software	Other
	$120	COMit (data), FaxWorks	Internal, software upgradeable, 16550 emulation
	$189	COMit (data), FaxWorks	External
	$137	COMit (data), FaxWorks	Internal
	$269	data and fax software for Mac	External for Mac
	$199	COMit (data), FaxWorks	External
	$154	COMit (data), FaxWorks	Internal
	$349	GlobalFax	For Macintosh PowerBooks
	$399	GlobalFax	For Macintosh PowerBook
	$319	GlobalFax	For Macintosh PowerBooks
	$279	GlobalFax	External, for Macintosh
	$349	GlobalFax	External, for Macintosh
	$279	GlobalFax	External, for Macintosh
5 years	$179	Smartcom LE (data), Smartcom FAX (for Mac or PC)	External, for Mac or PC

continues

Table 13.1 Continued

Manufacturer, Model Type	Speed	Compression Error Correction	Fax Modem/Speed
Hayes Accura 144B +FAX	14.4K	V.42bis, MNP 5/ V.32bis, MNP 2-4	send, receive/14.4K
Hayes Accura 288 V.FC+FAX	28.8K	V.42bis, MNP 5/ V.FC, V.32bis, MNP 2-4	send, receive/14.4K
Value Leader, 19.2K and above (tie)			
Hayes Accura 288B V.FC+FAX	28.8K	V.42bis, MNP 5/ V.FC, V.32bis, MNP 2-4	send, receive/14.4K
Hayes Accura 96 +FAX	9.6K	V.42bis, MNP 5/ V.32, MNP 2-4	send, receive/9.6K
Hayes Accura 96B +FAX	9.6K	V.42bis, MNP 5/ V.32, MNP 2-4	send, receive/9.6K
Hayes Optima 144 +FAX	14.4K	V.42bis, MNP 5/ V.32bis, MNP 2-4	send, receive/14.4K
Hayes Optima 144B +FAX	14.4K	V.42bis, MNP 5/ V.32bis, MNP 2-4	send, receive/14.4K
Hayes Optima 288 V.FC +FAX	28.8 K	V.42bis, MNP 5/ V.FC, V.32bis, MNP 2-4	send, receive/14.4K
Hayes Optima 288B V.FC+ FAX	28.8K	V.42bis, MNP 5/ V.FC, V.32bis, MNP 2-4	send, receive/14.4K
Hayes Optima 96 +FAX	9.6K	V.42bis, MNP 5/ V.32, MNP 2-4	send, receive/9.6K
Hayes Optima 96B +FAX	9.6K	V.42bis, MNP 5/ V.32, MNP 2-4	send, receive/9.6K
Intel Cellular Faxmodem for PCMCIA	14.4K	V.42bis, MNP 5/ V.32bis, MNP 2-4	send, receive/14.4K

Warranty	Price	Software	Other
5 years	$159	Smartcom LE (data), Smartcom FAX	Internal
5 years	$299	Smartcom LE (data), Smartcom FAX	External
5 years	$249	Smartcom LE (data), Smartcom FAX	Internal
5 years	$159	Smartcom LE (data), Smartcom FAX (for PC or Mac)	External, for PC or Mac
5 years	$149	Smartcom LE (data), Smartcom FAX	Internal
5 years	$519 (PC) $549 (Mac)	Smartcom LE (data), Smartcom FAX (for Mac or PC)	External, for Mac or PC
5 years	$519	Smartcom LE (data), Smartcom FAX	Internal
5 years	$579 (PC) $599 (Mac)	Smartcom LE (data), Smartcom FAX (for Mac or PC)	External, for Mac or PC
5 years	$499	Smartcom LE (data), Smartcom FAX	Internal
5 years	$479 (PC) $499 (Mac)	Smartcom LE (data), Smartcom FAX (for PC or Mac)	External, for PC or Mac
5 years	$479	Smartcom LE (data), Smartcom FAX	Internal
	$349	WinFax Lite, HyperAccess Lite (data)	Works with cellular or standard phone lines

continues

Table 13.1 Continued

Manufacturer, Model Type	Speed	Compression Error Correction	Fax Modem/Speed
Intel Faxmodem 144/144e	14.4K	V.42bis, MNP 5/ V.32bis, MNP 2-4	send, receive/14.4K
Intel Faxmodem 144/144i	14.4K	V.42bis, MNP 5/V.32 bis, MNP 2-4	send, receive/14.4K
Intel Faxmodem for PCMCIA 14.4	14.4K	V.42bis, MNP 5/V.32bis, MNP 2-4	send, receive/14.4K
Intel Faxmodem for PCMCIA 96	9.6K	V.42bis, MNP 5/ V.32, MNP 2-4	send, receive/9.6K
Intel SatisFAXtion 400	14.4K	V.42bis, MNP 5/ V.32bis, MNP 2-4	send, receive/14.4K
Intel SatisFAXtion 400/e	14.4K	V.42bis, MNP 5/ V.32bis, MNP 2-4	send, receive/9.6K
MultiTech MultiModem 1432ZDX	14.4K	V.42bis, MNP 5/ V.32bis, MNP 2-4	send, receive/14.4K
MultiTech MultiModem 1932ZDX	19.2K	V.42bis, MNP 5/ V.32terbo, V.32bis, MNP 2-4	send, receive/14.4K
MultiTech MultiModem II 1432BA	14.4K	V.42bis, MNP 5/V.32bis, MNP 2-4	send, receive/14.4K
MultiTech MultiModem II 1432BA-Mac	14.4K	V.42bis, MNP 5/V.32bis, MNP 2-4	send, receive/14.4K

Warranty	Price	Software	Other
3 years	$199	fax and data software	External
3 years	$169	fax and data software	Internal
3 years	$249	FAXability, HyperAccess Lite (data)	
3 years	$229	FAXability, HyperAccess Lite (data)	
3 years	$349	FAXability Plus, CrossTalk Communicator (data)	Internal, onboard 80186 with 512K RAM for enhanced background faxing
3 years	$399	FAXability Plus, CrossTalk Communicator (data)	External
10 years	$289	MultiExpress data and MultiExpressFax software	External
10 years	$299	MultiExpress data and MultiExpressFax software	External
5 years	$749	MultiExpress data and MultiExpressFax software	External, synchronous and asynchronous operation, leased line functions, UUCP "spoofing" for UNIX systems
5 years	$779	QuickLink II data and fax software	External for Macintosh, synchronous and asynchronous operation, leased line functions, UUCP "spoofing" for UNIX systems

continues

Table 13.1 Continued

Manufacturer, Model Type	Speed	Compression Error Correction	Fax Modem/Speed
MultiTech MultiModem II 1432BC	14.4K	V.42bis, MNP 5/V.32bis, MNP 2-4	send, receive/14.4K
MultiTech MultiModem II 1432LT	14.4K	V.42bis, MNP 5/V.32bis, MNP 2-4	send, receive/14.4K
MultiTech MultiModem II 1432MU	14.4K	V.42bis, MNP 5/V.32bis, MNP 2-4	send, receive/14.4K
MultiTech MultiModem II 1432MU-Mac	14.4K	V.42bis, MNP 5/V.32bis, MNP 2-4	send, receive/14.4K
MultiTech MultiModem II 1932BL	19.2K	V.42bis, MNP 5/ V.32terbo, V.32bis, MNP 2-4	send, receive/14.4K
MultiTech MultiModem II932 BA	9.6K	V.42bis, MNP 5/ V.32, MNP 2-4	
MultiTech MultiModem II 932BA-Mac	9.6K	V.42bis, MNP 5/ V.32, MNP 2-4	

Warranty	Price	Software	Other
5 years	$499	MultiExpress data and MultiExpressFax software	Internal, synchronous and asynchronous operation, leased line functions, UUCP "spoofing" for UNIX systems
5 years	$449	MultiExpress data and MultiExpressFax software	PCMCIA, UUCP "spoofing" for UNIX systems
5 years	$699	MultiExpress data and MultiExpressFax software	External, pocket-sized, battery or AC power, UUCP "spoofing" for UNIX systems
5 years	$699	QuickLink II data and fax software	External for Mac portables, pocket-sized, battery or AC power, UUCP "spoofing" for UNIX systems
5 years	$799	MultiExpress data and MultiExpressFax software	External, synchronous and asynchronous operation, leased line functions, UUCP "spoofing" for UNIX systems
5 years	$699	MultiExpress data and MultiExpressFax software	External, synchronous and asynchronous operation, leased line functions, UUCP "spoofing" for UNIX systems
5 years	$729	QuickLink II data and fax software	External for Macintosh, synchronous and asynchronous operation, leased line functions, UUCP "spoofing" for UNIX systems

continues

Table 13.1 Continued

Manufacturer, Model Type	Speed	Compression Error Correction	Fax Modem/Speed
MultiTech MultiModem II 932BC	9.6K	V.42bis, MNP 5/ V.32, MNP 2-4	
MultiTech MultiModem PCS ("Personal Communication System")	19.2K	V.42bis, MNP 5/V.32terbo, V.32bis, MNP 2-4	send, receive/14.4K
Practical Peripherals MC144MT II	14.4K	V.42bis, MNP 5/V.32bis, MNP 2-4	send, receive/14.4K
Practical Peripherals MC288LCD V.FC	28.8K	V.42bis, MNP 5/V.FC, V.32bis, MNP 2-4	send, receive/14.4K
Practical Peripherals MC288MT V.FC	28.8K	V.42bis, MNP 5/V.FC, V.32bis, MNP 2-4	send, receive/14.4K
Practical Peripherals PC144HC	14.4K	V.42bis, MNP 5/V.32bis, MNP 2-4	send, receive/14.4K
Practical Peripherals PC144LCD	14.4K	V.42bis, MNP 5/V.32bis, MNP 2-4	send, receive/14.4K

Warranty	Price	Software	Other
5 years	$499	MultiExpress data and MultiExpressFax software	Internal, synchronous and asynchronous operation, leased line functions, UUCP "spoofing" for UNIX systems
5 years	$949	MultiExpress PCS software, manages telephone, voice mail fax, and multimedia mail	External, includes telephone handset. Can establish simultaneous voice and data link with other PCS modems, allowing you to transfer files and talk to the remote operator at the same time. Upgradeable.
lifetime	$159	MacComCenter data and fax software	Mac-compatible external
lifetime	$429	MacComCenter data and fax software	Mac-compatible external, upgradable, 3-line LCD, synchronous and Hayes AutoSync operation, leased line operation
lifetime	$299	MacComCenter data and fax software	Mac-compatible external, upgradable
lifetime	$189	Quick Link II data and fax software, WinFAX Lite	PC-compatible, internal, Hayes Autosync and leased-line operation
lifetime	$299	Quick Link II data and fax software, WinFAX Lite	PC-compatible, external, 3-line LCD display, Hayes Autosync and leased-line operation, synchronous operation

continues

Table 13.1 Continued

Manufacturer, Model Type	Speed	Compression Error Correction	Fax Modem/Speed
Practical Peripherals PC144MT	14.4K	V.42bis, MNP 5/ V.32bis, MNP 2-4	send, receive/14.4K
Practical Peripherals PC288HC	28.8K	V.42bis, MNP 5/V.FC, V.32bis, MNP 2-4	send, receive/14.4K
Practical Peripherals PC288LCD	28.8K	V.42bis, MNP 5/V.FC, V.32bis, MNP 2-4	send, receive/14.4K
Practical Peripherals PC288MT	28.8K	V.42bis, MNP 5/V.FC, V.32bis, MNP 2-4	send, receive/14.4K
Practical Peripherals PM14400FX PKT	14.4K	V.42bis, MNP 5/V.32bis, MNP 2-4	send, receive/14.4K
Practical Peripherals PM14400FXSA	14.4K	V.42bis, MNP 5/V.32bis, MNP 2-4	send, receive/14.4K

Value Leader, 14.4K and below

Manufacturer, Model Type	Speed	Compression Error Correction	Fax Modem/Speed
Practical Peripherals PM144HC II	14.4K	V.42bis, MNP 5/V.32bis, MNP 2-4	send, receive/14.4K
Practical Peripherals PM144MT II	14.4K	V.42bis, MNP 5/V.32bis, MNP 2-4	send, receive/14.4K
Practical Peripherals PM288 PKT V.FC	28.8K	V.42bis, MNP 5/V.FC, V.32bis, MNP 2-4	send, receive/14.4K
Practical Peripherals PM288 PKT V.FC	28.8K	V.42bis, MNP 5/V.FC, V.32bis, MNP 2-4	send, receive/14.4K

Warranty	Price	Software	Other
lifetime	$199	Quick Link II data and fax software, WinFAX Lite	PC-compatible, external, Hayes Autosync and leased-line operation, synchronous operation
lifetime	$329	Quick Link II data and fax software, WinFAX Lite	PC-compatible, internal, Hayes Autosync and leased-line operation
lifetime	$429	Quick Link II data and fax software, WinFAX Lite	PC-compatible, external, 3-line LCD display, Hayes Autosync and leased-line operation, synchronous operation
lifetime	$349	Quick Link II data and fax software, WinFAX Lite	PC-compatible, external, Hayes Autosync and leased-line operation, synchronous operation
lifetime	$399	Quick Link II data andfax software	PC-compatible, pocket modem
lifetime	$549	Quick Link II data and fax software	PC-compatible, external, 12-character LED display, also provides for synchronous communications
lifetime	$149	Quick Link II data and fax software	PC-compatible, internal
lifetime	$159	Quick Link II data and fax software	PC-compatible, external
lifetime	$499	Quick Link II data and fax software	PC-compatible, pocket modem, supports Hayes Autosync operation
lifetime	$499	Quick Link II data and fax software	PC-compatible, pocket modem, supports Hayes Autosync operation

continues

Table 13.1 Continued

Manufacturer, Model Type	Speed	Compression Error Correction	Fax Modem/Speed
Practical Peripherals PM288HC II V.FC	28.8K	V.42bis, MNP 5/V.FC, V.32bis, MNP 2-4	send, receive/14.4K
Practical Peripherals PM288MT II V.FC	28.8K	V.42bis, MNP 5/V.FC, V.32bis, MNP 2-4	send, receive/14.4K
Practical Peripherals PM9600HC II	9.6K	V.42bis, MNP 5/V.32, MNP 2-4	send, receive/14.4K
Practical Peripherals PM9600MT II	9.6K	V.42bis, MNP 5/V.32, MNP 2-4	send, receive/14.4K
Practical Peripherals PractiCARD 144	14.4K	V.42bis, MNP 5/V.32bis, MNP 2-4	send, receive/14.4K
Supra COMCard 144 (PC)	14.4K	V.42bis, MNP 5/V.32bis, MNP 2-4	send, receive/14.4K
Supra FAXModem 144LC (Mac)	14.4K	V.42bis, MNP 5/V.32bis, MNP 2-4	send, receive/14.4K
Supra FAXModem 144LC (PC)	14.4K	V.42bis, MNP 5/V.32bis, MNP 2-4	send, receive/14.4K
Supra FAXModem 144PB (Mac)	14.4K	V.42bis, MNP 5/V.32bis, MNP 2-4	send, receive/14.4K
Supra FAXModem 288 (Mac)	28.8K	V.42bis, MNP 5/V.FC, V.32bis, MNP 2-4	send, receive/14.4K
Supra FAXModem 288 (PC)	28.8K	V.42bis, MNP 5/V.FC, V.32bis, MNP 2-4	send, receive/14.4K
Supra FAXModem 288i (PC)	28.8K	V.42bis, MNP 5/V.FC, V.32bis, MNP 2-4	send, receive/14.4K
Supra FAXModem 288PB (Mac)	28.8K	V.42bis, MNP 5/V.FC, V.32bis, MNP 2-4	send, receive/14.4K

Warranty	Price	Software	Other
lifetime	$279	Quick Link II data and fax software	PC-compatible, internal
lifetime	$299	Quick Link II data and fax software	PC-compatible, external
lifetime	$139	Quick Link II data and fax software	PC-compatible, internal
lifetime	$149	Quick Link II data and fax software	PC-compatible, external
lifetime	$349	Quick Link II data and fax software	PC-compatible, PCMCIA modem
5 years	$349.95	COMit, WinFax Lite, FaxTalk for DOS, CIM	PCMCIA
5 years	$189.95	MicroPhone LT, FAXstf, CIM, scripts for AppleTalk Remote Access	
5 years	$149.95	COMit, WinFax Lite, FaxTalk for DOS, CompuServe Information Manager (CIM)	
5 years	$269.95	MicroPhone LT, FAXstf, CIM, scripts	Internal modem for for AppleTalk Remote Access PowerBooks
5 years	$349.95	MicroPhone LT, FAXcilitate, CIM	LED status display, upgradable to voice
5 years	$349.95	COMit, FaxTalk, CIM	LED status display, upgradable to voice
5 years	$269.95	COMit, WinFax Lite, FaxTalk for DOS, CIM	LED status display, upgradable to voice
5 years	$349.95	MicroPhone LT, FAXcilitate, CIM	Internal modem for PowerBooks

continues

Table 13.1 Continued

Manufacturer, Model Type	Speed	Compression Error Correction	Fax Modem/Speed
Supra FAXModem (Mac)	14.4K	V.42bis, MNP 5/V.32bis V.32bis, MNP 2-4	send, receive/14.4K
Supra FAXModem (PC)	14.4K	V.42bis, MNP 5/V.32bis V.32bis, MNP 2-4	send, receive/14.4K
US Robotics, Sportster 28,800 Fax	28.8K	V.42bis, MNP 5/V.34, MNP 2-4	send, receive/14.4K
US Robotics, Sportster 28,800 Fax (Mac)	28.8K	V.42bis, MNP 5/V.34, MNP 2-4	send, receive/14.4K
US Robotics, Sportster 14,400 Fax	14.4K	V.42bis, MNP 5/V.32bis, MNP 2-4	send, receive/14.4K
US Robotics, Sportster 14,400	14.4K	V.42bis, MNP 5/ V.32bis, MNP 2-4	
US Robotics, MAC&FAX	14.4K	V.42bis, MNP 5/ V.32bis, MNP 2-4	send, receive/14.4K
US Robotics, MAC&FAX	28.8K	V.42bis, MNP 5/ V.32bis, MNP 2-4	send, receive/14.4K
US Robotics, Sportster 9600 Fax	9.6K	V.42bis, MNP 5/V.32, MNP 2-4	send, receive/9.6K
US Robotics, Sportster 9600	9.6K	V.42bis, MNP 5/V.32, MNP 2-4	
US Robotics, WorldPort 14,400 Fax/Data PC MCIA Modem	14.4K	V.42bis, MNP V.32bis, MNP 2-4	send, receive/14.4K
US Robotics, WorldPort Dual Standard Cellular FaxPCMCIA Modem	16.8K (12K over cellular connections)	V.42bis, MNP 5, HST/V.32bis, MNP 2-4	send, receive/14.4K
US Robotics, WorldPort 14,400 Fax/Data Modem	14.4K	V.42bis, MNP 5/V.32bis, MNP 2-4	send, receive/14.4K

Warranty	Price	Software	Other
5 years	$249.95	MicroPhone LT, FAXstf, CIM, scripts forAppleTalk Remote Access	LED status display, upgradable to voice
5 years	$229.95	COMit, WinFax Lite, FaxTalk for DOS, CIM	LED status display, upgradable to voice
5 years	$329 ext. $299 int.	QuickLink II FAX software (data, fax functions)	PC-compatible
5 years	$339 ext.	FAX stf, MicroPhoneLT (data, fax functions)	Mac-compatible
5 years	$199 ext. $169 int.	QuickLink II FAX software (data, fax functions)	PC-compatible
5 years	$189 ext. $159 int.	QuickLink II software (data functions)	PC-compatible
5 years	$209 ext.	FAX stf, MicroPhoneLT software	Mac-compatible
5 years	$339 ext.	FAX stf, MicroPhoneLT software	Mac-compatible
5 years	$189 ext. $159 int.	QuickLink II FAX software (data, fax functions)	PC-compatible
5 years	$179 ext. $149 int.	QuickLink II software (data functions)	PC-compatible
2 years	$339	QuickLink II FAX software (data, fax functions)	
2 years	$595	QuickLink II FAX software (data, fax functions)	
2 years	$329	QuickLink II FAX software (data, fax functions)	Battery-powered, pocket-sized

continues

Table 13.1 Continued

Manufacturer, Model Type	Speed	Compression Error Correction	Fax Modem/Speed
US Robotics, WorldPort Dual Standard Cellular Fax Modem	16.8K (12K over cellular connections)	V.42bis, MNP 5/V.32bis, MNP 2-4, HST	send, receive/14.4K
US Robotics, WorldPort 9696 Fax/Data Modem	9.6K	V.42bis, MNP 5/V.32, MNP 2-4	send, receive/9.6K
US Robotics, Courier Dual Standard V.34 Ready Data/Fax Modem	28.8K	V.42bis, MNP 5, ASL, HST, HST cellular/V.FC, V.32bis, MNP 2-4	send, receive/14.4K
US Robotics, Courier V.34 Ready Data/Fax Modem	28.8K	V.42bis, MNP 5, ASL/V.FC, V.32bis, MNP 2-4	send, receive/14.4K
US Robotics, Courier HST Dual Standard terbo Fax	19.2K (21.6K with other ASL modems)	V.42bis, MNP 5, ASL, HST/V.32terbo, V.32bis, MNP 2-4	send, receive/14.4K
US Robotics, Courier V.32 terbo Fax	19.2K (21.6K with other ASL modems)	V.42bis, MNP 5, ASL/V.32terbo, V.32bis, MNP 2-4	send, receive/14.4K
US Robotics, Courier V.32 terbo	19.2K (21.6K with other ASL modems)	V.42bis, MNP 5, ASL/V.32terbo, V.32bis, MNP 2-4	
US Robotics, Courier HST	16.8K (12K on cellular lines)	V.42bis, MNP 5, ASL/HST	
Zoom 14.4PC	14.4K	V.42bis, MNP 5/V.32bis, MNP 2-4	send, receive/14.4K

Warranty	Price	Software	Other
2 years	$545	QuickLink II FAX software (data, fax functions)	
2 years	$299	QuickLink II FAX software (data, fax functions)	Battery-powered, pocket-sized
2 years	$795 ext. $745 int.	QuickLink II FAX software (data, fax functions)	Free upgrade to V.3
2 years	$595 ext. $545 int.	QuickLink II FAX software (data, fax functions)	Free upgrade to V.34
2 years	$695 ext. $645 int.	QuickLink II FAX software (data, fax functions)	
2 years	$495 ext. $455 int.	QuickLink II FAX software (data, fax functions)	
2 years	$475 ext. $435 int.	QuickLink II FAX software (data, fax functions)	
2 years	$895 ext. $845 int.		
7 years	$119 int. $149 int.	fax and data for DOS and Windows or Macintosh	

continues

Table 13.1 Continued

Manufacturer, Model Type	Speed	Compression Error Correction	Fax Modem/Speed
Zoom PBK 14.4 Internal Modem for PowerBook	14.4K	V.42bis, MNP 5/V.32bis, MNP 2-4	send, receive/14.4K
Zoom PCMCIA 14.4C	14.4K	V.42bis, MNP 5/V.32bis, MNP 2-4	send, receive/14.4K
Zoom PKT 14.4 Pocket Modem	14.4K	V.42bis, MNP 5/V.32bis, MNP 2-4	send, receive/14.4K
Zoom VFP 14.4V	14.4K	V.42bis, MNP 5/V.32bis, MNP 2-4	send, receive/14.4K
Zoom VFP 19.2	19.2K	V.42bis, MNP 5/V.Fast, V.32bis, MNP 2-4	send, receive/14.4K
Zoom VFP 24K	24K	V.42bis, MNP 5/V.Fast, V.32bis, MNP 2-4	send, receive/14.4K

Value Leader, 19.2K and above (tie)

Manufacturer, Model Type	Speed	Compression Error Correction	Fax Modem/Speed
Zoom VFP 28.8	28.8K	V.42bis, MNP 5/V.Fast, V.32bis, MNP 2-4	send, receive/14.4K
Zoom VFP V.32	9.6K	V.42bis, MNP 5/V.32, MNP 2-4	send, receive/9.6K
Zoom VFP V.32bis	14.4K	V.42bis, MNP 5/V.32bis, MNP 2-4	send, receive/14.4K
Zoom VFX 14.4V	14.4K	V.42bis, MNP 5/V.32bis, MNP 2-4	send, receive/14.4K
Zoom VFX 14.4V for Macintosh	14.4K	V.42bis, MNP 5/V.32bis, MNP 2-4	send, receive/14.4K
Zoom VP V.32	9.6K	V.42bis, MNP 5/V.32, MNP 2-4	
Zoom VP V.32bis	14.4K	V.42bis, MNP 5/V.32bis, MNP 2-4	

Warranty	Price	Software	Other
7 years	$279	stfFAX, Microphone LT (data)	Internal for Macintosh PowerBook
2 years	$299	fax and data for DOS and Windows	PCMCIA, cellular-ready
7 years	$269	fax and data for DOS and Windows or Macintosh	Pocket-sized portable
7 years	$199	fax, voice, and data for DOS and Windows	Internal, with voice mail and Business Audio
7 years	$189 int. $219 int.	fax and data for DOS and Windows or Macintosh	
7 years	$199 int. $229 int.	fax and data for DOS and Windows or Macintosh	
7 years	$249 int. $269 int.	fax and data for DOS and Windows or Macintosh	
7 years	$129 int. $179 ext.	fax and data for DOS and Windows or Macintosh	Class 1 and 2 fax
7 years	$139 int. $189 int.	fax and data for DOS and Windows or Macintosh	Class 1 and 2 fax
7 years	$239	fax, voice, and data for DOS and Windows	External, with voice mail
7 years	$239	MacFax, MicroPhone LT (data)	External, with voice mail
7 years	$139 int. $169 int.	data for DOS and Windows or Macintosh	
7 years	$149 int. $179 int.	data for DOS and Windows or Macintosh	

continues

Table 13.1 Continued

Manufacturer, Model Type	Speed	Compression Error Correction	Fax Modem/Speed
ZyXEL U-1496 PLUS	19.2K	V.42bis, MNP 5/ Proprietary 19.2K, Proprietary 16.8K, V.32bis, MNP 2-4	send, receive/14.4K
ZyXEL U-1496B	16.8K	V.42bis, MNP 5/ Proprietary 16.8K, V.32bis, MNP 2-4	send, receive/14.4K
ZyXEL U-1496B PLUS	19.2K	V.42bis, MNP 5/ Proprietary 19.2K, Proprietary 16.8K, V.32bis, MNP 2-4	send, receive/14.4K
ZyXEL U-1496E	14.4K	V.42bis, MNP 5/ Proprietary 16.8K, V.32bis, MNP 2-4	send, receive/14.4K
ZyXEL U-1496E PLUS	19.2K	V.42bis, MNP 5/ Proprietary 19.2K, Proprietary 16.8K, V.32bis, MNP 2-4	send, receive/14.4K
ZyXEL U-1496P	16.8K	V.42bis, MNP 5/ Proprietary 16.8K, V.32bis, MNP 2-4	send, receive/14.4K

Chapter Summary

This chapter shows you many options for taking your computer on line. It lists several modems and fax-modems from the top manufacturers in the industry.

Warranty	Price	Software	Other
5 years	$749		External with 2-line LCD, with voice mail functions, for Mac or PC, supports leased lines, upgradeable
5 years	$329		External, with voice mail functions, for Mac or PC, supports leased lines, upgradeable
5 years	$479		External, with voice mail functions, for Mac or PC, supports leased lines, upgradeable
5 years	$349		External, with voice mail functions, for Mac or PC, supports leased lines, upgradeable
5 years	$499		External, with voice mail functions, for Mac or PC, supports leased lines, upgradeable
5 years	$529		Portable, with voice mail functions, for Mac or PC, supports leased lines and cellular connections

IN THE NEXT CHAPTER

CD-ROM is one of the fastest-growing areas of personal computing. The next chapter explains the technology, what to look for before you purchase, and lists several CD-ROM drives.

Chapter Fourteen

CD-ROM

CD-ROM is one of the most exciting things to happen to personal computers for quite a while. You can get huge reference materials (even whole encyclopedias), games with full-motion video and stereo sound, and even your photo album on a disc under 5 inches across and less than 1/16" thick.

CD-ROM stands for Compact Disc-Read-Only Memory. The key words here are *read only*. You cannot store data on a blank CD-ROM disc without an expensive mastering machine. Once written on, traditional CD-ROM discs can't be rewritten or even added to; the contents of the disc are fixed.

CD-ROM discs are growing in popularity because of their storage capacity. A CD-ROM disc holds about 660M of data, as much as you can fit on 450 1.44M floppy disks. And a CD-ROM disc only costs $1 to $2 to produce in quantity, so it is the cheapest way to distribute large amounts of data.

Data distribution has always been a popular use of CD-ROM. Many companies distribute databases of many kinds on CD-ROM, though different search software and indexing techniques can make it frustrating to move from one database to another. Your company may have one or more CD-ROM discs available on your company network for use in various kinds of research. More and more public libraries have publication indexes on CD-ROM. Much research that used to be done from remote databases via modem is now being done locally from CD-ROM.

Distribution of traditional software is now being augmented by the use of CD-ROM. You can buy CD-ROM versions of popular applications, especially Microsoft applications, that include extra utilities, templates, and even multimedia help.

Now CD-only software is becoming available; some of the most popular software titles available are found only on CD-ROM. *Compton's Interactive Encyclopedia*, the *New Grolier Multimedia Encyclopedia for Windows*, and *Microsoft Encarta* are three multimedia encyclopedias that have proven very popular. CDs for children's entertainment and education are also growing in popularity. CD-ROM-based games, interactive fiction, and beautifully illustrated and animated fiction and non-fiction books are all found on CD-ROM.

The decision to buy a CD-ROM drive depends greatly on your pocketbook, needs, and level of interest. The following sections address some of the technical issues that affect your buying decision and how to go about purchasing a CD-ROM.

CD-ROM Basics

CD-ROM drives are evolving along two directions. The first is raw performance—how much data can the drive hold and how fast can it transfer the data to the computer. The base CD-ISO standard is 660M of data on disc with a 150K/second transfer rate. This is an odd mix; the storage capacity is that of a very large hard disk, but the transfer rate is that of a slow floppy drive. CD-ROM capacity and speed are improving in much the same way that floppy disk capacity and speed have evolved—slowly, and with lots of attention to standards, but moving forward nonetheless.

Double-speed (300K/second) and triple-speed (450K/second) CD-ROM drives are the next step up the ladder. These drives come close to solving what may be the worst problem of CD-ROM drives—slow performance. Double-capacity CD-ROM drives are also appearing, but these drives are less generally needed and so will probably catch on first in high-end mass-storage applications.

Seek time (the time it takes the drive to find data on the disk) is also slow on CD-ROM drives. Many take about a second to find data before transferring it. Even a fast drive takes two- to three-tenths of a second to find data. A hard disk drive is 10 times faster than the fastest CD-ROM drive.

Raw performance is important because CD-ROMs are a very tempting delivery vehicle for multimedia. If you're playing a CD-ROM-based game, it can take a second or so just to start data transfer after a scene change, introducing annoying delays. After the data is found, it takes two seconds to transfer a full screen of VGA video from CD-ROM to the screen at 150K/second. Full-motion video requires 30 frames per second, so only the fastest CD-ROM drives can deliver acceptable animation. Audio is much less demanding, so it plays fine on CD-ROM drives (yes, they play your standard music CDs).

The other direction in which CD-ROM drives are evolving is writeability. Whereas traditional CDs are read-only, write once, CDs that you can add information to, but not erase, are starting to catch on. Kodak's Photo CD standard allows you to take film to a processing shop and get back a CD-ROM disc with photos on it. The disc can hold up to 100 images, and you can keep going back and adding images to the disc until it's full.

If you plan to use this capability, be sure that your CD-ROM drive will cooperate. Some can only access the first group of photos that were put on the disc, not additional photos that were added later. Discs that have more groups of photos added to them later are called *multisession CD-ROMs*, and drives that can handle these are often called "Kodak Multisession Compatible."

Of course, there are great advantages to write-once technology beyond storing photos. If you have used a CD-ROM drive, you have probably had to hassle with swapping discs to get at different applications or databases. Imagine a double-capacity CD-ROM drive that you could fill with just the bits and pieces you wanted—say, your three favorite multimedia applications and your favorite database. You would only need one write-capable drive per workgroup to make CD-ROM much more attractive to all the users in the group. Support for multisession Photo CD discs may be the first step in this direction.

There is an alphabet soup of CD-ROM standards that support varying levels of capability along these two axes, performance and writeability. The standards that matter most to personal computer buyers and users are as follows:

- *ISO 9660.* The base defining standard for CD-ROM data storage. Any CD you can buy today should be ISO 9660-compliant.

- *MPC.* This key standard specifies a CD-ROM drive that can find data in one second or less and transfer it at 150 kilobytes per second while using no more than 40 percent of the CPU's time. The base MPC standard is slow compared to high-end drives of today.

- *CD-ROM XA.* This standard is an extension of MPC that supports the interleaving of audio information and data. It is rare at this time, but it's becoming more common and is used in IBM's Ultimedia systems.

- *MMCD.* Multimedia CD is an extension of CD-ROM XA used by Sony in its portable Multimedia Player. This standard is used by *Compton's MultiMedia Encyclopedia for Windows*.

- *Photo CD.* This standard is another variant of CD-ROM XA that supports photo recording and playback. Multisession Photo CDs can access data recorded in two or more separate recording sessions.

- *Audio boards.* You may need an audio board to get good sound quality, or any sound at all, out of a CD-ROM. Some IBM-compatible drives that play back audio CDs need an audio board to do so—Macintoshes have this capability built in.

- *Compression.* JPEG, MPEG, fractal compression, and Video 1 are all ways to compress data going onto a CD-ROM drive and decompress data coming off it. Compression can greatly improve multimedia performance, although it can also introduce incompatibilities and add cost.

CD-ROM Problems

The problem with CD-ROM technology is that it's still relatively new; in the IBM-compatible world, at least, there are still too many competing standards to allow a true mass market to develop. Part of the reason for incompatibilities is that people's needs and desires are different. Some users are perfectly willing to settle for text, code, and limited multimedia. Others want, and are willing to pay for, discs and drives that can play back two hours of full-screen, full-motion video with stereo sound. Software developers try to appeal to high-end users by packing advanced features onto a disc, yet they still want to appeal to the majority of low-end users.

CD-ROM drives are also one of the major ways in which people learn about the increasing difficulty of upgrading today's complicated PC systems. Trying to add a CD-ROM adapter card, whether SCSI or some other type, can be a nightmare of incompatibilities and problems. CD-ROM drives that attach to the parallel port have slow performance but fewer compatibility problems.

Purchase Considerations

If you are a typical IBM-compatible user who does not have a strong need for any particular CD-ROM title, you may want to wait to buy a CD-ROM. $200 to $400 for a mid-range drive—plus more for a sound board and titles, plus the hassle of installing most drives—is an awful lot to go through for something that may or may not prove useful to you.

If you do decide to buy, go for a name brand CD-ROM drive that has high performance specifications, preferably CD-ROM XA. Sony and NEC are two of the market leaders. Hitachi and Toshiba also make well-regarded drive engines. If you buy from someone else, the CD-ROM drive you buy will likely use one of these companies' CD-ROM mechanisms under the hood, but you'll be depending on the vendor for installation instructions, service, and technical support.

If you are buying a new system soon, you may want to go ahead and get a CD-ROM drive for it. The drive is less expensive as part of a system, and the system manufacturer takes the responsibility for making it work. You can also get sound capability that works with the CD-ROM drive as part of the system; again, there's only one place you have to call if you are having problems. Get CD-ROM XA and multisession Photo CD capabilities if you can afford them.

If you are using or buying a Macintosh, consider buying a CD-ROM drive. The hardware and software base are more stable. Installation is easier if you have to do it yourself because the drive simply plugs into a SCSI port, and Apple can add a CD-ROM drive to a new system you are buying. Over one-third of mid-range Macintoshes sold today are ordered with a CD-ROM drive installed; if you have firm uses for CD-ROM in mind, it's probably a good time to get on the bandwagon.

CD-ROM Drive Listing

The CD-ROM drive is becoming increasingly popular because CDs can store large amounts of information. Especially outstanding are the amounts of information on CD-ROM that you can work with interactively. CD-ROM enables programs mixing graphics, animation, and sound to occupy just one disk.

To aid you in selecting a CD-ROM drive for your computer, table 14.1 lists many different models of CD-ROM drives from several manufacturers. This table is sorted by manufacturer. The following are descriptions of each column in the table:

- *Company, Model.* Use this information to purchase the correct CD-ROM drive that meets your needs.

- *Compatibility.* This information indicates the kind of computer to which you can attach the CD-ROM drive. Remember, however, that you must match the drive to the correct interface.

- *External/Internal.* With this information, you can determine whether the CD-ROM drive is meant to be installed internally or externally to your computer.

- *Interface.* All CD-ROM drives must attach to your computer via an interface. This column describes the type of interface that you must use for each drive.

- *Capacity.* Use this information to determine the maximum capacity CD-ROM that the drive can handle.

- *Cache Size.* To increase the speed at which your computer gets information from a CD-ROM drive, some drives have built-in cache memory. The information in this field enables you to see whether a drive has a cache built in and the capacity of the cache.

- *Transfer Rate.* Use this information to determine the speed at which information transfers from the drive to your computer. This speed is measured in kilobytes per second.

- *Access Time.* This column indicates the average time that it takes for the CD-ROM drive to find the next piece of information. This time is indicated in milliseconds, or thousandths of a second.

- *Warranty.* Displays the time that the manufacturer warrants the drive.

- *Price.* Displays the cost of the drive, enabling you to do a cost vs. performance evaluation.

Table 14.1 CD-ROM Drives

Company, Model	Compatibility	External/ Internal	Interface	Cache Size
Apple, AppleCD 300e Plus	Any SCSI-equipped computer	External	SCSI	256K
Value Leader, Double-speed drives				
Apple, AppleCD 300i Plus	SCSI-equipped computer with available 5-1/4" bay	Internal	SCSI	256K
CDTechnology Porta-Drive T3401	PC, Mac	External	SCSI	256K
CDTechnology Porta-Drive T4100	PC, Mac	External	SCSI-2/SCSI	64K
Chinon CDA-535	Mac	External	SCSI	256K
Chinon CDS-535	PC, Mac	Internal	SCSI	256K
Chinon CDX-535	PC	External	SCSI	256K
Hitachi CDR-1750S	PC, Mac	External	SCSI	64K
Hitachi CDR-1900S	PC, Mac	External	SCSI	128K

Transfer Rate	Access Time	Warranty	Price	Other
342K/sec	<290ms	1 year	$314	Multisession PhotoCD, 2 RCA jacks, headphone jack, caddyless
342K/sec	<290ms	1 year	$314	Multisession PhotoCD, 2 RCA jacks, head phone jack, caddyless
300K/sec	320ms		$850	Also acts as stand-alone audioCD player. Battery or AC powered. Weighs 3 lbs. PhotoCD multisession compatible. RCA and headphone jacks. Sealed mechanism
300K/sec	320ms		$500	Also acts as stand-alone audio CD player. Battery or AC powered. Weighs 1 lb. PhotoCD multisession compatible. Headphone jack
300K/sec	280ms		$795	Multisession PhotoCD, headphone jack, RCA jacks
300K/sec	280ms		$645	Multisession PhotoCD, headphone jack. Street price, ~$380
300K/sec	280ms		$795	Multisession PhotoCD, headphone jack, RCA jacks. Street price, ~$430
150K/sec	320ms		$600	PhotoCD, automatic lens cleaning, airtight chassis, caddy, headphone jack
300K/sec	260ms		$670	PhotoCD, automatic lens cleaning, airtight chassis, caddy, headphone jack

continues

Table 14.1 Continued				
Company, Model	Compatibility	External/Internal	Interface	Cache Size
Hitachi CDR-1950S	PC, Mac	External	SCSI	256K
Hitachi CDR-6700	PC	Internal	Proprietary	128K
Hitachi CDR-6750	PC	Internal	SCSI	256K
Liberty 100CD	PC, Mac	External	SCSI	
Mirror	Mac	External	SCSI	64K
NEC 3XE	PC, Mac	External	SCSI	256K
NEC 3XI	PC, Mac	Internal	SCSI	256K
Value Leader, Triple-speed drives				
NEC 3XP	PC, Mac	External (portable)	SCSI	256K
NEC 4XPRO	PC, Mac	External	SCSI	256K
Plextor 4Plex	PC, Mac	External	SCSI	1M
Plextor 4Plex	PC	External	SCSI	1M

Transfer Rate	Access Time	Warranty	Price	Other
307K/sec	235ms	2 years	$670	Multisession PhotoCD, automatic lens cleaning, airtight chassis, caddy, headphone jack. Burst transfer rate: 5M/sec
307K/sec	260ms		$515	Automatic lens cleaning, airtight chassis, caddy, headphone jack
307K/sec	245ms	2 years	$515	Multisession PhotoCD, automatic lens cleaning, airtight chassis, caddy, headphone jack. Burst transfer rate: 5M/sec.
330K/sec	200ms	1 year	$599	Multisession PhotoCD, volume control, headphone jack
300K/sec	320ms		$299	PhotoCD, RCA and headphone jacks, volume control
450K/sec	195ms	2 years	$499	Multisession PhotoCD, Quicktime, automatic lens cleaning, full audio controls, headphone jack
450K/sec	195ms	2 years	$465	Multisession PhotoCD, Quicktime, automatic lens cleaning, full audio controls, headphone jack
450K/sec	195ms	2 years	$415	Multisession PhotoCD, Quicktime, automatic lens cleaning, full audio controls, headphone jack
600K/sec	180ms	2 years	$995	Multisession PhotoCD, Quicktime, automatic lens cleaning, full audio controls, headphone jack
600K/sec	235ms	2 years	$649	Multisession PhotoCD, CD-I, caddy, headphone jack, volume control
600K/sec	235ms	2 years	$699	Multisession PhotoCD, CD-I, caddy, headphone jack, volume control. With adapter

continues

Table 14.1 Continued

Company, Model	Compatibility	External/Internal	Interface	Cache Size
Value Leader, Quadruple-speed drives				
Plextor 4Plex	PC	Internal	SCSI	1M
Plextor Double-Speed PLUS	PC, Mac	External	SCSI-2	64K
Plextor Double-Speed PLUS	PC	Internal	SCSI-2	64K
Procom, PICDP-DS	PC	Internal	Proprietary	64K
Procom, SICD-DS	PC	Internal	SCSI-II	
Procom, SICDN-3x	PC	Internal	SCSI-II	
Procom, SICD-TDS	PC	Internal	SCSI-II	
Procom, PXCDP-DS	PC	External	Proprietary	64K
Procom, MCD-DS	PC	External	SCSI-II	
Procom, MCDN-3x	PC	External	SCSI-II	
Procom, MCD-TDS	PC	External	SCSI-II	
Procom, ICD-MX/MQ	Mac	Internal	SCSI-II	

Transfer Rate	Access Time	Warranty	Price	Other
600K/sec	235ms	2 years	$599	Multisession PhotoCD, CD-I, caddy, headphone jack, volume control. With adapter
335K/sec	240ms	1 year	$409	Multisession PhotoCD, caddy, headphone jack, volume control
335K/sec	240ms	1 year	$299	Multisession PhotoCD, caddy, headphone jack, volume control.
300K/sec	<320ms	1 year	$265	Multisession PhotoCD, volume control, headphone jack, caddyless
330K/sec	<200ms	1 year	$545	Multisession PhotoCD, volume control, headphone jack, caddyless
450K/sec	<195ms	1 year	$565	Multisession PhotoCD, volume control, headphone jack, caddyless
300K/sec	<250ms	1 year	$353	Multisession PhotoCD, volume control, headphone jack, caddyless
300K/sec	<320ms	1 year	$315	Multisession PhotoCD, volume control, headphone jack, caddyless, RCA jacks
330K/sec	<200ms	1 year	$665	Multisession PhotoCD, volume control, headphone jack, caddyless
450K/sec	<195ms	1 year	$685	Multisession PhotoCD, volume control, headphone jack, caddyless
300K/sec	<250ms	1 year	$465	Multisession PhotoCD, volume control, headphone jack, caddyless
330K/sec	<200ms	1 year	$549	Multisession PhotoCD, volume control, headphone jack, caddyless

Chapter Summary

CD-ROM is an exciting technology that is only starting to become mainstream. This chapter explains how it works and lists several CD-ROM drives.

IN THE NEXT CHAPTER

The next chapter helps you deal with one of the classic axioms of personal computing: no matter how much storage you have, it's not enough. It explains several options for extra storage, including external hard drives, cartridge systems, and optical drives.

CHAPTER FIFTEEN

Storage

An old axiom says a project will expand to fill all the allotted time. In the same vein, your data will expand to fill your entire hard disk. No matter how much disk space you start with, you'll run out sooner or later (usually sooner). Today's software applications can take up dozens of megabytes, and if you work with pictures or sound files you'll fill up hundreds of megabytes in no time.

To combat the data explosion, many users have started to install additional, external hard drives. Others have chosen the "limitless" storage of a removable-media system. Either solution takes some of the crowding off of your internal hard drive, and can help you transport or back up large amounts of data safely.

In this chapter, you learn about some of the major storage technologies on the market today: external hard drives, floptical drives, magneto-optical drives, and removable cartridge drives. Some of the pros and cons of each method are listed, and you learn how much you can expect to pay for drives and cartridges.

Selecting an External Storage Device

As with any other buying decision, you first have to know what you want. Different storage devices meet different needs. Do you want very reliable storage, even if it costs more? If so, magneto-optical (MO) drives are a safe bet. Do you need fast retrieval of your data, or can you stand to wait a few extra milliseconds? External hard drives are quick, and removable cartridge drives follow close behind, but MO drives are a little slower.

Do you want to share large amounts of data with a service bureau or other users in your office? Removable cartridge drives from SyQuest or Bernoulli (Iomega) are standard equipment in service bureaus, letting you carry 44M, 88M, or more in a compact package, and some service bureaus have 128M or 256M magneto-optical drives. If you're looking for an inexpensive data backup system, a tape drive might suit your needs and budget better than any of the solutions in this chapter. Despite their differences, all of the drives discussed in this chapter are designed with a common goal: to expand your storage space. Therefore, there is a fair amount of overlap in their capabilities.

External hard drives are just like the hard drive inside your PC, only they have their own case. If you get a SCSI-based external hard drive, you may be able to carry it from one PC or Macintosh to another, never having to leave your data or software behind. Like internal hard drives, externals come in a huge range of sizes and speeds. They're more expensive than internal drives, because they have to include their own power and cooling subsystems, but external hard drives are a relatively inexpensive way to expand your storage options.

The "unlimited" storage solutions store data on self-contained cartridges, similar to floppy disks in some ways but with much higher capacities. When one cartridge fills up, you just buy a new one and pop it into the drive. Flopticals, magneto-optical drives, and removable cartridge drives fit into this category.

The following section describes the inner workings of each storage method, including advantages and disadvantages of each.

How It Works

External hard drives are internal hard drives with their own cases. The manufacturer of the hard drive inside your PC may sell external versions of the same hard drive. The external case is responsible for cooling and power, just like your computer's power supply. On a PC, external hard drives are typically a little slower because they have to transfer data over SCSI or other kinds of interfaces, which are slower than the direct IDE interface on most internal PC drives. Mac users won't see much speed difference at all. Speed is one of the main advantages of external hard drives over other storage solutions. Optical drives and even cartridge drives are from 2 to 10 times slower (or more) than most hard drives. They also last longer than some removable cartridges. The main disadvantage of an external hard drive also applies to internal hard drives—once they're full, you're stuck.

Floptical drives (a combination of *floppy* and *optical*) are something of a hybrid. Most can read standard 3 1/2-inch floppy disks formatted on your PC or Macintosh, but they also use special 3 1/2-inch disks that hold 21M or more. The "optical" part of their name comes from the optical tracking mechanism inside the drive—they use optics to find data on the drive but magnetic heads to read and write the data. Because the data is stored magnetically, it is susceptible to strong electrical currents and magnets.

Floptical drives are relatively inexpensive, and handy for backups of small amounts of data. The slow speed, however, makes them seem like little more than high-capacity floppy disks.

Magneto-optical (MO) drives, on the other hand, are about as safe as you can get. When they write data to the disk, they use a laser that actually heats the surface of the disk to well over 100 degrees Centigrade. When the disk is heated, a special magnetic head writes the data to the media. Once the disk cools, it is no longer susceptible to magnetic influence. You could set the disk directly on a magnet with no data loss. MO disks are shock-resistant and are rated at six times the life span of other removable cartridges (30 years versus 5 years). They also cost much less than SyQuest or Bernoulli disks. For all their advantages, MO drives have at least one major drawback—they are about 2/3 slower than removable cartridge drives.

Combining the bottomless storage concept with traditional hard drive technology are removable cartridge drives. They take the magnetic platters normally found in a standard hard drive and put them in a tough plastic cartridge. The drive contains all the read/write heads and electronics, so when you insert a cartridge into it, it becomes a true external hard drive. SyQuest and Iomega (Bernoulli) are the leaders in removable cartridge drives, making popular 44M, 88M or 90M, and 150MB models. This popularity is an advantage, as you can share large amounts of data with other users who have the same type of drive. Service bureaus typically accept data on SyQuest, Bernoulli, or both. The disadvantages include speed (slower than a standard external hard drive) and magnetic risks of the media.

Price and Costs

External hard drives vary, depending on their size and speed. They're not quite down to the "dollar-per-megabyte" level, like internal drives, but they're not far behind.

Floptical drives cost $300 to about $500; 21M floptical disks cost from $15 to $20.

Magneto-optical drives are expensive (starting around $700), but the media is cheap. Expect to pay about $60 for a 128M cartridge, which is less than half the cost per megabyte of a comparable hard drive.

Removable cartridges cost between $65 and $100 for everything from 44M to 150M capacities. In some cases, you can find 88M or 90M cartridges cheaper than 44M cartridges because of the increasing popularity of the higher capacity drives. The drives cost between $300 and $600, making them an excellent value.

Listings of Storage Devices

Table 15.1 lists popular external storage devices, including the following fields:

- *Company, Model.* Use this information to follow up on a product by calling the company or a dealer.
- *Capacity.* The amount of data you can fit on a cartridge or on the drive. When a device uses several kinds of cartridges, all available capacities are listed.
- *Ext. Media Cost.* If a drive uses cartridges, this field lists their "street" prices.
- *Compatibility.* Shows whether the device connects to a PC, Macintosh, or both.

- *Warranty.* All of the devices listed are expensive to repair. Make sure that you know who pays for repairs, labor, and shipping. In some cases, the manufacturer offers data recovery services for damaged cartridges or hard drives.
- *Price.* Manufacturer's suggested retail price.

Table 15.1 External Storage Devices

Company, Model	Capacity Cost	Ext. Media	Compatibility
Fujitsu DynaMO Drive	230M	$80 (230M)	PC, Mac
IOMEGA Bernoulli Dual 150	2x150M	$95	PC, Mac
IOMEGA Bernoulli Dual 90 Pro	2x90M	$95	PC, Mac
IOMEGA Bernoulli Insider 150	150M	$95	PC
IOMEGA Bernoulli Insider 150 SCSI	150M	$95	PC
IOMEGA Bernoulli Insider 90 PRO	90M	$95	PC
IOMEGA Bernoulli MacTransportable 150	150M	$95	Mac
IOMEGA Bernoulli MacTransportable 90	90M	$95	Mac
IOMEGA Bernoulli PC Powered 150	150M	$95	PC
IOMEGA Bernoulli PC Powered 90	90M	$95	PC
IOMEGA Bernoulli Transportable 150	150M	$95	PC, Mac
IOMEGA Bernoulli Transportable 90 Pro	90M	$95	PC, Mac

Storage

Warranty	Price	Other
	$1300 (PC)/ $1225 (Mac)	
2 years	$1299	External, holds 2 cartridges
2 years	$999	External, holds 2 cartridges
2 years	$589	Internal, IDE interface
2 years	$599	Internal, SCSI interface
2 years	$419	Internal, SCSI interface
2 years	$589	External, SCSI interface
2 years	$419	External, SCSI interface
2 years	$589	External, with interface
2 years	$419	External, with interface
2 years	$699	External
2 years	$499	External

continues

Table 15.1 Continued

Company, Model	Capacity	Cost	Ext. Media	Compatibility
IOMEGA Floptical Drive	21M	$20		PC
IOMEGA Floptical Drive	21M	$20		PC
IOMEGA Floptical Insider	21M	$20		PC
IOMEGA Floptical Mac	21M	$20		Mac
IOMEGA Floptical Parallel Port	21M	$20		PC
IOMEGA Floptical PC Powered	21M	$20		PC
IOMEGA LaserSafe Magneto Optical Drive	1.3G	$110		PC, Mac
Liberty 115S Cartridge Drive	150M	$95		Mac, PC
Liberty 115S Cartridge Drive	200M	$115		Mac, PC
Liberty 115S Optical Drive	1.3G	$110		Mac, PC
Liberty 115S Optical Drive	650M	$120		Mac, PC
Liberty 15+9 External Hard Drive	120M	n/a		Mac, PC
Liberty 15+9 External Hard Drive	160M	n/a		Mac, PC
Liberty 15+9 External Hard Drive	256M	n/a		Mac, PC
Liberty 30S External Hard Drive	120M	n/a		Mac, PC

Warranty	Price	Other
2 years	$499	Internal, SCSI, no interface, includes 21M shareware disk
2 years	$569	External, SCSI, no interface, includes 21M shareware disk
2 years	$569	Includes interface, 21M shareware disk
2 years	$599	External, includes 21M shareware disk
2 years	$739	For laptops and desktops, includes 21M shareware disk
2 years	$599	External, includes 21M shareware disk
2 years	$3995	External
1 year	$699	Bernoulli-compatible
1 year	$799	Syquest-compatible
1 year	$2699	
1 year	$1849	
2 years	$399	2.5" drive
2 years	$449	2.5" drive
2 years	$549	2.5" drive
2 years	$599	2.5" drive, built-in battery pack

continues

Table 15.1 Continued

Company, Model	Capacity Cost	Ext. Media	Compatibility
Liberty 30S External Hard Drive	160M	n/a	Mac, PC
Liberty 30S External Hard Drive	256M	n/a	Mac, PC
Liberty 50S Cartridge Drive	105M	$70	Mac, PC
Liberty 50S Cartridge Drive	270M	$90	Mac, PC
Liberty 50S External Hard Drive	170M	n/a	Mac, PC
Liberty 50S External Hard Drive	270M	n/a	Mac, PC
Liberty 50S External Hard Drive	340M	n/a	Mac, PC
Liberty 50S External Hard Drive	540M	n/a	Mac, PC
Liberty 50S Optical Drive	128M	$35	Mac, PC
Liberty 50S Optical Drive	230M	$80	Mac, PC
Liberty 70S External Hard Drive	1.23G	n/a	Mac, PC
Liberty 70S External Hard Drive	1.8G	n/a	Mac, PC
Liberty 70S External Hard Drive	2.1G	n/a	Mac, PC
Liberty 70S External Hard Drive	4.2G	n/a	Mac, PC
Mirror External Hard Drive	1.1G	n/a	PC, Mac
Mirror External Hard Drive	1.8G	n/a	PC, Mac

Warranty	Price	Other
2 years	$639	2.5" drive, built-in battery pack
2 years	$699	2.5" drive, built-in battery pack
1 year	$549	Syquest-compatible, built-in power supply
1 year	$749	Syquest-compatible built-in power supply
2 years	$449	3.5" drive, built-in power supply
2 years	$599	3.5" drive, built-in power supply
2 years	$699	3.5" drive, built-in power supply
2 years	$899	3.5" drive, built-in power supply
1 year	$999	
1 year	$1199	
2 years	$1399	5" drive, built-in power supply
2 years	$1499	5" drive, built-in power supply
2 years	$1999	5" drive, built-in power supply
2 years	$3899	5" drive, built-in power supply
5 years	$849	SCSI-2
5 years	$1219	SCSI-2

continues

Table 15.1 Continued

Company, Model	Capacity Cost	Ext. Media	Compatibility
Mirror External Hard Drive	170M	n/a	PC, Mac
Mirror External Hard Drive	2.1G	n/a	PC, Mac
Mirror External Hard Drive	270M	n/a	PC, Mac
Mirror External Hard Drive	3.4G	n/a	PC, Mac
Mirror External Hard Drive	340M	n/a	PC, Mac
Mirror External Hard Drive	520M	n/a	PC, Mac
Mirror External Hard Drive	540M	n/a	PC, Mac
Mirror Optical Drive	128M	$35	PC, Mac
Mirror Optical Drive	230M	$60	PC, Mac
Mirror Optical Drive	256M	$60	PC, Mac
Mirror SyQuest Drive	105M	$65	PC, Mac
Mirror SyQuest Drive	44M	$65	PC, Mac
Mirror SyQuest Drive	88M	$95	PC, Mac
Panasonic 5.25" Optical Drive	1.5G	~$160	PC, Mac
Panasonic 5.25" Optical Drive	1.5G	~$160	PC, Mac
Pinnacle Micro Sierra 1.3G Mac	1.3G	$110	Mac

Storage

Warranty	Price	Other
2 years	$249	
5 years	$1529	SCSI-2
2 years	$359	SCSI-2
5 years	$2249	SCSI-2
2 years	$369	SCSI-2
2 years	$629	SCSI-2
2 years	$599	SCSI-2
1 year	$799	
1 year	$979	
1 year	$999	
2 years	$429	
2 years	$299	
2 years	$439	
n/a	$3695	Internal
n/a	$3995	External
1 year	$2995	Includes interface

continues

Table 15.1 Continued

Company, Model	Capacity Cost	Ext. Media	Compatibilty
Pinnacle Micro Sierra 1.3G PC	1.3G	$110	PC
Pinnacle Micro Sierra 2.6G Mac	2.6G	$110	Mac
Pinnacle Micro Sierra 2.6G PC	2.6G	$110	PC
Pinnacle Micro Tahoe 130 Mac	128M	$35	Mac
Pinnacle Micro Tahoe 130 PC	128M	$35	PC
Pinnacle Micro Tahoe 230 Mac	230M	$80	Mac
Pinnacle Micro Tahoe 230 PC	230M	$80	PC
PROCOM, MRD 80C Cartridge Drive	88M	~$95	PC
PROCOM, MRD 80C Cartridge Drive	88M	~$95	Mac
PROCOM, MRD 270 Cartridge Drive	270M	~$90	PC, Mac
PROCOM, IRD 80C Cartridge Drive	88M	~$95	PC, Mac
PROCOM, IRD 270 Cartridge Drive	270M	~$90	PC
PROCOM, MEOD 130-E Erasable Optical Drive	128M	~$75	PC, Mac
PROCOM, MEOD 651 Erasable Optical Drive	650M	~$195	PC, Mac
PROCOM, MD 2003 External Hard Drive	2.03G	n/a	PC
PROCOM, MD 2101 External Hard Drive	2.1G	n/a	PC

Warranty	Price	Other
1 year	$3195	Includes interface
1 year	$5795	Includes interface
1 year	$5995	Includes interface
1 year	$899	Portable
1 year	$1099	Portable, includes interface
1 year	$999	Portable
1 year	$1199	Portable, includes interface
2 years	$795	
2 years	$695	
2 years		
2 years	$745	
2 years		
1 year	$1595	
1 year	$3195	
5 years	$2695	10ms access time, SCSI-2
5 years	$2795	10ms access time, SCSI-2

continues

Table 15.1 Continued

Company, Model	Capacityy Cost	Ext. Media	Compatibilty
PROCOM, MD 2103 External Hard Drive	2.1G	n/a	PC
PROCOM, MTD 2900 External Hard Drive	2.9G	n/a	PC
PROCOM MD 1003 External Hard Drive	1.05G	n/a	Mac
PROCOM MD 1071 External Hard Drive	1.07G	n/a	Mac
PROCOM MD 1331 External Hard Drive	1.33G	n/a	Mac
PROCOM MD 1601 External Hard Drive	1.6G	n/a	Mac
PROCOM MD 2003 External Hard Drive	2030M	n/a	Mac
PROCOM MD 2101 External Hard Drive	2.1G	n/a	Mac
PROCOM MD 2103 External Hard Drive	2.1G	n/a	Mac
PROCOM MD 240 External Hard Drive	240M	n/a	Mac
PROCOM MD 2900 External Hard Drive	2.9G	n/a	Mac
PROCOM MD 340 External Hard Drive	340 M	n/a	Mac
PROCOM MD 450 External Hard Drive	450M	n/a	Mac
PROCOM MD 531 External Hard Drive	525M	n/a	Mac
SyQuest SQ3105 3.5" Removable Cartridge Drive	105M	$65	PC, Mac

Warranty	Price	Other
5 years	$3195	9ms access time, SCSI-2
5 years	$4095	11ms access time, SCSI-2
5 years	$1895	10ms access time, SCSI-2
5 years	$1995	9ms access time, SCSI-2
5 years	$2095	9ms access time, SCSI-2
5 years	$2395	9ms access time, SCSI-2
5 years	$2695	10ms access time, SCSI-2
5 years	$2795	10ms access time, SCSI-2
5 years	$3195	9ms access time, SCSI-2
2 years	$695	12ms access time, SCSI-2
5 years	$4095	11ms access time, SCSI-2
2 years	$895	12ms access time, SCSI-2
2 years	$1195	12ms access time, SCSI-2
5 years	$1395	9ms access time, SCSI-2
2 years	~$335	

continues

Table 15.1 Continued

Company, Model	Capacity Cost	Ext. Media	Compatibility
SyQuest SQ3270 3.5" Removable Cartridge Drive	270M	$90	PC, Mac
SyQuest SQ5110 5.25" Removable Cartridge Drive	88M	$90	PC, Mac
SyQuest SQ5200 5.25" Removable Cartridge Drive	200M	$100	PC, Mac
SyQuest SQ555 5.25" Removable Cartridge Drive	44M	$65	PC, Mac

Chapter Summary

This chapter covers several ways that you can increase the storage capacity of your system. It explains the benefits and costs of external hard drives, floptical drives, magneto-optical drives, and removable cartridge drives. Several storage solutions are listed, including features and prices.

Warranty	Price	Other
2 years	~$500	
2 years	~$300	
2 years	~$600	
2 years	~$200	

IN THE NEXT CHAPTER

Chapter 16 talks about another way to store your data—tape backup drives. Though not suitable for quick access (like the drives discussed in this chapter), tape backup units are a valuable part of any computer system. It only takes one hard drive crash to make a believer out of most people.

Chapter Sixteen

Tape Backup Systems

Your workplace may offer you the capability of backing up your data over the network. Or, you may be conscientious enough to regularly back up to floppy disks; if so, keep up the good work. Otherwise, you need to seriously consider a tape backup system.

Hard disks fail, and they usually give no warning before they do. Perhaps more importantly, people make mistakes. Not all of the mistakes are of the DEL *.* variety—you may, for instance, find yourself desperately wishing to get back to your old Windows setup after installing one too many programs. Unless you are willing to lose your current setup and data files to accident or hardware failure, you need a backup strategy. Tape backup drives are the easiest to use and the least expensive way to do this.

As with ergonomics, backup is often paid attention to only by those who have already experienced pain from their computer use. In the case of backup, the pain is from data loss caused by a user error, software problem, or hardware crash. With ergonomics, though, solutions are complicated. With backup, they're simple: a regular backup plan will protect you from lost data.

The next few paragraphs quickly introduce some of the key considerations for personal backup. If you are a manager or LAN administrator who is backing up many systems, this section is a good place to start, but you'll need more sophisticated information and higher capacity products than are discussed here. For backup of your office PC, home system, or portable computer, you can learn everything you need to know in a few minutes.

Backup Background

The cheapest and most convenient kinds of tape backup are offered by QIC-40, QIC-80, and Teac drives. QIC, pronounced *quick*, stands for Quarter-Inch Cartridge. QIC tapes are small and convenient, but a QIC-40 drive can store up to 120M with extended tape and compression; a QIC-80 drive can store twice as much. Teac drives are available in 60M, 150M, and 600M capacities, with price varying accordingly.

The cheapest of these tape drives is around $300 for an external unit. Get the smallest, least expensive unit that will comfortably hold the contents of your entire hard drive. That way you can start a backup and leave it running overnight (backing up 100M can take several hours).

Macintosh tape drives typically attach to the SCSI port, which makes them very easy to connect and share. Many tape drives for PC-compatibles, however, use a controller card inside the PC, making it very difficult to use the tape drive on more than one machine. Some PC-compatible tape drives connect to the computer's parallel port, which means that you can share them among different desktop and portable computers.

Tape backup software is also important. If you use Windows, get Windows control software; it's generally quite a bit easier to use than DOS software. The software should make it easy to do small incremental backups as well as large, complete backups.

Purchase Considerations

If you're buying a new desktop system, consider getting a tape drive at the same time, built-in if possible. You'll be much more likely to back up regularly, and you can use communications software to connect your portable machine and back it up too. Built-in tape units are also cheaper than external ones.

Windows backup software can make a big difference for backing up IBM-compatibles because it is easier to use and some Windows packages can do backups while you're working. To prevent too big of a drain of system resources, do incremental backups of recently changed files during the workday and full backups during lunchtime or off hours. DOS backup software, though it lacks these features, can also get the job done.

Among manufacturers, drives from Colorado Memory Systems (CMS) and Maynard Electronics are well-regarded. The Backpack QIC 80 drive from Micro Solutions Computer Products is a solid drive that connects to a parallel port. Drives from many vendors are really relabeled versions of those from the companies mentioned previously or other reliable vendors; if you stick with a fairly well-known company, you will probably not go too far wrong.

Central Point Software's backup utilities for Macintosh and PC-compatibles is well-regarded, as is Norton's. You may want to pick a system that comes with such a utility package, not only for backups but for preventative maintenance on your hard drive.

Computer users are getting more and more serious about backup solutions. Take the time to make backup a part of your computing routine.

Fields for Tape Drive Listings

Table 16.1 lists tape drives, sorted by company. The following fields are used for each drive:

- *Company.* The organization that markets or manufactures the drive.
- *Capacity.* The size (in megabytes) of tapes that can be used with the system.
- *Connection.* Whether the drive requires a card inside your PC, connects to a SCSI port, or connects to a parallel port.
- *Speed.* Number of megabytes that can be backed up in one minute.
- *Price, Int./Ext.* Manufacturer's suggested retail price for internal and external drives.
- *Avg. Cartridge Cost.* Street price of high-quality tapes for the drive.

Table 16.1 Tape Backup Systems

Company, Model	Capacity	Connection
Colorado Memory Systems Jumbo 120	120M	Proprietary (PC)
Value Leader		
Colorado Memory Systems Jumbo 250	250M	Proprietary (PC)
Colorado Memory Systems Jumbo Trakker	120M	Parallel port (PC)
Colorado Memory Systems Jumbo Trakker	250M	Parallel port (PC)
Colorado Memory Systems PowerDAT 6000	4G	SCSI (PC)
Colorado Memory Systems PowerTape 1100	1G	Proprietary (PC)
Colorado Memory Systems PowerTape 2400	2.4G	SCSI (PC)
Colorado Memory Systems PowerTape 4000	4G	SCSI (PC)
Conner MS Cartridge System	1.35G	PC
Conner MS Cartridge System	1.35G	PC
Conner MS Cartridge System	525M	PC
Conner MS DAT 2G	2G	SCSI (PC)
Conner MS DAT 2G	2G	SCSI (PC)
Conner MS DAT 4G	4G	SCSI (PC)
Conner MS DAT 4G	4G	SCSI (PC)
IOMEGA Tape250	250M	Proprietary (PC)
IOMEGA Tape250 Parallel Port	250M	Proprietary (PC)
Value Leader		
Mirror DAT drive	2G	SCSI
Mirror DAT drive	4G	SCSI
Mirror DAT drive	8G	SCSI
PROCOM IDAT8000/E	2G-8G	SCSI
PROCOM ITD600/E	600M	SCSI
PROCOM MDAT8000/M	2G-8G	SCSI (Mac)

Tape Backup Systems

Price, Int/Ext	Avg. Cartridge Price	Other
$119	~$25	Internal, QIC-40
$199	~$25	Internal, QIC-80
$249	~$25	External, QIC 40
$399	~$25	External, QIC 40
$1695/$1895	~$15	
$799	~$40	Internal
$1295/$1495	~$55	
$1695/$1895	~$60	
$1745/$2045	~$60	Includes interface
$1795	~$60	External, drive only
$1095/$1345	~$50	Includes interface
$1825	~$15	External, drive only
$1825/$2155	~$15	Includes interface
$1995	~$15	External, drive only
$2395/$2825	~$15	Includes SCSI interface
$199 (int. only)	$25	QIC-80
$399 (ext. only)	$25	QIC-80
$799 (ext. only)	$20	
$1099 (ext. only)	$20	
$1399 (ext. only)	$20	
$1895/$1995	~$15	
$1295/$1595	~$80	
$1995 (ext. only)	~$15	

CHAPTER SEVENTEEN

Sound Devices

The heart of multimedia is sound. The best PC sound systems produce CD-quality digital sound that really shows off the bells and whistles in multimedia presentations and games, not to mention home-grown or prerecorded music.

In this chapter, you learn about the new generation of sound cards for the PC and how to choose one that's right for your needs and your budget. This chapter is exclusively aimed at present or future PC-compatible computer owners—Macintosh has had this technology, built in, for years.

Selecting a Sound Card

Sound cards can add lifelike sound effects to your favorite games, play your music CDs using your CD-ROM drive, and let you compose and play your own music. Some let you give voice commands to your computer through a microphone. Multimedia presentation programs can deliver sales pitches through your sound card, and now even word processors let you embed sounds in your documents. Whether your new PC comes with a sound system built-in or you add one later, you're likely to have a sound card on your PC in the near future.

When you start looking at sound cards, keep a realistic idea of what you want and what you want to spend. If you have never taken a piano lesson, you might not need advanced composition and mixing capabilities. If you just want to add more bang to your games, even low-end sound cards fill the bill. For a multimedia system, you may want to save a slot in your PC (and a little money) and get a sound card with a built-in CD-ROM interface. The market is booming, and the sound card companies are stuffing their cards with useful options to attract buyers.

How It Works

Sound cards work much like the "brains" of an electronic keyboard, creating sounds based on preprogrammed patterns. When your software tells the sound card to play an "A" note using a trumpet's voice, the card checks to make sure that it knows what a trumpet sounds like, and then plays a note with its internal trumpet sound, manipulating the pitch so that it sounds like an "A" note.

The cards use two technologies for creating these sounds: FM synthesis and Wave-table synthesis (also called Wave-table lookup). FM synthesis is the less expensive, lower quality method, using computerized approximations of instrument voices. FM synthesis has (for lack of a better term) a "computerized" sound, somewhat tinny and not quite realistic. Wave-table synthesis uses recordings of actual instruments to produce a richer, truer sound. Some cards support both methods, but if you can have only one, Wave-table synthesis is the way to go.

The genesis of PC sound was MIDI (Musical Instrument Digital Interface), the most widely used standard in computerized music. MIDI lets you control digital keyboards, drum machines, and sequencers. With sequencing software, you can create MIDI files that play an almost limitless number of instruments, simultaneously. The MIDI controller (the sound card, in this case) sends small signals to the instruments, which is much quicker than sending entire sounds in wave form. Because the commands are simple, MIDI files take up much less disk space than wave-form sounds. The instruments obey the commands of the controller, playing sounds from their internal data banks to the rhythm set by the controller. Make sure that your sound card has MIDI capabilities if you want to do professional composing.

Features to Look For

Because sound cards are designed to work within multimedia systems, they often include features that make multimedia integration easier, such as on-board CD-ROM controllers and digital signal processors (DSPs). The most valuable controller is SCSI-based, because you can connect up to seven peripherals (storage devices, scanners, and so forth) to its single port. DSPs are processor chips that take much of the sound processing load off of the main CPU (very important in a multimedia system that's trying to manage sound and animation and regular I/O functions at the same time). Many DSPs are also set up to manage real-time compression and decompression of sound files. Because a 1-minute sound file at 44.1 kHz (the most common quality speed) can take up over 10M of hard disk space, compression is very important.

Another important feature is an array of ports, including stereo speaker ports, microphone, joystick, MIDI, and (if possible) SCSI.

When purchasing a piece of new technology, you always have to look out for vendors who have cut corners to keep prices low. In the sound card market, a corner that is often cut is adequate recording functions. If you plan to do digital recording, your card should be able to record at 44.1 kHz ("CD-quality") or as much as 48 kHz. Be very careful, though, as many sound cards are advertised with those speeds, but only in *playback* mode, not record mode. Another often-overlooked quality is stereo sound. Most people assume that sound cards will provide stereo sound, but some cards are mono only. Even if the card has two inputs and/or two outputs, it may be mono only.

If you just want some spice for your games, an older, 8-bit sound card will work fine. Almost all new sound cards support 16-bit sound. For professional-quality sound, you need at least 16-bit recording and playback (the MPC2 standard).

Bundled software should include a sound mixer if you want to do recording and a sequencer if you want to create MIDI compositions. Some cards include simple voice-processing software to let you use voice commands to play games or activate keyboard macros. Some utilities, like sound file players and CD audio controllers, are readily available as shareware or freeware.

Manufacturers

The "standard" sound card is the Sound Blaster, by Creative Labs. The first widely successful sound card, Sound Blaster set the standard for PC sound several years ago. Today, all good sound cards are Sound Blaster compatible so that they can use the variety of software written to work with the Sound Blaster. Creative Labs still makes innovative sound products, but other companies are producing highly competitive products—driving prices on even the best-quality sound cards into the "more-than-affordable" range.

Several companies make multimedia kits, including sound cards, CD-ROM drives, amplified stereo speakers, and (usually) CD-ROM titles, such as encyclopedias and games. Media Vision is a leader in sound cards and kits, as is Turtle Beach. Typically focused on external storage, Procom Technologies has introduced a full multimedia kit as well.

Listing of Sound Cards

Table 17.1 includes the following fields:

- *Company, Model.* Use this information to follow up on a product by calling the company or a dealer.
- *Synth. Method.* FM synthesis, Wave-table synthesis, or both.
- *Speed.* The sampling and playback speed of the card. 44.1 kHz is excellent and 48 kHz is a (hardly noticeable) step up.
- *Compatibility.* Sound Blaster, Ad-Lib, Microsoft Windows Sound System, and others. Most multimedia applications can work with Sound Blaster; Microsoft Windows Sound System is a good second choice.

- *CD-ROM Interface.* An SCSI CD-ROM interface is the most flexible, but proprietary interfaces work fine if you already own (or plan to buy) the right kind of drive. Check with the manufacturer or dealer to find out which types of drives will work with a sound card before you purchase.

Table 17.1 Stereo Sound Cards

Company, Model	Synth. Method	Speed
Cardinal Digital Sound Pro 16	FM	48KHz
Cardinal Digital Sound Pro 16 PLUS	wavetable	48KHz
Value Leader		
Cardinal Digital Sound Pro 16	wavetable	48KHz
Cardinal Digital Sound Pro 16 PLUS	FM	48KHz
Creative Labs Sound Blaster 16 MultiCD	FM	44.1KHz
Creative Labs Sound Blaster 16 SCSI-2	FM	44.1KHz
Creative Labs Sound Blaster 16 Value Edition	FM	44.1KHz
Creative Labs Sound Blaster AWE32	wavetable	44.1KHz

- *Features*. An on-board Digital Signal Processor (DSP), microphone or headphones, and/or game port increase the value of a sound card—if you actually plan to use them.
- *Price*. Manufacturer's suggested retail price.

Compatibility	CD-ROM Interface	Features	Price
Sound Blaster, MIDI, Microsoft Sound System, Business Audio	Sony	DSP	$100
SoundBlaster, MIDI	SCSI-2 Microsoft Sound System, Business Audio	DSP	$209
Sound Blaster, MIDI, Microsoft Sound System, Business Audio	Sony	DSP	$159
Sound Blaster, MIDI, Microsoft Sound System, Business Audio	SCSI-2	DSP	$150
Sound Blaster, MIDI	Creative Labs, Mitsumi, Sony	Upgradeable	$199.95
Sound Blaster, MIDI	SCSI-2	Upgradeable	$249.95
Sound Blaster, MPU-401, MIDI	Creative Labs		$149.95
Sound Blaster, MPU-401, MT-32, Sound Canvas, MIDI	Creative Labs, Sony, Mitsumi	DSP, Q-Sound 180-degree soundscape, TextAssist text-to-speech synthesis, high-performance condenser microphone, advanced WavEffects (chorus, reverb, etc.)	$399.95

continues

Table 17.1 Continued

Company, Model	Synth. Method	Speed
Creative Labs Sound Blaster Pro Value Edition	FM	44.1KHz (mono)
Creative Lab Sound Blaster Value Edition	FM	22KHz
Diamond SonicSound	wavetable	44.1KHz
Diamond SonicSound LX	FM	44.1KHz
Logitech AudioMan	FM	44.1KHz (playback)
Logitech SoundMan Wave	wavetable	44.1KHz
Media Vision Premium 3-D MCD	FM	44.1KHz
Media Vision Premium 3-D SCSI-2	FM	44.1KHz
Media Vision Pro 3-D	wavetable	44.1KHz
Microsoft Sound System	FM	44.1KHz
Orchid GameWave 32	wavetable	48KHz (playback)
Orchid SoundWave 32	wavetable	48KHz

Compatibility	CD-ROM Interface	Features	Price
Sound Blaster, MIDI	Creative Labs		$115.95
Sound Blaster, MIDI			$79.95
Sound Blaster, Ad Lib	SCSI-2		$299
Sound Blaster, Ad Lib	Mitsumi, Sony, Panasonic		$149
Sound Blaster, Ad Lib		Portable, for laptops	$179
Sound Blaster, Sound Blaster Pro, Ad Lib, Roland MPU-401 MIDI, General MIDI	SCSI	Upgradeable	$299
Sound Blaster, Ad Lib, Roland MPU-401 MIDI, General MIDI, Roland MT-32	Panasonic, Mitsumi, or Sony	Three-dimensional sound	$199
Sound Blaster, Ad Lib, Roland MPU-401 MIDI General MIDI, Roland MT-32	SCSI	Three-dimensional sound	$199
Sound Blaster, Ad Lib, Roland MPU-401 MIDI General MIDI, Roland MT-32	SCSI	Three-dimensional sound	$379
Sound Blaster, MIDI		Headphones, microphones	$219
Sound Blaster, Ad Lib, Roland MPU-401 MIDI General MIDI, Roland MT-32	Sony and Mitsumi	DSP	$249
Sound Blaster, Ad Lib, MS Windows Sound System Roland MPU-401 MIDI, General MIDI	Sony and Mitsumi	DSP	$249

continues

Table 17.1 Continued		
Company, Model	Synth. Method	Speed
Orchid SoundWave 32+SCSI	wavetable	48KHz

Chapter Summary

This chapter covers the basics of sound card technology and some of the things you need to know to make an informed sound card buying decision.

Compatibility	CD-ROM Interface	Features	Price
Sound Blaster, Ad Lib, MS Windows Sound System Roland MPU-401 MIDI, General MIDI, Roland MT-32	SCSI-2	DSP	$279

IN THE NEXT CHAPTER

Scanners (which let your computer pick up pictures or words from already-printed pages) are becoming a popular item for computer users at all levels, whether those users are desktop publishers, photo enthusiasts, or business or home computer users. The next chapter explains scanning technology and what to look for in hand held and flatbed scanners.

Chapter Eighteen

Scanners

A scanner (a piece of equipment that lets your computer pick up pictures or words from already-printed pages) has long been a necessity for desktop publishers, but because of some developments in the industry, other PC users are now eyeing scanners to help in their work. The move to graphical user interfaces (GUIs) has made people more graphics-conscious, which has affected everything from reports to business letters. Improved quality in laser printing makes it possible to use photographs and other graphics (digitized with a scanner) to add professional-looking visual impact to all your documents. You can even use a scanner to digitize a copy of your signature, inserting it as a graphic at the end of correspondence.

As fax modems become more popular, people are starting to scan printed documents into their computers for faxing.

A major development in scanning has been the advances in optical character recognition (OCR). You can now have your scanner take a picture of typewritten copy (a book, a magazine, a letter, and so on) and have the OCR software "read" the picture, changing it into regular text for your word processor. The process is much quicker than entering the text manually, and the best OCR packages are very accurate at translating scanned text to regular text, even when the original uses several point sizes or fonts. If you have to enter copy from typewritten or other printed sources, you could save a great deal of time with a scanner and top-quality OCR software (like OmniPage from Caere Corp.).

In this chapter, you learn the major differences and buying considerations among scanners, how they work, and what companies make good scanners. The chapter also provides four tables of scanners (hand-held grayscale, hand-held color, flatbed grayscale, and flatbed color) listing features and prices of popular scanners.

Selecting a Scanner

Before you invest in a scanner, get a clear picture of how you'll use it and how your needs might change. If you work with desktop publishing, you probably will want a flatbed scanner, but will you need grayscale or color? If all your work is black and white now, do you foresee doing some color work in the future? If your scanner will be used solely to send faxes with your fax modem, a low-cost black-and-white scanner makes the most sense—don't spend the extra money for color or high resolution, because it won't show up on the faxes anyway. For occasional jobs (a monthly newsletter or quarterly reports, for example), you might not want to invest in an expensive flatbed scanner; you might prefer a high-quality hand held model (which saves you money and desk space).

Scanners don't vary greatly in features (though scanning software does), so there aren't many differences to consider between competing models. The factor most people notice is *resolution*, which is the number of dots the scanners pick up when they read a one-inch line of an image. (Resolution ranges from around 300 dots per inch (dpi) to 1,200 dpi or more.) The truth, however, is that even entry-level resolutions (300 to 400 dpi) are acceptable in almost every scanning application. Unless you're a professional image processor, you won't notice any difference between a 150 dpi grayscale image and a 1,200 dpi image except that the latter takes up a much bigger portion of your hard drive. As you use higher resolutions, the images on your hard disk take up more and more space. It is not unusual for a high-resolution color scan to take up 20M or more of disk space.

The secret to good scanning isn't in using the highest resolution, but the most efficient resolution for the output device (usually a printer or monitor). Your monitor, for example, is probably between 50 and 100 dpi, so scanning a photograph at a higher resolution can't improve what you see on-screen—it just eats up more disk space.

For printing grayscale pictures, lower resolutions may actually look better than higher ones. Single-color laser printers can show only black or white, so they use patterns of black and white areas to simulate grays. The dots in the picture must be considerably larger than the dots the printer uses to make the pattern, because the printer creates a separate gray pattern for each dot in the picture. If the picture has the same resolution as the printer (or higher), the printer has to abandon its gray patterns and print one dot (black or white) for each dot in the original picture. If you have a 600 dpi laser printer, for example, a 600 dpi grayscale picture will print out very dark and muddy, whereas a 150 dpi grayscale picture will show much more natural grayscales and even-looking tones.

In the next section, you learn how scanners work and how you can evaluate different buying considerations.

How It Works

This section provides a basic technical explanation of scanning. If you're interested in how the scanner works under the hood, take a look at this section. Otherwise, feel free to skip on to the next one.

The basic principle behind scanners is very simple—they project a light onto a point on an image and measure the amount of light reflected back. The measurements are recorded as numbers and the numbers are stored in a file on your hard disk. After the image is on your drive, you can use it in word processing documents, edit it, or send it to someone else over a modem (or fax modem).

For black-and-white scanning (as opposed to grayscale or color scanning), the scanner measures the reflection to see whether it's more light than dark (white) or more dark than light (black). Black-and-white scanning is also called "line-art" scanning because it provides the best results when scanning single-color graphics like pen-and-ink drawings rather than continuous tone graphics like photographs. Line-art scanning requires much less disk space than other methods because it can describe each dot with one bit of information.

Grayscale scanning measures the amount of light and dark in every dot in an image. Most grayscale scanners can detect 64 or more levels of gray. Depending on the number of gray levels, grayscale scans can take up considerably more hard drive space than line-art scans—6 times as much for 64 gray levels.

Color scanning uses the same basic concept (projecting light onto an image and measuring the reflection), but has to make some adjustments to separate one color from another. Almost all color scanners use the RGB (red, green, blue) method to detect colors. In some cases, the scanning element has one red filter, one green filter, and one blue filter, and it makes one pass over the image with each filter. This three-pass scanning creates good-quality color images and is fast enough for any application (faster than single-pass scanning, in some cases).

Single-pass scanning uses one of two color separation methods: triple filters or prisms. Triple filters are scanning mechanisms with a distinct element for each scan color (red, green, and blue). As the mechanism passes over the image, each element measures its color. Color scanners that use prisms project white light at their images and catch the reflection with a three-sided prism. The prism separates the reflected light into the colors of the spectrum (like a rainbow), projecting the light onto special receptors that measure the amount of red, green, and blue in it. Color scans take up a lot of hard drive space—three times or more that required by grayscale scans. If you want to do a great deal of color scanning, see Chapter 15, "Storage."

Price and Costs

Hand-held scanners are considerably less expensive than flatbed scanners ($150 to $300, compared to $700 or more for flatbeds), and their quality can be acceptable if you're careful. For professional work, though, flatbed scanners really earn their cost; hand-held scanners aren't worth the hassle if you do high-volume work.

Scanners are inexpensive to operate. You may have to replace the bulb once every few months (or longer), but even in color scanners, that expense is relatively small. You should keep some good-quality optical glass cleaner (from the photography shop) and lint-free cloth handy for cleaning flatbed scanners.

Resolution

Both hand-held and flatbed scanners start at about 300 dpi, and 400 dpi is becoming more and more common. Top end resolution on a wide-use scanner is about 1,200 dpi. Professional scanners (costing thousands of dollars) reach 2,400 dpi or more. Most scanners now include resolution-enhancement software, which can drive the scanners at even higher effective resolutions, turning a 400 dpi scanner into an 800 or 1,200 dpi scanner. When an advertisement boasts about high resolution, it's usually talking about this "enhanced" resolution rather than the native, or "optical" resolution.

The best scanners listed in this chapter have an optical resolution of 600, 800, or 1,200 dpi, which produce better quality images than software-enhanced scanners with lower optical resolutions.

For fax and OCR applications, resolution isn't much of an issue. The highest resolution standard fax is 200 dpi, so even the lowest resolution scanner can create a good image for faxing. Optical character recognition benefits only marginally from high-resolution scanned input, and in some cases cannot interpret the scan correctly above a certain resolution. Check with your OCR software maker for the optimum scanning resolution.

Drivers

All scanners require special drivers, which are included when you purchase the scanner. In Macintosh and Windows, most scanner drivers are available to any scanning software you decide to install, but DOS users should stick with only the leading brands (Hewlett-Packard and a few others) to make sure that your scanning software is compatible with your scanner.

Many scanners work with the "TWAIN" standard, which lets you bypass the scanning software and scan images directly into desktop publishing, graphics, or word processing programs. TWAIN compatibility saves you the time you normally would spend working in the scanning software, saving the scanned file, and inserting it into your document.

Size

Hand-held scanners are about four inches across and up to six inches long, enabling them to fit easily in a briefcase or desk drawer. Flatbed scanners take up about as much space as a laser printer.

Manufacturers

The biggest name in flatbed scanning is also the biggest name in laser printing: Hewlett-Packard. The Scanjet series for both Macintosh and PC-compatibles is very popular and consistently rated at the top of quality surveys. Apple also makes scanners for Macintoshes, employing its typically high standards in quality and features. Other players in the scanning market include Epson, Microtek, Mustek, and Umax (which is very strong in the Macintosh market).

In the hand-scanner category, Logitech is a leader, with several others in the running. Mouse Systems, Umax, Mustek, and others make quality hand-held scanners. Optical character recognition giant Caere bundles a high-quality hand-held scanner with its powerful OCR, image editing, and fax software as the "OmniSCAN" system, available for PC or Macintosh.

Listings of Scanners

The scanner listings are broken down into four categories: hand-held grayscale, hand held color, flatbed grayscale, and flatbed color. Each table lists specifications about each scanner, including the following fields:

- *Company, Model.* Use this information to follow up on a product by calling the company or a dealer.

- *Resolution/Enhanced Res.* The optical resolution and the software-enhanced resolution.

- *Max. Image Size.* For hand-held scanners, this is the width of the scanning area; for flatbed scanners, it is both dimensions of the scanning area. Be aware that most hand held scanners come with software that lets you scan wide areas in strips and combine the strips into a single image.

- *Compatibility.* Shows whether the scanner connects to a PC, Macintosh, or both.

- *Bundled Software.* Look for image editing software, with OCR and fax software as an added bonus. A popular item is "trainable" OCR software that can "learn" to read different fonts (rather than just typewritten text and a few basic fonts).

- *Warranty.* Scanners rarely break down, but repairs can be a very large expense if the warranty is too short. If you buy mail-order, check to see who pays for repairs and shipping.

- *Price.* Manufacturer's suggested retail price.

Table 18.1 B/W and Grayscale Hand Held Scanners

Company, Model	Resolution/ Enh. Res.	Max. Image Size	Compatibility
Caere OmniScan	400 dpi		Mac or PC
Logitech ScanMan 256	400x400	15" x 22"	PC
Logitech ScanMan 256/OmniPage	400x400	15" x 22"	PC
Logitech ScanMan 32DOS/CatchWord	400x400	15" x 22"	PC (DOS)
Logitech ScanMan 32WIN/OmniPage	400x400	15" x 22"	PC (Windows)
Logitech ScanMan Easy Touch/OmniPage	400x400	15" x 22"	PC

Value Leader

UMAX MiniLook Gray	400 dpi, 800 dpi	unlimited (automatic stitching, 4.3" width)	PC

Table 18.2 Hand-Held Color Scanners

Company, Model	Resolution/ Enh. Res.	Max. Image Size	Compatibility
Logitech ScanMan Color	400x400	15" x 22"	PC
Logitech ScanMan Color/ OmniPage	400x400	15" x 22"	PC
MicroTek ScanMaker Scooter	800 dpi	8.5" x 11"	PC

Value Leader

UMAX MiniLook Color	400 dpi, 800 dpi	unlimited (automatic stitching, 4.3" width)	PC

Scanners

Software	Warranty	Price	Other
OmniPage Direct, Fax-Master, Image Assistant GS		$449	Automatic image stitching, non-skid rollers
FotoTouch	1 year	$349	256 gray levels
FotoTouch, OmniPage (OCR)	1 year	$399	256 gray levels
GrayTouch, CatchWord (OCR)	lifetime	$199	32 gray levels
FotoTouch, OmniPage (OCR)	lifetime	$299	32 gray levels
FotoTouch, OmniPage (OCR)	1 year	$399	256 gray levels, attaches to a parallel port (includes pass-through connector for printer), motorized for correct speed and alignment
ProImage Plus, Perceive OCR		$145	Edge guide

Software	Warranty	Price	Other
FotoTouch	lifetime	$649	16.8 million colors, TWAIN compliant
FotoTouch, Omni-Page (OCR)	lifetime	$699	16.8 million colors, TWAIN compliant
ImageStar II, Isis OCR		$549	Includes TrackPad for stability
ProImage Plus, Perceive OCR		$295	Edge guide

Table 18.3 B/W and Grayscale Flatbed and Page Scanners

Company, Model	Resolution/ Enh. Res.	Max. Image Size	Compatibility
Apple OneScanner	75-1200	8.5" x 14"	Mac
Apple OneScanner for Windows	75-1200	8.5" x 14"	Windows
Value Leader			
Hewlett-Packard ScanJet IIp	300x300, 1200x1200	8.5" x 11"	Mac, PC
Logitech ScanMan PowerPage	400x400	8.5" x 11"	Mac, PC
Value Leader			
MicroTek ScanMaker IIG	300x600, 1200x1200	8.5" x 14"	Mac, PC
Panasonic FX-RS307U	300x600	8.5" x 14"	Mac
Panasonic FX-RS307U	300x600	8.5" x 14"	PC
Panasonic FX-RS506U	400 dpi	8.5" x 14"	Mac
Panasonic FX-RS506U	400 dpi	8.5" x 14"	PC

Table 18.4 Color Flatbed Scanners

Company, Model	Resolution/ Enh. Res.	Max. Imager Size	Compatibility
Apple Color OneScanner	75-1200	8.5" x 14"	Mac
Epson ActionScanning System	600x600, 1200x1200	8.5" x 11"	Mac, PC
Epson ES-800C Pro	800x800	8.5" x 11"	PC
Hewlett-Packard ScanJet IIcx	400x400, 1600x1600	8.5" x 14"	Mac, PC

Software	Warranty	Price	Other
Ofoto	1 year		
Ofoto	1 year		Includes SCSI inter-face
DeskScan II, Photo-Styler SE (PC version also includes Calera WordScan)	1 year	$599	
FotoTouch	1 year	$799	small footprint (2.75" x 12")
OmniScan (text, image, faxing)		$649	
Scan-Do/M		$1485 (w/ interface)	
PanaScan Plus		$1035 (w/ interface)	
Scan-Do/M		$1485 (w/ interface)	
PanaScan Plus		$1035 (w/ interface)	

Software	Warranty	Price	Other
Ofoto and ColorSync	1 year		
Adobe PhotoShop LE	1 year	$999	
Micrografx Picture Publisher	1 year	$1499	
DeskScan II, PhotoStyler SE	1 year	$1179	

continues

Table 18.4 Continued

Company, Model	Resolution/ Enh. Res.	Max. Image Size	Compatibility
MicroTek ScanMaker II	300x600, 1200x1200	8.5" x 14"	Mac, PC
Value Leader			
MicroTek ScanMaker IIHR	600x1200, 2400x2400	8.5" x 14"	Mac, PC
MicroTek ScanMaker III	600x1200, 2400x2400	8.5" x 14"	Mac, PC
MicroTek ScanMaker IISP	300x600, 1200x1200	8.5" x 14"	Mac, PC
Nikon AX-1200 ScanTouch	565x1200, 2400x2400	8.5" x 14"	Mac, PC
Panasonic FX-RS308C	300x600	8.5" x 14"	Mac
Panasonic FX-RS308C	300x600	8.5" x 14"	PC
UMAX PowerLook	1200x600, 2400x2400	8.5" x 14"	Mac, PC
UMAX UC1260 Color Scanner	1200x600, 2400x2400	8.5" x 14"	Mac, PC
UMAX UC630LE Color Scanner	600x300, 1200x1200	8.5" x 14"	Mac, PC
UMAX UC840 Color Scanner	800x400, 1600x1600	8.5" x 14"	Mac, PC
Value Leader			
UMAX Vista VT-600	600x300, 1200x1200	8.5" x 14"	PC
UMAX Vista-S6	600x300, 1200x1200	8.5" x 11"	Mac, PC

Software	Warranty	Price	Other
Adobe Photoshop LE			
DCR color correction, Adobe Photoshop		$1499	
DCR color correction, Adobe Photoshop		$3499	36-bit color, single pass
DCR color correction, Adobe Photoshop LE			single-pass
TWAIN drivers	1 year	$1535	SCSI-II compatible
Scan-Do/M		$1485 (w/interface)	
PanaScan Plus		$1035 (w/interface)	
Adobe Photoshop		$3495	sealed case for dust-free optics, enhanced speed
Adobe Photoshop		$1395	
(PC) Adobe Photoshop LE, (Mac) Adobe Photoshop LE and PhotoFlash		$795	
Adobe Photoshop		$995	
ImageFolio (image editing), Power Reader (OCR)		$695	
Adobe Photoshop LE, OmniPage Direct OCR, MagicMatch color matching		$945	enhanced speed

Chapter Summary

This chapter shows the variety of scanners on the market today. It explains scanning technology and common uses, and describes the main manufacturers of flatbed and hand held scanners. Four tables list specifications and prices for hand-held and flatbed scanners, grayscale and color models.

IN THE NEXT CHAPTER

The next chapter shows you how to keep your system well-fueled. Special protective power supplies and laptop batteries are covered.

CHAPTER NINETEEN

Feeding Your System

This chapter deals with a very important aspect of your computer system: its fuel. Next to viruses, power problems are about the most dangerous thing for a computer. Power spikes can fry the internal components, and unexpected power outages can dump the file you're working on into the bit bucket.

Your laptop runs out of fuel quicker than your car. The last thing you need when you're miles from a battery charge is a lifeless laptop battery.

In this chapter, you learn about keeping your computer steadily supplied with power. The first section deals with power conditioners and uninterruptible power supplies (UPS's). The last section gives you some options for purchasing extra laptop batteries or repairing old ones.

Secure Power Supplies for Your PC

Personal computers are very sensitive pieces of electronic equipment. Plugging yours directly into the wall outlet is like using cheap gas in your car—it'll work fine most of the time, but costs dearly when it doesn't. The power surging through your walls fluctuates slightly when appliances and lights are turned on and off; major appliances cause more significant fluctuations. Sometimes the power will spike for a split second, sending a huge burst of current to all appliances—sometimes too much for sensitive equipment like a computer to handle. Other times, the power will disappear or be reduced for a time (like in a blackout or brownout), stopping all the processes in your computer without giving you a chance to save your work.

With some advance planning, though, you can protect your computer from power problems. Power protection comes in three main forms: surge protectors and two types of uninterruptible power supplies.

Surge protectors are like fuses or circuit breakers, but rather than cutting off the power completely, they absorb the spikes internally. This leaves a relatively steady level of electricity on the line going to the computer. Surge protectors are inexpensive but offer some measure of protection for your computer.

Uninterruptible Power Supplies (UPS's) are the next step up in protection. They protect your equipment from all fluctuations, both spikes and power drops. A UPS is able to absorb power spikes like a surge protector, but it also can add power (from its internal batteries) when the levels go too low. UPS's are able to power your computer even during a blackout or brownout. All UPS's give you at least enough time to save your work, and some can power your machine for over an hour in an emergency. Many network file servers use UPS's because shutting them down abruptly causes expensive problems.

UPS's come in two flavors: backup and in-line. Backup UPS's let power pass through from the wall outlet to your computer until the power goes out, then (within a few milliseconds) they switch over to power the computer with their internal batteries. In-line UPS's always power the computer with their internal batteries, constantly recharging with power from the wall outlet. Both types offer high levels of protection.

Table 19.1 lists some equipment that will keep your PC, its data, and your peripherals safe. Most of the manufacturers listed carry a wide range of power protection devices. For more detailed information, use the addresses and phone numbers in Appendix B to contact them.

Table 19.1 Power Protection Equipment

Company	Product Description	Price
American Power Conversion	Personal SurgeArrest (Per3), 3-outlet surge protector with lifetime warranty, $2500 in lifetime equipment protection insurance	$24.95
American Power Conversion	Personal SurgeArrest (Per7), 7-outlet surge protector with lifetime warranty, $2500 in lifetime equipment protection insurance	$29.95
American Power Conversion	Professional SurgeArrest (Pro7), 7-outlet surge protector with lifetime warranty, $10,000 in lifetime equipment protection insurance	$49.95
American Power Conversion	PowerManager (Pow6), single-source power manager/surge protector for computer and up to five peripherals, with static protection, noise supression, lifetime warranty, lifetime $25,000 equipment protection insurance	$119.99
Value Leader		
American Power Conversion	PowerManager (Pow6T), single-source power manager/surge protector for computer and up to five peripherals, includes modem/fax protector, with static protection, noise supression, lifetime warranty, lifetime $25,000 equipment protection insurance	$134.99

Company	Product Description	Price
American Power Conversion	Line-R, power conditioner, $25,000 in lifetime equipment protection insurance	$179
American Power Conversion	The Smart UPS 250, uninterruptible power supply, 250 VA load, $25,000 in lifetime equipment protection insurance	$299
American Power Conversion	The Smart UPS 400, uninterruptible power supply, 400 VA load, $25,000 in lifetime equipment protection insurance	$399
American Power Conversion	The Smart UPS 600, uninterruptible power supply, 600 VA load, $25,000 in lifetime equipment protection insurance	$499
American Power Conversion	The Smart UPS 900, uninterruptible power supply, 900 VA load, $25,000 in lifetime equipment protection insurance	$799
American Power Conversion	The Smart UPS 1250, uninterruptible power supply, 1250 VA load, $25,000 in lifetime equipment protection insurance	$999
American Power Conversion	The Smart UPS 2000, uninterruptible power supply, 2000 VA load, $25,000 in lifetime equipment protection insurance	$1,699
Kensington	Power Tree 10 surge protector outlet strip, six outlets, $5,000 in equipment protection, 5-year warranty	$29.95
Kensington	Power Tree 20 surge protector outlet strip, six outlets, includes noise filtering, $5,000 in equipment protection, 5-year warranty	$49.95
Kensington	Power Tree 50 surge protector outlet strip, six outlets, includes noise filtering and phone line/modem protection, $10,000 in equipment protection, 5-year warranty	$69.95
Kensington	MasterPiece compact power control center, four outlets (for three peripherals and your computer) with master switch, includes noise filtering, $20,000 in equipment protection, 5-year warranty	$99.95

continues

Table 19.1 Continued		
Company	Product Description	Price
Kensington	MasterPiece power control center, five outlets (for our peripherals and your computer) with master switch, includes noise filtering, anti-static protection, $25,000 in equipment protection, 5-year warranty	$149.95
Kensington	MasterPiece Plus power control center, five outlets (for four peripherals and your computer) with master switch, includes fax/modem surge protection, noise filtering, anti-static protection, $25,000 in equipment protection, 5-year warranty	$159.95
Kensington	MasterPiece Plus Remote power control center, five outlets (for four peripherals and your computer) with master switch, one outlet continuously powered for a clock or other device that should be left powered while the system is turned off, two-part compact design, includes fax/modem surge protection, noise filtering, anti-static protection, $25,000 in equipment protection, 5-year warranty	$169.95
Kensington	Power Backer Plus 300, uninterruptible power supply, can power equipment from 8-95 minutes during loss of commercial power, up to 300 VA load (typical lower end desktop PC and monitor), surge protection (with fax/modem surge protection) and noise filtering, 2 year warranty with $25,000 in equipment protection	$349.95
Kensington	Power Backer Plus 450, uninterruptible power supply, can power equipment from 8-95 minutes during loss of commercial power, up to 450 VA load (typical mid-range desktop PC and monitor), surge protection (with fax/modem surge protection) and noise filtering, 2 year warranty with $25,000 in equipment protection	$449.95
Kensington	Power Backer Plus 600, uninterruptible power supply, can power equipment from 8-95 minutes during loss of commercial power, up to 600 VA load (typical high-end desktop PC with monitor), surge protection (with fax/modem surge protection) and noise filtering, 2 year warranty with $25,000 in equipment protection	$649.95

Company	Product Description	Price
Kensington	Power Backer Plus 800, uninterruptible power supply, can power equipment from 8-95 minutes during loss of commercial power, up to 800 VA load (typical high-end PC, mini, or server with monitor), surge protection (with fax/modem surge protection) and noise filtering, 2 year warranty with $25,000 in equipment protection	$849.95
Value Leader		
Global	Telecom Surge Protector, 6-outlet surge protector with fax/modem surge protection, includes noise filtering	$32.95
Global	Power Master II, 5-outlet power control center (for four peripherals and your PC) with master switch, includes fax/modem surge protection, with noise filtering	$99.95
Global	Voltage Regulator AC4901, 2-outlet power conditioner, regulates against undervoltages, with noise filtering	$99.95
Global	Voltage Regulator AC4902, 4-outlet power conditioner, regulates against undervoltages and overvoltages, with noise filtering	$169.95
Global	Voltage Regulator AC4903, 6-outlet power conditioner, regulates against undervoltages and overvoltages, with noise filtering	$249.95
Global	PowerRite Pro 97934, uninterruptible power supply, provides constant power from batteries (to eliminate switchover time from commercial to battery power), up to 400VA load, 10-year warranty	$329
Value Leader		
Global	PowerRite Pro 97935, uninterruptible power supply, provides constant power from batteries (to eliminate switchover time from commercial to battery power), up to 600VA load, 10-year warranty	$399
Global	PowerRite Pro 97936, uninterruptible power supply, provides constant power from batteries (to eliminate switchover time from commercial to battery power), up to 1000VA load, 10-year warranty	$639

continues

Table 19.1 Continued		
Company	Product Description	Price
Global	PowerRite Pro 97937, uninterruptible power supply, provides constant power from batteries (to eliminate switchover time from commercial to battery power), up to 1440VA load, 10-year warranty	$749
Global	PowerRite Pro 97938, uninterruptible power supply, provides constant power from batteries (to eliminate switchover time from commercial to battery power), up to 1920VA load, 10-year warranty	$1,249
Global	PowerRite Pro 97939, uninterruptible power supply, provides constant power from batteries (to eliminate switchover time from commercial to battery power), up to 2200VA load, 10-year warranty	$1,299
Global	On-line UPS 7112, includes power conditioning features and noise filtering, up to 600VA load, 1-year warranty	$479
Global	On-line UPS 7113, includes power conditioning features and noise filtering, up to 900VA load, 1-year warranty	$759

Laptop Batteries

When you plug your laptop (or notebook, subnotebook, or PDA) into a wall outlet, it can run forever without a glitch. As soon as you move away from the safety of that outlet, though, the clock starts ticking. The effective life of a portable battery pack (regardless of advertising claims) can be as little as two hours or less. If you plan to take to the road (or the skies) with your portable PC, take some extra batteries and a quality battery charger.

Your portable PC might use standard alkaline batteries (Hewlett-Packard's OmniBooks use several AA batteries, Apple's Newton can use AAA batteries), but probably uses a special battery pack. Though most battery packs are square or rectangular, most just contain one or two rows of cylindrical cells that look like regular "C" or "D" cells.

NiCad (Nickel Cadmium) battery packs are fairly standard, but they aren't as powerful or environmentally sound as some other types. The typical NiCad battery pack can be recharged up to 700 times, but has an effective life span of about 1,000 hours (1-1/2 years of regular use). NiCad batteries are popular for all types of portable equipment (camcorders and cellular phones, for example) because they are relatively inexpensive.

Apple uses the more powerful NiHy (Nickel Hydride) batteries in their lower end portables. These batteries recharge much quicker than NiCads. You can recharge a NiHy battery in about one and a half hours and use it for up to four hours, compared to NiCad's charging time of eight or more hours.

The next step up in battery technology is nickel-metal-hydride (NiMH), which is about 30 percent more powerful that NiCad. NiMH batteries typically last about a year in regular use. Apple uses nickel-metal-hydride batteries in their higher end portables.

Two higher end technologies are emerging in the battery market: Lithium Ion and Zinc Air. Lithium Ion batteries, boasting more power and longer life than NiMH, should be available in 1995. Zinc Air batteries are already available, typically in external battery packs, in configurations that can power an average laptop up to 20 hours.

Your portable PC may be able to take advantage of these advanced battery technologies, but it may not. Check with the manufacturer before purchasing any third-party batteries.

You may find that, after a while, your battery's capacity drops drastically. This is typically due to the "memory effect," caused by not charging the battery completely, either because the battery wasn't completely discharged before it started recharging or because the recharging process was interrupted. If, for example, the battery still has 50 percent of its power when you start to recharge it, it will only receive a 50 percent charge. Later, when you try to recharge it again, the memory effect could cause it to allow only a 50 percent recharge, even if the battery was completely discharged and needed a 100 percent charge. NiCad batteries are especially prone to the memory effect. To combat the memory effect, always run your batteries completely out of power before recharging them, and remove the battery when running the computer on AC current. Some battery chargers have a "power drain" or "conditioning" feature built in, which discharges the battery completely before recharging. Check with the manufacturer to make sure that this feature is included before purchasing a battery charger.

If you have had your portable PC for over a year, or if you don't have enough spare batteries, contact the companies listed in table 19.2 for new batteries and chargers. Some can even repair worn-out batteries, and all will accept your old batteries for recycling.

Table 19.2 Battery Suppliers

Company	Products/Services
Battery Technology (800.982.8284)	Replacement batteries, chargers, auto adapters, external battery packs for extending battery life
Power Express (800.POWER.EX)	Replacement batteries, chargers, auto adapters, AC adapters, external battery packs for extending battery life, power management software
House of Batteries (800.432.3385)	Replacement batteries, custom design, battery repair, chargers
TNR Technical (800.346.0601)	Replacement batteries, custom battery packs

Chapter Summary

Your computer needs a steady stream of electricity to function properly. This chapter covered several methods of protecting your PC from getting too much or too little power, including uninterruptible power supplies, power conditioners, and surge protectors. It also discussed laptop batteries and chargers, and listed sources for both.

IN THE NEXT CHAPTER

In Chapter 20, "Putting Together a System to Meet Your Needs," you'll learn how to look at your needs and available equipment objectively, and try to come up with a good match.

PART IV

Buying a System

Includes

Putting Together a System to Meet Your Needs

Making the Purchase

Planning for the Future

Vendor Information

CHAPTER TWENTY

Putting Together a System To Meet Your Needs

When you're deciding on the specifications for the system you want to buy, it's easy to make expensive mistakes. If you're too hasty or not well-enough informed, you can buy a system that costs too much and does far more than you need, or you can buy a system that's too limited and has to be replaced too soon.

However, you are the primary expert on what you need from a computer. With a little bit of forethought, you can translate those needs into a list of specifications that describe the computer system you should buy.

If you pick a middle-of-the-road base system, you are likely to be ready to meet the needs of today as well as the near future. This chapter will help you decide what kind of base system you should look for, and then describe how to fine-tune that system for your own specific requirements.

Know Your Operating Environment

You should get the same operating environment as the people you work with most closely. If most of your friends or coworkers use Macintosh, Windows, DOS, or any other operating system, you may get valuable help from them by following their lead. Of course, you may choose to purchase a system that supports multiple operating environments, like a PowerPC-based Macintosh (which runs Macintosh and Windows programs) or a PC-compatible with OS/2 (which runs OS/2, Windows, and DOS programs).

Chapter 4, "Deciding What Kind of Computer You Want," discussed at some length how to decide on the right kind of operating environment for your needs. It also looked into the question of whether a portable or desktop system is a better choice. Please look at that chapter again if you don't yet have a firm idea of what kind of system will fit your needs.

If that chapter isn't enough to help you decide, talk to friends and colleagues who use computers and get their advice. Reach at least a tentative decision before you start considering the specifications for your computer system; otherwise, the process of deciding on the details will include too many unanswered questions to end up with useful results. Don't make your purchase without first making some basic decisions about what your needs are and what products might best fit those needs.

General-Purpose Desktop PCs

In buying a PC, you want to buy a system that will meet your needs today and be flexible enough to keep up with the demands of tomorrow. A typical mid-range IBM-compatible or Macintosh system can handle most of today's software and still give you the capability to expand if needed.

A Mid-Range System

This section looks at the characteristics of a middle-of-the-road system first, in each of the important areas that you will have to specify to make an intelligent buying decision. Then it discusses what to do if you want either a little less cost or a little more power.

Processor

A mid-range Macintosh today uses a 68030 or 68040 microprocessor; a mid-range IBM-compatible PC uses an 80486SX or non-accelerated 80486. Clock speeds range from a low of 20 MHz up to a high of 33MHz, at this writing. To run more than one or two programs under Macintosh System 7.1 or Windows, you need the kind of power offered by such a mid-range system. Within these guidelines, choose a system that has the microprocessor and clock speed that make sense for your needs and budget.

Many IBM-compatible PCs offer inexpensive processor upgrades as well. This capability is worthwhile to have and is free from some vendors; look for processor upgradability if you believe that you may need more processor power in the next couple of years.

Slots

A key factor in the kind of PC you want is expandability, indicated by the number of slots. Related factors include the number of drive bays and the size of the power supply. Tower and mini-tower systems, which look like a regular desktop PC turned on its side, are usually the most expandable. The premium for a tower configuration over a regular desktop may be just a few hundred dollars. Some full-size desktop machines are quite expandable as well, with as many as eight expansion slots. Some compact desktop systems, by contrast, have one slot or none.

Even if you think you have your needs figured out pretty well, always buy a system that has one more slot and one more drive bay than you think you will need. You will be very frustrated if you need some new device and have to replace a several thousand-dollar system for want of a place to put it. Of course, you can solve the problem by getting external devices, but these cost more and take up more desk space.

Memory

For a system running Windows or System 7.1, get 8M of RAM memory. If you run just one or two applications, 4M may be enough. 2M is only a good idea if you're going to run DOS rather than Windows.

The motherboard of the machine you buy should be able to handle 16M of memory, minimum. Even if you never add this much memory, the resale value of your system will benefit. Having room for 32M or even 64M is better.

Video Adapter

Unless you're sure you will need a high-powered graphics adapter card, look for a system with video support on the motherboard. For an IBM-compatible PC, look for SuperVGA support with at least 512K of video memory. For faster video, look for a system with a VESA VL-bus or PCI local bus slot. Don't pay extra for the possibly higher performance and flexibility of PCI unless you are buying a Pentium system. You can put a very fast video card in a local bus slot at the time you purchase the system or later.

A Macintosh should have built-in support for Macintosh video and 512K of video memory. The only exceptions are the older Macs like the Macintosh Classic, which have a built-in 9-inch screen. Used early Macs are inexpensive and easy to find, but be sure that you're ready to spend the next couple of years squinting at a tiny screen before buying one of these. For faster video, look for a system with a PDS (Processor Direct Slot). Not all PDS devices are compatible with all PDS slots, so make sure that there's an appropriate affordable video card from a major manufacturer for the Macintosh that you buy.

Floppy Drives

IBM-compatible buyers should look for a system with dual floppy drives. The more commonly used 3 1/2-inch drive should be drive A, and the older 5 1/4-inch drive should be drive B. It's nice, but not necessary, that the 3 1/2-inch drive can read a 2.88M disk as well as the more common 1.44M format. You should only leave off the 5 1/4-inch drive if you're sure that you won't need to run old software or share data with someone who uses an old system.

Macintosh users do just fine with a single 3 1/2-inch drive because Macintoshes can read and write IBM-compatible 3 1/2-inch disk as well as all previous Macintosh disk formats with this drive.

Hard Drives

Because adding a hard drive or replacing your present one after you have been using your system for a while is expensive and often difficult, buy a big hard drive. Bigger hard drives are sometimes faster, too, so there's a dual benefit to buying more than you think you will need.

For IBM-compatible systems, buy the biggest drive you think you will need without counting on the file compression software in DOS. Then, if you surprise yourself and fill up the drive, you can turn on the file-compression capability and still have room to grow. A Windows system should have at least 100M of hard disk available after you install Windows and a few applications, and 200M is preferable.

For the Macintosh, a 160M internal drive is a good size to start out with; you may be able to get by with 80M. If you need further expansion after you buy your machine, you can just plug a second hard drive into the built-in, always-compatible SCSI port. If you want file compression, you have to buy this capability from a third party because there's no file compression built into the Macintosh operating system.

This book tries to avoid recommending hardware you don't really need, but many users end up buying a hard drive that turns out to be too small and too slow. Stretch a bit on this one; you're unlikely to regret it.

CD-ROM Drives

If you're ever going to get a CD-ROM drive, the best way to go is to get a built-in one at the time you buy your system. This way you don't have to worry about installation or finding desktop space for it, and it's clearly the responsibility of your system vendor to make sure that the CD-ROM drive works with the rest of your system. Also, the added cost of a CD-ROM drive included in a complete system is lower than the cost of buying a separate drive later.

Some are hesitant to buy a CD-ROM drive because a device that reads all the popular formats, plays audio CDs, and runs fast may still be a year or two away. However, many users can have a great deal of fun with a CD-ROM right away. Most Mac buyers should seriously consider a CD-ROM because Macintosh systems have fewer problems using CD-ROMs than IBM-compatibles, and some of the better titles come out on the Macintosh first. If you're buying an IBM-compatible system, find out the cost of getting a CD-ROM included, and go for it if the added cost is within your budget.

Input Devices

Most PC-compatible systems come with a cheap keyboard and mouse thrown in. If you're buying from a dealer or retail store, you can try the keyboard and mouse on the system you're buying and take that into account in your purchase. You may also be able to negotiate an upgrade for a moderate amount of money. If you're buying mail order, you're stuck with whatever the vendor sends you.

Many IBM-compatibles from lesser-known companies are shipped with very poor keyboards and mice. Unless you buy from the best companies (like those discussed in Chapter 7), you should plan on getting a better keyboard right away. Go to a dealer and check out several models. Look for key placement that works well with your software and for a comfortable feel. The keys should feel stable and shouldn't require heavy pounding to work. When you press the keys, they should make the right amount of noise to suit you—some people prefer a loud click and others prefer no sound at all. Also, buy a wrist rest ($5 to $10) for the keyboard to reduce strain.

You should also get a replacement for the mouse. Microsoft has worked hard to make its mouse ergonomic, but some users like alternatives even more. You may want to have both a mouse and a trackball and switch between them for different kinds of work or for variety.

The Macintosh ships with a choice of high-quality keyboards and a pretty good mouse. You can also get a special ergonomic keyboard that has two rotating halves for greater comfort. With the Mac, it's easy to hook up a trackball in series with your mouse. Then you can switch from one to the other easily for the sake of variety. Get a wrist rest for both your keyboard and your mouse.

Pay attention to input devices and how you use them; the highest-performance machine you can buy won't do much good if you can't use it because your wrists, elbows, or shoulders are too sore.

Monitor

For a mid-range system, strongly consider a 16- or 17-inch monitor. You can't beat a monitor this size or larger for working with a graphical user interface. Vendors advertise prices that include either a 13- or 14-inch monitor, or no monitor at all, so the extra money for a good-quality, decent-size monitor really does seem, well, extra. Remember that a large, high-quality monitor may enhance your enjoyment of a system more than any other single element, so dig deep at purchase time, or upgrade at some point after you buy your system. See Chapters 7 and 8 for detailed information about monitors.

Printer

Print quality will be very important to you from day one, so consider an inkjet printer over a dot-matrix printer unless cost is of foremost concern. A low-end laser printer that uses TrueType for its fonts is fairly expensive, especially for an individual, but price/performance-wise is probably a bargain. If you do any kind of artwork or use fonts heavily and can stretch to afford a 4- or 8-page-per-minute PostScript printer, you won't be sorry. See Chapters 9 and 10 for information about printers.

A Low-End Desktop System

You may want or need to spend less than the cost of a typical mid-range system. One or all of the following reasons may apply:

- You are on a tight budget and have to trade off some performance for price.
- Your needs are limited and you want the amount you spend to reflect that.
- You're not sure how much use you will get from the system and want to start small.

The first thing to realize is that you're not going to get away for a whole lot less than someone who buys a middle-of-the-road system. The economics of mass production and mass marketing are such that the group in the middle gets the best price/performance deal. It takes savvy and extra thought and research to buy a system that saves you money without compromising too much on performance or quality.

Many people on a tight budget try to stretch their dollars by buying from a less reputable manufacturer. Unless you really know what you're doing, however, you need the service, support, and upgradability that are more likely to be offered by a name-brand system. The best way to really save money in the long run is to buy a slightly less capable system from a name-brand manufacturer, and then upgrade or replace the system as your needs require and your budget allows.

For a low-end system, look at the lower end for each of the elements that make up a system. For an IBM-compatible, think about starting out with DOS, or accept that you will be running Windows with mediocre performance. Look for an 80386-based system; a slow one can handle DOS; you need a faster one for Windows. One or two slots may be enough to meet your needs, and 4M of memory should be enough to get you started.

Get a system with SVGA support on the motherboard, and consider settling for 256K of video memory. A single 3 1/2-inch floppy drive may be enough to get you started, and you can look at a smaller hard drive—60M to 80M for DOS, 100M to 120M for Windows. Skip the CD-ROM drive unless you're certain you will need it. If you will be using the system for more than a couple hours a day, do spend the money for a better keyboard and mouse. Get a low-cost 13- or 14-inch monitor instead of a larger one, and buy an inkjet printer if you can afford it; otherwise buy a dot-matrix model.

Buying a low-end Macintosh is easier than buying a low-end IBM compatible because choices are fewer, and even the cheapest systems have the reputable Apple name behind them. System 7.1 just about requires a 68030 and 4M of memory, but that setup runs almost anything you can think of fairly well. Every Macintosh has a SCSI port for external expandability, so you can be comfortable buying a system that has only one open slot.

Try to find a system with video on the motherboard and 256K of video memory. One 3 1/2-inch floppy is plenty, and an 80M internal hard drive may be enough for quite a while. If your budget can handle it, get a CD-ROM drive. Get a low-cost 14-inch monitor and an Apple or HP inkjet printer, and you will have an affordable, low-end system.

A High-End Desktop System

You may need a bigger, more powerful system than the middle-of-the-road offerings. One or more of the following reasons may apply:

- You want to run demanding applications like multimedia or high-end graphics.

- You need to run an advanced operating system like OS/2 or NT, or advanced Apple system extensions like collaboration.

- You want a system that can meet a wide range of possible future needs without having to add to it in bits and pieces later.

Realize that you can easily spend more money than you planned when you buy a high-end system. Also, the amount of extra bang you get for every extra buck diminishes rapidly as you get away from the mid-range. High-end users often pay twice what a mid-range user pays for a system that only offers a small increment of improvement in overall performance. Finally, there are a tremendous number of options at the high end, and each choice you make affects other choices.

Unless you're willing and able to spend time debugging your system, buy a high-end system from a reputable manufacturer. Advanced operating systems are compatible with less hardware than DOS, Windows, or plain-vanilla System 7.1. So unless you have a lot of experience, you need to get a name-brand system and peripherals and look for assurances from the system vendor that the combined system will be backed by warranty. The best way to get this assurance is to buy a complete system with the peripherals you need connected and the operating system software you need already loaded on the hard disk by the vendor. Make sure that documentation for the system as a whole and for each component is provided.

For a high-end system, consider the higher end of each of the specifications discussed previously. Your system, most likely a tower configuration, should have two to three open slots after all the peripherals you need to get started have been installed. For an OS/2 or NT-capable system, 16M of memory is a good starting point. You should have a local bus or PCI slot for video and another for a very fast hard disk controller. You should have an accelerated video card that has a driver for your operating system and a fast hard disk controller; consider using IDE for the internal drive and SCSI for expandability.

You need both 3 1/2-inch and 5 1/4-inch floppy drives for compatibility. You can't get too big a hard disk for a high-end system; 250M is a good size for daily work, although some systems have a 1G (gigabyte) hard drive. A CD-ROM drive is nearly a requirement just for loading in the operating system. Consider adding removable storage, like rewritable optical drives or Bernoulli-type removable hard drives. This option gives you unlimited storage and enables you to send large amounts of data to business associates who have the same types of drives.

A high-end Macintosh system needs the same things as a high-end IBM-compatible computer, but you also may need a PDS slot for high-end graphics. Look for SCSI-2 for expansion. A single 3 1/2-inch SuperDrive is enough, but you will need a big hard disk and a CD-ROM drive.

The long hours you will be putting in on your high-end system mean that you need a top-notch keyboard, mouse, and probably a trackball. Get a 16- or 17-inch monitor, or a larger one if you will be doing publishing work. Your printing needs depend greatly on the kind of work you're doing; consider a local 4-page-per-minute laser printer if you have access to a faster printer over the network.

General-Purpose Portables

Portable machines used to be poor relations to their desktop cousins. They were painfully limited in screen size and readability, memory size, hard disk size, and every other significant factor. Now, however, portable computers have grown up. If you shop carefully, you can find a portable system that meets most low-end or mid-range needs for a reasonable price.

The advantages of a portable system are portability and simplicity. A portable system should come with everything installed. It's hard to upgrade, so your choices are fewer. The challenge of getting adequate performance is met by the fact that portables tend to have lower-resolution screens than desktop systems. Fewer pixels to update means faster screen performance.

Portables have some significant disadvantages, though. At a given price point, a portable system is noticeably less powerful than a mid-range desktop system. You have to choose your software more carefully because a portable computer has less memory and hard disk space available.

A Mid-Range Portable System

A mid-range portable is one that can run Windows or the Mac's System 7.1 well, but not as fast as a typical desktop system. A mid-range portable can serve as a replacement for a desktop machine, but it imposes more restrictions on what you can do. Buying considerations for a full-time desktop replacement system are discussed in the section on high-end portable systems.

Processor

Portable pricing is such that a mid-range portable machine has a less powerful processor than a mid-range desktop system. Also, the processor is usually not upgradable. For IBM-compatible systems, try to stretch for a 486SLC if you need to run Windows. A Macintosh portable does fine with a 68030.

PCMCIA Slots

Portable systems usually have some expandability through proprietary internal peripherals, such as modems, and through external peripherals. IBM-compatible portables are now gaining internal expandability in the form of PCMCIA slots. A PCMCIA (Personal Computer Memory Card International Association) slot enables you to insert a card that adds functionality, such as more memory or a modem, into the computer. Unfortunately, there are three different kinds of such slots, and devices for them are still at somewhat of a premium as compared to an external device. Look carefully to make sure that the peripherals you need, with the performance you need, are available in one form or another before buying a portable system.

Memory

If you're running Windows or System 7.1, opt for at least 4M of memory. If you don't have enough memory, your software will have to go to the hard disk all the time, wasting power. Along the same lines, make sure that you can upgrade your portable to at least 8M of memory and that prices for the memory upgrade are at least somewhat reasonable.

Video Adapter and Built-In Screen

Look for a 9-inch or larger screen with 640 by 480 resolution (not the widely offered, but less-usable 8-inch and 640 by 400 resolution) and 16 shades of gray. This setup isn't great if you're used to a SuperVGA, 800 by 600 display with color, but you will get used to it. Getting a color screen for a portable adds to the price and reduces battery life, though this situation is improving.

Floppy Drives

Some systems come without a built-in floppy drive. They depend on an externally connected unit that you carry only if you need it. This setup is impractical for most users, though. Look for a portable system with a built-in floppy drive.

Hard Drives

For a system running Windows or System 7, don't settle for a 40M hard drive; it's just too small for heavy use. All the new Macintoshes come with at least an 80M hard drive, but used Macs (especially portables) may have 40M drives. (Macintosh software is a little less sprawling than Windows software, so 40M might be just enough for a Macintosh portable.) 60M is OK, and 80M is pretty good. Anything much larger is nice, but adds to cost, size and weight, and power usage.

CD-ROM Drives

If you want to use a CD-ROM drive with your mid-range portable, it will have to be an external unit. Shop carefully for a portable system and CD-ROM drive that work together and that enable you to use the CD-ROM drive with a desktop system as well.

Input Devices

Most portable systems have OK keyboards and bad pointing devices that can quickly cause strains and pains. Look for a portable that has a mouse port so that you can use a regular mouse or a full-size trackball whenever possible. You should also try to use a full-size keyboard when you can, but this feature is less important than using a real mouse or trackball.

Portables are bad ergonomically because they have substandard input devices and are often used in cramped positions by tired, harried people. When you have to use the built-in keyboard and pointing device, take frequent breaks to give your arms and hands a chance to recuperate. Try not to put yourself in a situation in which you have to do a lot of work in a hurry using a portable's built-in keyboard and pointing device.

Monitor

Most portables now come with a video-out port that you can use to hook up a desktop-type monitor. Look for this feature and use it whenever you can; it will make your software easier to use and cause less strain on your eyes. Using a portable that has a standard keyboard, mouse, and monitor plugged into it combines the ease of use of a desktop system with the portability and convenience of a portable.

Printer

There are more and more options for transportable printers and even true portable units that run on batteries and can print anywhere. See Chapters 9 and 10 for information about printers.

A Low-End Portable System

If you don't have much money to spend, you can make a few tradeoffs in buying a portable system. However, even a middle-of-the-road portable is low-powered compared to a typical desktop system; a low-end portable really limits what you can do. Also, the laws of mass production and mass marketing affect the portable market even more than the desktop market—if you lower your sights enough to save much money, you will probably end up trading away most of the things that contribute to the usefulness of the system.

There aren't any truly cheap Macintosh-compatible portables. An inexpensive IBM-compatible portable might be a system with a 286 microprocessor, 1M or 2M of RAM, a

20M or 40M hard disk, and no built-in pointing device. Such a system can't do much with Windows but is suitable for running DOS. If you use Windows on your desktop system, you may be able to pick DOS applications that you can use with the data files from your Windows programs. This way, at the possible cost of some file-conversion hassles, you will end up with a system that runs with acceptable performance.

You might also want to consider a system that is incompatible with your desktop PC but that can exchange files with it. Such a system might be very inexpensive and suitable for some word processing and even spreadsheet work. In addition to its low cost, a portable of this type might also be much lighter in weight and have longer battery life than an IBM-compatible or Macintosh portable. The worst remaining tradeoff with such a system is screen size. Many have 8-line screens, which are too small for most work; try to get a larger screen.

A High-End Portable System

A high-end portable system is one that most closely approximates a mid-range desktop system. This kind of portable can easily run Windows or System 7.1 and can serve as a replacement for a desktop machine. A high-end portable might have an 80486 microprocessor or, for a Macintosh, a relatively fast 68030 or lower-speed 68040. Memory size of 8M will help keep you from going to the hard disk too much, and a hard disk 80M to 100M in size will let you store a full range of applications and data files. Additional features of a high-end machine include a color screen and one or more PCMCIA slots, which you can use for connecting to your office network or for other purposes.

If you have this kind of system, you may also want to consider a docking station. This is a device that sits on your desk at home, work, or both and connects to external devices such as a standard monitor, keyboard, and mouse. The docking station can also connect your portable to your office network. You insert the portable into the docking station when you are at your desk, gaining access to all the devices it's connected to, and remove it when you leave.

Selecting a Model Based on a Major Application

The kind of system you get depends most heavily on your overall computing needs and your budget. However, the kinds of applications you intend to run can also affect the type of system you choose. In particular, your choice of peripherals might be affected by the one or two applications you use the most.

This section discusses considerations that affect desktop systems and the peripherals you might attach to a portable system that you also use at a desk. Portable system configurations are much less flexible than desktop ones. Compare the considerations discussed here to your own needs as you choose a system.

Word Processing

A system used mainly for word processing deals mostly with text, so it doesn't have the storage and memory requirements of a system that is used to do lots of calculations or to display and store graphics. However, word processing benefits greatly from a WYSIWYG environment that enables you to see how your document will look as you work on it. Also, the tremendous number of options available in today's mid-range word processing systems are much easier to access through a GUI such as Windows or the Macintosh interface than from DOS.

If you are willing to live without a GUI and advanced features, a number of low-end options open up. Some DOS word processors have WYSIWYG interfaces, or close to it, and run well on a system with little memory and a small hard disk. Any Macintosh system can run a WYSIWYG word processing program. So for low-end word processing you may be able to get by with an inexpensive system. You may even be able to buy a dedicated word processor, which combines a PC-type system unit with a printer and a floppy drive for about $500. Such systems are good for students and others with relatively simple needs.

For business use, however, a really good word-processing system can get pretty expensive. This is one application in which you can skimp a little bit on the computer itself and spend more on peripherals. A big screen is a big help, especially if you work on more than one document at a time. You may want to consider a portrait display, about the same size as a printed page. A big 20-inch or 21-inch gray-scale monitor that can show two pages at once is even better, especially if you need to compare documents to each other.

A precise, powerful printer is also a top priority. An inkjet printer is the minimum you should consider. A personal laser printer is the best price/performance choice, and having PostScript capability further increases your options.

If your needs evolve into the desktop publishing arena, you will need to look at a base system of at least average capability. If you plan to do color work, take the time to learn about the requirements of this highly technical area before making a purchase decision.

Spreadsheets

Spreadsheet programs are now much more capable than they used to be. Even mid-range programs include charting capabilities that were once the province of stand-alone business graphics programs. With 3-D spreadsheets, you can combine great masses of data into a single model. The number of options and functions in a typical program is huge.

If you spend most of your time in a spreadsheet working with relatively simple models, your needs might not be that much different from those of a word processing user. If, however, you use the more advanced mathematical and graphical capabilities of a spreadsheet, your system needs may be substantial.

A graphical user environment like Windows or the Macintosh is perfect for spreadsheets. The vast number of options you have in building and formatting the spreadsheet are much easier to access in a graphical environment. In addition to the fairly powerful system you need anyway to run Windows or System 7.1, you should get a system with a math coprocessor. A 486DX, 68040, or PowerPC microprocessor will serve you best. These microprocessors are very powerful and include fast, built-in math coprocessor capability.

You will also need additional memory and hard disk space if you build large, complicated spreadsheets or do much with graphics. 8M of memory and a 120M or larger hard disk may be about right. You will also want a large, high-resolution screen. A 16- or 17-inch monitor is probably about right. A Radius Pivot, a portrait-style monitor you can turn sideways for spreadsheet use, is a good compromise if money is too tight for a large monitor. The best thing of all is a 20- or 21-inch color monitor. Unfortunately, a color monitor of this size is big, heavy, and expensive.

For spreadsheet work, you end up printing a lot as you think of new things to put in the spreadsheet and get new ideas for using graphics. You need a printer with speed and precision, which means a laser printer.

The needs of advanced spreadsheet users have long spurred personal computer power to greater heights. If you plan to do lots of complicated spreadsheets and graphics, or want to combine presentation work with your spreadsheet modeling, the sky's the limit. Consider a high-end system and a color printer as well.

Educational Software, Games, and Multimedia

Educational software is usually written to run on less expensive systems. Even a low-end system that can run a graphical user interface, however slowly, is more than adequate for most educational software. The same system can be used to write reports and even to do research, on-line or from a CD-ROM drive.

A typical mid-range system that can run a graphical user interface is a good middle-of-the-road gaming system. The trouble is that Super Nintendo is also a good gaming system, and it costs thousands less. Don't buy a computer primarily for games unless you have plenty of money. It's perfectly acceptable, though, to use the system you already have for games.

On the high end, a gaming system needs to include a CD-ROM drive. The trouble is that the slow access times that characterize CD-ROM drives are a serious impediment to good game play. The basic CD-ROM technology is not really built for fast, random-access graphics, but higher-end CD-ROM drives (double- and triple-speed drives) are finally gaining enough speed for acceptable performance. Remember, you can get a CD-ROM drive and CD-based games much cheaper for Sega Genesis or Super Nintendo than you can for a personal computer.

Another hardware component that adds a great deal to gaming is a sound board. You can get 8-bit or higher quality 16-bit boards that work to a variety of different standards. If you buy a sound board, look for one that's compatible with the widest possible range of programs, including the ones that you want to start using.

A mid- to high-end gaming system is about the same thing as a multimedia system. A fast CD-ROM drive, a sound board, and fast video are the main elements. A mainstream multimedia system is different from a multimedia authoring system, which may need to be extremely powerful and upgradable, depending on your needs. Take the time to do some research before trying to get into multimedia authoring.

Many of the best games have a strong educational element, and many of the best educational programs are like games. Multimedia programs are largely for education or gaming, or are special editions of business programs with additional help and other files. Get a solid mid-range system that you can use for games, education, and multimedia software, all of which overlap each other, and then only buy the software that runs well on it.

Considering a Used Computer

The good news is that you can get a good deal on a used computer. Models from a major manufacturer usually are pretty reliable, so a system that's in good working order the day you buy it has a good chance of having some useful life left in it. If the computer does break down, you can probably get it repaired fairly readily.

The bad news is that prices on high-end and mid-range systems have dropped so fast lately that unrealistic sellers of used computers often ask as much for their worn-out system as a comparable system costs new. A used system is going to lack features commonly found in new systems, such as processor upgradability, a local-bus slot for video, and a long warranty, yet it may still have a high price on it. Only on the low end are you likely to find a very good deal. Warranties on new systems are being steadily increased, in many cases to three years; you won't get this kind of warranty on a used computer. The cost of repairs on a used system is such that one moderately serious problem will probably be expensive enough to wipe out the cost savings from your purchase.

Another problem is that the demand for power has grown so fast that yesterday's powerhouse systems are today's dogs. A 33 MHz 386 system, considered fast a year or two ago, is now seen as only good enough for running DOS, not Windows. Just recently, Apple was selling many 68000- and 68020-based systems; now only 68030- and 68040-based systems can be had, with PowerPC at the high end. Almost any system that you're likely to be able to buy used is a low-end system that should be available at a low-end price.

Before buying a used system, consider a local dealer who sells new systems at bargain-basement prices. Your chances of satisfaction, while not the same as for a name brand, are higher than for a used system. User's groups sometimes sell used systems and include a warranty.

Even if you're looking for a low-end system, don't buy something that can't run today's software. For a desktop IBM-compatible, don't get anything less than an 80386 microprocessor, VGA graphics, and a 60M hard disk. You may be able to get by with little memory and a small hard disk if you're willing to restrict yourself to running DOS and an integrated or low-end software package or two.

For a desktop Macintosh, things are more complicated. You need at least a 68020 microprocessor with a memory management chip, or a 68030 microprocessor, to use all the capabilities of System 7.1. You need 4M of RAM and at least a 20M hard disk as well.

On balance, buying a used system is probably not a good idea unless you are looking for a lower-end system to run DOS or undemanding Macintosh software and are very low on money. If you know how to do testing and repairs yourself, or are willing to learn, that's a plus. Remember that you will still need a printer and software for your system, which may bring the total price up out of your range.

Beware when buying used software, even if it's included with a used system. Software manufacturers sometimes restrict the licensing of software to anyone but the original purchaser, which means you might have trouble getting upgrades and support.

If you do decide to buy a used system, there are a few specific considerations you should keep in mind for the particular type of system you're interested in:

- *IBM compatible.* An IBM-compatible desktop system is your best chance for getting a bargain. Only buy a name brand and try to get a printer or other peripherals included in the deal.

- *Macintosh.* Macintoshes hold their value better than most other computers. Unfortunately, this can make Macintosh owners a little unrealistic about the true resale value of their used systems. Some ask more for their used system than today's price for the same system brand new. Before you buy a used system, find out what comparable new systems cost so that you can be sure that you get the best deal.

- *Portables.* Price/performance has improved so much for portables that you're unlikely to find a low price except on the lowest of the low-end machines.

If you do look for a used computer, one possible source for a good deal is a company that you, a family member, or a friend works for. Computer people within corporations are usually more realistic in their pricing than individuals. Check around for a deal from this source.

Otherwise, you're out in the open market. People who are more experienced than you in evaluating used systems are scanning the same ads you are, looking for a deal. If you don't move fast, you're likely to get stuck with an underpowered or overpriced system. Look for any computer-oriented publications in your area and start calling advertisers as soon as the new issue comes out. Try to see the system and make a decision soon after you call.

There are several utility programs that will give you an idea of the health of a system, especially the hard disk. If you are serious about buying a used computer, buy one or more of these programs and run them on the machine you're considering.

To check comparable prices, call the Boston Computer Exchange at (617) 542-4414. They should be able to point you to a good source for used computer prices. Many free computer magazines list prices of used computers for comparison purposes. While you're at it, you can compare the used system to the price of a similar new system as well.

Chapter Summary

This chapter pulls together many of the system features and options covered in previous chapters into a set of recommendations you can use in buying a personal computer. It discusses how to put together a useful general-purpose desktop or portable PC for mid-range, low-end, or high-end requirements. Then it describes specific considerations for some of the most important application areas. Finally, some key facts to consider in looking for a used computer are listed. The information and recommendations provided here should give you a solid start in making system purchasing decisions.

IN THE NEXT CHAPTER

You now have a pretty good idea of what you want in terms of both hardware and software. The next chapter describes the different options you have in choosing where to buy a system and the major concerns you should make sure to address in doing so. It concludes with a checklist that will help you get just the system you want.

CHAPTER TWENTY ONE

Making the Purchase

By now you should have a good idea of the type of personal computer system and peripherals you want. This chapter describes some of the different kinds of places that sell computers and peripherals so that you can decide where to make your purchases. It also lists questions you should ask about support, training, warranties, and package deals. Finally, it describes how to pull all of the different concerns together into a buying decision that gets the right equipment with the right kind of support for the right price.

Where To Purchase Computers and Peripherals

You can easily waste a lot of time and money by buying from the wrong source from among the many available. Different brands of computers and peripherals are available in only certain kinds of outlets; to get the system you want, you have to shop in the right kind of outlet. This section goes into detail about each of the choices you have.

A Brief History of PC Buying

Personal computers were once sold almost exclusively through computer dealers. At first, computer dealerships were started and run largely by enthusiasts—people who got into the business because they enjoyed putting a system together and figured they could make money doing it for others. Customers came into the store to buy a computer and came back again and again for peripherals, upgrades, software, and more computers. Customers appreciated their knowledge and personal touch, and as computer sales exploded in the early 1980s, small-to-medium dealerships thrived.

By the mid-1980s, computer dealerships began to consolidate. Huge chains, like Businessland and Computerland, grew by buying up some smaller stores and driving others out of business. The dealerships began to offer ongoing service contracts, training, and more. Dealerships were able to charge top dollar for their wares because of two factors: demand for services and products was very high, and the industry was so new that customers were afraid to venture into the world of computers without a helping hand nearby. High prices were tough on end users and small businesspeople, so they sought alternatives while big businesses supported the dealerships.

Mail order was an alternative and quickly became a favored way to buy software. People quickly figured out that every shrink-wrapped package of software was the same, whether you paid the suggested retail price (say, $650 for a business word processor) or the mail order price ($350-$375 for the same product). Hardware, however, didn't offer the same standardization at that time. "Box-builders" often created computer systems from the cheapest available components, regardless of quality or performance. Many people were drawn into bad experiences with mail order hardware, attracted by the low, low prices but disappointed with the products or unable to get support after the sale. Michael Dell, founder of Dell Computers, was one of the early leaders in changing this situation. Dell and a small number of other vendors ran professional, honest operations that sold complete systems at relatively low prices. The popularity of buying by mail order quickly grew. Innovations, such as on-site service and support, preconfigured systems with software already installed, and top-quality phone support, continue to make mail order attractive to more and more users today.

As computers became less exotic and more of a commodity, other kinds of retail outlets began to carry them too. (Packard Bell is a leading provider of systems through non-computer-store retail outlets.) Warehouse stores that carried dry goods, tires, televisions, and so on began to stock computers and peripherals as well. Department stores like Sears, electronics stores, and computer superstores have also prospered in the personal computer business.

Today's computer consumer is more educated, so most of the computer sellers have changed drastically in the past few years. In the following sections, you learn what you can expect from the dealers, mail order, superstores, electronics stores, and department stores in 1995.

Computer Dealers

Computer dealers are still the single leading source for computer purchases. Some stores mostly focus on inside sales to large corporations, and others have specific areas of expertise, such as networking, training, and so on. Some dealers, however, still do a good job of selling to individual end users and supporting what they sell.

Computer Dealer Advantages

Why go to a computer dealer? The following list details some of the reasons:

- ✔ *Convenience.* A computer dealer offers a very convenient way to buy systems, peripherals, or software. You walk in, look at the offerings, get some competent advice, choose one, and walk out. You then have a handy source for service, advice, and support.

✔ *Hands-on.* You can try things out at a computer dealer, which is a great advantage for evaluating things like video display quality, print quality, and so on. If you're not comfortable plunking down a few hundred dollars on something you have never seen up close, local computer dealerships are for you. If you use this resource, though, make sure that you support it—don't take up the salesperson's time asking questions at a store, and then use another channel to make the actual purchase.

✔ *Personal relationship.* Some computer dealer employees know their facts well enough to help you make good buying decisions. When you establish a relationship with these employees, they can keep you up-to-date on the latest hardware and software and answer questions.

✔ *Many services.* Many dealers offer training, consulting, and repair services all under one roof.

✔ *Comfort for the novice buyer.* If you're relatively inexperienced with computers, a good dealer can help bridge the gap between what you already know and what you need to know to have a positive experience with computers.

Computer Dealer Disadvantages

Buying from a computer dealer, just like buying through any other channel, has its disadvantages too:

- *Higher prices.* Prices from a computer dealer tend to be slightly higher. Use tools like this book and recent magazines to figure out if you're really getting what you pay for. If the prices are a lot higher than the value warrants, take your business elsewhere.

- *Limited selection.* You can only buy what the dealer stocks. Sure, the dealer can order things for you, but then you lose the convenience of local shopping.

- *Varying-quality salespeople.* Your local dealer could staff their store with people of little experience or those who are highly trained, and sometimes both types of people work on the same sales floor. Because a local store doesn't have the benefit of the standard training programs you find in nationwide chains, the salespeople's skills and knowledge vary widely.

Computer Dealers and Products

The following list explains other important things to consider when shopping at a computer dealer as compared to other ways of buying computer equipment:

- *Macintosh.* Apple was once solely dependent on the dealer channel, but now you can get the same high-quality products at many chains and superstores. Shop at several places, if possible, before making a buying decision.

- *IBM compatibles.* Big sellers of IBM compatibles through the dealer channel include IBM, Compaq, and AST. With these and other top brands available at reasonable prices, think long and hard before buying an off-brand system. Remember, product quality is worth more than up-front savings.

- *Peripherals.* You can tell a lot about a dealer by the peripherals it carries and how much its employees know about them. Look for top-name monitors, printers, and so on at reasonable prices.

- *Software.* A dealer usually charges a little more for software, but the extra cost is worth it if the dealer can give you good advice about what to buy and what to avoid. Occasional visits to buy software are also a good way to keep up your relationship with the dealer between major purchases. You can, however, get better immediately available selection (although the dealer can order anything you need) and probably lower prices elsewhere.

How To Get the Most Out of a Computer Dealer

If you decide to shop at a computer dealer, ask around for recommendations and visit several local dealers. A dealer who offers consulting or training services usually has more on the ball than one who doesn't. Find a large dealer with a friendly, knowledgeable staff. Ask a few technical questions to check for competence and willingness to spend some time with you. If you get vague or hard-to-understand answers, go elsewhere.

If you have a chance, make some small purchases and see whether you get good advice and service. If so, and if the price and selection are good, consider making your purchases at that dealer. Don't expect even the best dealer to solve all your problems, however; the dealer won't know enough about your needs to do everything for you. Build up your own knowledge to the point where you can eventually consider the dealer as one of several sources for computer equipment and support.

Mail-Order Vendors

Mail-order vendors are the fastest-growing channel for computer sales. To buy products from a mail-order vendor, you simply place a call to them (usually toll-free), specify what you want, and place an order. Although the vendors buy large ads featuring specific configurations, you can buy a system to meet any set of specifications you please. Vendors often sell computers under their own label and peripherals with their own label or from other manufacturers. Increasingly, mail-order vendors also sell a wide range of software and other computer-related products.

Although there are still a few fly-by-night mail-order dealers out there, and some honest businesses are struggling to regain profitability, the most successful mail-order vendors are among the solid citizens of today's computer marketplace. There are both strong advantages and disadvantages to this method of buying computer products, but many buyers, especially individuals and small businesses, are finding that mail order is the way to go.

Mail-Order Vendor Advantages
Some of the most important benefits of a mail-order vendor include the following:

- ✔ *Low prices.* Prices from mail-order vendors range from low to middle-of-the-road. In many cases, a dealer or superstore may be able to match these prices if you negotiate or wait for a sale, but mail-order vendors put their prices in print, and they're available all the time.

- ✔ *Convenience.* With mail order, you can pick up the phone and place an order without even leaving your desk. The vendor can put together any configuration you want, and you can complete the whole transaction in a few minutes.

- ✔ *Able salespeople.* Because mail-order vendors often sell a single line of systems and each employee does a lot of business, it's worth it to the vendors to train their people well on the available choices and hold on to top people.

- ✔ *Competent support.* Mail-order vendors live and die on the quality and availability of their phone support. The best vendors put top people on the support lines and have large enough staffs to handle the phone traffic without putting customers on hold for a long time. Many vendors charge for support, though, so make sure that you know about any possible support costs before you buy.

- ✔ *Preconfigured systems.* The best mail-order vendors will put together the hardware you order, configure your system for you with the drivers you need and the operating system and applications you order, and get the whole thing out to you a few days later. Then they will back up the system with service and phone support.

- ✔ *On-site service.* Many mail-order vendors offer on-site service with quick guaranteed arrival times as part of the price of a system. "On-site" means at *your* site—if you have problems with the system, a service representative comes to your home or business to fix it. This kind of service guarantee inspires the vendors to sell reliable systems so service costs are kept low.

- ✔ *Liberal return policy.* Most mail-order vendors give you 30 days or even longer to try out a system and return it if you're not completely satisfied. This way you can make sure that a system really meets your day-to-day needs. Make sure that you know who pays for shipping on any returns before you buy, though, because computers are usually expensive to ship.

- ✔ *Innovation.* The mail-order channel is extremely competitive, and vendors work very hard to come up with new ways to make customers happy, such as preconfiguring systems and offering liberal return policies. These innovations have led to financial troubles for some vendors, but the more prosperous ones do a lot to make the experience of buying and using a system pleasant and productive.

- ✔ *Help for the novice buyer.* Preconfigured systems and the service and support offered by mail-order vendors can be a real boon for the novice buyer. Although the best dealers can match or exceed this kind of service, it takes a lot of work to find and cultivate a relationship with such a dealer. Top-notch mail-order vendors are as close as the phone.

Mail-Order Vendor Disadvantages

There are also disadvantages to buying from a mail-order vendor. The following concerns may cause you to look elsewhere for a computer:

- *Limited selection.* Many mail-order vendors only carry one line of systems, their own. The type of system and configuration you need may not be a good price/performance choice from that vendor, and you can't choose from among several models in a price range.

- *Package deals.* The flip side of mail-order convenience is that you're dependent on the vendor for everything: a well-built system, a good price, and good support. You can't choose a monitor, graphics card, hard disk drive, or other component except those offered by the vendor. If one element is out of whack, you have to accept it or go elsewhere.

- *No hands-on.* You can't try the system until you buy and receive it. Even though return policies are liberal, this situation is a key disadvantage for many buyers.

- *Telephone only.* Phone lines get crowded, and the lack of face-to-face contact when you do get through can be alienating. If you enjoy developing a personal relationship with your vendor, as many buyers do, mail order won't work for you.

- *Waits for systems.* As mail order has become more popular, waits for some configurations have become extremely long—sometimes weeks or even months. This kind of delay happens in other channels as well, but mail-order vendors often have fewer alternatives to offer.

Mail-Order Vendors and Products

The plusses and minuses of buying mail order vary depending on the kind of product you're buying:

- *Macintosh.* As of this writing, Apple doesn't sell its complete line of products through mail order in North America. Some systems and configurations are offered through an Apple catalog, but prices are high—don't do it. Peripherals and software are available from third parties at good prices.

- *IBM compatibles.* The top mail-order vendors of IBM-compatibles are Dell, Gateway, and DEC. Some of these systems are relabeled from other vendors, which is not a problem except when it drives prices higher or quality lower.

- *Peripherals.* You can't look at monitor sharpness or print quality before you buy, so buying peripherals from a mail-order vendor can be frustrating. Many buyers do it, though, and just return anything they're dissatisfied with. Remember to find out whether you can return products at the vendor's expense or whether you have to pay for the shipping—monitors and printers are heavy, and therefore expensive to ship.
- *Software.* Mail-order vendors are offering more software, peripherals, and so on through their catalogs. Prices are good and convenience is pretty high.

How To Get the Most Out of a Mail-Order Vendor

The top mail-order vendors are a very good source for computer systems, peripherals, and software. If you have doubts, you probably will be pleasantly surprised by the experiences you have with a mail-order vendor.

A mail-order vendor has to do everything right, from making good systems at fair prices to offering excellent service and support, or customers can become unhappy fast. You only have a single point of contact—the phone. If lines are busy or the people at the other end aren't competent, you're really stuck.

You can increase your chances of having a positive experience by only buying from top-rated vendors. Much of the middle tier of mail-order is in financial trouble, and a few of the little guys are crooks. When a mail-order vendor starts to have financial problems, they begin to have difficulty providing the service and support that buyers depend on so much, which can be a real headache for you.

Look at magazine reviews for the system you're considering before buying it because you can't try out the system independently. You may be tempted to go to a dealer and ask a lot of questions, and then make your purchase from a mail-order dealer. This is tacky; do your research through books, magazines, friends, and coworkers instead.

Don't call until you know what you want, or you may end up making a poor purchase decision. When making a purchase or calling for support, ask to speak to a supervisor if the first person who answers doesn't seem knowledgeable, or call back and try your luck again.

If the vendor tells you there's a wait for a system, take any dates you're quoted with a grain of salt; the vendor is motivated to be optimistic. If you really need your system soon, as most people do, try another source. If you're buying peripherals or software and have to wait, go elsewhere.

Computer Superstores

Computer superstores are a very fast-growing and popular way to buy computers, add-on devices, and software. Well-known superstores include CompUSA, BizMart, and

Computer City. Ordinary consumers find a wide selection and low prices, and even businesses that are used to having their hands held find superstores a good deal for small- to medium-sized purchases.

Computer Superstore Advantages

The advantages of going to a computer store are pretty clear-cut:

- ✔ *Low prices.* Prices at a superstore may be the lowest you can find.

- ✔ *Convenience.* The best superstores are like super-dealerships. You can see a wide range of products on display, look at the offerings, choose one, and walk out. Service and support may be less than what a dealer offers, though.

- ✔ *Hands-on.* Again, like a dealership, you can check video display quality, print quality, and so on before you make the purchase. The availability and knowledge of the salespeople may be less than you can find at a dealer, but many more products are available for you to try.

- ✔ *Repair services.* Many superstores have a repair department right in the store. This service can be very convenient, and, of course, you can always pick up any new stuff you need while you're dropping off or picking up your system from the repair department.

- ✔ *Fun.* If you're even a little bit of a computer nerd, it's a lot of fun to walk around and look at hundreds of different computer products on display at once, relatively unbothered by salespeople. You can even get ideas for ways to use your existing system better by just walking around.

Computer Superstore Disadvantages

If you need anything but the lowest price and greatest convenience, there are real disadvantages to buying at a superstore:

- *Buyer beware.* You can easily make a bad system, peripheral, or software purchase at a superstore because the lousy products are right there on display with the good ones, and you may not be able to tell the difference. Do any needed research before you make a purchase.

- *Odd configurations.* Not only can you buy bad products at a superstore, you also can buy bad configurations. Who's going to tell you that the monitor you just got bundled with your system is fuzzy? Again, be careful.

- *Not for the novice.* The combination of disadvantages means that a novice buyer can really get burned by buying a system or major peripheral in a superstore. Stick to name brands, despite their higher prices, unless you really know what you're doing.

- *No relationships.* You're not investing in building up a source for support and advice when you shop and buy at a superstore, although, over time, your increased knowledge of the store's layout may help you get in and out faster.

- *Poor salespeople.* Computer superstore salespeople aren't expected to know much about any one group of products, so take their advice with a big grain of salt. You're on your own.

Computer Superstores and Products

Computer superstores now have the widest possible range of products, but there are still some limitations:

- *Macintosh.* You can now buy Macs in superstores. If you have bought a Macintosh before, or have a lot of experience as a user, a superstore may be a good place to buy another one. (Macintosh dealers are better than most, though.)

- *IBM compatibles.* You can get all sorts of IBM compatibles, including true-blue IBM systems, at superstores. Only a few true believers like AST stick exclusively to the dealer channel anymore. Even leading mail-order vendors like Dell sell through superstores as well. As with dealers, think long and hard before buying a no-name system or add-on device.

- *Peripherals.* You can see and compare dozens of monitors, printers, or other devices at one convenient location. If it's an add-in peripheral, ask how much the cost is to have it installed by the superstore's repair department.

- *Software.* Prices are low and convenience is high. Know what you want before you go in, though; reading the backs of boxes is no way to choose one software package over another. A store or salesperson may push the package with the best margins for them, not the best fit for you.

How To Get the Most Out of a Computer Superstore

The way to get the most out of a computer superstore is to know what you want before you go in. If you're a novice buyer, you're likely to need more help and support, like that offered by a top-notch dealer, than you can get at a superstore. (Even mail-order may be a better choice for new buyers.) If you're an experienced buyer who has a good understanding of the points made in this book and keeps up with recent computer magazine reviews, a superstore may meet your needs very well.

You may want to shop around for a superstore that seems cleaner, better organized, and has a friendlier and more helpful staff than others. Still, shifts change and staff turns over, so don't count on a personal connection. Know what you want and go in to get it. You can browse for some other things, but don't make additional buying decisions that you should research first.

Consumer Electronics Stores and Departments

Consumer electronics stores, electronics departments of warehouse stores, such as Price Club, Sam's Club, and CostCo, and electronics areas of office supply stores carry computer systems as part of their stock, but they don't give them much special attention in most cases. Consumer electronics stores and departments tend to stock complete systems, sold at a low fixed price, and a few popular peripherals and software packages. They may service the systems they sell, or refer you to the manufacturer. If you want a low-end system for the lowest price, you may want to consider buying at a consumer electronics store.

Consumer Electronics Store Advantages

Buying a system, peripheral device, or software package at a consumer electronics store has a few advantages:

- ✔ *Low prices.* Consumer electronics stores, and electronics departments in warehouse stores, often have the lowest available prices on the relatively small range of items they carry. This low price may outweigh disadvantages in terms of selection, service, and support, especially for peripherals and software.

- ✔ *Simplicity.* The small number of choices at consumer electronics stores makes buying a system or other computer-related equipment simple. If you see something you like among the offerings, you can be confident that you're getting a good price.

- ✔ *Bundled software.* Many systems sold at consumer electronics stores come with software already bundled. If the software is of the kind you want, this package can be a real bargain. However, this option is available through other outlets as well.

- ✔ *Not intimidating for novice buyers.* New buyers often favor consumer electronics stores as a place to buy a computer because they aren't intimidating in the way that more specialized computer outlets are. Unfortunately, it's the novice buyer who's most likely to need the service and support that are almost completely absent in this setting.

Consumer Electronics Store Disadvantages

Unless you know exactly what you want and happen to find it, there are real disadvantages to buying at a consumer electronics store:

- *Small selection.* Consumer electronics stores sell only the most popular, most profitable items they can get their hands on. This strategy leaves you with few choices. Buy only if what's on hand is just what you want.

- *Fixed configurations.* A consumer electronics store is not going to customize a system configuration for your needs; you have to buy the system as offered. Too often this situation means buyers compromise on what they want, and then don't have an easy way to upgrade.

- *Poor salespeople.* Consumer electronics store salespeople often aren't expected to know much about their products, so any advice you get may be mere speculation. Don't depend on the salespeople to help you decide what to buy.
- *Repair services.* The repair departments of consumer electronics stores may or may not know much about how to repair computers. Some may ship items back to the manufacturer, meaning you wait days or weeks before you see your system again. Check carefully into repair policies before buying.
- *Not for the novice buyer.* Although consumer electronics stores are appealing to new buyers, they don't have the service and support that new buyers need more than others. Know what you want before buying at a consumer electronics store.

Consumer Electronics Stores and Products

Consumer electronics stores carry only a few products, so you have to be careful that what they have is exactly what you want.

- *Macintosh.* Although Apple may start selling in more of these outlets, a consumer electronics store is the last place you want to buy a Mac. In mass-market outlets, Apple sells specific configurations with bundled software for slightly lower prices than through other outlets, but you will have trouble getting a custom configuration.
- *IBM compatibles.* Packard Bell is a real force in consumer electronics stores and departments. Packard Bell is known for middle-of-the-road systems at low prices. Although this is not necessarily the best company to buy from, it's a better choice than no-name systems from less-reputable vendors.
- *Peripherals.* There are usually few peripheral devices on display, so it's hard to compare one to another. If you already know just what you want and can find it at a consumer electronics store, the low price may be attractive.
- *Software.* Choices may be few, but prices are low, and there are no configuration hassles to worry about as there are with computer systems. If you know what you want, the consumer electronics store may be as good a place as any to buy software.

How To Get the Most Out of a Consumer Electronics Store

A consumer electronics store isn't really the place to go computer shopping if you have a choice. A computer superstore has all the advantages of a consumer electronics store, except possibly for slightly higher prices, with much better selection and repair services. Even salespeople will be more able to help at a superstore. A consumer electronics store may be a worthwhile choice if it has just what you want at a lower price than other local outlets.

Consumer electronics stores ring up much of their sales through impulse buying, which is the wrong way to buy computers. If you're in a consumer electronics store and get a sudden urge to buy a computer or peripheral you see on display, go somewhere, get a cool drink, and think it over. Then do some research on what you really need before deciding whether to buy the item you saw.

Department Stores

Buying a computer system and related equipment at a department store is much like making a purchase at a consumer electronics store, except that the environment is even less threatening and the selection and on-hand expertise is even poorer. You may be able to make a satisfactory purchase at a department store, but you probably won't get the lowest price and you certainly won't get the widest selection.

Department Store Advantages

Buying a system, peripheral device, or software package at a department store has a few advantages, similar to those of a consumer electronics store:

- ✔ *Simplicity.* It's simple to make a choice from among the small number of offerings you will find in a department store.

- ✔ *Bundled software.* Many systems sold at department stores come with software already bundled, further reducing total price and increasing simplicity. However, if the bundled software isn't what you need or want, it may have little value to you.

- ✔ *Not intimidating.* A department store is a very relaxed and comforting environment, especially for those who are new to computers.

Department Store Disadvantages

Unless the low-tech atmosphere of a department store is especially important to you, the disadvantages of buying there outweigh the advantages:

- *Prices.* Department stores tend to have slightly higher prices than other outlets.

- *Little selection.* Department stores sell only the most popular and most profitable items. You're likely to either pay a premium for a name brand or an average price for a below-average system.

- *Fixed configurations.* Department stores don't offer custom configurations. If you need something more or less than what's in the box, you will have to go elsewhere.

- *Poor salespeople.* If you have read this book up to this point, you know more about computers than most people, including the typical department store salesperson.

- *Repair services.* You're likely to have to depend on the manufacturer for repairs and technical support. If the department store service department does anything, it will just ship things back and forth while you wait. Check repair policies carefully before buying.
- *Not for the novice buyer.* Despite the comforting atmosphere, department store customers are on their own more than other computer buyers. This situation is OK if you're experienced but not if you're new to the field.

Department Stores and Products

Department stores are an easy way for computer hardware and software manufacturers to move products with decent profit margins, so they have created products to meet the needs of this market.

- *Macintosh.* Apple now sells some Macintosh systems in department stores, offering specific configurations with bundled software for slightly lower prices than through other outlets. The systems are typically lower end Macs, geared toward the student or the first-time computer user.
- *IBM compatibles.* IBM's PS/1 series is often found in mass-market outlets, such as department stores, as are offerings from Packard Bell and others. Software bundles are common; make sure that they include products that meet your needs. Don't buy from a no-name manufacturer.
- *Peripherals.* Choices are few, and prices may be high for the quality you're getting. Be careful.
- *Software.* Few products are offered, and prices may be high. Except for the bundled software that comes with systems, go elsewhere to buy software.

How To Get the Most Out of a Department Store

A department store is a comforting environment in which to buy a computer, and prices, although slightly higher than other outlets, are unlikely to be too far out of line. However, it's hard to get the configuration you want or a good deal in price/performance. Service and support offerings are poor, or dependent on the manufacturer, and there's no on-site expertise. You may want to consider buying at a department store if you see a really low price on a low-end system that you're interested in.

Be especially careful not to make an impulse buy at a department store. Easy credit terms and ready-made bundles may make a system attractive, but the lack of service, support, and expertise make it quite likely that the system you buy will do less than you want it to, and it may even end up on the shelf. This is an expensive way to get an education in computer buying principles. Be cautious when making a computer purchase in a department store.

Vendor Summary

This section sums up the major advantages of each channel. Look in the previous sections for detailed descriptions.

- *Computer dealer.* The best dealers have reasonable prices, knowledgeable and helpful salespeople, and good in-store repair services. If you can find a dealer near you who carries the products you want, building up a relationship with that dealer may be the best way to ensure long-term success in buying and using a computer.

- *Mail-order vendor.* The top mail-order vendors are easy to buy from and back up their low-priced, high-quality systems and related products with on-site service and top-notch phone support. Unless you have a strong preference for a system that's sold through dealers, or have a good relationship with a dealer already, mail order may be the best way to go.

- *Computer superstore.* Computer superstores have huge selections of products at reasonable prices and back them up with good on-site service. You won't usually get a lot of pre-sale help at a superstore, and it's easy to be confused by the plethora of products. If you know what you want, however, this may be the best place to go get it.

- *Consumer electronics store.* These stores, and electronics departments in warehouse stores, are comfortable places to go. The limited selection and fixed configurations they offer take the burden of choice off the buyer, but repair policies may be poor and salespeople aren't knowledgeable. You're probably better off buying from a different source.

- *Department store.* Department stores offer even fewer products than consumer electronics stores and have similar problems with unknowledgeable salespeople and lack of on-site repair service. Unless the exact configuration you want shows up at a very low price, you are probably better off buying elsewhere.

More Things To Consider in Buying a System

This book has discussed most of the important information you need to consider in buying a computer system: how a computer works, price, performance, the peripheral devices you need, upgradability, and where you can buy the system from. Additional factors include warranties, setup, support, and training. The following sections discuss these important concerns.

Warranties

No one wants their computers to break down, and everyone wants instant service when they do. The good news is that today's computer manufacturers are building more reliable machines, and more and more vendors are offering long warranties with on-site or carry-in service and fast turnaround.

There are several things to think about in looking at warranties, however. One is that a warranty is only as good as the company standing behind it. If your vendor goes out of business, the warranty may or may not be honored. With prices continuing to drop, some smaller vendors on the edge of bankruptcy, and larger vendors trying to drive smaller vendors out of business, this is a real concern.

Make sure that the vendor you buy from will be around for a while. The easiest way to do this is to buy from one of the top vendors listed in this book. Local vendors with healthy bottom lines and roots in the local computer community may also be a good bet. The middle-tier clone makers are the most likely to have problems.

Some unscrupulous vendors offer short warranties, hoping that some buyers won't notice and won't care. Others can't afford to offer long warranties because they sell less-reliable systems that break down often; the vendor can't afford to fix them multiple times for free. A long warranty means the company is willing to bet that the system they sell you won't break down.

You have to look out for confusion between the warranty offered by the manufacturer and that offered by the vendor. The vendor you buy from may not back the length of warranty that you think you're getting from the manufacturer. Find out whose warranty you're getting and who's responsible for backing it up.

Another important concern is the cost and terms of the service contract that you will be able to buy after the warranty expires. Even if you get a long, three-year warranty, you or the person you sell the computer to will probably want to buy a service contract for it when the warranty expires. If the service contract is expensive, the vendor is betting against the longevity of their system. Ask about the price of a service contract and compare it to the terms offered by other vendors.

The following list contains some additional things to look for in a warranty:

- ✔ *Length*. The length of the warranty is of primary importance. Make sure that you are really getting the full warranty you're entitled to. Then make sure that the vendor will last longer than the warranty.

- ✔ *On-site vs. carry-in service*. Carry-in service is not necessarily a bad deal if the repair site is close to you. But if the repair site is far away, you're faced with mailing heavy, bulky systems, monitors, and printers; look for on-site service instead. One exception may be if you're buying a portable system, which is easier to ship.

- ✔ *Right of return*. Mail-order vendors have led the way in offering the right to return anything you're not satisfied with for credit or a full refund, no questions asked. Other vendors may match this policy. Such a policy is worth seeking out, especially if you are unsure about the price/performance tradeoffs you're making in choosing a computer system.

- ✔ *Replacements.* Many vendors will ship or give you a replacement device in exchange for the broken one you give them. Then you don't have to wait for the broken unit to be repaired. This approach guarantees fast turnaround and may make mail-in service worth considering.

- ✔ *Printers.* Printers have many moving parts and are more likely to break down than other components. Look for a warranty with on-site service and fast response time, especially for a printer that's shared by several users.

- ✔ *Sale items.* Sometimes vendors reduce warranty protection for items on sale. Check to make sure that this isn't the case, and don't go along with it if so.

The following is a list of warranty-related questions to ask when buying a system from a computer dealer, computer superstore, consumer electronics store, department store, or other retail outlet:

- Where does the system go for repairs—the store or the manufacturer?
- If the store handles repairs, are there some it can't handle? What happens then?
- Do you have to mail anything anywhere? If so, who pays for shipping? Does the vendor ship you a replacement?
- If the vendor ships a replacement, does it wait until it receives the damaged equipment? (The vendor should ship the replacement when it receives the call from you.)
- What's the longest you might be without your system? Will the store give you a replacement once some specific amount of time passes?
- When does the warranty start? (It shouldn't start until the day you receive the system.)
- Who backs the warranty? (The manufacturer and the seller should both back it.)
- Who tracks the warranty? (The store should track it.)
- What is the money-back period? (This should be at least 30 days.)
- What level of training or certification does the store require of its technicians? (Manufacturer's training is best.)

The following similar questions are ones you should ask of a mail-order vendor, or in other cases where on-site service from a major service vendor is offered:

- How long do you have to wait for a repairman? (This may vary depending on your location.)
- What repairs can be handled on-site?
- What repairs can't be handled on-site? What happens then?

- What's the longest you might be without your system? Will the service provider give you a replacement once some specific amount of time passes?
- When does the warranty start? (It shouldn't start until the day you receive the system.)
- Who backs the warranty? Who tracks it? (The mail-order vendor should do both.)
- What is the money-back period? (This should be at least 30 days.)
- What level of training or certification does the mail-order vendor require of its technicians? (Manufacturer's training is best.)

Setup

One of the biggest potential hassles in buying a computer is setting it up. This process includes both connecting and installing hardware components and installing software onto the hard disk. If nothing goes wrong, setting up a computer can easily be done in an hour. If there are problems, however, it can turn into a confusing, frustrating task that can take hours.

The vendor that sells you your computer should do everything possible to set up your system for you and to give you clear, concise instructions on how to do any remaining steps. Phone support should be available, with no long waits or busy signals, to help if you have problems. Luckily, vendors are being forced to realize their obligations and are taking action.

Early leaders in this area are Dell Computer in the IBM-compatible world, and Apple Computer with its Macintoshes. The "Happy Mac" project at Apple videotaped selected users who were setting up systems, watched where they had problems, and then sought to remove as many obstacles as possible. (The assembled ease-of-use experts were appalled when one user cut herself badly trying to get the top off a system.) Besides improvements in packaging and documentation, a key step was for Apple to install system software on the hard disk before shipping. This way, when you turn on a brand-new Macintosh, you quickly see the "Happy Mac" face that indicates that system software is available and being started up.

Dell has gone even further by installing not only the operating system and drivers but also any and all applications that are bundled with your system, or that you specify when you order it. The actions of Apple, Dell, and others have embarrassed the rest of the industry into taking long overdue steps to make setup easier.

The computer system you buy should already have the operating system and graphical user environment, if any, installed. The vendor should take it on themselves to install any additional hardware you buy, such as a video card, and the needed drivers for it. The vendor should also test that important options, such as high-resolution graphics modes, work once your system is set up. If you buy application software along with your system, the vendor should install it. Testing the applications is probably not necessary unless one or more applications have strong hardware dependencies, such as the demands that a CAD program places on a graphics card.

If the vendor does not do configuration, software installation, and initial testing for you, ask them to. If they refuse, take some time to decide whether a system that you have to spend several hours setting up, backed by a sullen and uncooperative vendor, is really a good buy. A refusal to take on the responsibility for setup may indicate a lack of confidence by the vendor that everything they sold you will really work together or a lack of knowledge on how to do the setup, neither of which is a good sign.

Unfortunately, even the most cooperative vendor can only do so much for you. If you already have a graphics card and monitor, for instance, it's a rare vendor who will offer to install it for you in the system you just bought. You will have to move any applications and data that you already have on an existing system onto the hard disk of your new system yourself. If your computer will be connected to a network, or you need to dial in to a network remotely, you probably will have to handle setup for these things yourself. Make sure that the vendor does everything that they can for you, and then be prepared to spend some time getting your system set up to your exact needs and making sure everything works.

Phone Support

The availability of phone support is becoming important for hardware as well as for software. Whereas many manufacturers have long pointed users to dealers for any kind of support, including phone calls, more and more are taking on the responsibility themselves.

Currently, phone support policies are a patchwork of different approaches, from those who stick with the standard "call your dealer" to mail-order computer system vendors who are committed to providing support themselves. When you do get free, long-term phone support, the next issue to worry about is whether you will be able to get through when you do have a question. If phone support is your main way to get help, and you can't get through, you're really stuck. Once you do get through, you need to get someone on the other end who can really help. Some companies have competent front-line personnel and policies that bring in more and more expert help until even the most difficult questions are answered; others have poor hiring and training practices and are not much help when you call.

Another problem is keeping track of all the different sources of support you have for your hardware and software and the different terms of the support, with the period of free support ending more quickly for some products than others and wildly varying options for what you have to pay after the free support expires. Again, mail-order companies are taking the lead, supporting not only all the hardware you buy from them, but in many cases serving as the first line of support for software that's included in your system as well. If phone support is a big concern for you, consider looking for this kind of all-inclusive policy.

For hardware, look for companies that offer between one and, preferably, three years of free phone support, and reasonable rates for additional years after the free period ends. (Ideally, hardware companies should offer free phone support for their products forever, to whoever owns or uses the product.) Software companies should have a fairly long free support period, at least several months, and then reasonable rates for additional support. Support is expensive and difficult for the companies to provide, but as companies sell to more and more novice users, and as users of all levels of experience take on more and more complicated tasks, it's becoming increasingly important.

In addition to phone support, some companies offer fax support and support through on-line services. This option is nice to have if you have access to a fax machine or if you already use the on-line service in question, but don't consider these alternatives as replacements for live phone support. For instance, an on-line service can cost about $10 a month for basic service, which is a pretty expensive form of support. Make sure that these additional services are offered in addition to, not instead of, live phone support.

To evaluate the quality of phone support for both hardware and software, read trade magazines like *InfoWorld* and *PC Magazine*, both of which are among the many journals that rate phone support in articles and reviews. Also consider the difficulty of dealing with a great number of companies; part of the popularity of mail-order vendors for hardware, and application suites for software, is the fact that you get support for several pieces of your system from a single source. Also, consider the capability of the vendor to back up its promises. If the vendor is experiencing financial difficulties, well-staffed, competent phone support may be among the first things to go.

Training, Training, Training

Training is probably the most neglected aspect of personal computer use. As a personal computer owner, you have as much processing power on your desktop as was found in a powerful minicomputer ten years ago. You're expected to understand and be able to use several applications, an operating system, and a graphical user interface, all of which are complicated in their own right and which have sometimes unpredictable interactions with each other. If you are also on a network, the possible complexities multiply.

In order to cope with all this, you should invest time in getting trained in the use of your operating system, graphical user interface (unless you're a DOS-only user), and your top few applications. Even getting this training won't solve all your problems, of course; no one can predict what problems may come up in your particular configuration of hardware and software, especially in a networked environment. Training is also notorious for covering only the basics of a particular application, not the details that power users want to know. If you at least take the time to pick up the basics, however, you will get the most out of your applications and operating environment, and have a base of understanding that you can apply to your work on your specific setup.

Start by getting training in your particular operating environment. If you use DOS, OS/2, or the Macintosh, get training in that; if you use Windows, you will need training in that and some DOS basics as well. This training will give you competence in basic, daily interactions with your computer and will have an overall positive effect on your ability to install new applications, back up your system, and troubleshoot problems, either on your own or with help from technical support. If you don't get some training or pick up the knowledge slowly and painfully on your own, you will quickly feel helpless when confronted with a problem. If you do take the time to learn the basics, your overall computer use will be greatly enhanced.

After you learn your way around your operating environment, pick your most-used application and get training on it. This training can have added benefits because most applications, especially for the Macintosh and, to a lesser extent, Windows, work very much alike, so learning one application will give you a leg up on all the others. The confidence you get from knowing your main application well will spill over into everything else you do with your computer.

There are several ways to get training in a particular application or operating environment. If you are very self-disciplined, you can learn most of what you need to know by using the documentation that comes with each of your software packages. Work through any on-line or written tutorials first. Then figure out the basics of using the software. When you have put a little time in with the program, page through the documentation, looking for tips and procedures for the things you already do or want to know how to do. When you find relevant information, read it in detail. When you have learned what you can from the documentation, or as an alternative to the documentation, buy a third-party book or two and go through it. Especially valuable are books that are specific to using the software in the way it's used in your own profession or discipline.

However, few people are willing to really plunge into the depths of documentation and third-party books. Other forms of training are application-specific classes from computer stores, training companies, and user groups. Take at least one half-day to full-day class for each major application you plan to spend much time on; the investment will repay itself many times over. Other forms of training are on-line and videotaped training courses from third-party vendors. Though the quality and target audience of these products varies, you may find they are a very valuable source of training.

A Buyer's Checklist

When you're ready to actually buy a system, gather information from a variety of sources: the chapters and tables in this book, computer magazine articles and ads, other books, and friends and coworkers. Spend a little time looking at systems in a computer superstore or other outlet. Then fill out this checklist to use as you make your purchase. Note that this checklist covers computer systems and graphics systems, but not peripherals.

For peripheral purchasing considerations, see the following chapters:

- Chapter 8, "Monitors and Adapters"
- Chapter 10, "Printers"
- Chapter 11, "Ergonomic Devices"
- Chapter 12, "Pointing Devices"
- Chapter 13, "Modems and Fax Modems"
- Chapter 14, "CD-ROM"
- Chapter 15, "Storage"
- Chapter 16, "Tape Backup Systems"
- Chapter 17, "Sound Devices"
- Chapter 18, "Scanners"

What Kind of Computer?

The first question you have to answer is which operating environment you want: Macintosh, Windows, or DOS? (For detailed information on these alternatives and on less common environments, such as NT and OS/2, see Chapter 4.)

If you will be using your computer for work and there is one predominant environment among your coworkers, you should get that environment. Otherwise, buy Macintosh for ease of setup, ease of use, and for student use. Buy DOS for lowest system cost. Buy Windows for access to the most applications (DOS plus Windows). Windows is easier to use than DOS, but less so than Macintosh.

1. Operating environment (Macintosh, Windows, DOS, other):
   _____

The other question you have to answer before you get started is whether you want a desktop or portable system. Choose a desktop system if you don't need portability and you want the lowest cost for performance and expandability. Otherwise, consider a portable, with a dock if you plan to use it on a desktop much.

2. Type of system (desktop, portable): _____

IBM-Compatible Systems

If you choose to run DOS or Windows, your specific buying considerations are covered here. The next section lists Macintosh-specific questions. This checklist covers desktop systems primarily because they are still the most common. Portable-related considerations are also covered wherever necessary.

In the IBM-compatible arena, computers are rated first and foremost by their microprocessor. Get a 486SX or full 486 for Windows; a 386SX or 386 for DOS. If you need math coprocessing for a spreadsheet, CAD, fast graphics, etc., buy a full 486, not an SX. Don't buy a Pentium system except for the highest-powered applications.

Portable systems are increasingly required to do as much as their desktop cousins, so consider buying the same class of microprocessor for a portable as you would for a desktop. Even for portables, try to get a 486 or 486SX to run Windows. Consider an SX instead of a full 486 to keep the price down. Also look for a microprocessor with power-saving features.

1. Microprocessor (386SX, 386, 486SX, 486, Pentium): _____

The speed of your microprocessor also affects performance. Although options are changing constantly, choices at this writing are listed in the question. Pick a speed that seems right, but be willing to consider slightly higher or lower speeds if other price/performance tradeoffs seem to justify it. Consider dropping down a notch or two for a portable to keep the price reasonable.

2. Microprocessor speed 386SX/33 (which means 33 MHz 386SX); 386/33; 386/40; 486SX/33; 486/33; 486/50; 486/66; 486/100; Pentium/66: _____

Additional microprocessor-related considerations are low power consumption (especially important for portables) and whether the microprocessor can be replaced or have a clock-doubling or clock-tripling upgrade chip added.

3. Additional capabilities: (low power, replaceable, clock-doubling or -tripling):

_____

The number of slots makes a big difference for IBM-compatibles because there are so many add-ons available. You need to have at least one slot open after all the add-on devices you need are installed. Three slots total is enough for most systems; five or six gives maximum expandability. You also want at least one drive bay open so you can add another internal hard disk, a CD-ROM drive, or an additional floppy disk drive. For an expandable portable system, you want at least one PCMCIA slot that isn't already in use.

4. Expandability (number of slots, open drive bays):

_____

Memory is an important consideration. The amount of memory the system comes with is important; you should start with 2M for DOS and at least 4M for Windows. 8M is better for Windows. The memory capacity of the system is important too; this capacity limits the amount of memory you can add on the motherboard. 16M is the minimum; 32M or 64M is better. Adequate memory is especially important for portables in helping you avoid running the hard disk too much when on battery power.

5. Memory installed (2M for DOS, 4M or 8M for Windows):

_____

6. Memory capacity (16M minimum):

_____

It's a lot harder and more expensive to replace an existing hard disk or add a new one than it is to add memory, so getting a big enough hard disk to start out with is important. You may want to add a second, 5 1/4-inch floppy drive to the standard 3 1/2-inch drive for backward compatibility with old floppies. Be willing to consider a slightly smaller hard disk for a portable, but make sure that it includes a floppy drive.

7. Hard disk space (40M-plus for DOS, 100M-plus for Windows), number of floppy drives (one 3 1/2-inch drive and possibly one 5 1/4-inch drive as well):

_____

The graphics subsystem is a very important factor in how happy you are with your system. SuperVGA capability should be adequate for most needs. You will want a local bus or other accelerated video card for Windows. A 13- to 14-inch monitor is fine for DOS, but try to find money in your checking account and space on your desktop for a 16- to 17-inch monitor for Windows. If you do graphics-intensive work, consider an accelerated video card.

8. Video adapter (on-board SuperVGA with 256K of video memory for DOS; local bus SuperVGA video adapter with 512K of video memory for Windows; accelerator for graphics-intensive applications).

   _____

9. Video monitor (Non-interlaced, 13- to 14-inch, 800 by 600 for DOS; 16- to 17-inch, 1,024 by 768 for Windows):

   _____

For a portable system, look for a 9-inch or larger screen and color if you can afford it, 16 gray scales if you can't. Make an active-matrix display a requirement. Also make sure that there's a VGA or better video-out port.

10. Video for portables: (screen size, color, active-matrix, VGA video-out port):

    _____

Macintosh Systems

Buying a Macintosh system is somewhat easier than buying an IBM compatible because there's only one manufacturer rather than hundreds. This checklist covers desktop systems first, and then adds portable-related considerations wherever necessary.

Like IBM compatibles, Macintosh computers are rated first and foremost by their microprocessor: either the Motorola 68030 or 68040 chips, or the newly released IBM PowerPC chips (see Chapter 6 for more information about these microprocessors).

If you're wary of new technology, you may want to stick with the 68030 or its faster counterpart, the 68040. Either runs all the standard Macintosh programs adequately, but 68040-based systems offer more possibilities for higher end graphics, music, animation, and math-intensive work. PowerPC's are, arguably, the next step up from the 68040's performance. Possibly their most touted feature is their capability to run Microsoft Windows as well as Macintosh system software. If you use both Windows and Mac at work, the PowerPC Macintosh is definitely a better choice than 680x0-based Macs. Another important consideration is Apple's announcement that all their Macintosh computers will be PowerPC-based in the near future. This move probably won't leave 680x0 owners out in the cold, but they would have to buy processor or motherboard upgrades to use new PowerPC-specific software.

1. Microprocessor (68030, 68040, PowerPC):

   _____

The speed of your microprocessor also affects performance. Although options are changing constantly, choices available at this writing are listed in the question. Pick a speed that seems right, but be willing to consider slightly higher or lower speeds if other price/performance tradeoffs seem to justify it. Consider dropping down a notch or two for a portable to keep the price reasonable.

2. Microprocessor speed (68030/20, 68030/25, 68030/33, 68040/25, 68040/33, PowerPC/60, PowerPC/66, PowerPC/100):

_____

Additional microprocessor-related considerations are low power consumption (especially important for portables) and whether the microprocessor can be replaced in favor of a faster one later. You may want to consider one of the systems with a digital signal processing (DSP) chip for multimedia work.

3. Additional capabilities: (low power, replaceable microprocessor, DSP chip):

_____

The number of slots is less important for a Macintosh than for an IBM compatible because more capabilities are built into the base system. A highly expandable Mac might have three open slots; a non-expandable one might have a single processor direct slot (PDS). You may want a built-in CD-ROM drive, and you may want an open drive bay for additional internal expandability. However, standardized SCSI makes it easy to expand with external devices instead.

4. Expandability (number of slots, CD-ROM drive, open drive bays):

_____

Memory is an important consideration. Virtual memory isn't particularly well-implemented on the Macintosh, so try to get enough "real" memory for your needs. 4M is enough to run System 7, one application, and some desk accessories; 8M is enough to do several things at once without having to use virtual memory. The memory capacity of the system is important too; this limits the amount of memory you can add on the motherboard. 16M is the minimum; 32M or 64M is better. Adequate memory is especially important for portables; it lets you avoid running the hard disk too much when on battery power.

5. Memory installed (4M to 8M):

_____

6. Total memory capacity (16M minimum):

_____

With built-in SCSI, adding an additional external hard disk if the internal one runs out of space is no big deal. Still, it's convenient to have enough space on your internal drive to last a while. As for floppy drives, the standard, 3 1/2-inch SuperDrive is enough. Be willing to consider a slightly smaller hard disk for a portable, but make sure that a floppy drive is included.

7. Hard disk space (80M to 160M or more), floppies (one): _____

The graphics subsystem is very important in how happy you are with your system. Look for built-in video with 512K or more of video memory. You will want an accelerated card that goes in a PDS slot for graphics-intensive applications, such as illustration work or color desktop publishing. Try to find money in your checking account and space on your desktop for a 16- to 17-inch monitor.

8. Video adapter (built-in video with at least 512K of video memory; accelerated card for graphics-intensive applications): _____

9. Video monitor (16- to 17-inch or even larger): _____

For a portable system, look for a 9-inch or larger screen, and color if you can afford it, 16 gray scales if you can't. Make an active-matrix display a requirement. Also make sure that there is a video-out port.

10. Video for portables: (screen size, color, active-matrix, video-out port): _____

Making the Purchase

When it comes time to actually buy your system, you can do several things to make a purchase you will be happy with for a long time. Start by using the preceding checklist to make sure that the system you're considering has everything you need. Also look through this book for ideas about add-ons you may want to buy as part of your system.

Then look at the section in this chapter on warranties. Check that the system you're buying has all the warranty protection that you want and that there's at least a 30-day return period so you have time to try the system out.

Check policies on phone support and other forms of support to make sure that they're satisfactory. Make sure that the system is fully configured with operating system software and any other software you buy, as well as drivers to support your graphics card and monitor. If the vendor will not configure the system for you, consider whether you'd be better off buying elsewhere.

Make sure that you haven't talked yourself into, or haven't been talked into, buying a no-name brand from a manufacturer who may not be here tomorrow. If you are heading down this path, make sure that you're willing to take the risks involved and that you're getting a good enough deal to justify passing up a brand-name system.

If everything looks good, make the purchase. If possible, use a credit card; it's easier to avoid paying a disputed bill with a credit card than with a check. Also, some credit card companies will automatically extend the warranty of any item you buy with their card. If you are dissatisfied with your purchase, contact your credit card company immediately; they should agree not to pay the vendor until the dispute is resolved. Some will also negotiate a resolution with you and the vendor. Your rights will vary depending on the state or country you're in.

As soon as you get your system, put it together, plug it in, and make sure that everything works. Format a floppy disk; copy and delete some files on your hard disk; run some programs. (Game programs can be good stress tests for your system.) The sooner you find and complain about a problem, the easier it is to get it fixed. Check that your software works, that options like high-resolution graphics modes are available, and anything else you can think of.

After you do an initial check to ensure that everything works, run everything a lot for a week or two. If your hardware makes it through this "burn-in period" without failing, it's likely to last a long time.

Chapter Summary

This chapter covers the information you need to actually make your purchase. It describes where to buy a system, important factors to consider in making a purchase, including warranties and support, and offers checklists to use in shopping for a system and guidelines for making the purchase.

IN THE APPENDIX

This is the last chapter of the book; following is Appendix A. The appendix covers maintaining your computer equipment and software, upgrading it, and repairing a computer system.

APPENDIX A

Planning for the Future

After you purchase a system and have it working properly, you want to keep it running smoothly. This appendix describes how to keep your system unit, disk drives, keyboard, mouse, monitor, and printer in top condition. It also describes how to upgrade the different pieces that make up your computer. Getting your system repaired is important, and in this appendix you learn about in-warranty and out-of-warranty repairs. Finally, it describes ways to keep track of what is going on in the personal computer industry and recommends magazines and on-line sources of up-to-date computing information.

Maintaining Your Computer System

Periodic preventive maintenance is as important for your computer as for your car. By keeping your computer in good condition, you can avoid costly repair bills, as well as loss of valuable data.

Maintaining the System Unit

The computer system unit needs little maintenance. However, you need to be aware of dust and smoke that can get into your system unit. A blanket of dust or smoke residue acts as an insulator on the chips, causing them to run at higher temperatures. In a normal environment, you can avoid heat-induced chip failure by cleaning the chips once a year with canned compressed air or a hand vacuum designed for electronic components. If you work in a dusty or smoky environment, vacuum the inside of the system unit every two months. (Vacuuming does not completely remove the smoke residue, but it is your best defense against it.) Another good way to remove dust is with a can of spray air, available in most electronics stores.

Many computer systems contain one or more batteries. IBM-compatible and IBM AT computers use a battery to power the CMOS chip, which holds the setup information needed to operate the computer. Your computer cannot start correctly when the CMOS battery is dead. To restore the setup information that your computer needs, replace the battery and run a setup program. The setup program can reside in ROM or on a setup disk (usually included with your computer). If the setup program is in ROM, you start the setup program by turning on your computer and pressing a key or key combination that is indicated by an on-screen message (something like Press Escape to run Setup). It's a good idea to write down all the setup information in case you or a computer repairperson need it in the future.

Battery life varies from one to five years. Your vendor can give you some idea about probable battery life and about the cost and availability of replacement batteries. Always keep the documentation that comes with your system unit and components; it contains information that can be valuable when replacing the battery and restoring setup information.

Maintaining Floppy Disk Drives

Clean the magnetic heads in the floppy disk drive once a year. Cleaning is simple when you use a kit from a company like Curtis Manufacturing. Cleaning kits for 3 1/2-inch or 5 1/4-inch floppy disk drives are available at computer retail stores and cost about $10. Make sure that the cleaning system is a wet system rather than a dry system. A dry system may damage your disk drive recording heads.

You may need to have the floppy disk drive realigned periodically. If the drive starts to detect a lot of errors on floppy disks, check the disks on another system before throwing them out; it may be that the drive is the problem, not the disks. Programs like System Sleuth (Dariana, Inc.) and Check It (Touchstone Software Corp.) can tell you if the drive controller or the drive itself is failing. If the drive is the problem, don't hesitate to toss it out in favor of a new one. New floppy drives are inexpensive (often less than the price it takes to repair an old one) and easy to install.

Maintaining Hard Disk Drives

The hard disk is the most vulnerable part of a personal computer system. If your hard disk crashes, you may lose the use of your hard disk and all or part of the data on the disk. (The term crash originally meant that the read/write head on a hard disk hit a platter, causing irreparable damage to the disk and its data. Today, the term more loosely describes any problem that causes the hard disk to stop working.) To ensure against the loss of important data and programs because of a crash, back up the data on your hard disk onto floppy disks or tape periodically.

> **MS-DOS Utilities**
>
> This section talks about several third-party utilities you can purchase for DOS, Windows, and Macintosh, but owners of DOS 6 and above can put their checkbooks away for the most part. DOS 6 includes virus scanning and virus protection, several disk utilities, and a very good backup/restore application. Don't let yourself get talked into buying a lot of extra utilities with a PC if it includes DOS 6 or above.

PC Fullback+ (West Lake Data) and Fastback Plus (Fifth Generation Systems) are programs that back up hard disks for IBM and IBM compatible computers. There's also a Fastback Plus for the Mac. PC Tools Deluxe and Mac Tools Deluxe (Central Point Software), collections of useful disk utilities, also include hard disk backup software. This capability is found in many other programs as well. In general, these programs are faster and easier to use than the backup utilities that come with DOS 5.0 and below (though DOS 6.0 and above include backup software that is more than adequate), or the comparable program included with the Mac. Because the third-party programs also compress data, you can store the contents of your hard disk on fewer floppy disks.

For best results, back up any new or newly changed information on your hard disk daily or weekly, depending on how much data you enter and how costly the loss of the data would be. Hard disks, on the whole, are reliable and work for many years, yet every hard disk, no matter how reliable, will crash eventually if you keep using it long enough. Your backup strategy should reflect this level of dependability, as well as the amount and value of data on your computer.

Several products for IBM-compatible computers prevent hard disk failure by examining the surface of the hard disk platter for defects. SpinRite (Gibson Research) is one example of a preventive program. As anyone who has lost hours, days, or weeks of work to a hard disk crash can tell you, though, nothing should replace making regular backups.

Computer viruses recently have received a great deal of press. Viruses are small programs that can damage other programs or data files on your system. They are usually carried by programs that are copied from an infected system to a healthy one. A virus may be non-destructive, causing minor annoyances, such as messages on your screen. Other viruses, however, destroy some or all of the data on your hard disk.

If you download programs by modem from information services or bulletin-board systems or exchange disks with someone who does, there's a possibility of exposure to a computer virus. Even shrink-wrapped software programs from reputable manufacturers have been carriers of computer viruses on rare occasions. To protect yourself from computer viruses, purchase an anti-viral program like Norton Anti-Virus for the PC or SAM AntiVirus for the Macintosh (both from Symantec) or Central Point Anti-Virus for both PC and Mac. There are also shareware programs that stop viruses, including McAffee VirusScan for the PC. Virus-detection programs sometimes interfere with the operation of other software, such as installation programs, so you have to learn how to turn them on and off.

The more you use a hard disk, the more slowly the disk operates. This slowdown is caused by file fragmentation, which occurs when program and data files are divided and distributed randomly over available space on the hard disk. To bring your disk up to speed again, you need an optimizing program. Disk-optimizing software collects the scattered pieces of a program or file into one block on the hard disk. Good choices for disk-optimizing software are OPTune (Gazelle Systems) and Norton Utilities (Symantec) for

IBM and IBM compatibles and Disk Express II (ALSoft) and Mac Tools Deluxe (Central Point Software) for the Macintosh. Such programs are also included in many other utilities packages. Run a disk-optimizing program every month. You can also defragment your files by copying them from one disk to another and back, but then you run the risk of accidentally deleting a file. A disk-optimizing program is more efficient.

No matter how much data your hard disk can hold, you eventually may fill the disk to capacity. How quickly or slowly you fill your hard disk depends on the number of software programs you install on the hard disk and the size of the files you create with those programs. You occasionally need to reorganize the files to keep from overloading the hard disk. You can move some files from the hard disk to floppy disks for archival storage and erase unnecessary files.

If you work only with MS-DOS on an IBM or IBM-compatible computer, these housekeeping chores can be tedious. You can use a program, such as XTree Pro Gold (XTree), however, to complete this task quickly and effectively. If you use Windows on an IBM or compatible computer, or if you use a Macintosh computer, you may not need a special program to help you remove files from the hard disk. How frequently you need to do housekeeping depends on the space available on your disk and the size and number of files you create daily.

Maintaining the Keyboard, Mouse, and Video Monitor

The keyboard, mouse, and video monitor need little maintenance. You can clean the keyboard surface as needed with a cloth dampened with a mild cleaning solvent. (Never spray a solvent directly on the keyboard.) Remove and clean the mouse ball with a mild solvent every six months. At the same time, clean the rollers that come into contact with the mouse ball with a cotton swab and a mild solvent like rubbing alcohol. Clean the monitor display area (with the monitor turned off) once a week with ordinary glass cleaner. If the glass is covered with an anti-glare coating, use a special screen cleaner, such as Clean Screen (Curtis Manufacturing Company). The documentation that comes with the monitor tells you whether the screen is coated and needs such special cleaners.

Maintaining the Printer

Printers need periodic maintenance, primarily replacing ribbons and cartridges. If you have a dot-matrix printer with a nylon ribbon, the print becomes lighter with use. Print a page when the ribbon is new, and use that page as a visual guide to indicate when you should replace the ribbon. Otherwise, you may not notice the degradation until the print has become quite faint.

Clean your dot-matrix printer each time you change the printer ribbon. Use a vacuum or a can of spray air to clean out the paper dust that tends to collect in the printer. Periodically, perhaps every fifth time you change the ribbon, you should use a cotton swab and mild solvent like rubbing alcohol to clean the printer head; then use a soft cloth to clean the platen (the rubber-like cylinder against which the paper rests).

A laser or inkjet printer signals you when to replace the toner cartridge or ink cartridge. Plan to keep an extra toner or ink cartridge handy. These printers do not give you much warning before the ink runs dry. For example, an inkjet printer signals you only a few pages before the ink runs out. If you don't have an ink cartridge on hand, you may be unable to complete your printing task until you can get one. As with a dot-matrix printer, clean your laser or inkjet printer each time you change the toner or ink cartridge. Because the black toner powder can spread through the machine, you need to clean the inside of a laser printer regularly. The documentation for the laser printer gives you the proper cleaning procedures. Inkjet printers do not require much maintenance.

Maintaining Your Software

Maintaining your software is not something that most users give much thought to, but it's an important part of owning a computer system. It's also an important part of the cost of owning a computer because software manufacturers are making less of their money from new product sales and more from sales of upgrades to existing users. Read magazine articles and watch advertisements to learn what you can about upgrade policies and costs.

The first rule of software maintenance is to register your software. Software is an asset worth hundreds or even thousands of dollars, and registering it helps you protect that asset. (If the cost of the software isn't sufficient motivation, think of the value of your data!) Each software package you buy comes with a registration card; always send it in immediately. (If you own unregistered software, call the company and find out how you can register it.) Many companies respond to your registration card with a thank-you card and even, in some cases, a free gift.

After your software is installed and registered, be sure to keep the original floppy disks that you loaded it from. (Resist the temptation to use them for backup or file transfers.) You may well need to reinstall the software at some point because of a hard disk crash or a more minor problem that causes the software not to work. In many cases, the installation program allows you to specify what features to install or not to install; you may want a different mix of features later. Or you may upgrade or replace your computer and need to reinstall to different hardware. When any of these things happen, you'll be glad to have the original disks on hand.

Keep a file with information about registration and upgrades. For each program you own, you should have the name, address, and phone number of the company that sold you the software and the serial number of your copy. This information makes it easy for you to get technical support and to let vendors know if you change your address. It can be valuable if you want to sell some of your software, either separately or when you sell your system. Keep the upgrade offers that you receive from companies in this file as well.

When an opportunity to upgrade comes along, wait a month or two to take advantage of it; this time gives the company a chance to hear from other, more eager users who will upgrade immediately and discover any bugs in the upgrade. After some time has passed, send in the upgrade offer if you need some feature contained in the upgrade. (Some companies put a time limitation on the upgrade offer to frustrate this kind of approach; be sure to respond within the time limitation.) Even if you don't take advantage of the offer in the short term, save it until later; you may need some new feature down the road or find that you need to upgrade to maintain compatibility with other software or new hardware that you purchase.

Long-Term Troubleshooting Strategies

After your system is up and running, you may not experience problems with components for several months, or even years. If you suspect a problem, however, the diagnostic software that comes with your computer may be able to pinpoint the problem for you. Although you may not be able to solve the problem, you will have information to give to your dealer or a technical support person. The documentation that accompanies the computer should discuss how to operate the diagnostic software.

You can purchase diagnostic software that is more thorough and easier to use than the software that comes with the system. One good choice for IBM-compatibles is Check It (Touchstone Software). Check It tests the system board, RAM, hard disk drive, floppy disk drive, video circuits, serial and parallel ports, keyboard, mouse, joystick, and printer. Check It also indicates whether a problem is caused by hardware or software. If Check It locates a problem, you can give the information to a repairperson or use the information to repair the computer yourself. Macintosh computers come with a program called Disk First Aid that will help you diagnose problems on your hard and floppy disk drives.

Not all computer problems are caused by system components. Problems are sometimes caused by human errors, such as erasing a file or reformatting a hard disk. Such problems can be devastating if you don't have the appropriate software to rescue you. Utility software is designed to perform important tasks of this sort: to recover erased files, to reverse problems caused by reformatting a hard disk, to reconstruct damaged files, and to repair a corrupted hard disk.

When you look for utility software, notice what features the program offers. A unique feature may make one utility program more suitable for your purposes than another program. Utility software includes maintenance programs. For IBM and IBM-compatible computers, utility options include PC Tools Deluxe (Central Point Software), Norton Utilities (Symantec), and Mace Utilities (Fifth Generation Systems). For Macintosh computers, choose a utility program like Mac Tools Deluxe (Central Point Software), or Norton Utilities for the Macintosh (Symantec).

Upgrading Your Computer

One of the great advantages of desktop personal computers is the fact that they can easily be upgraded. The expansion slots inside a PC can support almost any kind of electronic device, even a whole additional computer more powerful than the PC itself. The ports that come with your computer are also avenues of expansion.

This promise of upgradability is not easy to take advantage of, however, especially in the IBM-compatible world. The combination of DOS and Windows makes for a complex software environment that must run on thousands of subtly different brands and configurations of personal computers. Getting an add-in device and its driver to work with the hardware and software you already have can be anything from very easy to excruciatingly complicated and difficult.

A Macintosh is quite a bit easier to upgrade, for several reasons. There are far fewer models of Macintosh than of IBM-compatibles and fewer hardware and software combinations to worry about. Many Macintosh peripherals are SCSI-based, which means you just run a SCSI cable from one into the next, up to seven at a time. Apple also works with third-party vendors to help them design add-ons that are compatible with various Macs and with each other.

Many of the concerns described in this book that relate to buying a PC come into play when you want to upgrade your system. A computer dealer can do the upgrade for you, at some extra cost; if you bought from a mail-order vendor, that vendor can talk you through any problems over the phone. (If you buy the add-in device from the same vendor, the vendor will be even more willing to help.) The manufacturer of the add-in device may be able to help you as well.

There are some general rules to keep in mind when doing upgrades:

- *Get information.* Make sure you either get a look at the system's documentation or contact the vendor or manufacturer of the system before doing an upgrade. Every system has a few quirks that make some easy-sounding operations difficult or impossible.

- *Back up your data.* A problem during an upgrade, even one done by an experienced technician, can cause your system to be out of action for some period of time. Having a current backup may save you a lot of grief.

- *Unplug the system.* Never open a system unit without having unplugged it; otherwise, you may be electrocuted.

- *Ground yourself.* Never touch a chip without grounding yourself first by touching metal, such as your computer's power supply; the static electricity on your body can burn out a microprocessor, memory chip, or other component. It's not a bad idea to get an anti-static wrist strap, available in electronic stores.

- *When in doubt, give up fast.* If you are starting an operation and believe that you may be doing something wrong, put everything back the way it was, go back to work, and wait to do the upgrade until you can get assistance. You're a lot better off waiting a little while than doing something that may cause your system or data to be damaged.

Many of the upgrade options described in the following sections may not apply to portable computers. The requirements of more computing power in less space means that smaller and often less-common parts are used. Check your system's documentation or check with the vendor to see what's upgradable and what's not.

If you aren't knowledgeable about computers, consider buying add-on equipment only from a dealer or store that will do the upgrade for you. You can also turn to a friend or coworker who has done similar upgrades for help and advice. Be careful, however, and try not to do any harm; that way, even if you aren't able to make the upgrade work, you're no worse off than when you started and can get a vendor to help you complete the upgrade.

Adding Memory

Consider adding memory as a way of increasing performance. On an IBM-compatible running DOS, add memory when you run out of memory space for your programs. When running Windows, add memory when your system is going to disk a lot to take advantage of virtual memory. On a Macintosh, try to have enough memory so that you can run all the programs you need while leaving virtual memory turned off; this will greatly improve performance.

On some systems, adding memory is simple. You just unplug your machine so as to avoid electrocuting yourself, open the system unit, touch metal to discharge electricity, gently plug in SIMMs into empty sockets, and restart your computer.

Life is not so kind in other cases, however. Systems that run DOS need to be reconfigured to recognize the additional memory. Many systems need SIMMs of specific sizes to be put in specific slots, or performance will suffer. Some SIMMs are a little hard to snap in; others are impossible to snap in without a special tool. It's easy to cause damage trying to remove old SIMMs by hand or snapping in new ones.

Read the documentation that comes with your system carefully to see how to put in memory. Try to get help from a knowledgeable friend or coworker. If you don't have the documentation or a knowledgeable friend, or if the task looks difficult, buy your memory from a source that will install it for you. There's no sense in having a five-minute installation process take hours, or even damage your system, because you don't know what you're doing.

Adding a Math Coprocessor

Adding a math coprocessor to your system gives it a moderate boost in performance for a relatively small price. Most Macintosh and 386SX, 386DX, and 486SX systems have a math coprocessor socket just waiting for a math coprocessor to be installed. (68040, 486DX, PowerPC, and Pentium microprocessors already have a math coprocessor built in.) Macintosh systems need a 68882 math coprocessor; IBM-compatible systems need a 387, 387SX, or 487SX math coprocessor. (The number of the math coprocessor is the same as the number of the main processor, but with a seven in place of the six.) Get a math coprocessor that runs at the same clock speed as the main microprocessor. Intel is the biggest provider of these chips for IBM-compatibles, but there are several competitors who use similar numbering schemes.

You need a math coprocessor to speed up spreadsheet recalculations, other math-intensive operations, and graphics. Only software that can take advantage of a math coprocessor, including most spreadsheets, CAD programs, graphics programs, and Windows drivers, will benefit from it. If you need a big boost in this area, look at upgrading your microprocessor. The on-chip math coprocessor of a 486 is much faster than a 386/387 combination; the same is true for a 68040 over a 68030/68882 pair.

To add a math coprocessor, make sure your system has an empty socket for one. Then buy it, unplug your system, ground yourself, and plug the coprocessor in. If there is no socket, you may be able to add it anyway, using a daughtercard that plugs into the microprocessor's socket. You may need to reconfigure your system and your software to recognize the chip; check your system's and programs' documentation to be sure.

Upgrading the Processor

Consider upgrading your microprocessor if you're looking for a quick performance boost. The upgraded system usually won't perform as well as a new system built around the new microprocessor, but it's nearly certain to run faster than it used to.

Look for information in your system's documentation or call the vendor for information if you are interested in upgrading your computer's microprocessor. The difficulty of doing such upgrades ranges from easy to impossible.

Apple does not provide microprocessor-only upgrades for Macintosh systems. The best options are to buy an add-in board from a third-party vendor or a motherboard replacement from Apple. The add-in boards give a quick and often substantial performance boost; the motherboard replacement effectively upgrades your system from one type to another. You can usually handle the add-in board upgrade yourself, but motherboard replacements should usually be done by a technician.

Motherboard replacements are also available for IBM-compatibles, but they can be quite expensive. If you want to replace only the microprocessor, the simplest microprocessor upgrades are to systems that have an Overdrive socket installed. (Many 486-based desktop systems have this kind of socket.) You simply buy the Overdrive chip and install it, following the previous general rules and the specific rules in your system's documentation. The installation process may involve moving a jumper or updating your system's BIOS, so don't proceed without finding out the facts.

If there is no Overdrive socket, you may be able to pull out a 386 or 486 microprocessor and replace it with a faster one. The system's BIOS must support the new chip; check your system's documentation or ask the manufacturer. Some systems use ZIF (zero insertion force) microprocessor sockets that make it easy to remove one microprocessor and insert another. Some use old-style sockets that may be harder to get the chip out of; it's easy to bend the chip's legs or even break them off when removing or installing a chip, which can make the socket or the chip useless. Some systems solder the microprocessor to the motherboard so that you can't remove it. Take a look at your system's motherboard, and then get help if you're concerned about possible problems in upgrading your system's microprocessor.

Upgrading a 486-based system to Pentium may be problematic. Many systems have a special socket that allows you to remove the 486 and plug in an Overdrive Pentium chip instead. The performance improvement will only take you part of the way to what a "true" Pentium system can do, and you won't have the multiprocessor capability that some native Pentium systems will have, but you'll get a noticeable performance boost. If you compare the price to the performance increase, though, you probably will decide it's not worth the extra money. Some systems will need replacement or additional fans to help dissipate the heat from the Pentium (and there's a lot of it); others may require special versions of the Pentium chip. Contact your vendor before upgrading your system to Pentium to find out what's involved.

Upgrading the Hard Disk

You may need to upgrade your hard disk once or more during the life of your system. When a disk gets 3-4 years old, it's only a matter of time before it dies, taking your data with it. (The diagnostic programs listed earlier in this appendix can warn you of any impending problems and prevent most of them.) You may also need more capacity or more speed from your hard disk; remember, larger hard disks are generally faster than smaller ones, and newer ones are generally faster than older ones.

If you need more capacity but not more speed, consider buying a compression program. This kind of utility can roughly double the capacity of your hard disk at the cost of a slight decrease in speed. (Compressing the data as it is stored and decompressing it as it is retrieved takes a little time.) There is also a slightly increased chance of data loss if there is a disk problem or a power outage. Many users of compression programs consider the trade-offs to be well worth it.

A special word of warning for hard disk upgrades: always back up your data before doing anything with your hard disk.

Upgrading your hard disk may be relatively simple. The speed and capacities of hard disks are increasing constantly, so you should be able to find a disk that's the same physical size as your old one, and that has the same type of connection to the system, but that holds much more data and runs faster. If your current hard disk controller supports it and you have an open drive bay, you can add another internal hard drive. The easiest upgrade is from an existing IDE or SCSI drive to a new one or an additional one of the same type, because it doesn't require a new card. Most new hard drives are IDE or SCSI-based, but older computers might have MFM or RLL drives and controllers that would have to be replaced.

If you need or want a new controller, the upgrade is more complicated; follow instructions that come with the product. Don't be afraid to get help on this one.

If you have a SCSI connector or are willing to add one, all the better. When you get the connector working right and get a hard drive compatible with the connector, you can simply connect up an external drive. Then you have the use of both the internal drive and the external one, which can also be carried to other systems with a SCSI connector. Some IBM-compatibles do not like to boot from a SCSI disk, so keep your internal IDE or other drive. An advanced operating system like Microsoft Windows NT may be able to access your internal IDE drive and your external SCSI drive simultaneously, which will enable some operations to proceed very fast.

Upgrading the Keyboard and Mouse

If you don't currently have a mouse, you will need one to run today's newer software, even DOS software. If you already have a mouse, you may want to upgrade both your keyboard and your mouse so that you can work with greater comfort and less risk of soreness and injury from poorly-designed input devices.

If you have an older IBM-compatible system with no mouse port, you will have to either use up a serial port to plug in your mouse, or install a small add-in card that has a port you can plug the mouse into. Many of today's systems have a built-in mouse port in addition to the keyboard port. Macintoshes have one or more Apple Desktop Bus (ADB) ports that accept a keyboard plug; the mouse then plugs into the keyboard.

Upgrading your keyboard and mouse, once you have a mouse port, is easy; just unplug the old and plug in the new. Keep the old devices, especially your mouse; using a variety of devices over time can be an effective way to reduce strain. Learn to use your mouse with your weaker hand part of the time if you get soreness in your stronger hand, again for the sake of variety.

Upgrading the Video System

Unless you use an accelerated video card with its own graphics processor, such as a TI 34020, the speed of your system's microprocessor is the biggest factor in graphics speed. Next may be the quality of your software's drivers; make sure you have the latest drivers for Windows or for individual DOS applications. (This is less of a concern with Macintosh systems.) The next concerns are whether the card is in a fast slot, such as a VL-bus slot, whether acceleration features are built into the card, and whether VRAM (fast Video RAM) or standard DRAM chips are used for the card's memory. The more colors and higher resolution you run the card at, the more work the processor has to do to keep graphics going.

Most users who move to Windows either get a new system or upgrade several aspects of their old one in order to improve performance. Possibly the most common upgrade is video, running neck and neck with upgrading the CPU. A graphical user interface, such as the Macintosh or Windows both enables and requires a large, colorful screen to run multiple simultaneous applications on while retaining some access to the desktop. Demanding applications like screen savers, games, and graphics programs will make you want to add more color capability to your system as well.

Picking the right video upgrade for your system is difficult. After you pick a video card, installing it and getting the drivers right is another challenge, the nature of which varies from system to system. Follow the manufacturer's instructions carefully and don't be afraid to call technical support. Do some informal before-and-after speed tests with your own software to make sure that you're getting the speed you deserve.

Long-Term Upgrade Strategies

In formulating a long-term upgrade strategy, you need to decide when it makes sense to add power to your existing system and when it makes sense to ditch your existing system and move on to a new, more powerful one.

Your overall purpose in upgrading and, eventually, replacing your system is to maintain a balanced system that lets you run your software with good performance. The requirement that your system be balanced means that you shouldn't do a bunch of different, expensive upgrades; replace your system with a new, more powerful one instead. If there are one or two things you can do that fix particular bottlenecks in your system's performance or that involve the purchase of components (such as a large monitor) that you can take forward with you to your next system, by all means consider them.

Keep long-term pricing trends in sight while making upgrade decisions. For instance, prices have dropped dramatically in the last two to three years. If your system is older than that, you'd be much better off to replace it than to try to use upgrades to bring it up to par. For instance, nothing you can do to your older system is going to give it a local bus slot for video, but this slot is practically a standard feature in today's systems.

Unfortunately, the same factors that render your older system out-of-date mean that it won't bring in much, compared to its purchase price, when you resell it.

When you buy a system, set a period of time that you plan on keeping it, typically 2-3 years. If you have an existing system, decide about how much longer you will keep it. Then make your upgrading decisions against your planned replacement date. If you are more than a year away from replacement time, upgrading makes sense. If you're closer than that to buying a new system, only the least expensive or most urgently needed upgrades are a good idea.

Someday, systems will be completely modular, so you will be able to buy a personal computer and keep it for many years, upgrading parts as they wear out and become obsolete. The PC industry is rapidly changing today, from yesterday's AT bus and non-upgradable microprocessors, to today's VL-bus and upgradable processors, to the PCI bus, 64-bit memory access, and multiprocessor capability that may be common on the systems of tomorrow. Be conservative in your buying and upgrading decisions today so that you'll have the flexibility to be able to buy the systems of tomorrow.

Repairing a Personal Computer System

Personal computer systems are generally reliable and can give you many years of trouble-free service; nevertheless, electronic and mechanical components are susceptible to breakdown. During the warranty period, you need only return the computer to the dealer for repair or contact the manufacturer. When the computer or components are out of warranty, you have several options, described in the following sections.

When you do have a problem and take your system in for service, be careful. Technicians may do more work than is needed due to incompetence or in order to increase profits. You can often head this off by running a diagnostic program before taking the system in. Another, more subtle problem is that service technicians will often suggest upgrades to your computer, sometimes hinting that the new piece of equipment will be more reliable than the old. Keep your eyes open when offered these suggestions, and investigate them independently before buying any expensive equipment or software. You should upgrade your computer because you decide it's a good idea, not because a technician turns your problem into a sales opportunity.

In-Warranty Repairs

The warranty period differs among components and from computer to computer. Most computer manufacturers offer one-year warranties, but a substantial number offer longer warranties. The warranty period may be longer for additional components you buy for your computer, such as a modem, than for the system unit. Keep accurate records of purchase dates and warranty periods; make sure that you have dated copies of your receipts. You must prove that your computer or component is in warranty to obtain a warranty repair.

Keep a record of procedures to follow if your computer or a component breaks down during warranty. For best repair service, return the computer or component to the dealer from whom you purchased it or to an authorized dealer repair center. IBM, Compaq, and Apple, for example, have authorized dealer repair centers that honor the manufacturer's warranties.

Your warranty may provide on-site service for a period of time. Having the repairman come to your business or home to repair your computer eliminates the need to disconnect and move the computer. If your warranty provides on-site service, find out what procedures you must follow when you need a repairman.

If you are not located near an authorized service center, you may need to mail the computer or the component to the manufacturer for repair. Find out whether the manufacturer offers telephone support to help you verify that your computer really needs repair. Make sure that you have proper authorization from the company to return the computer. The manufacturer also may recommend a carrier or a means of shipment. If possible, pack your computer in the original packing cartons. Some, but not all, manufacturers may return the repaired components to you by air. Although some manufacturers provide fast, reliable service, the downtime and uncertainty of sending your system away for repair, plus the possible added costs of shipping, make this a service method to be avoided if possible.

Ask your dealer or the manufacturer if a warranty repair extends the warranty. The replacement part may carry a warranty of its own. For example, suppose that your computer carries a one-year warranty and you need to replace the disk drive after six months. If the new disk drive carries a one-year warranty of its own, it may have six months of coverage beyond the computer warranty. Keep all documentation relating to warranty repairs.

Out-of-Warranty Repairs

When you need to repair your computer after the warranty period, be selective about the repair service you choose. Your dealer may charge a premium price for the repair, all too often more than you would pay to replace the machine or faulty components. Find a good technical repair shop that charges reasonable rates or consider making the repair yourself. Once you have an estimate or two on the repair, check the cost of replacing the broken component altogether. As component prices continue to drop, it's often cheaper to replace a worn-out piece of equipment than to fix it.

Finding a Reliable Repair Center

The dealer who sold you your system may not be the only reliable service center in your area. Other repair shops may have better prices or offer bonuses that your dealer does not offer. For example, some repair shops offer loaner or rental equipment while your computer or component is being repaired.

Where do you look for repair shops? Ask a friend or someone you trust. Word of mouth often is the best way to find reputable service centers. Check the yellow pages under Computers & Computer Equipment—Service & Repair. Many service centers advertise this way. Their ads may tell you which computers and other products they service. Check the prices and the services available at several service centers near you. Ask the following questions:

- Do you charge by the hour or by the job?
- Do you provide loaner or rental equipment?
- Do you use replacement parts from the original manufacturer?
- Do you provide on-site service?
- Do you provide pick-up and delivery services?
- What is the minimum charge for on-site service or pick up and delivery?
- How long will the repair take?
- Will you guarantee a time for completion?
- Do you offer a warranty on the repair?

Generally, the cost is less—and easier for you to budget—when a repair is charged by the job. Loaner or rental equipment can help you keep up your productivity, especially if the repair takes several days or longer.

Major computer manufacturers, such as IBM, Compaq, and Apple, have specially designed components in their systems. These components often are sized or shaped so that only parts from the original manufacturer work well in the computers. Discuss the options with your repair center before you decide whether to use original manufacturer components or generic, or third-party, components made by other manufacturers.

On-site service usually is the fastest way to have your computer fixed and to keep computer downtime to a minimum, although you pay a premium price. A service center that picks up and delivers also saves you travel time.

An estimate of how much time the repair will take can help you make decisions, especially if your business depends on your computer. If the repair takes less than one or two days, you may not need to borrow or rent another computer. When your computer goes down in the middle of a time-essential task, however, you may have no other choice than to rent a replacement for the duration of the repair. Rentals can be expensive, so shop around for the facility that offers the fastest repairs and for a rental company that offers the most reasonable rates.

Repairing the Computer Yourself

Computers are mostly modular. A computer is made up of a main circuit board (the motherboard) with smaller circuit cards plugged into it, so (contrary to the fears of many new computer owners) you don't have to wade through an intricate maze of wiring to repair it. The video circuitry, for example, often resides on a video card (although this circuitry may be on the motherboard), which can be replaced rather easily. Of course, if you use some common sense when a problem arises, you often won't have to replace anything. For example, your computer may fail to display anything on-screen for several reasons; the monitor may be unplugged, the monitor may not be turned on, or you may have a faulty monitor. If the problem is not with the monitor, you can check the video card (the one to which you attach the cable from the monitor).

Opening a desktop IBM-compatible system unit is simple. Sometimes, a few screws on the rear of the computer hold the case together. After you remove the screws, the cover slides off. Other models have removable tops. You can pop off the top of any computer in the Mac II line easily. Opening a compact Macintosh like the Classic or Classic II requires special tools and is more difficult than opening a standard PC. Check the manufacturer's documentation to make sure that you don't void any warranties by opening your computer. Make sure that you don't open any units sealed with a label because you may void your warranty if you do.

If you plan to make repairs yourself, look for software and books to help you. Check It (Touchstone Software) is an aid to diagnosing computer problems. A widely-used do-it-yourself repair book from Que is *Upgrading and Repairing PCs*, written by Scott Mueller.

Keeping Pace with New Developments

Flexibility makes buying a personal computer different from buying any other piece of electronic equipment. A personal computer is not limited to one purpose. For example, you can use a personal computer for word processing and for spreadsheets. You can use the computer to manage your personal finances or to play games. For this reason, you should keep abreast of new developments in personal computer hardware and software. Computer magazines and on-line services are two good ways to keep current with developments in the personal computer industry.

Subscribing to Computer Magazines

Many computer magazines are available, each devoted to a different aspect of computing. *PC Magazine*, for instance, has many comparative reviews of similar products in each issue. *PC Magazine*, however, is geared toward the person who buys equipment and software for corporations, so the information can be overwhelming to a novice. *Computer Shopper* and similar magazines specialize in ads from hundreds of mail-order suppliers of personal computer systems, components, and software. *Home Office Computing* is good if you have a computer set up at home that you use for business. *Computer Craft* is a good source of information for anyone interested in upgrading or enhancing a personal computer system.

Some magazines focus on a specific product. For example, *WordPerfect* magazine concentrates on articles about the WordPerfect word-processing program. If you are interested in a specific area of computing, such as desktop publishing or music, look for magazines like *Publish* or *Electronic Musician*.

When you consider buying or subscribing to a magazine, keep in mind the magazine's slant—what readers the magazine addresses. Some magazines are intended for computer technicians, whereas others are aimed more toward the general reader. A quick glance through the table of contents of a magazine and one or two articles should give you a feel for its audience.

Most magazines cover only one kind of computer. For example, *PC Magazine* and *PC World* cover IBM-compatible computers; *MacWorld* and *MacUser* cover Macintosh computers. All these magazines are good sources of information for using and buying products associated with a particular brand of personal computer.

Some of the most interesting magazines are the controlled-circulation weeklies, such as *InfoWorld*, *PC Week*, and *MacWeek*. To get one of these magazines, first get a subscription card from the issue of a friend or coworker. The card will ask you your job title, company size, and, most important, how many hardware and software purchases you make yourself or influence. Answer honestly, but remember that you influence any purchase that you have some input into. After you fill out the card, mail it in. The company that runs the magazine decides whether you qualify for a subscription.

Joining an On-Line Service

You may want to contact other people who have similar computer systems and software in order to ask them questions or to discuss a particular topic. Consider signing up for an on-line service, such as CompuServe, America Online, GEnie, or Prodigy. Computer hardware makers increasingly use these services to deliver support; consider joining the one that your system vendor uses. These services have hundreds of conferences, specific areas where you can leave messages and get responses to questions about computing topics. You also can chat with other members of the service. Chatting takes place when you and other users type short messages into a shared area of the on-line service; you see other users' messages as they appear. Chatting can lead to fascinating, humorous conversations or meandering wastes of time.

To connect to an on-line service, you need communications software and a modem, and you generally pay an hourly fee for using the service. The information you receive, however, can be well worth the cost. Find out what hours are peak and off-peak for calling the service; peak rates can be two to three times the cost of off-peak rates.

Another kind of on-line service is a local bulletin-board service (BBS). BBSs allow you to leave messages that others can read and respond to and allow you to upload and download software. BBSs often keep a computer on-line so that you can leave messages at any time. Some BBSs cater to IBM-compatibles only, Macintoshes only, or other special areas (even non-computer related areas). Some charge a membership fee, but many are free. Contact your local user groups to find out about BBSs.

Appendix Summary

This appendix offers advice for planning for the future in four key areas: maintenance, upgrades, repair, and keeping up with new developments. The first section includes advice on how to maintain the different components of a computer system; the second section describes different ways in which you can upgrade your system; the third explains what to do when your computer needs repair—with or without a warranty in effect. The final section describes two ways to keep abreast of new products introduced for personal computers: computer magazines and on-line services. These sources help you obtain information about computing and locate people with interests similar to yours.

APPENDIX B

Vendor Information

Ambra
3200 Beechleaf Court
Raleigh, NC 27604-1063
Phone: 919-713-1550
Fax: 919-713-1599

Amdek
9020-II Capital of Texas Highway N.
Suite 400
Austin, TX 78759
Phone: 800-792-6335
Fax: 800-742-6335

American Power Conversion
132 Fairgrounds Road
West Kingston, RI 02892
Phone: 800-800-4APC
Fax: 401-789-3180

Anthro
10450 SW Manhasset Drive
Tualatin, OR 97062
Phone: 800-325-3841
Fax: 800-325-0045

Apple Computer, Inc.
20525 Mariani Avenue
Cupertino, CA 95014
Phone: 408-996-1010

ATI Technologies, Inc.
33 Commerce Valley Drive East
Thornhill, Ontario I3T 7N6
Canada
Phone: 905-882-2626 (Support)
       905-882-2600 (Office)
Fax: 905-882-2620

Austin Direct
2121 Energy Drive
Austin, TX 78758
Phone: 800-752-1577
Fax: 512-454-1357

Battery Technology
5700 Bandini Blvd.
Commerce, CA 90040
Phone: 213-728-7874
Fax: 213-728-7996

Brother International Corporation
200 Cottontail Lane
Somerset, NJ 08875-6714
Phone: 800-284-4357
       908-356-8880
Fax: 908-469-4415

Canon U.S.A., Inc.
One Canon Plaza
Lake Success, NY 11042
Phone: 800-848-4123

Cardinal Technologies, Inc.
1827 Freedom Road
Lancaster, PA 17601
Phone: 800-775-0899

CD Technology, Inc.
766 San Aleso Avenue
Sunnyvale, CA 94086
Phone: 408-752-8500
Fax: 408-752-8501

Chinon America, Inc.
615 Hawaii Avenue
Torrance, CA 90503
Phone: 310-533-0274
Fax: 310-533-1727

Citizen America Corporation
P.O. Box 4003
Santa Monica, CA 90411-4003
Phone: 310-453-0614 ext. 435 (Support)
       800-556-1234 ext. 34 (Literature)
Fax: 310-453-2814

Colorado Memory Systems
800 South Taft Avenue
Loveland, CO 80537
Phone: 303-669-8000
Fax: 303-667-0997

Compaq Computer Corporation
P.O. Box 692000
Houston, TX 77269-2000
Phone: 800-345-1518 (Dealer)
       800-652-6672 (Tech. Support)

Conner
36 Skyline Drive
Lake Mary, FL 32746
Phone: 407-263-3500
Fax: 407-263-3555

Creative Labs
1901 McCarthy Blvd.
Milpitas, CA 95035
Phone: 408-428-6600
       405-742-6622 (Support)
Fax: 408-428-6611

Curtis
30 Fitzgerald Drive
Jaffrey, NH 03452-1931
Phone: 603-532-4123
Fax: 800-955-5544

Dataproducts Corporation
6219 De Soto Avenue
P.O. Box 746
Woodland Hills, CA 91365-0746
Phone: 800-334-3174 (Literature Division)
       800-283-7227 (Support)
       818-887-8000
Fax: 818-887-4789

Dell Computer Corporation
9505 Arboretum Blvd.
Austin, TX 78759-7299
Phone: 800-879-3355
Fax: 512-338-8700

Diamond Computer Systems, Inc.
1130 E. Arques Avenue
Sunnyvale, CA 94086
Phone: 408-736-2000
Fax: 408-730-5750

Digital Equipment Corporation (DEC)
146 Main Street
Maynard, MA 01754-2571
Phone: 800-344-4825
Fax: 508-493-8780

Epson America, Inc.
20770 Madrona Avenue
Torrance, CA 90509-2842
Phone: 310-782-0770

Fujitsu Computer Products of America
2904 Orchard Pkwy.
San Jose, CA 95134
Phone: 800-626-4686
       408-432-6333
Fax: 408-894-1709

Gateway 2000
610 Gateway Drive
North Sioux City, SD 57049
Phone: 800-523-2000
Fax: 605-232-2023

GCC Technologies, Inc.
209 Burlington Road
Bedford, MA 01730-9143
Phone: 800-422-7777
Fax: 800-4GCC-FAX

Genoa Systems Corporation
75 E. Trimble Road
San Jose, CA 95131
Phone: 800-934-3662
　　　　408-432-9090
Fax: 408-434-0997

Global
2249 Windsor Court
Addison, IL 60101
Phone: 800-845-6225
　　　　708-627-8800
Fax: 708-627-1742

Global Village
685 East Middlefield Road
Mountain View, CA 94043
Phone: 800-736-4821 (Sales)
　　　　415-390-8200
Fax: 415-390-8282

Hayes Microcomputer Products, Inc.
5923 Peachtree Industrial Blvd.
Norcross, GA 30092
Phone: 800-96-HAYES
　　　　404-441-1617
Fax: 404-449-0087

Hewlett-Packard Company
19310 Pruneridge Avenue
Cupertino, CA 95014
Phone: 800-752-0900

Hitachi
1290 Wall Street W.
Lyndhurst, NJ 07071
Phone: 201-935-8980
Fax: 201-935-4869

House of Batteries
16512 Burke Lane
Huntington Beach, CA 92647
Phone: 800-432-3385
Fax: 714-375-0235

IBM PC Direct
3039 Cornwallis Road
Building 203-CC113
Research Triangle Park, NC 27709
Phone: 800-426-2968

Infogrip
1145 Eugenia Place
Ste. 201
Carpinteria, CA 93013
Phone: 805-566-1049
Fax: 805-566-1079

Intel Corporation
5200 Elam Young Parkway M.S. C03-07
Hillsboro, OR 97124-6497
Phone: 800-538-3373
       503-629-7354
Fax: 800-525-3019

Iomega
1821 West Iomega Way
Roy, UT 84067
Phone: 800-777-6654

Jefferson
23454 25th Avenue S.
Seattle, WA 98198
Phone: 206-824-1111
Fax: 206-824-0941

Kensington Microware, Ltd.
2855 Campus Drive
San Mateo, CA 94403
Phone: 800-535-4242
       415-572-2700
Fax: 415-572-9675

Keytronic
P.O. Box 14687
Spokane, WA 99214-0687
Phone: 509-928-8000
Fax: 509-927-5383

Kodak
901 Elm Grove Road
Rochester, NY 14653-5415
Phone: 800-344-0006

Kurta
3007 East Chambers
Phoenix, AZ 85040
Phone: 602-276-5533
Fax: 602-276-9007

LaserMaster
6900 Shady Oak Road
Eden Prairie, MN 55344
Phone: 612-944-9330
Fax: 612-944-0522

Lexmark International
1221 Alverser Drive
Midlothian, VA 23113
Phone: 800-438-2468
Fax: 800-522-3422

Liberty
375 Saratoga Ave, Ste. A.
San Jose, CA 95129-1339
Phone: 408-983-1127
Fax: 408-243-2885

Logitech, Inc.
6505 Kaiser Drive
Fremont, CA 94555
Phone: 800-231-7717
       510-795-8500
Fax: 510-792-8901

MAG InnoVision, Inc.
4392 Corporate Center Drive
Los Alamitos, CA 90720
Phone: 800-827-3998
       714-827-3998
Fax: 714-827-5522

Mannesmann Tally
P.O. Box 97018
Kent, WA 98064-9718
Phone: 206-251-5524
Fax: 206-251-5520

Media Vision
47300 Bayside Parkway
Fremont, CA 94538
Phone: 800-845-5870
Fax: 510-770-9592

Microsoft Corporation
One Microsoft Way
Redmond, WA 98052-6399
Phone: 800-426-9400
Fax: 206-883-8101

MicroSpeed, Inc.
5005 Brandin Court
Fremont, CA 94538-3140
Phone: 800-232-7888
       510-490-1403
Fax: 510-490-1665

MicroTek
3715 Doolittle Drive
Redondo Beach, CA 90278
Phone: 800-654-4160
       310-297-5000
Fax: 310-297-5050
     310-297-5101 (Automated FaxBack System)

MicroTouch
300 Griffin Park
Methuen, MA 01844
Phone: 508-659-9000
Fax: 508-659-9100

Mitsubishi Electronics America, Inc.
(Information Systems Division)
5665 Plaza Drive
Cypress, CA 90603-0007
Phone: 800-843-2515
       714-220-2500
Fax: 714-236-6172

Mouse Systems Corporation
47505 Seabridge Drive
Fremont, CA 94538
Phone: 510-656-1117
Fax: 510-770-1924

Multi-Tech Systems, Inc.
2205 Woodale Drive
Mounds View, MN 55112
Phone: 800-328-9717
612-785-3500
Fax: 612-785-9874

NEC Technologies, Inc.
1414 Massachusetts Avenue
Boxborough, MA 01719
Phone: 800-632-4636
508-264-8000
Fax: 508-264-8245

Nikon Electronic Imaging
1300 Walt Whitman Road
Melville, NY 11747-3064
Phone: 516-547-4355
800-526-4566
Fax: 516-547-0305

Okidata Corporation (Division of
Oki America, Inc.)
532 Fellowship Road
Mt. Laurel, NJ 08054
Phone: 800-654-3282
609-235-2600
Fax: 609-778-4184

Orchid Technology, Inc.
45365 Northport Loop West
Fremont, CA 94538
Phone: 800-767-2443
510-683-0300
Fax: 510-490-9312

Panasonic Communications & Systems Company
1707 North Randall Road
Elgin, IL 60123
Phone: 800-447-4700 (Service)
       708-468-4900
       800-222-0584 (Tech. Support)

Plextor
4255 Burton Drive
Santa Clara, CA 95054
Phone: 408-980-1838
Fax: 408-986-1010

Pinnacle Micro
19 Technology
Irvine, CA 92718
Phone: 714-727-3300
Fax: 714-727-1913

Polaroid
1 Upland Road N2
Norwood, MA 02062
Phone: 800-225-2770
       800-225-1618
Fax: 617-446-4600

Power Express
4976 Stuckey Drive
San Jose, CA 95124-5120
Phone: 800-769-3739
       408-559-4848
Fax: 408-559-5969

Practical Peripherals, Inc.
375 Conejo Ridge Avenue
Thousand Oaks, CA 91361
Phone: 800-442-4774
Fax: 805-374-7200

Procom Technology, Inc.
2181 Dupont Drive
Irvine, CA 92715
Phone: 800-800-8600
       714-852-1000
Fax: 714-852-1221

QMS, Inc.
One Magnum Pass
Mobile, AL 36618
Phone: 205-639-4400
        800-523-2696 (Product Information Line)
Fax: 205-633-4866

Radius Inc.
1710 Fortune Drive
San Jose, CA 95131
Phone: 800-227-2795
Fax: 408-954-1927

RasterOps Corporation
2500 Walsh Avenue
Santa Clara, CA 95051
Phone: 800-729-2050
        408-562-4200
Fax: 408-986-1362

Samsung Information Systems America, Inc.
105 Challenger Road
Ridgefield Park, NJ 07660-0510
Phone: 201-229-4000
Fax: 201-229-4110

Sharp Electronics
Sharp Plaza
Mahwah, NJ 07430
Phone: 800-237-4277

Sony Corporation of America
3300 Zanker Road
San Jose, CA 95134
Phone: 800-352-7669
        408-432-0190
Fax: 408-943-0740

Star Micronics America, Inc.
420 Lexington Avenue, Ste. 2702
New York, NY 10170
Phone: 800-447-4700

SuperMac Technology
215 Moffett Park Drive
Sunnyvale, CA 94089
Phone: 408-541-6100
Fax: 408-541-6150

Supra
7101 Supra Drive SW
Albany, OR 97321
Phone: 503-967-2400
Fax: 503-967-2401

SyQuest
47071 Bayside Parkway
Fremont, CA 94538
Phone: 800-245-2278
Fax: 510-226-4102

Tektronix, Inc.
P.O. Box 1000
MS 63-630
Wilsonville, OR 97070-1000
Phone: 800-835-6100
Fax: 503-682-2980

Texas Instruments Incorporated
P.O. Box 6102
MS 3255
Temple, TX 76503
Phone: 800-527-3500

Toshiba America Information Systems, Inc.
P. O. Box 19724
Irvine, CA 92713-9724
Phone: 800-334-3445
       714-583-3000
Fax: 714-583-3140

UDS Motorola
5000 Bradford Drive
Huntsville, AL 35805
Phone: 800-451-2369
Fax: 205-430-8926

UMAX
3353 Gateway Blvd.
Fremont, CA 94538
Phone: 510-651-8883
Fax: 510-651-8834

U.S. Robotics, Inc.
8100 North McCormick Blvd.
Skokie, IL 60076-2999
Phone: 800-342-5877
Fax: 708-982-5800

ViewSonic
20480 Business Pkwy.
Walnut, CA 91789
Phone: 800-888-8583
       909-468-5800
Fax: 909-468-5838

Western Digital Corporation
8105 Irvine Center Drive
Irvine, CA 92718
Phone: 800-832-4778
       714-932-4900
Fax: 714-932-4012

Zeos International
1301 Industrial Blvd. NE
Minneapolis, MN 55413
Phone: 800-423-5891
       612-623-9614
Fax: 612-633-1325

Zoom Telephonics
207 South Street
Boston, MA 02111
Phone: 800-666-6191
Fax: 617-423-9231

ZyXel
4920 East La Palma Avenue
Anaheim, CA 92807
Phone: 714-693-0808
Fax: 714-693-0705

INDEX

14,400 bps (bits per second) fax speeds, 276
16-bit/32-bit external interfaces, processors, 39
24-pin dot-matrix printers, 226
2,400 bps (bits per second) fax speeds, 276
486 and Pentium-based portable PCs, 120-134
486DX-based IBM-compatibles, 102-104
486DX2-based IBM-compatibles, 104-110
486DX4-based IBM-compatibles, 112-114
486SX-based IBM-compatibles, 96-100
601/603/604 chips (PowerPC), 47
6100 Power Macintoshes, 140
680X0-based Macintoshes, 136-138
68882 math coprocessor, 46
7100/66 Power Macintosh, 140
80286 microprocessor, 41
80386 microprocessor, 42
80386SX microprocessor, 41
80486 microprocessor, 43
8086 microprocessor, 41
8088 microprocessor, 40-41
80X86-compatible microprocessors, 44
8100 Power Macintoshes, 140

A

ABCOM wrist pads, 259
acceleration of Windows performance, 158
accounting programs, 21
accuracy and PCs, 12
Acer America PCs, 90
active-matrix screens, portable PCs, 163
Adobe PostScript laser printers, 211
ALSoft Disk Express II, 418

Ambra Corp., 85, 433
   486 and Pentium-based portable PCs, 120
   486DX2-based PCs, 104
   486DX4-based PCs, 112
   486SX-based PCs, 96
   Pentium-based PCs, 116
   subnotebooks/PDAs, 148
AMD coprocessors, 45
Amdek monitors, 176, 180, 433
America Online, 431
American Power Conversion, 433
   surge protectors, 362
   UPS, 363
AMLCD (active-matrix LCD), portable PCs, 164
annual reports, 20
Anthro, 433
anti-glare screens, 256-257
anti-glare visors for monitors, 262
anti-radiation screens, 257
Apple Computer, Inc., 83, 433
   authorized dealer repair centers, 428
   CD-ROM drives, 308
   color flatbed scanners, 356
   dot-matrix printers, 228
   inkjet printers, 232
   large monitors, 182
   Macintosh, 83
      display standards, 167-169
      operating systems, 69
   medium monitors, 180
   microprocessor upgrades, 423
   office laser printers, 242
   personal laser printers, 238
   PowerBooks, 69
   Power Macs, 83
   scanners, 353, 356
   small monitors, 176
   subnotebooks/PDAs, 148
   system setup assistance, 403

AppleTalk, 22
applications, 58, 406
    see also programs; software
archival file storage, 418
AST Research PCs, 86
ATI Technologies, Inc., graphics adapters, 188, 434
audio boards for CD-ROMs, 305
Austin Direct portable PCs, 122, 434
authorized dealer repair centers, 428
AUTOEXEC.BAT file, device drivers, 58

B

back pain, 261
back rests, 264
Backpack QIC 80 drive (Micro Solutions), 335
backup UPSs, 362
backup utilities, 335
backups of hard drives, 416
batteries, 366-368, 415
Battery Technology batteries, 367, 434
BBSs (bulletin-board services), 432
Bernoulli external storage drives, 317-318, 377
BIOS (Basic Input/Output System), motherboards, 48
bits, processor handling, 39
black-and-white scanning, 351, 354-356
blackouts, protecting against, 362
bps (bits per second), fax speeds, 276
brands of computers, 63
Brother International Corp., 434
    dot-matrix printers, 228
    inkjet printers, 232
    office laser printers, 244
    personal laser printers, 238
brownouts, protecting against, 362
budget considerations for PC purchase, 64
buffers for printers, 224
built-in video, Macintosh, 156
buses, 51
business uses for PCs, 26-27
buyer's checklist, 407-412
Byte magazine, User's Column, 14

C

caches
    CD-ROM drives, 307
    microprocessors, 48

Caere scanners, 354
CalComp thermal wax color printers, 248
Canon U.S.A., Inc., 434
    486-and Pentium-based portable PCs, 124
    486DX2-based PCs, 106
    486SX-based PCs, 96
    inkjet printers, 232
    office laser printers, 244
    personal laser printers, 238
Cardinal Technologies, Inc., 434
    modems, 280
    sound cards, 342
carpal tunnel syndrome, 258
cartridge drives, 315-317
CD Technology, Inc., 434
CD-only software, 303
CD-ROM drives, 54, 304-305
    gaming systems, 383
    IBM-compatibles, 306, 374
    Macintosh, 306, 374
    manufacturer/model listings, 307-312
    portable PCs, 380
    sound cards, 342
    technological problems, 305
CD-ROM XA, 305
CDTechnology CD-ROM drives, 308
Central Point Software
    Anti-Virus, 417
    backup utilities, 335
    hard drive backup programs, 417
    Mac Tools Deluxe, 418-420
    PC Tools Deluxe, 420
Centronics parallel ports, dot-matrix printers, 199
Check It (Touchstone Software), 420
checklist for PC buyers, 407-412
Chinon America, Inc., CD-ROM drives, 308, 435
chip sets for video, 167
Citizen America Corp., 435
    dot-matrix printers, 228
    inkjet printers, 234
    thermal printers, 226
Clean Screen screen cleaner (Curtis Manufacturing), 418
clip art, 24
clock speed, processors, 38
CMOS chip battery maintenance, 416
CMS (Colorado Memory Systems) tape backup systems, 335-336, 435

Index **449**

college uses for PCs, 28
color monitors, 161
color printers, 214-218, 248-250
   dot-matrix printers, 203, 227
   drivers, 217
   graphics, 216
   inkjet printers, 208, 232
   laser printers, 214-215
   manufacturers, 217
   memory, 217
   paper handling, 217
   presentations, 221
   prices, 216
   resolutions, 216
color scanners, 351, 354-356
colors, video memory support, 159-160
command-line interfaces, DOS, 66
communications and PC capabilities, 27
Compaq Computer Corp., 83-84, 435
   486-and Pentium-based portable PCs, 124
   486DX2-based PCs, 106
   486SX-based PCs, 98
   authorized dealer repair centers, 428
   QVision video accelerator, 84
   subnotebooks/PDAs, 148
compatibility
   microprocessors, 39
   monitors/video adapters, 174
   software/hardware, 79
compilers, 26
compression
   CD-ROMs, 305
   modems, 276
CompuServe, 431
Computer Craft, 431
computer dealerships, 387-390
computer games, 24
computer magazines, 430
Computer Shopper, 430
computer superstores, 393-395
CONFIG.SYS file, device drivers, 58
configuration of systems, 403
Conner tape backup systems, 336, 435
consumer electronics stores, PC purchases, 396-398
conventional memory, 50
coprocessors
   graphics, 188
   math, 42, 46, 383, 423
   spreadsheet programs, 383

cost benefits of PCs, 13
Creative Labs, 435
   sound cards, 342
   SoundBlaster sound card, 341
credit cards, PC purchases, 413
cross-platform PC operations, 26, 40
Curtis Manufacturing, 435
   Clean Screen screen cleaner, 418
   floppy drive cleaning kits, 416
   wrist rests, 259
Cyrix
   80X86-compatible coprocessors, 45
   math coprocessors, 42

D

data compression and modems, 276
data storage on PCs, 18
database programs, 21-22, 171
Dataproducts Corp. color inkjet printers, 248, 436
dealer repair centers, 428
DEC (Digital Equipment Corp.), 89, 436
   486-and Pentium-based portable PCs, 124
   486DX-based PCs, 102
   486DX2-based PCs, 106
   486DX4-based PCs, 112
   486SX-based PCs, 98
   dot-matrix printers, 228
   office laser printers, 244
   Pentium-based PCs, 116
   personal laser printers, 238
Dell Computer Corp., 436
   486-and Pentium-based portable PCs, 126
   486DX4-based PCs, 112
   486SX-based PCs, 98
   mail-order PCs, 88
   Pentium-based PCs, 116
   system setup assistance, 403
department stores and PC purchases, 398-399
desks, ergonomically-sound, 262
desktop PCs, 372-378
desktop publishing programs, 20
   display recommendations, 171
   printers, 220
   system recommendations, 382
diagnostic software, 420
Diamond Computer Systems, Inc., 436
   graphics adapters, 190
   sound cards, 344

digital recording, sound cards, 340
DIP (dual-in-line package) memory chips, 50
direct PC purchases (mail order), 88
discharging batteries before charging, 367
disk drives, 52-55
Disk Express II (ALSoft), 418
Disk First Aid (Macintosh), 420
disk-optimizing, 417
displays, 155, 165-169
docking bays on portable PCs, 73, 381
documents, word processors, 19
DOS operating system, 64-67
    startup description, 59
    training in system use, 406
    word processors, 382
dot pitch of monitors, 162, 174
dot-matrix printers, 198-204, 226-230
    color, 227
    color printing, 203
    draft speed, 200
    drivers, 201
    emulation, 227
    Epson, 203
    fonts, 201
    graphics, 201
    manufacturers, 204
    memory, 203
    noise level, 227
    paper handling, 202
    resolution, 200
    speeds, 200, 227
double-speed CD-ROM drives, 304
draw programs, 23
drive bays, 56
drive controller problems (floppy drives), 416
drivers, 58
    color printers, 217
    dot-matrix printers, 201
    inkjet printers, 206
    laser printers, 212
    scanners, 352
    video display, 169
drum of laser printers, 209
DSPs (digital signal processors), sound cards, 340
dye sublimation color printers, 215
dynamic RAM, 49

E

E-Machines
    monitors, 180, 184
    Macintosh graphics adapters, 192
e-mail, files transfers, 66
educational software, 25, 172, 383
EISA bus standard, 51, 84
Electronic Musician, 431
electronics stores and PC purchases, 396-398
emulation
    and printers, 227, 237
    software, 83
Epson America, Inc., 436
    color flatbed scanners, 356
    dot-matrix printers, 203, 228
    inkjet printers, 234
    personal laser printers, 238
ergonomic equipment, 255, 261
ergonomic mice, 258
expanded memory, 51
expansion slots, 51-52, 372
extended memory, 51
extensions, 58
external CD-ROM drives, 307
external hard drives, 315-317
external interfaces, 16-bit/32-bit processors, 39
external modems, 276
external storage devices, 317-330
eyestrain, 256

F

Fargo dye sublimation color printers, 248
fax modems, 275
Fifth Generation Systems
    Fastback Plus for the Mac, 417
    Fastback Plus program, 417
    Mace Utilities, 420
files
    archival storage, 418
    AUTOEXEC.BAT, device drivers, 58
    CONFIG.SYS, device drivers, 58
    MIDI, 340
financial viability of vendors, 81
Finder (Macintosh), 69
firmware (ROM), 57
flat screens on monitors, 175

flat-file databases, 21
flatbed scanners, 349-351, 356
floor-standing tower systems, 56
floppy drives, 53
    IBM-compatibles, 373
    Macintosh, 373
    maintenance, 416
    portable PCs, 379
    realigning, 416
floptical drives, 316-317
FM synthesis, sound cards, 340
fonts
    dot-matrix printers, 201
    inkjet printers, 206
    laser printers, 211
    printers, 225
footrests, 263
fragmentation of hard drives, 417
Fujitsu external storage drives, 318, 436
full-page monitors, 161

G

games, 24, 172, 383
gas plasma displays, portable PCs, 164
Gateway
    486DX-based PCs, 102
    subnotebooks/PDAs, 148
Gateway 2000, 90, 436
    486- and Pentium-based portable PCs, 126
    486DX2-based PCs, 108
    486DX4-based PCs, 114
    486SX-based PCs, 98
    Pentium-based PCs, 118
Gazelle Systems OPTune program, 417
GCC Technologies, Inc., 437
    dye sublimation color printers, 248
    thermal printers, 226
GEnie, 431
Genoa Systems Corp, 437
Gibson Research, SpinRite program, 417
Global, 437
    mouse wrist rest, 260
    surge protectors, 365
    UPS, 365
    wrist rests, 259
Global Village modems, 280, 437
grammar checkers, 12
graphics
    color printers, 216
    coprocessors, 188
    display recommendations, 171

    dot-matrix printers, 201
    laser printers, 211
    processors, 426
graphics adapters, 173, 188-194
graphics programs, 23
graphics tablets, 267
graphs in spreadsheet programs, 20
grayscale monitors, 161
grayscale scanners, 351, 354-356
groupware, 22
GUI (graphical user interface), 23
    display recommendations, 171
    Macintosh, 83
    Microsoft Windows, 68

H

hand-held scanners, 350-351, 354
hand/finger-related pain, 258
happy Mac icon, 59
hard drives, 53
    external, 315-317
    failure prevention, 417
    IBM-compatibles, 374
    Macintosh, 374
    maintenance, 416-418
    portable PCs, 379
    spreadsheet programs, 383
    upgrades, 424-425
hardware
    compatibility with software, 79
    phone support, 79, 404-405
    service and support policies of vendors, 79-80
    upgrades, 421-427
Hayes Microcomputer Products, Inc., modems, 280, 437
Hewlett-Packard Company, 437
    inkjet printers, 236
    office laser printers, 244
    PCs, 90
    personal laser printers, 238
    scanners, 353, 356
    subnotebooks/PDAs, 150
high-end desktop PCs, 377-378
high-end portable PCs, 381
Hitachi CD-ROM drives, 308, 437
Home Office Computing, 430
home uses for PCs, 28
home-office operating environment considerations, 65
House of Batteries batteries, 367, 438

I

IBM Corp.
    486-and Pentium-based portable PCs, 128-130
    486DX-based PCs, 102
    486DX2-based PCs, 110
    486DX4-based PCs, 114
    486SX-based PCs, 100
    authorized dealer repair centers, 428
    dot-matrix printers, 228
    inkjet printers, 236
    Intel microprocessors, 40-44
    office laser printers, 244
    OS/2 operating system, 64, 71
    PCs, 84-85
    Pentium-based PCs, 118
    personal laser printers, 240
    PS/1 and PS/2 PCs, 85
    subnotebooks/PDAs, 150
    Valuepoint PCs, 85
    XGA (Extended Graphics Array), 166
IBM PC Direct, 438
IBM Personal Computer Company, 84
IBM-compatibles, 64
    486DX-based, 102-104
    486DX2-based, 104-110
    486DX4-based, 112-114
    486SX-based, 96-100
    buyer's checklist, 408-410
    CD-ROM drives, 54, 306, 374
    Compaq, 83
    display standards, 166-167
    expansion bus, 51
    floppy drives, 53, 373
    graphics adapters, 189-192
    hard drives, 53, 374
    hard drive backup programs, 417
    keyboards/mouse, 375
    low-end models, 376
    manufacturer/specification listings, 93
    math coprocessors, 423
    memory upgrades, 422
    microprocessors, 372, 423
    modems, 278
    monitors, 173
    operating systems, 67
    Pentium-based, 116-118
    portable PCs, 378
    ports, 55
    power supply, 56
    ROM BIOS, 48
    self-repair, 430
    sound cards, 339
    Super VGA video support, 156
    tape backup systems, 334
    training in system use, 405-406
    upgrades, 421-422
    used systems, 385
    VGA video support, 156
    word processors, 382
icons, happy Mac, 59
IIT math coprocessors, 42
in-line UPSs, 362
in-warranty repairs, 427-428
InfoGrip BAT keyboard, 260, 438
information storage and PCs, 12, 18
InfoWorld, **431**
injuries, preventing with ergonomic equipment, 255
inkjet printers, 230-236, 375
    color, 232
    drivers, 206
    fonts, 206
    graphics, 206
    manufacturers, 208
    memory, 207
    noise level, 233
    paper handling, 207
    prices, 205
    print quality, 205
    resolution, 205
    speed of printing, 205
input devices, 267, 375, 380
installation of systems, 403
Intel Corp., 438
    math coprocessors, 42
    microprocessors, 39-45
    modems, 282
interfaces, CD-ROM drives, 307
interlaced monitors, 163
internal CD-ROM drives, 307
internal modems, 276
IOMEGA, 438
    external storage drives, 317-320
    tape backup systems, 336
ISA bus, 51, 85
ISO 9660 CD-ROM drives, 305

J-K

Jefferson Company ergonomic keyboards, 260, 438
Kensington Microware, Ltd., 438
    mice/trackballs, 268
    surge protectors, 363
    UPS, 364
keyboards, 374
    maintenance, 418
    ports, 55
    portable PCs, 380
    upgrades, 425
KeyTronic, 439
    ergonomic keyboards, 260
    ergonomic mice, 268
    trackballs, 261, 268
Kodak dye sublimation color printers, 248, 439
Kurta graphics tablets/PenMouse, 270, 439

L

LANs (local-area networks), 22
large monitors, 173, 182-186
laser printers, 208-214, 375
    color printing, 214
    drivers, 212
    drum, 209
    fonts, 211
    graphics, 211
    manufacturers, 214
    memory, 213
    paper handling, 212
    PCL (printer control language), 211
    prices, 210
    print quality, 210
    printer engine, 209
    printing speed, 210
    resolution, 210
LaserMaster printers, 439
    color inkjet, 248
    office laser, 246
    personal laser, 240
LC Macintoshes, 136
LCDs (liquid crystal display), portable PC screens, 163
letter-quality speed, dot-matrix printers, 200
LexMark International office laser printers, 246, 439

Liberty, 439
    CD-ROM drives, 310
    external storage drives, 320-322
light-emitting diode (LED) array printers, 210
line-art scanning, 351
liquid-crystal shutter (LCS) printers, 210
Lithium Ion batteries, portable PCs, 367
local bus video, 157
Logitech, Inc., 439
    child mouse, 270
    ergonomic input devices, 258
    mice, 270
    scanners, 354-356
    sound cards, 344
    trackball, 270
long-term upgrade strategies, 426-427
Lotus Notes program, 23
low-end PCs, 376
low-end portable PCs, 380
low-power microprocessors, 45
lumbar rolls, 264

M

Mac Tools Deluxe (Central Point Software), 417-420
Mace Utilities (Fifth Generation Systems), 420
Macintosh (Apple), 83
    680X0-based desktop models, 136-138
    built-in video, 156
    buyer's checklist, 410-412
    CD-ROM drives, 54, 306, 374
    Disk First Aid, 420
    display standards, 167-169
    expansion bus, 52
    floppy drives, 53, 373
    graphics adapters, 192-194
    happy Mac icon, 59
    hard drives, 54, 374
    low-end models, 376
    magazines, 431
    manufacturer/specification listings, 93
    math coprocessors, 423
    memory upgrades, 422
    microprocessors, 46, 372, 423
    modems, 278
    monitors, 173
    operating system, 69
    PDS (processor direct slot) slot, 373

portable PCs, 140-146, 378
ports, 55
power supply, 56
ROM, 49
self-repair, 430
small monitors, 176
system setup assistance, 403
systems, 64
tape backup systems, 334
training in system use, 405-406
upgrades, 421
used systems, 385
video support, 373
word processing systems, 382
macros, 25
MAG InnoVision, Inc., 439
large monitors, 184
medium monitors, 180
small monitors, 176
magazines on computers, 430
magneto-optical (MO) drives, 316-317
mail order PC purchases, 88, 388, 390-393
maintenance of PC systems, 415-420
Mannesmann Tally, 440
dot-matrix printers, 228
office laser printers, 246
thermal printers, 226
manufacturers
color printers, 217
dot-matrix printers, 204
inkjet printers, 208
laser printers, 214
PCs, 77, 81
math coprocessors, 42, 46, 383, 423
Maynard Electronics tape backup systems, 335
MCA (Micro Channel Architecture) bus, 51, 84
McAffee VirusScan for the PC, 417
Media Vision sound cards, 344, 440
medium monitors, 178-182
memory
color printers, 217
conventional, 50
DIP (dual-in-line package) chips, 50
dot-matrix printers, 203
expanded/extended, 51
inkjet printers, 207
laser printers, 213
low-end PCs, 376

mid-range PCs, 373
personal laser printers, 237
portable PCs, 379
SIMMs (single-in-line memory modules), 50
SIP (single-in-line package) chips, 50
spreadsheet programs, 383
upgrading, 422
video adapter, 159
virtual, 51
MHz (megahertz), processor speeds, 38
Micro Solutions Backpack QIC 80 drive, 335
microprocessor cache of motherboards, 48
microprocessors, 372
16-bit/32-bit external interfaces, 39
compatibility, 39
Intel, 39-44
low-power, 45
Motorola, 39, 46
NEC, 41
personal laser printers, 237
PowerPC, 40, 46
spreadsheet uses, 383
superscalar, 38
upgrading, 423-424
Microsoft Corp., 440
DOS operating system, 66
Microsoft Windows, 64, 68
sound cards, 344
trackball/mouse, 270
Windows NT, 64, 68, 71
MicroSpeed trackball/mouse, 270, 440
MicroTek scanners, 354-358, 440
MicroTouch touchscreen, 272, 440
mid-range PCs, 372
mid-range portable PCs, 378
mid-size monitors, 173
MIDI (Musical Instrument Digital Interface), 340
mini-tower systems, 56
minimum specifications
DOS systems, 67
Microsoft Windows, 68
Microsoft Windows NT, 71
OS/2 operating system (IBM), 71
Mirror
CD-ROM drives, 310
external storage drives, 322-324
tape backup systems, 336

Mitsubishi Electronics America, Inc.,
    monitors, 176, 180, 184, 440
MMCD, CD-ROM drives, 305
modems, 275-278
monitor arms, 262
monitors, 160-165, 173-174, 375
    anti-glare visors, 262
    display standards, 165-169
    dot pitch, 162
    flat screens, 175
    maintenance, 418
    monochrome, 161, 175
    portable PCs, 162-163, 380
    radiation from, 256-257
    Radius Pivot, 383
    resolution, 161
    scan rate, 162
    spreadsheet programs, 383
    tilt-swivel bases, 175
motherboards, 47-52
Motorola microprocessors, 39, 46
mouse, 267-268, 374
    ergonomic, 258
    maintenance, 418
    on-screen movement, 23
    ports, 55
    portable PCs, 380
    upgrades, 425
Mouse Systems Corp., 441
MPC standard, CD-ROM drives, 305
Multi-Tech Systems, Inc., 441
multimedia
    authoring systems, 384
    display recommendations, 171
    programs, 24
    sound cards, 340
multiscanning monitors, 163
multisession CD-ROMs, 304
multisynchronous monitors, 163
MultiTech modems, 284

N

name recognition in PC purchasing, 78
NEC Technologies, Inc., 91, 441
    CD-ROM drives, 310
    large monitors, 184
    medium monitors, 180
    microprocessors, 41
    office laser printers, 246
    personal laser printers, 240
    small monitors, 176
networking, 22
networks and modems, 278
newsletters, 20
NiCad batteries for portable PCs, 366
Nikon color flatbed scanners, 358
Nikon Electronic Imaging, 441
NiMH batteries for portable PCs, 367
noise levels
    dot-matrix printers, 227
    inkjet printers, 233
noninterlaced monitors, 163
Norton (Symantec)
    Anti-Virus for the PC, 417
    backup utilities, 335
    Norton Utilities, 417, 420
NuBus slots for Macs, 52

O

OCR (optical character recognition),
    scanners, 349
office laser printers, 242-246
office uses for PCs, 26-27
office-home operating environment
    considerations, 65
Okidata Corp., 441
on-line services, 22, 277, 431
operating systems
    DOS, 66
    environments, 63, 371
    IBM OS/2, 71
    IBM-compatibles, 67
    Macintosh, 69
    Microsoft Windows, 68
    Microsoft Windows NT, 71
    software, 57
optical drives, 377
optimizing programs for hard drives, 417
OPTune (Gazelle Systems), 417
Orchid Technology, Inc., 441
    IBM-compatible graphics adapters, 190
    sound cards, 344
OS/2 operating system (IBM), 64
    high-end systems, 377
    minimum specifications, 71
    training in system use, 406
out-of-warranty repairs, 428

P

Packard Bell PCs, 87
pain, hand/finger-related, 258
paint programs, 23
palmtops, 74
Panasonic Communications & Systems Company, 442
    external storage drives, 324
    printers, 230, 240, 246
    scanners, 356-358
paper handling
    color printers, 217
    dot-matrix printers, 202
    inkjet printers, 207
    laser printers, 212
paper sizes for printing, 224
parallel ports, 55
    dot-matrix printers, 199
    printer connections, 224
PC Fullback+ (West Lake Data), 417
PC Magazine, 430
PC Tools Deluxe (Central Point Software), 417, 420
PCC use, training in, 14, 405-406
PC Week, 431
PC World, 431
PCI bus, 52
PCI local bus slot, 373
PCL (printer control language), laser printers, 211
PCMCIA
    cards, 52
    modems, 277
    slots for portable PCs, 379
PCs
    desktop models, 372-378
    repair, 427-430
    top manufacturers, 81-91
PDAs (personal digital assistants), 74, 146-152
PDS (processor direct slot) slot, 52, 373
Pentium processors (Intel), 43
    IBM-compatibles, 116-118
    portable PCs, 120-134
performance considerations in PC purchases, 78
personal finance programs, 21
personal laser printers, 236-240
personal need and PC purchase, 30

phone support
    hardware/software, 79
    system setup, 404-405
Photo CDs, multisession, 305
Pinnacle external storage drives, 324-326, 442
Plextor CD-ROM drives, 310, 442
PMLCD (passive-matrix LCD), portable PCs, 164
pointing devices, 267
Polaroid, 442
portable PCs, 27, 73-75, 378-381
    486- and Pentium-based, 120-134
    batteries, 366-368
    CD-ROM drives, 380
    docking bays, 73, 381
    drives, 379
    ergonomic input devices, 258
    fax modems, 277
    high-end, 381
    IBM-compatibles, 408
    keyboards, 380
    low-end, 380
    Macintosh, 140-146, 169
    manufacturer/specification listings, 93
    memory, 379
    monitors, 162-163, 380
    mouse, 380
    PCMCIA slots, 379
    trackballs, 380
    used systems, 385
    video support, 157
portrait monitors, 161
ports, 55
PostScript (Adobe) printers, 211, 216, 375
Power Express batteries, 367, 442
Power Macintosh (Apple), 83, 140
power supply for computers, 56, 361
power surge protection, 361
PowerBooks (Apple), 69, 142-146
PowerPC microprocessors, 40, 46
Practical Peripherals, Inc., modems, 288, 442
presentation programs, 23
presentations and color printers, 221
preventing injuries with ergonomic equipment, 255
preventive PC maintenance, 415-420
prices
    color printers, 216
    dot-matrix printers, 199

inkjet printers, 205
laser printers, 210
PC purchases, 78
print quality
    inkjet printers, 205
    laser printers, 210
printer drivers, 201
printer engine, laser printers, 209
printers, 29, 197-198, 223, 375
    buffers, 224
    color, 203, 208, 219
    desktop publishing, 220
    dot-matrix, 198-204
    emulation, 224
    fonts, 225
    inkjet, 204-208
    laser, 208-214
    maintenance, 418-419
    noise levels, 225
    paper sizes, 224
    purchasing guidelines, 218
    reports, 221
    resolution, 224
    serial/parallel port connections, 224
    speeds, 224
    spreadsheets, 221
    warranties, 225
    word processing, 220, 382
problems with systems, 420
processors, 372
    IBM-compatible PCs, 372
    Macintosh, 372
    portable PCs, 378
    upgrading, 423-424
    see also microprocessors
PROCOM Technology, Inc., 442
    CD-ROM drives, 312
    external storage drives, 326-328
    tape backup systems, 336
Prodigy, 431
programming, 25
programs, 58
    accounting, 21
    Check It (Touchstone Software), 420
    database management, 21-22
    desktop publishing, 20
    determining needs, 65
    Disk Express II (ALSoft), 418
    draw, 23
    educational, 25

    Fastback Plus (Fifth Generation Systems), 417
    graphics, 23
    Lotus Notes, 23
    Mac Tools Deluxe (Central Point Software), 418-420
    Mace Utilities (Fifth Generation Systems), 420
    modem/communications, 29
    multimedia, 24
    Norton Utilities (Symantec), 417, 420
    OPTune (Gazelle Systems), 417
    paint, 23
    PC Fullback+ (West Lake Data), 417
    PC Tools Deluxe (Central Point Software), 420
    personal finance, 21
    presentation, 23
    SpinRite (Gibson Research), 417
    spreadsheet, 18, 20-21, 382-383
    Symantec anti-virus, 417
    tax, 21
    training in use, 406
    word processing, 19-20
    XTree Pro Gold (XTree), 418
    see also applications; software
PS/1, PS/2 PCs (IBM), 85
***Publish* magazine, 431**
purchasing PCs, 30-32

Q

QMS, Inc., color printers, 248
Quadra Macintosh models, 136-138
quality of work with PCs, 11
QVision video accelerator (Compaq), 84

R

radiation from monitors, 256-257
Radius Inc., 443
    Macintosh graphics adapters, 192
    monitors, 383
        large, 184
        small, 178
RAM (random-access memory)
    graphics adapters, 188
    motherboards, 49
RasterOps Corp., 443
    IBM-compatible graphics adapters, 190
    large monitors, 184

Macintosh graphics adapters, 194
medium monitors, 180
small monitors, 178
realigning floppy disk drives, 416
recording, sound cards, 340
records
databases, 21
storage and PCs, 12
refresh rates for monitors, 174
registration of software, 419
relational databases, 22
removable cartridge drives, 315-317
repairing PCs, 427-430
repetitive tasks and PCs, 12
resolution
color printers, 216
dot-matrix printers, 200
graphics adapters, 188
inkjet printers, 205
laser printers, 210
monitors, 161, 174
personal laser printers, 237
portable PCs, 163, 379
printers, 224
scanners, 350-352
video memory support, 159-160
retail purchases, 86
ROM (read-only memory)
firmware, 57
motherboards, 48

S

sales brochures, 20
sales channels for PC purchases, 80
SAM AntiVirus for the Macintosh, 417
Samsung Information Systems of America, Inc., 443
scan rate of monitors, 162
scanners, 349
Apple, 353
black-and-white, 351
color, 351
components of/operations, 349-353
drivers, 352
flatbed, 349
grayscale, 351
hand held, 350
Hewlett-Packard, 353
listings of manufacturers, 353-358
resolution, 352

screen shades, 256
screens, 161, 174
anti-glare/radiation, 256-257
flat, 175
MicroTouch touchscreen, 272
portable PCs, 379
SCSI ports/tape drives, 52, 55
seek time, CD-ROM drives, 304
Sega Genesis, 383
Seiko dye sublimation color printers, 250
self-repair of PCs, 430
serial ports, 55, 199, 224
service/support policies of hardware/ software vendors, 79-80
setup of systems, 403
setup programs, battery replacement, 416
shared modems, 277
sharing work over networks, 22
Sharp Electronics, 443
SIMMs (single-in-line memory modules), 50
single-pass scanning, 351
SIP (single-in-line package) memory chips, 50
sizes of screens, 174
slots for expansion, 372
small monitors, 173-178
software, 57-58
CD-only, 303
compatibility with hardware, 79
diagnostic, 420
emulation, 83
maintenance, 419-420
modem control, 276
modem/communications, 29
phone support, 79, 404-405
purchasing from computer dealerships, 390
service and support policies, 79-80
sound mixers, 341
tape backup, 334
training in use, 406
upgrades, 420
video display drivers, 169
see also applications;programs
solid ink color printers, 215
Sony Corp. of America, 443
sound connectors, 55

sound cards, 339-341
    CD-ROM drives, 342
    DSPs (digital signal processors), 340
    gaming systems, 384
    recording, 340
SoundBlaster sound card (Creative Labs), 341
speed considerations
    microprocessors, 38
    modems, 276
    printing, 200, 205, 224, 227
spell-checkers, 12
SpinRite (Gibson Research), 417
spreadsheet programs, 18-21, 171, 221, 382-383
Star Micronics dot-matrix printers, 230, 443
static RAM, 49
stereo sound cards, 341
STN (Supertwist-nematic), portable PCs, 164
storage devices, external units, 315-316
subnotebooks, 74, 146-152
Super Nintendo, 383
Super VGA video support, IBM-compatibles, 156, 166
super-portable PCs, 74
SuperMac Technology, 444
    dye sublimation color printers, 250
    IBM-compatible graphics adapters, 190
    large monitors, 186
    Macintosh graphics adapters, 194
    medium monitors, 180
superscalar microprocessors, 38
superstores and PC purchases, 80
SuperVGA, IBM-compatibles, 373
Supra modems, 292, 444
surge protectors, 361
swivel bases for monitors, 160, 175
Symantec
    anti-virus programs, 417
    Norton Utilities, 417, 420
SyQuest external storage drives, 317, 328, 444
System (Macintosh), 69
system clock of motherboards, 48
system extensions, 58
system unit of PCs, 55-57, 415-416

T

Tandy PCs, 87
tape drives/backup systems, 55, 333-336
tax programs, 21
TekTronix, Inc., dye sublimation color printers, 250, 444
tendonitis, 258
testing used systems, 386
Texas Instruments Inc., 444
thermal printers, 215, 225-226
three-pass scanning, 351
tilt-swivel bases for monitors, 175
time-based media, 24
TNR Technical batteries, 368
Toshiba America Information Systems, Inc., 444
    PCs, 88
    portable PCs, 132
    subnotebooks/PDAs, 150
Touchstone Software, Check It, 420
trackballs, 258, 267-268, 375, 380
training in PC use, 14, 405-406
transportability of PCs, 29
traveling and working, 73
triple-speed CD-ROM drives, 304
troubleshooting problems, 420
TrueType laser printer fonts, 220, 375
TWAIN compatibility in scanners, 352
two-page monitors, 161

U

U.S. Robotics, Inc., 445
UDS Motorola, 444
UMAX scanners, 354, 358, 445
upgrades
    hardware, 421-427
    memory, 422
    software, 420
UPSs (uninterruptible power supplies), 362
U.S. Robotics modems, 294
used computers, 384-386
User's Column, *Byte* magazine (Jerry Pournelle), 14
utilities, 58
    system maintenance, 420
    testing used systems, 386

V

Valuepoint PCs (IBM), 85
vendors
  compatibility of hardware/software, 79
  financial viability, 81
  mail-order, 81, 390-393
  service and support policies, 79-80
  superstores, 80
VESA
  local bus standard, 52
  VL-bus, IBM-compatibles, 373
VGA video support, 156
video
  chip sets, 167
  display systems, 155-165
  Macintosh support, 373
  memory, 373
  monitors, 418
  output ports, 55
  QVision video accelerator (Compaq), 84
video adapters, 156-160, 173-174
video cards, 426
video-out ports, portable PCs, 380
ViewSonic, 445
  large monitors, 186
  medium monitors, 182
  small monitors, 178
virtual memory, 51
viruses, 417
VirusScan for the PC (McAffee), 417
visors for monitors, 262
voltage regulators, 365
VRAM (video memory), 159

W

WANs (wide-area networks), 22
warehouse stores, PC purchases, 396
warranties, 400-403
  CD-ROM drives, 307
  graphics adapters, 188
  in-warranty repairs, 427-428
  monitors, 174
  printers, 225
wave-table synthesis, sound cards, 340
West Lake Data, PC Fullback+ program, 417
Western Digital Corp. graphics adapters, 190, 445

Windows (Microsoft)
  accelerator cards, 158
  minimum system specifications, 68
  operating system, 68
  startup description, 59
  tape backup software, 334
  training in system use, 406
Windows NT (Microsoft), 64, 68
  high-end systems, 377
  minimum specifications, 71
  operating system, 71
word processing, 11, 19-20, 220
  desktop systems, 382
  display recommendations, 171
WordPerfect **magazine, 431**
working at home/while traveling, 73-74
wrist pain, 258
wrist rests, 258, 375
WYSIWYG (What You See Is What You Get), 220

X-Y-Z

XGA (Extended Graphics Array), IBM, 166
XTree Pro Gold (XTree), 418
ZEOS International, 91, 445
  486- and Pentium-based portable PCs, 134
  486DX-based PCs, 104
  486DX2-based PCs, 110
  486DX4-based PCs, 114
  486SX-based PCs, 100
  Pentium-based PCs, 118
  subnotebooks/PDAs, 150
Zinc Air batteries, portable PCs, 367
Zoom modems, 296
ZyXEL modems, 300